E. Thiessen
Free Desk Copy

RELIGION: CLASSIC SOCIOLOGICAL APPROACHES

McGRAW-HILL RYERSON SERIES IN CANADIAN SOCIOLOGY

General Editor - Lorne Tepperman

A STATISTICAL PROFILE OF CANADIAN SOCIETY,
Daniel Kubat and David Thornton

IDEOLOGICAL PERSPECTIVES ON CANADA, 2nd Edition,
M. Patricia Marchak

SOCIAL MOBILITY IN CANADA,
Lorne Tepperman

CANADIAN SOCIETY IN HISTORICAL PERSPECTIVE,
S.D. Clark

CRIME CONTROL: THE URGE TOWARD AUTHORITY,
Lorne Tepperman

THE DISREPUTABLE PLEASURES: CRIME AND DEVIANCE IN CANADA,
John Hagan

UNDERSTANDING DATA,
B.H. Erickson and T.A. Nosanchuk

THE MAKING OF THE CANADIAN MEDIA,
Paul Rutherford

SOCIAL PSYCHOLOGY AS POLITICAL ECONOMY,
W.P. Archibald

THE NEW URBAN POOR,
S.D. Clark

SOCIOLOGICAL THEORIES OF EDUCATION,
Raymond Murphy with the collaboration of Ann Denis

DEMOGRAPHIC BASES OF CANADIAN SOCIETY, 2nd Edition
Warren Kalbach and Wayne McVey

FRAGILE FEDERATION: SOCIAL CHANGE IN CANADA,
Lorna Marsden and Edward Harvey

THE CANADIAN CLASS STRUCTURE, 2nd Edition,
Dennis Forcese

THE SURVIVAL OF ETHNIC GROUPS,
Jeffrey G. Reitz

WOMEN, FAMILY AND THE ECONOMY,
Sue Wilson

THE URBAN KALEIDOSCOPE: CANADIAN PERSPECTIVES,
Leslie W. Kennedy

RELIGION: CLASSIC SOCIOLOGICAL APPROACHES,
Roger O'Toole

RELIGION: CLASSIC SOCIOLOGICAL APPROACHES

ROGER O'TOOLE
University of Toronto

McGraw-Hill Ryerson Limited

Toronto Montréal New York Auckland Bogotá Cairo Guatemala Hamburg
Johannesburg Lisbon London Madrid Mexico New Delhi Panama Paris
San Juan São Paulo Singapore Sydney Tokyo

For Winnie and Frank

Religion: Classic Sociological Approaches

ISBN 0-07-548560-5

1 2 3 4 5 6 7 8 9 0 W 3 2 1 0 9 8 7 6 5 4

Printed and bound in Canada

Canadian Cataloguing in Publication Data

O'Toole, Roger, date
Religion: classic sociological approaches

(McGraw-Hill Ryerson series in Canadian sociology)
Includes index.
ISBN 0-07-548560-5

1. Religion and sociology. I. Title. II. Series.

BL60.085 1984 306'.6 C83-099288-X

CONTENTS

EDITOR'S INTRODUCTION

So far, neither science nor modern technology — not the new pain-killers millions of people take every day, not the trimmer automobiles, not the miracles of instant world-wide communication, not the funniest television comedies or the most revealing clothing in easy-to-launder fabrics, not the "big bang" theory nor genetic engineering nor the new ways of painfully prolonging life with expensive machines, not even the pleasures of PAC-MAN in your own home — so far, I repeat, neither science nor technology has managed to eliminate religion.

This fact would have come as a shock to the philosophers of the Enlightenment, who blamed so many social abuses and errors of thinking, directly or indirectly, on religion. They expected progress in reason, in science and in technology to eliminate the despair and ignorance that supposedly made people invent religions and allowed them to spread. Increasing individualism, through the exercise of informed choice, would presumably cut the bonds of collective, repressive and customary action, of which religious observance was a prime example.

Yet here we are, two centuries since the Industrial Revolution began to unpack the lunch pail of the physical world, witnessing not fewer but more religions, indeed new and different kinds of religions: hybrids of Eastern and Western thinking, of sacred and secular, primitive and advanced, magical and metaphysical, hybrids scarcely imaginable two centuries ago. The growth of knowledge and choice have led, not to eliminating religion, but to a more careful choice of religious views and to more sophisticated believing. This is not to say that blind faith and emotionalism are gone from all religions today; simply, there is more variety. Religions today vary on the dimension of heated emotionalism versus cool cerebralism almost as widely as the music available at a local record store.

This being so, one is far from surprised that the sociology of religion continues to attract the interest of undergraduate students and scholarly researchers alike. Yet the new work in this area has not lost touch with the old. We can easily locate current research in terms of older ideas and debates, and thus link current researchers to the founding spirits of sociology: to Durkheim, Weber and Marx, and to the founders of allied disciplines, especially anthropology, psychology and philosophy. The sociology of religion shows not only great persistence but also great continuity with past concerns.

The present book makes much of this continuity. We are plunged into debates that are centuries old, that have been carried on across continents and across disciplines by the best minds of their time. Professor O'Toole's elegant writing and impeccable scholarship are themselves a source of pleasure, quite aside from the interesting and sometimes surprising ideas we learn about. We find, too, that in the sociology of religion, all the important questions, if followed back to their historical roots, reveal difficult and still unresolved debates about the nature of social reality and of sociology itself. Thus, issues like the usefulness of functional analysis, or the merits of sociologistic versus psychologistic models, continue to stalk these pages, as they do, perhaps less obviously, all sociological research.

In short, reading this book I found myself having to confront a number of very basic issues in sociology, in the context of what turns out to be, excuse me Voltaire, a still timely topic: religion. You will enjoy doing the same.

LORNE TEPPERMAN

PREFACE

This text attempts to introduce the undergraduate student to the sociology of religion through an exposition of some of the main classic approaches associated with the founding fathers of the sociological tradition.

Far from being a scholastic or antiquarian activity, the study of the sociological classics is still an essential prerequisite of significant work in the discipline of sociology in general and in the subdiscipline of the sociology of religion in particular. It is clear that sociological scholarship has not evolved to the point at which the contributions of such giants as Marx, Weber or Durkheim can be consigned to the custody of the historian of ideas. Indeed, as the eminent American sociologist Talcott Parsons observed at the end of his long career, it is impossible for sociology to advance without a continuous revisiting of its intellectually rich tradition.

Thus, the best work within the sociology of religion is still undertaken as part of what C. Wright Mills called the Classic Tradition. This intellectual inheritance, in Lewis Coser's terms, sensitizes investigators to what to look for and what to ignore generally at the same time as it provides methods for initiating specific inquiries.

In providing a brief insight into classic sociological approaches to religion and in sketching the impact of the classics on contemporary sociological theory and research, it is hoped that this book may prove useful, not only to students specializing in sociology but to those pursuing religious or theological studies who wish to become familiar with the foundations of the sociological approach to religion.

In offering this book to students, I wish to acknowledge my intellectual debts to my own teachers: to Bryan Wilson and Roland Robertson, who introduced me to the sociology of religion; to John Rex and Herminio Martins, who inspired my interest in the sociological classics; and to Lewis Feuer, who encouraged my fascination with ideology and those murky areas which border the fields of religion, science and politics. In making such acknowledgements, of course, I hasten to offer an author's *mea culpa* regarding the contents of the present volume.

The completion of this book has been greatly facilitated by the typing skills of Ruth Barrow and by the editorial counsel and assistance of Joan Blishen and Wendy Thomas of McGraw-Hill Ryerson.

My debt to my wife, Margaret, must be acknowledged but cannot be adequately expressed.

ROGER O'TOOLE

CHAPTER ONE
INTRODUCTION

An enlightened and progressive social thinker of the eighteenth or nineteenth centuries granted a miraculous, brief and tantalizing glimpse of the intellectual future would perhaps have found the spectacle of numerous scholars of our own day expending their energies in the study of religion among the most baffling of the revelations accorded him. This intimation that our scientifically sophisticated post-industrial society, inheritor of a century or more of enlightenment, progress or evolution might still harbour beliefs and practices of a religious nature would have been surprising and profoundly disquieting. As he hurriedly revised his blueprints of the future in the light of the wonders he had seen, our imaginary sage may have ruminated on the ruins of a cherished but shattered certainty that the term "religion," if it persisted at all, was shortly destined to purely pejorative usage.[1]

By no means all social thinkers of the last two centuries have penned epitaphs to religion. Nonetheless, it is true that even before the intellectual revolution precipitated by the publication of Charles Darwin's *Origin of Species,* the days of religion (and specifically European Christianity) had seemed, to a number of influential social commentators, to be numbered.[2] Self-styled antagonists of religion rejoiced at mounting evidence of the alienation of the masses from the churches and gloated over the apparently terminal nature of a sickness whose symptoms were rank corruption followed by a growing social, political and intellectual disrepute, and the final ignominy of complete irrelevance. Meanwhile, though reluctant to accept a diagnosis of incurability and imminent demise, many within the fold of traditional organized religion undoubtedly felt placed on the defensive in a seemingly more precarious social order and peered into the future with apprehension and foreboding.[3]

With the wisdom of hindsight it is easy to be smug about the naïvete of our intellectual forebears, particularly regarding their misplaced optimism, dire prophecies and unfulfilled "unscientific" predictions. We now know that organized religion proved somewhat more capable of effective defence, counterattack and tenacious adaptation in the face of modernization than its opponents anticipated, just as we need no reminder that scientific and industrial "progress" has failed to prove the universal, unmixed blessing anticipated by its proponents. Yet it would be rash to completely dismiss the opinions of our predecessors concerning the long-term prospects of religion. While it may be true that in the long run we are all dead, an effort to assess the predictions of the last two centuries in terms of a "long view" of historical development is not manifestly misguided. Such an attempt is at least likely to engender a certain intellectual humility and an increased sympathy for those eighteenth- and nineteenth-century observers who struggled to peer into the future by reading the signs of their own times.

It is abundantly clear that, in perhaps the most radical formulation of the issue, the last king has not yet been strangled with the entrails of the last priest.[4] In more subtle terms, however, it is nonetheless conceivable that forecasts of the demise of religion were not mistaken. Sentence of death having been passed, it is arguable that a mere stay of execution has been granted or that the condemned is experiencing a death agony of unexpectedly prolonged duration. From such a viewpoint, obituaries to religion, while premature, may still be regarded as appropriate.

In criticism, it might be retorted that such an argument repeats the classic procedure of having one's cake and eating it, and that a "prediction" so vague and open-ended is unworthy of the name. In addition, it might also be maintained that what one observer diagnoses as a drawn-out death agony may, to a more sanguine eye, have the appearance of fair, even robust health, particularly under circumstances of generally inhospitable climate.

The problems encountered even in such a superficially simple task as assessment of the predictive accuracy of antique epitaphs indicate the extreme difficulty of calm, clear and careful consideration of the condition of religion. In particular, they instil an appreciation that such appraisal may merely reflect what an observer *expects* to perceive; a snare that is no less dangerous for the modern scholar than for those who have trodden the same intellectual path before him. By comparison with his predecessors, however, the contemporary analyst has at his disposal a far richer treasury of fact and opinion upon which to draw; so much so, indeed, that it may sometimes seem a mixed blessing. Whether such a state of affairs attests to the continued vitality of religion or merely to similar magnetic powers as possessed by withering tribes, endangered species and dead cities, the perils of winding through the labyrinthine ways of conflicting contentions, contradictory evidence, inconsistent language and rival interpretations render firm and definitive conclusions hard to attain.

An attempt to read the auspices of religion and to interpret the signs of the times in a contemporary religious context is, therefore, fraught with danger; a fact emphasized by even the most cursory examination of current themes in popular and scholarly literature.

Thus, from one vantage point, the life of religion appears belatedly, remarkably peacefully, but nonetheless inexorably, to be drawing to its close, at least in modern societies.[5] In this reading of the evidence, the only real uncertainties involve the precise hour of death and likely consequences for the bereaved after the final death knell has been sounded. This interpretation draws upon mounting evidence of disheartened decline and disarray in the churches and invokes proofs of the growing irrelevance of organized religion in the social, political and cultural life of modern societies. More than this, however, it also perceives the rapid disappearance of religious content from the hearts and minds of ordinary men and women. For some commentators the imminent extinction of religion is cause for satisfaction or even celebration, while for others it occasions bitter regret. For these and for more disinterested observers, however, conclusive proof of impending doom seems to reside in the widespread, undisguised indifference with which the news itself is greeted.

Completely at odds with the preceding description, though, is a vision of contemporary religion vouchsafed other concerned spectators.[6] In this alternative scene there is neither deathbed nor cause for tears; faith and hope prevail, righteousness reigns and the mood is one of festivity rather than grief. To those who thus perceive the continuing vitality of religion, the communications media appear to shriek daily supportive testimony as international events topple the claim that religion is dead. Thus, revolution in Iran, inspired and led by Muslim clergy, shatters the political stability of the region, challenges the power of the United States and threatens international relations; in Northern Ireland, conflict between religious minority and majority persists and escalates to the point of social chaos and civil war; while in Poland, proletarians who refuse to bow their heads to their government wave religious banners and bend their knees as the demands of trade-unionism are granted benediction in religious ceremonial. Oversimplified as such examples may prove, they nonetheless serve their purpose in evincing the vivacity of religion in the contemporary age, for better or worse.

Other evidence of religious vitality is derived from the aggressive refusal of many religious bodies to be dismissed either from the world stage or from the every-day lives of ordinary people. The "ecumenical" and "renewal" movements in Christianity since the Second Vatican Council represent examples of such determination,[7] while the unwillingness of religious bodies in the Third World to make their exit quietly is another.[8] Such a widespread commitment to preventing the script of the *Communist Manifesto* from replacing the scriptures of the Old and New Testaments is regarded as unshakeable evidence of a religious will to survive, and indeed to triumph. Those who seek confirmation that religion persists in good health even in the most "advanced" societies are able to elicit eloquent testimony favourable to their cause by focussing attention upon the United States, the nation that has sent men to the moon and rockets to the farthest reaches of space. There, it can be argued, religion, and for that matter "old-time religion," is still a vital element in the national life.[9] In the most recent presidential election, for example, all three major candidates laid explicit emphasis on their commitment to Christianity, while two of them also indicated their joy at being "born again." In such circumstances it can be argued that the social, political and cultural influence of such militant, avowedly religious lobbies as the "Moral Majority" may not be easily dismissed.[10]

Accumulation of evidence that obituaries to religion have been, to say the least, exaggerated[11] inevitably draws attention to the fact that a yearning for religion is by no means confined to the middle-aged and middle-class. In this regard the commitment of young people to religion, "old time" or not, is viewed as particularly significant.[12] Thus, while (as the lyric states) "old-time religion" may be "good enough" for many people, it is decidedly not good enough for others who, nonetheless, fervently regard themselves as "religious." Some, particularly among the affluent and alienated young have therefore been drawn to, or have created, more exotic variants of religiosity; drawing inspiration from sources as diverse as Eastern mysticism, medieval witchcraft and science fiction.[13] While these beliefs and practices may appear alien or offensive to adherents of more established religious organizations they can, however, be interpreted as new manifestations of a religious impulse that is unquenchable even in the midst of a widespread materialism.

Perhaps the only firm conclusion that might be drawn from the foregoing discussion concerns the impossibility of deriving any firm conclusions from the facts and arguments thus presented. Possession of the highest moral and intellectual qualities by those involved in such debate no more guarantees the self-evident truth of propositions than do eloquence and fervor in their expression. Thus, bombardment by contradictory facts and contrary interpretations of the same facts is likely to leave the ordinary believer or unbeliever, as well as the student approaching the scholarly literature for the first time, battle-fatigued rather than enlightened. Reeling from a barrage of assertion and counter-assertion, he may understandably be inclined to retreat into the sanctuary of prior predilection.

Yet the brief excursion into the labyrinth undertaken in the preceding pages has been neither frivolous nor unrewarding. On the contrary, appreciation of the scene of confusion that it has revealed is the fundamental prerequisite of any fruitful further analysis, while identification of the sources of this confusion is the first necessary step toward some measure of enlightenment.

The primary source of confusion is perhaps least obvious because it is so basic. Bluntly, this may be expressed as a state of affairs in which nobody seems to know, understand or care what anybody else is talking about, while more delicately, charitably and accurately it may be diagnosed as a lack of any conceptual consensus. Endemic even in use of the key term "religion" itself, conceptional cloudiness so pervades many discussions as to render them at best inconsistent and at worst meaningless.[14]

But what, in turn, are the underlying sources of this conceptual chaos? A partial answer may be suggested by indicating firstly the nature of religion as a general societal concept, and secondly by emphasizing its accompanying value-laden character.[15] It may now be obvious that a definition of religion has been deliberately avoided throughout the preceding discussion in an attempt to lure the reader into subjective utilization of the term. If this strategy has been successful, the meaning of religion will have been taken for granted and its referents assumed simply because "everybody knows what it is." The earlier discussion strongly suggests, however, that what "everybody knows" may be problematic in the extreme and subject to wide variation. Like "the family" that is observed, known and understood by ordinary people in the course of, and as a consequence of, their involvement in every-day social life, "religion" involves and evokes meanings rooted in particular social contexts. For most of its users, this term is not an antiseptic scientific tool[16] but rather an element of common discourse packed with an intellectual and emotional content that varies with social and, by implication, psychological circumstances.

That religion is the locus of deeply held emotions and biases in a broad range of circumstances is an observation that should provoke little dissent. In North American and European societies, the historically close identification of Christianity and values has intensified the connection between religion and emotional commitment to a point of apparent inextricability. This does not imply that those with strong religious (or indeed anti-religious) emotional commitments are thereby incapable of sensible or rational discussion of religion, nor does it necessarily assert the superiority of objective, disinterested or "value-free" statements on the topic. It does, however, suggest that a value-laden and emotionally charged atmosphere clouds rather than clarifies conceptually, thereby inhibiting genuine communication and meaningful conversation concerning "religious" matters.

While the kind of problems discussed above are by no means confined to a religious context,[17] they are particularly acute therein. Appreciation of this fact is thus the beginning of wisdom in any attempt at social-scientific or sociological investigation of the phenomenon of religion. Indeed, the very existence of such problems is itself a crucial fact that should not escape the sociologist's attention, given the broadly defined aim of understanding religion as a social phenomenon.[18] In the following chapters, more detailed attention will be paid to the nature of religion and its sociological interpretation. At this point, however, it seems strategically appropriate to place initial stress upon the character of the sociology of religion as one among diverse ways of understanding religion. Notwithstanding the assumptions and assertions of some of its detractors, it stakes no claim to being either a unique, all-embracing metaperspective or even *primus inter pares* among sundry other approaches.[19] It has no pretensions to superseding, overriding or rendering irrelevant other strategies of enquiry, nor does it presume either to debunk or legitimate all or any religious beliefs and practices. In endeavoring merely to secure a limited glimpse of reality from a specific vantage point, it regards the validity and utility of its observations as matters for investigation, criticism and dispute, while readily acknowledging its intellectual debts to scholars and others outside its fold. It should not go unstated, however, that as a distinct, richly productive scholarly enterprise, the sociology of religion is able to draw on a vast intellectual capital that is more than sufficient to ensure fulsome repayment of debts incurred, as well as to guarantee the generation of new forms of intellectual wealth.

Footnotes to Chapter One

[1] Scepticism regarding "official" religion is, of course, not a new phenomenon. It has existed in classical antiquity and "primitive societies," and the "village atheist" appears to be a universal social type. The rise of a scientific world-view in the eighteenth and nineteenth centuries was accompanied by a scepticism of orthodox religious world views on a hitherto unprecedented scale. The influence of such "freethinking" is evident in the embryonic social sciences as well as in the European and Anglo-American political thought of the period. See Thomas Paine, *The Age of Reason,* New York: The Liberal Arts Press, 1957 (first published in 1794 and available in many editions); David Hume, *Dialogues Concerning Natural Religion,* Indianapolis & New York: The Bobbs-Merrill Co. Inc., 1974 (first published 1779 and available in many editions); Edward Royle (ed.), *The Infidel Tradition: From Paine to Bradlaugh,* Toronto: Macmillan of Canada and Maclean-Hunter Press, 1976; Frank E. Manuel, *The Eighteenth Century Confronts the Gods,* New York: Atheneum, 1967 (first published in 1959); A.D. White, *A History of the Warfare of Science with Theology in Christendom* (2 Volumes), New York: Dover Publications, 1960 (first published 1896); and Owen Chadwick, *The Secularization of the European Mind in the Nineteenth Century,* Cambridge: Cambridge University Press, 1975.

[2] See C.C. Gillispie, *Genesis and Geology: The Impact of Scientific Discoveries upon Religious Beliefs in the Decades Before Darwin,* New York: Harper and Row, 1959; Ian G. Barbour, *Issues in Science & Religion,* New York: Harper and Row, 1966; Reginald Stackhouse, "Darwin and a Century of Conflict" in Richard D. Knudten (ed.), *The Sociology of Religion:*

An Anthology, New York: Appleton-Century-Crofts, 1967, pp. 430–435; and Frank Manuel, *The Prophets of Paris: Turgot, Condorcet, Saint-Simon and Comte,* New York: Harper and Row, 1965. Darwin's *Origin of Species* was published in 1859.

[3] A major concern was, of course, the loss of the "lower orders" sustained by organized Christianity throughout the eighteenth and nineteenth centuries and only partly offset by occasional "revivals" of Christianity such as Methodism, Evangelicalism and the rise of such bodies as the Salvation Army. The fear that political radicalism would fill the void created by the absence of religion was not misplaced, though alliances between the churches and forces of political reaction were doomed to be self-defeating from the standpoint of revitalizing lower-class religiosity. See K.S. Inglis, *Churches and the Working Classes in Victorian England,* London: Routledge and Kegan Paul, 1963. It is instructive to consider the retreat into reaction of Roman Catholicism during the reign of Pope Pius IX (1846–1878) as a case study in the profound impact of secularism upon traditional religion. See, e.g., A.B. Hasler, *How the Pope Became Infallible: Piux IX and The Politics of Persuasion,* (trans. P. Heinegg), Garden City, New York: Doubleday and Co., 1981 (first published in German in 1979); Bill McSweeney, *Roman Catholicism: the Search for Relevance,* Oxford: Basil Blackwell, 1980, pp. 22–60; and J. Derek Holmes, *The Triumph of the Holy See,* London: Burns and Oates, 1978.

[4] In Marat's famous French revolutionary formula.

[5] See, for example, the work of the British sociologist Bryan R. Wilson, especially his *Religion in Secular Society: A Sociological Comment,* Harmondsworth: Penguin Books, 1969; and *Contemporary Transformations of Religion,* London: Oxford University Press, 1976. Wilson concludes the latter work with the statement: ". . . religions are always dying. In the modern world it is not clear that they have any prospect of rebirth" (p. 116). For further discussion of the phenomenon of "secularization" see Chapter 6 of this book.

[6] For sceptical attitudes to the "demise" of religion, see Andrew M. Greeley, *Unsecular Man: the Persistence of Religion,* New York: Dell Publishing Co., 1972; and Andrew Greeley and Gregory Baum (eds.), *The Persistence of Religion,* New York: Herder & Herder, 1973. See also Chapter 6 of this book.

[7] See, for example, McSweeney, *op. cit.*, pp. 165–255; Peter Hebblethwaite, *The Runaway Church: Post-Conciliar Growth or Decline,* New York: The Seabury Press, 1975; and Peter G. McCaffery, "A Sociological Analysis of the Concerns of Pressure Groups in the Roman Catholic Church in the Netherlands and in England" in *The Contemporary Metamorphosis of Religion?* (Acts of the 12th International Conference on the Sociology of Religion), Lille, France, C.I.S.R. Secretariat, 1973, pp. 239–255.

[8] See, for example, McSweeney, *op. cit.* pp. 198–209; Hebblethwaite, *op. cit.* pp. 179–194; Guenter Lewy, *Religion and Revolution,* New York: Oxford University Press, 1974, pp. 504–536; David H. Levine, *Religion and Politics in Latin America: the Catholic Church in Venezuela and Columbia,* Princeton, N.J.: Princeton University Press, 1981; Emmanuel DeKadt, *Catholic Radicals in Brazil,* London: Oxford University Press, 1970; J.G. Davies, *Christians, Politics and Violent Revolution,* London: SCM Press, 1976; and Alistair Kee (ed.), *A Reader in Political Theology,* London: SCM Press, 1974.

[9] Discussions of the pertinence of the work of Will Herberg and of the notion of "civil religion" are relevant here. See Herberg's *Protestant – Catholic – Jew: An Essay in American Religious Sociology,* Garden City, N.Y.: Doubleday and Co., (Revised Edition), 1960; R.E. Richey and D.G. Jones (eds.) *American Civil Religion,* New York: Harper and Row, 1974; and R.N. Bellah and P.E. Hammond, *Varieties of Civil Religion,* San Francisco: Harper and Row, 1980.

[10] Two recent papers by John H. Simpson are useful in this context. See "Is there a Moral Majority?" presented at the annual meeting of the Society for the Scientific Study of Religion, Baltimore, October 1981 and "Some Observations on the Current Vitality of Conservative Religion" presented at the annual meeting of the American Association for the Advancement of Science, Toronto, January 1981.

[11] Mark Twain noted that reports of his death had been "greatly exaggerated." Peter Berger has adapted the comment to refer to reports of God's demise. See Peter L. Berger, "Second Thoughts on Defining Religion," *Journal for the Scientific Study of Religion,* Vol. 13, 1974, p. 133.

[12] Such significance is by no means discovered only in a supposed rekindling of interest among the young in established religious organizations. Some commentators also perceive in the "counter-culture" of the 1960s and the vitality of contemporary Christian and non-Christian cults, evidence of religious rebirth. See Charles Y. Glock and Robert N. Bellah (eds.), *The New Religious Consciousness,* Berkeley: University of California Press, 1976, and Daniel Bell, "The Return of the Sacred? The Argument on The Future of Religion," *British Journal of Sociology,* Vol. 28, 1977, pp. 419–449. For sceptical views on religious return or rebirth see B.R. Wilson, *Contemporary Transformations of Religion* (cited above), p. 116; B.R. Wilson, "The Return of the Sacred," *Journal for the Scientific Study of Religion,* Vol. 18, 1979, pp. 268–280; and Roy Wallis, "The Rebirth of the Gods? Reflections on the New Religions in the West," Inaugural Lecture, Queen's University, Belfast, (New Lecture Series No. 108), 1978. See also Chapter 6 of this book.

[13] See Glock and Bellah, *op. cit.*; Wallis, *op. cit.*; Robert Wuthnow, *The Consciousness Reformation,* Berkeley: University of California Press, 1976; Robert Wuthnow, *Experimentation in American Religion: The New Mysticisms and their Implications for the Churches,* Berkeley: University of California Press, 1978; Irving I. Zaretsky and Mark P. Leone (eds.), *Religious Movements in Contemporary America,* Princeton, N.J.: Princeton University Press, 1974; and Thomas Robbins and Dick Anthony (eds.), *In Gods We Trust: New Patterns of Religious Pluralism in America,* New Brunswick, N.J.: Transaction Books, 1981. See also Chapter 6 of this book.

[14] One writer has referred to "inarticulate mumbo jumbo" as characterizing some discussions of religion, but even the most articulate discussions are fruitless if nobody uses the same words to mean the same things. See G.E. Barnhart, "Is One's Definition of 'Religion' Always Circular?" *International Yearbook for The Sociology of Knowledge & Religion,* Vol. 9, Westdeutscher Verlag, 1975, p. 122. See also Chapter 2 of this book.

[15] The "societal" conception of religion refers to its conventional meaning in every-day life, as distinct from its meaning in a specialized, scholarly context. The extent to which sociological concepts should reflect societal usage is, of course, a perennial matter for concern. The starting point for most discussions of the problem of values in sociological work is Max Weber, *The Methodology of the Social Sciences* (Trans. E.A. Shils and H.A. Finch), Glencoe: The Free Press, 1949. Weber's discussion has provoked a vast critical literature.

[16] This is not to imply, however, that "scientific" definitional uses are immune to conventional, emotional, ethnocentric and personal bias in their formulation.

[17] Students of, for example, the sociology of the family, politics or deviant behaviour may feel that the sociologist of religion is far from alone in the difficulties of defining his subject matter and freeing his work from extra-scientific bias.

[18] The sociologist of religion must be aware of the varied forms and biases of conventional uses of the term "religion," not only insofar as they inhibit or make difficult the formulation of scholarly definitions, but as social and cultural facts that possess sociological importance in their own right. The overlapping of "ordinary language" and scientific usage is a theme that is explored in more detail in the next chapter, but at this point it should be noted that the present chapter deliberately attempts to suggest such overlap. In trying, as far as possible, to capture the state of mind of an observer of the religious scene who relies largely on facts and opinions derived from the mass media, together with occasional glimpses of scholarly thought (obtained often at second-hand), it endeavours to appeal to the student taking the first steps towards more disciplined inquiry. The portrayal of conceptual chaos in the discussions of "educated laypersons" is also intended to prepare the student for the equally apparent defini-

tional disharmony that will be encountered in the scholarly literature discussed in the next chapter.

[19] Obviously relevant parallel enterprises are the anthropology, psychology and philosophy of religion, and the disciplines of theology, comparative religion, and history of religion or *religionswissenschaft*. The anthropologist Raymond Firth has noted: "We can no longer afford to neglect the more professional theoretical analysis of religion not only by sociologists, with whom we have kept in comparative general touch, but also by psychologists, historians, philosophers, theologians and other students of comparative religion, some of whom have displayed a growing sociological awareness," "Problem and Assumption in an Anthropological Study of Religion," *Journal of the Royal Anthropological Institute* (Vol. 89, 1959, p. 136). This sentiment may be applauded in the present context, although what Runciman has termed "the condescension implicit in the concluding phase" must be disclaimed. See W.G. Runciman, "The Sociological Explanation of Religious Beliefs," *Archives Européennes de Sociologie*, Vol. 10, No. 2, 1969, pp. 172n–173n. (Note also Runciman's other pertinent comments on disciplinary delusions of grandeur.)

CHAPTER TWO
WHAT IS RELIGION?

General Problems of Definition

In the previous chapter, the consequences of the definitional anarchy characterizing many popular discussions of "religion" were briefly denoted. It is clear that in such circumstances meaningful conversation is difficult, if not impossible, and that even the most painfully achieved agreement or consensus may be illusory. What is less clear, however, is the way out of this linguistic labyrinth. The builders of the Biblical Tower of Babel were at least aware of their inability to communicate, whereas many modern discussions are bedevilled by the erroneous belief that participants are engaged in genuine communication because they share a common language and require no translators or interpreters. This is perhaps the least obvious but most effective way in which the Devil merits his title "the Father of Lies."

The attempt to achieve definitional clarity and consistency in a religious context is in itself a strictly philosophical enterprise, although it is a fundamental prerequisite of any systematic understanding of the phenomenon of religion. In the immediate postwar years the eminent British philosopher Dr. C.E.M. Joad established "It all depends on what you mean" as his personal "catch phrase" in a popular radio-discussion program, and although his views were hardly representative of contemporary British philosophy, his constant incantation of this preliminary formula undoubtedly was. Modern philosophers have indeed been so preoccupied with the meaning of words that some have viewed philosophy itself as nothing more nor less than the unravelling of language. It is unnecessary, however, to subscribe to such iconoclasm, or to imbibe the wisdom of Austin or Wittgenstein in order to appreciate the value of clearly defined terms as the foundation of sound thinking, productive argument and genuine consensus in any intellectual context.[1]

Serious students of religion have not been slow to recognize this fact nor, in consequence, to offer a variety of definitional strategies calculated to induce intellectual clarity. While their efforts have undoubtedly succeeded in encouraging self-conscious circumspection in the scholarly use of "religious" terminology, they have, however, failed notably to engender any broad conceptual consensus even within distinct disciplines or subdisciplines. Depressing or discouraging as such a state of affairs might appear to a natural scientist, it provokes less concern from the scholar in the humanities or social sciences who may, indeed, regard the achievement of a generally accepted vocabulary of religion as a lost cause: unlikely at best, undesirable at worst.[2]

Students of the social sciences, perhaps sociologists most of all, are highly sensitive to questions of consistency and consensus in conceptual clarification. The most cursory investigation of the most elementary sociological textbooks uncovers conceptual cloudiness and contradiction rather than clarity and consistency, while more sophisticated analysis of contemporary sociological theory reveals chaos more than consensus.[3] To the sociologist, therefore, the difficulties involved in formulating an appropriate definition of religion may not appear more surprising or any different in kind from those to be encountered, for example, in attempts to define "family" or "work" satisfactorily.

Though definition is a philosophical activity, it is in no way the private preserve of professional philosophers. Thus, in the case of the word "religion," definitions are offered by sociologists, psychologists, theologians and historians, among others. In such a situation the temptation to engage in rather glib assertions of the benefits of intellectual interchange should be counterbalanced by a warning that hasty and indiscriminate interdisciplinary lending and borrowing may result in confusion. Such a strategy serves a general as well as a specific purpose by bringing into focus the nature of definition itself.

Definitions are grounded in utility as much as in truth, for although intended to facilitate the perception of reality and "knowing the truth," they are themselves neither true nor false but only more or less useful.[4] Their utility, however, is not universal but dependent upon the demands of an observer, which means, in practice, that it is determined within the framework of a particular discipline or subdiscipline. From this point of view it is not unlikely that a "useful" definition developed in one discipline may be regarded as less useful (or useless) in another, and that difficulties may attend the transplanting of definitions across disciplinary borders. This is not to maintain the automatic invalidity of definitions estranged from their original context, but to emphasize the relativity of utility. The revelation of a vital truth in one discipline may appear an odd and irrelevant exercise from the perspective of another, and the conceptual scheme that makes it possible may therefore seem unworthy of wider interest or application.[5]

The theologian, for example, might strive for a definition of religion that captures the yearning of the human soul for God, the source of life, the principle of universal harmony or salvation, as well as expressing God's love for mankind. Though such a definitional quest might not necessarily be irrelevant to sociologists or psychologists and might even be a source of useful insights, its central focus is unlikely to be immediately appreciated. Again, the psychologist might wish to apprehend the varieties of religious experience in terms of a definition that involves the workings, predispositions, structure, propensities and even pathologies of the human mind. This approach might, however, appear uninteresting or irrelevant to a sociologist whose definition is likely to stress the collective aspect of religion: its nature as a group rather than an individual phenomenon.[6]

At this point, it seems appropriate to summarize briefly and plainly the explicit and implicit propositions of the preceding discussion as they relate to the definition of religion. Firstly, it is apparent that a universally useful "all-purpose" definition is difficult if not impossible to attain, its intellectual desirability being, in any case, by no means self-evident. Secondly, it is clear that religion may logically be defined from any number of specific vantage points, none of which need presuppose the ontological accuracy or inaccuracy of religious knowledge in general or particular terms. In a definitional context, the only meaningful religious reality or truth is that implied by the terms of the definition itself, whether these are expressed in the language of the social scientist, the theologian, the mystic or the poet. Thirdly, whatever its divine connotations, religion is incontrovertably a human phenomenon, with both individual and collective aspects. This observation, which may appear simultaneously both trite and profound, is of special import to social science though its significance is by no means confined to such a context.

Social-Scientific Definitions

As noted above, the quest for an adequate definition of religion is hardly a new venture even within the social-scientific intellectual enterprise. Indeed, the problem of defining religion was faced by both of the major "founding fathers" of modern sociology in the early years of the present century. Thus, in a famous (or infamous) statement, the great German sociologist Max Weber underlined the difficulty of formulating a definition of religion by his reluctance to undertake the task at the outset of his treatise on the sociology of religion:

> To define "religion," to say what it *is,* is not possible at the start of a presentation such as this. Definition can be attempted, if at all, only at the conclusion of the study.[7]

Though Weber's French counterpart, Emile Durkheim, exhibited no such reluctance, he likewise emphasized the difficulty of conceptualizing religion. Indeed, his brilliant, original and ultrasociological tour de force continues to incite rather than dispel definitional disagreement.[8]

It is fitting that discussion of the social-scientific definition of religion should begin with the ideas of Weber and Durkheim, not merely because they still provide the major sources of intellectual inspiration in the "scientific study of religion," but because their contrasting approaches to the problem of definition are as instructive in their weaknesses as in their strengths.

Durkheim "set out quite explicitly to say what religion *is* and to put forward a general theory of its origin,"[9] and he did so, in the first instance, by an incisive critique of prevailing anthropological wisdom. Though indebted to Robertson Smith for elements of his approach,[10] Durkheim deserves credit for accomplishing a radical revision of the intellectual ground rules for the sociological study of religion by his rejection of a substantive conception of this phenomenon and his attempt to replace it by one that was functional in nature. His dissatisfaction with substantive definition was provoked concretely by the apparent inadequacies of the influential definition proposed by the eminent English anthropologist Sir Edward Tylor.[11] This definition, whose substantive referent "belief in spirits" seemed, to Durkheim, incapable of incorporating the great world "religion" of Buddhism (an arguably atheistic and materialistic view of the universe), was thereby rendered redundant.[12] In putting forward as its successor his own celebrated formulation, therefore, Durkheim included two main themes:

> . . . a religion is a unified system of beliefs and practices relative to sacred things, that is to say, things set apart and forbidden – beliefs and practices which unite into one moral community called a Church, all those who adhere to them.[13]

The first theme involved distinguishing "the sacred" as the focus of "religious" belief and activity, while the second, in Durkheim's view "no less essential than the first," concerned the nature of religion "as an eminently collective thing," indeed as the thing that serves to unite the collectivity. Regarding Tylor's definition as indefensibly exclusive, Durkheim offered a conceptualization that is inclusive in both its utilization of the supposedly universal category of the "sacred" and its assertion of a universal social function for religion.

Yet, despite the confidence with which Durkheim promulgated his new, radically derived sociological definition and the enthusiasm with which it was received and transmitted in some quarters, it failed to provide the theoretical base line for the scientific study of religion that its author envisaged. Moreover, it is not difficult to discern the roots of this failure in that very quality of inclusivity that promised to be the most stimulating characteristic of the new definition. Thus, initially alluring though it is, the distinction between the sacred and the profane appears less attractive when subjected to closer scrutiny. For, while its ubiquity is hypothesized rather than asserted *a priori* and is, in principle, subject to the same fate as Tylor's "belief in spirits," circumstances in which the absence of the distinction could ever be confidently established are difficult to conceive. Indeed, the assumed relativity and infinite variation of the distinction make the basis upon which its recognition occurs unclear and uncertain; a problem intensified by Durkheim's insistence that this dichotomy is not merely sociological but essentially societal.[14] Thus, even allowing for the vagueness of the categories of the sacred and profane, it is essential that their existence be recognized not merely by a sociological observer or interpreter but by the members of the particular group under observation. Under the circumstances, the danger of arbitrary substitution of the latter by the former seems ever present, ensuring that those who seek sociologically may surely find the sacred.

Likewise, the inclusive intent of the functional aspect of Durkheim's definition carries with it the dangers of vagueness and circularity. If religion is defined in terms of its effect, and its main effect is the maintenance of "moral communities," the existence of such communities both assumes and demonstrates the existence of "religion." This point is further underlined, moreover, when the inextricable union between religion and society is made even more explicit in Durkheim's own formulations:

> The gods are nothing else than collective forces, incarnated, hypostatized under a material form. At bottom, it is society which the faithful worship; the superiority of the gods over men is that of the group over its members.[15]

Thus, religion is:

> . . . a system of beliefs by means of which individuals represent the society of which they are members and the relationships, obscure but intimate, which they have with it.[16]

In arguing that religious experience cannot be founded upon an error or a lie, and that his "entire study rests upon the postulate that the unanimous sentiment of the believers of all times cannot be purely illusory," Durkheim appears concerned to justify as much as to explain the nature of religion.[17] For him, religion is, in some sense, "society worshipping itself," so that "society" is the symbolic referent of religious ritual. This means, if Parsons' interpretation is accepted, that religion celebrates the common ultimate-value attitudes of a group, and that, therefore, not only is religion a social phenomenon, but (as for Auguste Comte) society itself may be viewed as a religious phenomenon.[18] From a definitional viewpoint, such inclusivity is a mixed blessing and has met a theoretical reception varying from the ecstatic to the dismissive. To some scholars it is evidence of Durkheim's analytic brilliance, while to others it illustrates that his "claims are much, much too sweeping" and that his sociology of religion is fundamentally "misconceived."[19] For thinkers of the latter kind, such a broad definition suggests that the very persistence of society implies the existence of religion. In their view, such demonstration of the universality of religion may, however, entail the redundancy of the term "religion" as a useful conceptual tool.[20]

Though Weber was conceptually cautious where Durkheim was courageous, this by no means allowed him to circumvent the difficulties of definition. Indeed, his approach created its own problems. Weber's unwillingness to construct a definition (even a "working definition") at the outset of his researches has been noted earlier. The fact that his approach is not completely unique or idiosyncratic also seems worthy of note, however, as evidence that this is one form that a concern for flexibility in definition may typically take. In a work published in the same year as *The Elementary Forms of The Religious Life,* and evidently influenced both by Durkheim and English anthropology,[21] the classicist Jane Harrison condemned any approach to the study of religion that began with a general preconceived notion of "religion" and then squeezed into its confines those facts that came its way and appeared susceptible to such treatment. Rejecting preliminary definition, she announced her intention to "collect the facts that admittedly are religious and see from what human activities they appear to have sprung."[22]

Similarly, the late Professor S.F. Nadel, an influential figure in British social anthropology, observed in a monograph on African religion:

> Whichever way we propose to describe the province of things religious, we are bound to encounter a border zone which defies precise *a priori* allocation on this or that side of the boundary. To be sure, this residue of inaccuracy is entailed in the broad view of religion which we made our starting point. But no other starting point seems feasible. Bluntly stated, what we set out to do is to describe everything in a particular culture that has a bearing on religion. And since "religion" is precisely one of those words which belong to the more intuitive portions of our vocabulary, and hence cannot be given a sharp connotation, we have no choice but to feel our way towards the meaning it should have in given circumstances. We must not risk omitting anything that might be relevant . . .[23]

A consideration of these approaches to the problem of definition leads to the conclusion that they both incorporate a fundamental methodological error by assuming implicitly what they are not prepared to express explicitly.[24] The temptation to side-step the frustrating business of formulating even a "working definition" of religion at the beginning of a project is great, especially in a broad, comparative enterprise. But, as Jack Goody has argued, the refusal to delimit one's universe of discourse provides no escape from anticipated problems, and indeed the dangers of such abdication of responsibility may well "outweigh the advantages."[25] Such a judgment is underlined by another anthropologist, Robin Horton, who observes:

. . . to go ahead with the comparative study of religion while leaving the scope of the term undefined is to behave in a self-stultifying way; for until some fairly precise criteria of inclusion of phenomena in the denotation of "religion" have been given, it is impossible to specify those variables whose behaviour we have to try to explain in our study. Until such criteria have been given, it is also possible to carry on an endless and entirely barren argument about whether a given item of human behaviour is or is not religious.[26]

Returning to Weber's refusal to provide initial boundaries for his field of discourse, it is apparent that despite his towering status in intellectual history, the foundation of his sociology of religion is only as strong (or as weak) as that constructed by Harrison or Nadel. The shakiness of its foundations is well-expressed by Peter Berger:

Max Weber . . . took the position that a definition of religion, if possible at all, can come only at the end, not at the beginning of the kind of task he had set for himself. Not surprisingly, he never came to such an end, so that the reader of Weber's opus waits in vain for the promised definitional payoff. I am not at all convinced by Weber's position on the proper sequence of definition and substantive research, since the latter can only proceed within a frame of reference that defines what is relevant and what is irrelevant in terms of the research.[27]

It is worth emphasizing, however, that the major methodological flaw in Weber's approach is not that the "promised definitional payoff" fails to materialize, for, after all, he acknowledges that possibility. It is rather that it never could materialize in the way he suggests. For, it may be argued, Weber no more than anyone else was capable of analysing something without having any criteria for its identification. Thus, in the absence of explicit criteria, his readers are justified in inferring the existence of implicit "religious" referents, and in regarding these as crucial in determining the nature of any definition that might finally emerge.

In fairness to Weber, it should be emphasized that his decision to proceed in his work as he did was clearly not taken lightly. This is not merely to imply that Weber had an acute appreciation of the perils of premature abstract categorization; it is also to insist that his strategy has nothing in common with a convenient, cynical or cavalier contempt for conceptual clarification as an obstacle to "real work." It might also be added (with Durkheim particularly in mind) that Weber's conviction that the consequences of conceptual caution may be less pernicious than the results of over-ambitious conceptualization is not necessarily misplaced.[28]

This brief consideration and comparison of the definitional approaches of Durkheim and Weber is no sterile chapter in the history of ideas. It is, rather, a convenient and fruitful way of raising a number of key conceptual issues that face the modern scholar no less than his illustrious predecessors. In the absence of any broad, scholarly, conceptual consensus, it is inevitable, for example, that students of religion will be drawn again and again to Weber's formulation of the definitional problem, his critics notwithstanding. Evidence of the intrinsic appeal of such an approach, as opposed to an attraction based merely on Weber's scholarly authority, may be found in an article by James Dagenais.[29] In arguing that the "scientific" study of religion is "a lost cause," Dagenais has recourse to a very "Weberian" line of attack, though at no time does he directly invoke Weber's name. In presenting a phenomenological critique of attempts to define religion, Dagenais attempts to rescue the study of religion from the clutches of sociology, science, positivism, formalism and nominalism as he perceives them. It is significant that, in his heated attack, he draws not only upon the writings of the "phenomenological movement" and contemporary critics of science, but upon sources crucial in the formulation of Weber's methodology. It is even more significant, in the present context, that his reading of Dilthey, his espousal of the distinction between *Naturwissenschaft* and *Geisteswissenschaft* and his approval of the method of *Verstehen* should result in a strategy for dealing with "religion" that closely parallels that of Max Weber. Thus, while eschewing the quest for the "phenomenal essence" of religion, Dagenais advocates an "empathic understanding" whose aim is "to make the intentionality of the scholar coincide with that of the religious participant." Such is to be achieved by taking "the risk of not having a theory or definition to begin with and rest upon" and "the risk of having to follow the data 'in act' . . ." In his view, the search for formal definition is misplaced, leads only to "scientific misunderstanding" and overlooks "descriptive statements of 'religious activity towards', that is, expressions of religious intentionality from the point of view of the 'observer'." Thus, viewing both scientific and theological interpretations of religion as failures by virtues of "their hidden presuppositions," Dagenais proposes that scholars "proceed by indirection."[30]

It is somewhat surprising that a scholar so sensitive to the danger of hidden presuppositions and so dedicated to the activity of "unconcealment" should be so apparently unaware of his own presuppositions. Yet Dagenais's argument undoubtedly rests upon an assumption that "the religious participant," religious "data," "activity" and "intentionality" are all immediately and unambiguously identifiable by the scholar seeking empathic understanding Such an argument therefore involves (as a hidden presupposition) an implicit working definition of religion, in this case one that rests upon the very shaky assumption that religion is rooted in the workings of the right hemisphere of the human brain. In such circumstances, it is not surprising that the conclusion is reached that "religion is what religion does," a formulation that appears less "untraditional and outrageous" than neo-functionalist and circular.[31]

Though its dangers may outweigh its attractions, the Weberian definitional strategy vis-à-vis "religion" remains sharply provocative and stimulates consideration not merely of the nature of religion but of the nature of definition in general. Some questions that naturally follow from the contemplation and criticism of Weber's approach are the following:

(a) Is it better to start with or finish with a definition in the process of research?
(b) Is a "clean" rather than an "untidy" definition to be preferred?
(c) Is a broad definition more useful than a narrow one?
(d) Is it the case that various kinds of definitions may possess utility at different stages of the research process? (It might be argued, for example, that a broad definition might be appropriate only to the early stages of research.)
(e) Is a definition of religion to be based primarily upon the subjective conceptions of observers or participants?
(f) To what extent should a sociological definition of religion entail a societal plausibility? Should it, for example, be consistent with the "folk-categories of European societies"?[32]

Before these questions are given further attention, it is appropriate to consider the profound impact of the Durkheimian definition upon the study of religion. While it might be argued that this definition involves an important substantive component in its category of the "sacred,"[33] its major effect is to shift attention from the substance to the functional significance of religion. By denying the intrinsic quality of phenomena regarded as sacred, Durkheim underlines, as Talcott Parsons notes, their *symbolic* character. The search for the referents of such symbols leads to the famous assertion that the real object of religious veneration is society, and to the interpretation of religious ritual as "a mechanism for expressing and reinforcing the sentiments most essential to the institutional integration of society."[34] Although Durkheim's insights into symbolism, the sacred and society are expressed brilliantly, his approach tends to underplay the importance of variation in the specific forms of society and the specific content of religious beliefs in favour of a general conception of society and religion that, at times, reaches the point of circularity. As Parsons observes, "he tends to treat religious patterns as a symbolic manifestation of 'society', but at the same time to define the most fundamental aspect of society as a set of patterns of moral and religious sentiment."[35]

Though this state of affairs has led some scholars to perceive his definition as no more helpful than Weber's non-definition, Durkheim's legacy is a rich one, particularly among sociologists and anthropologists of religion. Through the influence, especially, of the British social anthropologist A.R. Radcliffe-Brown and the American sociologist Talcott Parsons, the ideas of Durkheim percolated into the English-speaking intellectual world and became a key component in the perspective of "structural-functionalism." As the dominant social-scientific perspective in the two decades following World War II, structural functionalism exerted an influence on the study of religion that persists up to the present day.[36] In this context, it is no exaggeration to remark that *The Elementary Forms of The Religious Life* represented the starting point for nearly all textbook discussions of religion within the discipline of sociology for more than a quarter of a century, so that, in consequence, definitions of the subject-matter were overwhelmingly functional in character.[37] In such circumstances, therefore, Thomas F. O'Dea was understating the case when he commented, in 1966, that "much that is worthwhile in the growing research into the sociology of religion has been significantly influenced by a sociological point of view called 'functional theory'."[38] He was articulating the prevailing dogma much more accurately when he remarked:

> It is an axiom of functional theory that what has no function ceases to exist. Since religion has contrived to exist from time immemorial it obviously must have a function, or even a complex of functions.[39]

In a similar vein, Elizabeth Nottingham spoke for many others when she observed that "from the point of view of the sociologist . . . religion may be regarded as a cultural tool by means of which man has been able to accommodate himself in his total environment . . .[40] The identification of the sociological with a functionalist perspective in this passage is unambiguous and unequivocal.

Though the most obvious aspect of the Durkheimian legacy has undoubtedly been the neglect of substantive definitions in favor of functional ones, the other definitional issues illuminated by this perspective on religion are also worth noting briefly at this point:

(a) What is the utility of the "sacred-profane" dichotomy as a basis for understanding religion?

(b) What is the importance of the distinction between "beliefs" and "practices" in a religious context?

(c) What are the respective merits of "inclusive" and "exclusive" (broad and narrow) definitions? Can the problem of circularity be avoided in inclusivist formulations?

(d) Must religion be understood from a collectivist viewpont? Is a religion without a "church" (in Durkheim's sense) an impossibility?

(e) Is morality a necessary element in the definition of religion?

(f) Should religion be defined in terms of an observer or of its adherents?
(g) Is religion universal, and is it necessary for the survival of human society? If so, what is the definitional consequence?

The enduring relevance of the Durkheimian definitional strategy may be inferred as much from the animosity it still generates in some quarters as from the variety of functional interpretations it has spawned in others. Thus, despite the fact that, in the last two decades, the fortunes of functionalism have suffered a notable decline not restricted to the study of religion, definitional debate in a religious context still proceeds, to a considerable degree, as a dialogue with the ghost of Durkheim.

The outlines of a substantivist position are etched against a background of Durkheimian functionalism, while the spirits of Durkheim's old anthropological adversaries are summoned to aid in an intellectual counterrevolution.[41]

Probably no topic in the social sciences has been discussed at greater length or explored in greater detail than that of "functionalism."[42] For present purposes, therefore, it should suffice to discern and describe the kinds of functional definitions utilized in the analysis of religion. Elizabeth Nottingham provides the basic elements of such description in her classic structural-functional textbook of the 1950s:

> As students of sociology our main concern with religion . . . is with its function in human society. The term function . . . refers to the contribution of religion, or of any other social institution, to the maintenance of human societies as going concerns. Our interest, then, is in the part that religion has played and still plays in furthering their survival.[42]

A functional definition, then, as Roland Robertson has noted, "uses as the criteria for identifying and classifying a phenomenon the functions which that phenomenon performs; the functions which a system requires are stipulated and then observed; social and cultural phenomena are classified and identified on the basis of the functions which they perform."[43]

Although such characterizations would not likely be challenged by functionalists, it would be surprising to find in their social-scientific writings any monolithic conformity and consistency in their application of basic functionalist principles. Thus, close scrutiny of functionalist definitions and analyses of religion reveals a number of related, parallel and frequently overlapping approaches, rather than any clearly circumscribed consensus.

Some writers, for example, attempt to identify the essential requirements for the survival of human societies, and proceed to investigate the contribution of religion in this regard. Nottingham, for example, regards "some degree of common agreement, or consensus, about the nature of . . . crucial obligations, as well as the existence of power sufficient to constrain individuals and groups to fulfill them" as "a minimum essential for the persistence of the social order."[44] Not surprisingly, she turns to the work of Durkheim, which "has done more than that of any other single sociologist to throw light on the nature of [the] interaction between social values and related norms and the habitual fulfilment of social and moral obligations by most members of human societies."[45] Thus, religion is seen as providing values that promote agreement about the nature and content of social obligations, as ensuring the integration and coherence of such values and as reinforcing these values as a constraining power. The social function of religion is, therefore, an integrative one. Religion "promotes a binding together both of the members of societies and of the social obligations that help to unite them."[46]

In similar vein, O'Dea credits Durkheim with indicating "the strategic social function of religion" by emphasizing the reaffirmation of the group and the sanctification of social norms in a religious context as a "strategic basis for social control in the face of deviant tendencies and expression of impulses dangerous to the stability of society."[47] Not content with repeating Durkheimian formulae, however, he attempts to understand religion in terms of the "adaptive and expressive needs of human beings," and discovers its contribution to societies and cultures to be based upon its "central characteristic" of "transcendence of everyday experience in the natural environment." The human need for such a transcendental reference is rooted in conditions of contingency (or uncertainty), powerlessness, and scarcity and their consequences of frustration and deprivation. Religion functions to assist human beings in facing these "brute facts;" existential characteristics of the "human condition" inherent in human societies. More technically, O'Dea describes religion as "the most basic 'mechanism' of adjustment to the aleatory and frustrating elements."[48]

In pursuing his analysis, O'Dea raises two other matters of great importance in the functional approach to religion. They both emerge in the following statement:

Functional theory focuses our attention on the functional contribution of religion in the social system. Religion, by its reference to a beyond and its beliefs concerning man's relationship to that beyond, provides a supraempirical view of a larger total reality. In the context of this reality, the disappointments and frustrations inflicted on mankind by uncertainty and impossibility, and by the institutionalized order of human society, may be seen as *meaningful in some ultimate sense,* and makes acceptance of and adjustment to them possible.[49] (emphasis added)

By referring to questions of meaning and ultimacy, O'Dea invokes two other distinct though related functionalist approaches that require consideration.

Religion, in O'Dea's view, answers "the problem of meaning" by sanctifying the norms of the social order, and it does so by providing a grounding for beliefs and orientations "in a view of reality that transcends the empirical here-and-now of daily experience."[50] It takes little sophistication to trace such a perspective to the work of Max Weber; indeed, Weber's work is an important foundation of this variant of functional analysis. Weber's discussion of the manner in which "solutions to the problem of meaning, must be grounded in increasingly generalized, and 'fundamental' philosophical conceptions" is traced by Parsons to a basic "drive" toward meaning and the resolution of "discrepancies" presented by such facts as frustration, suffering and error.[51] In Weber's view, the development of culture involves propulsion by the continual search for "grounds of meaning" that can resolve discrepancies and that become progressively "more 'ultimate' reference points . . . further removed from the levels of common sense experience on which the discrepancies originally arise."[52]

So central is the conception of "meaning" to Weber's work on religion that it forms the core of his implicit "definition" of religion. For not only did Weber stress the necessity of understanding the "meaning" of religion in a general sense: his prime concern was clearly with what Parsons has termed "grounds of meaning." These may be understood as "a pattern or programme *for life as a whole,* which is given meaning by an existential conception of the universe, and within it the human condition in which . . . action is to be carried out."[53] Expressed somewhat more simply, it might be said that Weber was interested in "the basic perspectives around which a group or society of individuals 'organize' their life – their basic orientations to human and social life, conceptions of time, the meaning of death; in fact the basic cosmological conceptions in relation to human existence."[54]

The influence of this perspective is not hard to perceive in the work of both Talcott Parsons himself and of Robert Bellah, scholars equally indebted to both Durkheim and Weber.[55] In their view, as Robertson notes, individuals are controlled by norms prescribed by the social system, while the cultural system of beliefs, values and symbols controls the social system and "performs the function of providing the general guidelines for human action."[56] At the highest, most general level of the cultural system are the (somewhat unsuitably termed) "grounds of meaning," which may be identified with religion and which provide the means of defining it. Implying, as it appears to, that "grounds of meaning" are necessary for societal survival, this perspective assumes the universality of "religion" in human societies. Consistent with this is Parsons' observation that religion is "as much a human universal as language or an incest taboo, which is to say a kinship system."[57]

The inherent link between the problem of meaning and the question of "ultimacy" is apparent from the preceding discussion. Yet the functionalist approach, which defines religion in terms of a solution to "ultimate problems," finds its inspiration as much in the theology of Paul Tillich as in the sociology of Max Weber.[58] Seeking "the functions that distinguish religion as a human activity," J. Milton Yinger regards Tillich's statement that religion is that which concerns us ultimately as a "good starting point for a functional definition."[59] Acknowledging the difficulty of deciding just what an "ultimate problem" is, he suggests the following as "among the fundamental concerns of human societies and individuals:"

How shall we respond to the fact of death? Does life have some central meaning despite the suffering, the succession of frustrations and tragedies? How can we deal with the forces that press in on us, endangering our livelihood, our health, the survival and smooth operation of the groups in which we live - forces that our empirical knowledge is inadequate to handle? How can we bring our capacity for hostility and our egocentricity sufficiently under control that the groups within which we live, without which indeed, life would be impossible, can be kept together?[60]

Religion functions, therefore, to meet these "deep-seated emotional needs, springing from the very nature of man as an individual and as a member of society." It is, accordingly, best defined as "a system of beliefs and practices by means of which a group of people struggles with these ultimate problems of human life. It is the refusal to capitulate to death, to give up in the face of frustration, to allow hostility to tear apart one's human associations."[61]

While aspects of his analysis parallel Weber's discussion of the problem of suffering and evil, Yinger underlines his openness to theological influences by identifying religion with Reinhold Niebuhr's "citadel of hope built on the edge of despair." In a world in which the good die young and the evil flourish as the green bay tree, religion is, for Yinger, a refuge built on faith and hope.[62]

While it is clear from the foregoing discussion that different "styles" of functional analysis are applied to the study and definition of religion, it is equally apparent that the perspectives already investigated are, essentially, variants on a single theme. Thus, the differences between these perspectives provide little preparation for the distinctive character of the last functional definition to be discussed here.

Arguing that "a functional definition of religion avoids both the customary ideological bias and the 'ethnocentric' narrowness of the substantive definition of the phenomenon," Thomas Luckmann attempts, in his controversial work *The Invisible Religion*,[63] to provide a unique and uncompromisingly "functional" definition of his own. Acutely sensitive to the problems of definition in this context, he exhibits courage and conviction in charting a course that owes little to the American tradition of structural functionalism and much to the direct inspiration of Emile Durkheim.[64] Luckmann's startling shift in definitional direction is perhaps best captured by direct quotation:

The organism - in isolation nothing but a separate pole of "meaningless" subjective processes - becomes a self by embarking with others upon the construction of an "objective" and moral universe of meaning. Thereby the organism transcends its biological nature.

It is in keeping with an elementary sense of the concept of religion to call the transcendence of biological nature by the human organism a religious phenomenon . . . this phenomenon rests upon the functional relation of self and society. We may, therefore, regard the social processes that lead to the formation of self as fundamentally religious.[65]

In this view, everything that is human is, *ipso facto,* religious. The "transcendence of biological nature" is, by definition, a universal human characteristic and thus, notwithstanding the outrage of substantivist or theological critics, religion may be regarded as an "all-encompassing phenomenon." Pleading guilty to the charge that his analysis "fails to provide a specific account of the 'objective' and institutional forms of religion in society," Luckmann stresses his deliberate preoccupation with identifying "the general source from which sprang the historically differentiated social forms of religion." In his judgment, this strategy represents a "necessary first step in the sociological theory of religion," for, by demonstration of the religious quality of the "processes by which consciousness and conscience are individuated," the "universal yet specific anthropological condition of religion" may be identified.[66]

By extending Durkheim's analysis to its logical conclusion in what his critics might regard as a *reductio ad absurdum,* Luckmann promulgates the broadest, most inclusive of all sociological definitions of the phenomenon of religion. While it maintains a militant "functionalist" stance against the attacks of substantivists, therefore, his approach may in no way be considered representative of functionalism in general, and his definition remains outside the functionalist mainstream.

At this point, it is appropriate to summarize some of the main advantages and disadvantages of functionalist definitions of religion, especially as they relate to some of the questions raised in the context of both the Weberian and Durkheimian definitional traditions.

It is inappropriate to consider here whether definitional strategies based on the premise that "religion is what religion does" involve a complete or merely partial view of the nature of religion. As I have argued, the worth of definitions in the present discussion is measured in terms of utility; under such circumstances, partial insights into reality appear worthy and inevitable. The real merit of a definition, therefore, is best gauged in its own terms and within its own circumscribed boundaries.

From this point of view it may be noted that some functionalist analyses exhibit uncertainty regarding their point of view, particularly regarding their individual or collective (psychological or sociological) focus. In both Yinger's and O'Dea's discussions for example, sociological analysis tends to drift at times into a version of psychological functionalism reminiscent of the work of the anthropologist Bronislaw Malinowski.[67] Such functional analysis is no less psychological for referring to "Man" rather than to a specific human being.

Consideration of the functionalism associated with Parsons and Bellah reveals an intentionally broad and inclusive conception of religion that, while not as inclusive as Luckmann's, is nonetheless open to the criticism that it is too vague to be a tool of sociological analysis and too "circular" to make "religion" anything more than a redundant category. It is hard to believe that these authors do not themselves acknowledge the merit in such attacks, for in their writings they fail to provide a consistent identification of "religion" with "grounds of meaning." Indeed, while in their social commentaries the term is accorded a conventional, every-day use, its pure definitional conceptualization is confined to the lofty realm of abstract theorizing. This evident gap between theory and application seems to cast doubt upon the utility of the definition in question.[68]

A fortiori, what is true of the Parsons-Bellah formula may also be argued with respect to Luckmann's. Thus, while Luckmann clearly acknowledges and defends the gap between his underlying "anthropological" conception of religion and its objective and institutional forms, it may be questioned whether an appreciation of the former is really of any great assistance in identifying and understanding the latter.[69]

An important matter raised by functional definitions of religion relates to the content of religion. If religion is, indeed, what religion does, its existence is therefore to be inferred from the fact that its "job" is done. Thus, whatever "does its job" (i.e. performs its functions) is "religious." A strict functionalist definition, therefore, rules out conceptions like "pseudo-religion" or "quasi-religion," no matter how apt such usage seems in ordinary conversation.[70] The notion of a "secular religon" is not, in this context, a contradiction in terms, and systems of beliefs and practices such as communism, fascism, nationalism, Americanism, humanism or psychoanalysis may be termed "religious" in the full sense of the definition.[71] If they perform "religious" functions, for example by providing solutions to the "problem of meaning," by integrating a social group through shared "grounds of meaning," or by answering "ultimate problems," they are, by definition, "religious." Introduction of the idea of "functional equivalents" to religion is thus a departure from a strict functional analysis, for it introduces an implicit, substantive element into the definition of religion. It assumes a substantive element in "religion proper" that is lacking in its equivalent performing exactly the same functions.

Functionalist thinkers tend to be inconsistent in dealing with the degree of inclusiveness implicit in their perspective. Occasionally (like Luckmann), they hold firmly to their beliefs, but perhaps more frequently they take refuge in conventional usage, availing themselves of the convenient escape hatch of the "functional equivalent" or "functional alternative," as if "genuine" religion had an agreed and readily recognizable specific content.

The meaningfulness of such concepts as "secular religion," "political religion" and even "scientific religion" is entailed by the functionalist approach and underscores its inclusivism. Whether this quality is to be celebrated or bemoaned is, of course, a matter of opinion. Thus, while one scholar may exult in the universal applicability of an inclusive definition, another may perceive it as incorporating everything, and consequently nothing, under its rubric.[72]

The same problem is highlighted by consideration of the viewpoint that reveals the solution of "ultimate problems" as the basic function of religion. While the conception of a universal, existential concern with the ultimate on the part of humankind has an intellectual and emotional appeal to the scholar in search of a broad foundation for religion, its attraction tends to diminish the more closely it is scrutinized. It may be questioned, for example, whether there exists any clear, cross-cultural human consensus on what is of ultimate concern.[73] Alternatively, such questioning may be regarded as irrelevant because "ultimate problems" are to be defined sociologically rather than societally. However, if social scientists rather than ordinary human beings living in societies are empowered to decide what it is that concerns humanity ultimately, it is unclear on what basis a choice is to be made, or whether any worthwhile scholarly consensus is ever likely to emerge. If, as might plausibly be argued, one society's ultimate concern is another's irrelevance, the odds against the compilation of a social-scientific short list seem formidable.

A further difficulty in defining religion in terms ot "ultimacy" is suggested by Yinger's comment that religion is not alone in dealing with the ultimate problems of human life.[74] This seems to introduce an implicit conventionalism and substantivism into his functionalist argument, and to involve a retreat from the logic of his own perspective in a manner that would certainly elicit condemnation by Luckmann. Yinger's unwillingness to pursue a functionalist analysis to its logical limit in order to avoid the inclusion of, for example, medical or scientific practices under a "religious" heading parallels Parsons' and Bellah's attempts to have their functionalist cake and eat it, and is not redeemed by invocation of the hybrid conception of "quasi-religion." Thus, if religion is what religion does, and if religion is defined as that which addresses "ultimate problems" (however these may be defined), then whatever adresses such problems is religious, no matter how much such an interpretation violates every-day understandings of the term. Retreat from such a position appears to deny the whole purpose and utility of a functional definition of religion at the same time it exposes the difficulty of assimilating normative theological concepts such as "ultimacy" into social-scientific discourse.[75]

A final observation that must be made regarding functional definitions concerns "religious" participants' awareness of the functional character of their beliefs and practices. While not of immediate concern in the evaluation of the merits of functionalism in a religious context, this matter is extremely relevant to the task of "explaining" religious beliefs and actions. In the present discussion it may merely be noted that analysis of functional definitions entails contemplation of the relative utility and validity of participants' and observers' accounts of the nature of religion.[76]

For a number of years, functional definitions of religion attained the status of orthodoxy in the fields of anthropology and sociology. But mounting attacks upon functionalism as a general social explanatory scheme have inevitably engendered criticism of functional definitions of religion. It would, indeed, be no exaggeration to state that, within the discipline of sociology at least, proponents of functional definitions have been intellectually on the defensive for a considerable time.

During the functionalist (or, more precisely, structural-functionalist) ascendancy, it was as foolhardy to utilize a substantive definition of religion as it was to exhibit interest in religious origins. Both were associated with an outmoded, disreputable and speculative Victorian anthropology, beyond whose ethnocentric intellectualist and evolutionary assumptions social sciences had progressed irrevocably. In an intellectual atmosphere that encouraged the revival of Herbert Spencer, the reappraisal of Sir Edward Tylor and Sir James Frazer could not long be denied.[77] Thus, inspired especially by Tylor, a highly effective substantivist reaction has emerged to challenge the functionalist definitional monopoly in the sphere of religion.

Though it is, of course, quite possible to hold a substantive conception of religion without recourse to Tylor (or, indeed, without knowledge of him), his description of religion as "belief in Spiritual Beings" is widely regarded as the classic substantive definition of the phenomenon.[78] Whatever its merits or faults, this definition focusses clearly on the substance of religion as a particular kind of belief that might be readily apprehended in the social world. It therefore provides a convenient starting point from which analysis of substantive definitions in general may proceed, as well as an appropriate finishing point for the deliberations of some advocates of substantivism.[79]

As Tylor's definition hints, substantive definitions, like their functionalist counterparts, may be psychological or sociological in orientation. Definitions of the former sort focus on a "distinct kind of experience which is religious by virtue of its content."[80] In practice, concern with the identification of such an organic "religious thrill" (in the anthropologist Lowie's terminology)[81] tends to broaden into a compilation of a variety of psychological states associated with "religion," and finding common ground with psychological functionalism and its preoccupation with "needs."[82] In this context, the lines drawn between the psychological and the sociological, the functional and the substantive, are, of necessity, extremely fine. Though he does not define religion in psychological terms, Durkheim, for example, undoubtedly associates religion with particular psychological states such as feelings of awe and exultation inspired by participation in crowd behavior, and such feelings are crucial both to his substantive notion of the "Sacred" and to consequent inference of its functions.[83]

Interestingly enough, what is perhaps the classic case of psychological substantivism exhibits a number of similarities to Durkheimian religious psychology. The German theologian Rudolf Otto's assertion of the idea of "the Holy" or "numinous" as the "real innermost core of all religion" involves an "experience in feelings" of a "wholly other" that is outside the realm of "the usual, the intelligible, and the familiar" and that overpowers the individual with mixed emotions of dread, unworthiness and fascination.[84]

The strange harmony of contrasts that Otto detects in individiual consciousness of the "Holy" is reflected in many attempts to describe or define religion in terms of peculiar psychological states, even though the quest for some elusive yet universal religious thrill has been singularly unsuccessful. Thus, a varied literature explores such psychological themes as fear, powerlessness, awe, loneliness, suffering, frustration, dependency, helplessness, hopelessness and humility in the search for the intellectual and emotional characteristics of "religious" mentality.[85] One such exploration, in which the theologian Paul Tillich portrays religion as dealing with "what concerns us inescapably, ultimately, unconditionally" has already been noted.[86] It merits reconsideration, however, as a link between the theological psychology of Otto and sociological functionalism in a number of guises. In Tillich's view, religious experience involves a personal encounter with "the holy, the numinous presence of that which concerns us ultimately," and an intellectual or cognitive drive from level to level of philosophical analysis "to a point where we cannot speak of level anymore, where we must ask for that which is the ground of all levels, giving men their structure and their power of being."[87]

From a very different background, the anthropologist Edward Sapir contributes a number of psychological insights into a definition founded on the assumption that the core of religion is the pursuit of "ultimate serenity."[88] Revealing, like Otto, a strange harmony of contrasts, he observes that religion is "man's never-ceasing attempt to discover a road to spiritual serenity across the perplexities and dangers of daily life," and that it involves "omnipresent fear and a vast humility paradoxically turned into bedrock security." Religion thus assures "the triumph of human consciousness" in an inscrutable world.[89]

As may already be apparent, the substantive definition of religion in psychological terms is a difficult enterprise. The search for a distinct and identifiable "religious mentality" or "religious experience" having been conducted, apparently, in vain, attention is shifted to a variety of psychological states assumed to be associated with religion; none of them, however, may be confidently utilized in isolation as a substantive definitional referent for the term. Though frequently misreported, the psychologist William James recognized the inevitability of this state of affairs at the turn of the century. In his classic and, in this context, aptly named book *The Varieties of Religious Experience,*[90] James considers "the 'religious sentiment' which we see referred to in so many books, as if it were a single sort of mental entity," and comments:

> In the psychologies and in the philosophies of religion, we find the authors attempting to specify just what entity it is. One man allies it to the feeling of dependence; one makes it a derivative from fear; others connect it with the sexual life; others still identify it with the feeling of the infinite; and so on. Such different ways of conceiving it ought of themselves to arouse doubt as to whether it possibly can be one specific thing; and the moment we are willing to treat the term "religious sentiment" as a collective name for the many sentiments which religious objects may arouse in alternation, we see that it probably contains nothing whatever of a psychologically specific nature.[91]

Observing that while it undoubtedly makes sense to talk about "religious love," "religious fear," "religious joy," "religious awe" and the like, James insists that religious love is only "man's natural emotion of love" directed to a religious object, that religious fear is merely ordinary fear aroused by the notion of divine retribution and that religious awe is the same "organic thrill" that may be triggered, for example, by the beauty of natural surroundings, "only in this case it comes on us at the thought of our supernatural relations."[92] The same conclusion may be drawn of "all the various sentiments which may be called into play in the lives of religious persons:"

> As concrete states of mind made up of a feeling plus a specific sort of object, religious emotions . . . are psychic entities distinguishable from other concrete emotions; but there is no ground for assuming a simple abstract "religious emotion" to exist as a distinct elementary mental affection by itself, present in every religious experience without exception.[93]

In James' view, the fact that there is "no one elementary religious emotion" but rather a "common storehouse of emotions upon which religious objects may draw"[94] has even broader definitional implications than are immediately apparent. Thus, it is conceivable that there might "also prove to be no one specific and essential kind of religious object [or] religious act,"[95] a suggestion with serious consequences for substantivism in general.

Writing at about the same time as James, the German sociologist Georg Simmel also perceives that "religious" feelings and impulses, "faith," for example, are by no means restricted to conventional religious contexts.[96]

Thus, although faith is "usually understood as the essential and specific expression of religion, as its substance," it is also evident that there is an every-day "relation among men which is expressed by the same term" and permeates many kinds of social relationships.[97] For Simmel, there are no distinctively religious feelings, impulses, attitudes or relationships, for "religion" is merely an outgrowth of ordinary human relations, albeit one that heightens, isolates, refines and completes aspects of them. Like his American contemporary, therefore, he regards the search for specifically religious psychological phenomena as futile.

In the final analysis, of course, the utility of a substantive definition of religion (whether psychological or sociological) will depend, not just upon the nature of its content or objective referent, but on the clarity and precision with which this referent is identified and described. The pitfalls of vagueness and circularity, therefore, threaten the substantivist no less than the functionalist. For this reason (to take a convenient example), the experience of contact with "the ultimate" may be perceived as an extremely shaky substantive foundation for a useful definition of religion for the same reasons that render "ultimacy" a problematic concept in a functional definitional context.[98] Thus, while Sapir defines religion in terms of a quest for "ultimate serenity," he readily acknowledges that "what constitutes spiritual serenity must be answered afresh for every culture and for every community - in the last analysis, for every individual." If this is so, however, and if indeed "the ultimate problems of an Ojibwa Indian are different as to content from those of the educated devotee of modern science,"[99] it may be questioned whether the notions of "ultimacy" or "serenity" have any consistent meaning. If, as appears possible, general criteria by which they might be recognized are unavailable, their utility for definitional purposes must be seriously doubted. In these circumstances, "religion" necessarily becomes as elusive a concept as "ultimacy," and both are entrapped in a logical vicious circle in terms of which they may be interpreted as meaning anything and everything.

Substantive definitions of the sociological kind, both inclusive and exclusive in form, have attained a new respectability in recent years and merit particular attention. In criticizing the most widespread functional approaches to defining religion, their proponents refreshingly provoke reconsideration of some issues involved in the explanation of religion.[100] Some of these have already been noted, and others will be raised in the discussion that follows and in the next chapter.

A very loose version of substantivism is advocated by the British sociologist W.G. Runciman and, given his preference for a Weberian rather than a Durkheimian analysis of religion, it is hardly surprising that his definition bears a strong affinity, in practice, to Weber's "non-definition" of the phenomenon.[101] Thus, although Runcimen disapproves of the temptation to give up at the outset in the quest for a useful definition, he believes strongly that the "religious" is unlikely "to furnish a significantly rewarding theoretical category" for the understanding of beliefs, and that, for explanatory purposes, it might be better abandoned. He is unwilling to discard the term "religion," however, but only when used in a context where the term "ideology" would be equivalent, that is:

> in denoting those distinctive combinations of factual with ethical beliefs which constitute the "religion" of the Nuer, Dinka, Tokugawa Japanese, Homeric Greeks, Roman Catholics, Benthamite Utilitarians, Jews, Muslims, Anarchists, Narodniks, Christian Scientists, Dialectical Materialists and all the rest. In other words, if there is a general distinction to be retained between "non-religious" and "religious" beliefs, it is merely a distinction between what may be loosely called "matter-of-fact" beliefs on one side and beliefs about the conduct of life on the other.[102]

The vagueness of this approach is undeniable, for not only is Runciman's list heterogeneous, it is also entirely open-ended. Hence, while at first it seems inclined toward commonsense societal meaning, closer inspection reveals it as too broad and inclusive to represent conventional usage. The substantive distinction (roughly paralleling Durkheim's sacred-profane dichotomy) between "matter-of-fact" and "conduct-of-life" beliefs presents similar difficulties. Thus, while the latter are, in Runciman's view, "a universal and unambiguous category," the identification and isolation of such beliefs about *Lebenspraxis* is less easy than he assumes, given their "many different sorts of relation" to beliefs of a more prosaic kind. Finally, it is by no means clear on what basis "matter-of-fact" beliefs are so neatly and conveniently divorced from "religion" or "ideology" which, even in Runciman's own terms, combine the prescriptive with the cognitive.[103]

Whether his pragmatic definitional strategy is useful in the explanation of religion, or whether it is "at any rate unlikely to make the task of explanation any more difficult than otherwise,"[104] a consideration of Runciman's views is an appropriate means of introducing discussion of substantive sociological definitions of religion. To his credit, Runciman is extremely aware of the danger of sinking into a bottomless conceptual swamp by losing sight of the fact that a definition is to be evaluated in terms of its utility as an explanatory tool. From this point of view, his cautious attempt to combine "ordinary-language" usage and inclusivism with a loose, substantive dichotomy between religious and non-religious beliefs is understandable. Viewed more negatively, it illustrates that fuzziness, circularity, implicit conceptual bias, hazy theoretical distinctions and oscillation between societal and sociological usage are by no means confined to functionalist discourse. Whether "conduct of life" is a clearer concept than, for example, "grounds of meaning" or "ultimate problem" is a moot point.

"Dissatisfaction with Durkheim's definition of religion," Runciman notes, "has led to a revival of Tylor's usage, which has at least the merit of seeming more immediately suited to the practising anthropologist's needs." But, he also observes, "its revival is more for want of a better than for any newly discovered merits of its own."[105] He is undoubtedly correct in tracing Tylor's intellectual resurrection to a reaction against Durkheimianism and functionalism, and it is probably true to say that Tylor offers a convenient symbolic starting point for those wishing to reinstate substantivism. However, such an acknowledgement should not tempt us to a hasty dismissal of the utility of the Tylorian definition. Its revival may indeed owe nothing to "newly discovered merits" but, as the British anthropologist Robin Horton indicates, it has survived "the come-and-go procession of more exotic ideas with its robust closeness to common usage."[106]

It is hard to interpret the return to Tylor in terms of mere *faute de mieux* when so competent an anthropologist as Horton confesses, of his own attempt at a definition of religion, that "the definition I shall put forward is so close to Tylor's that I hesitate to call it in any way new."[107]

Beginning with a rejection of Durkheimianism, Horton flatly refuses to constrict religion within the confines of social structural symbolism:

> In effect, defining religion as structural symbolism comes to much the same thing as defining the substance "linen" in terms of its occasional use as a flag: the symbolic function is as incidental to the nature of the first as it is to that of the second.[108]

Though he admits that, within particular cultures, certain religious activities and beliefs have become associated with specific statuses or social groups so that eventually they come to symbolize them, he regards this symbolic function as merely a by-product of religious activity. As the results of non-symbolic "prior structural associations," what Horton calls "the impressive system of god-to-group co-ordination" evident in many societies may be satisfactorily explained, in his view, on the basis of a definition of religion that is in line with general usage. Turning to Tylor's definition, therefore, Horton is at pains to distinguish its misleading implications from those that have more value.

"Belief in spirits" can be an unprofitable substantive referent if it leads to perception of "spirits" as a distinct "class of objects characterized by a specific mode of existence" or if it involves "specific conditions of knowledge relevant to the making of true statements about them."[109] Through analysis of some examples from African cultural contexts, Horton indicates the futility of attempting to distinguish religious from non-religious phenomena in this particular manner because "the epistemological characteristics of any religious object one can think of are shared with some class of non-religious objects."[110] Available evidence convincingly demonstrates the danger of overgeneralization regarding spirits and suggests that such phenomena may have either a non-material or a down-to-earth material character. The "commonsense" notion of the immaterial nature of spirits, which is almost true by definition in Western cultures, is certainly not, therefore, of universal applicability. The Kalabari Water-People spirits discussed by Horton, for example, exhibit a "thorough-going materiality" in the eyes of their beholders and, open to the experience of the ordinary senses, are existentially of the same order as human beings or common, every-day physical objects. Yet, even if "spirits" were, *ipso facto,* confined to a realm beyond the reach of the ordinary senses, it would be foolhardy to identify their habitat as exclusively the domain of the "religious." As Horton notes, such entities would "fall into an epistemological category with others which are not religious," as even the most superficial consideration of modern theoretical physics makes abundantly clear.[111]

Thus the Nuer conception of "Spirit" described by Evans-Pritchard[112] emerges as the unlikely epistemological bedfellow of atoms, molecules, alpha particles and other theoretical entities whose existence is postulated by modern science. These scientific entities are "defined as incapable of direct observation, and statements about them can only be said to be verified by the behaviour of certain characteristics of observable phenomena which are assumed to be 'symptoms' of variations in the unobservables."[113] In the same way as exhibited by the Nuer in their accounts of "Spirit," contemporary scientists infer the truth of something that is in principle unobservable from the behavior of observable objects. Thus the domain of the non-material and unobservable is by no means the exclusive preserve of "spirits."

In Horton's view, the misleading aspect of Tylor's definitional criterion of "belief in spirits" is more than redeemed by its value in leading us to compare interaction with religious objects and interaction with human beings, and it is by following this lead that he is enabled to forge his own definition of religion:

> For purposes of the definition put forward here, it will be assumed that in every situation commonly labelled religious we are dealing with action directed towards objects which are believed to respond in terms of certain categories - in our own culture those of purpose, intelligence and emotion - which are also the distinctive categories for the description of human action. The application of these categories leads us to say that such objects are "personified." The relationships between human beings and religious objects can be further defined as governed by certain ideas of patterning and obligation such as characterize relationships among human beings. In short, religion can be looked upon as an extension of the field of people's social relationships beyond the confines of purely human society. And for completeness' sake we should perhaps add the rider that this extension must be one in which human beings involved see themselves in a dependent position vis-à-vis their non-human alters - a qualification necessary to exclude pets from the pantheon of gods.[114]

In appraising how well his own formulation measures up as a good definition in this sphere, Horton lays down two criteria:

. . . we are concerned with a term which has a clear common usage in our own culture. To avoid confusion, therefore, any definition which we put forward as the basis of its use in anthropology should conform as closely as possible to the usage of common sense. At the same time, we must look for the universal aspect of the phenomena commonly denoted by the term: for a culture-bound label is of no use in cross-cultural comparisons. . . . Secondly, we should bear in mind that members of several other academic disciplines – notably Psychology and History – are also bent on the study of "comparative religion"; and our definition should be sufficiently congruent with their assumptions for the results they achieve to be compared with our own findings.[115]

On these grounds, he determines that the definition "seems to measure up fairly well" as it "sticks close to common sense in preserving the connexion between 'religion' and other terms such as 'god' and 'spirit'; and it tallies closely with the assumption of psychoanalysts and historians."[116]

In an article that appeared almost on the heels of Horton's, Jack Goody also acknowledges that, "with all its limitations," a Tylorian definition "appears to offer the nearest approach to a resolution of our problems."[117] While he reaches this conclusion after arguments similar to Horton's, it is noteworthy that he finds particular significance in the fact that "in one of the most thoughtful of recent contributions to the study of the religion of a non-literate people, Evans-Pritchard has defined his field of discourse in Tylorian terms."[118] Like Horton, Goody is dissatisfied with the Durkheimian domination of discourse in social-anthropological and sociological contexts, and perceives the sacred-profane dichotomy as especially vague and misleading. Noting that a distinction between the "natural" and "supernatural" in the Western sense is by no means universal, he attacks what might be termed a loose substantivism in favor of a tighter, more specific substantive approach closely paralleling Horton's suggested new definition. Thus, turning his back on a natural-supernatural dichotomy that fails to account for the inextricability of "natural" and "supernatural" in specific cultural contexts, and rejecting a sacred-profane distinction whose cultural relativity denies it any universal substantive referent, Goody constructs his own definition. Combining the insights of Marett and Frazer with a basic acceptance of Tylor's definition, he suggests that "religious beliefs are present when non-human agencies are propitiated on the human model."[119] Religious activities include, however, not just acts of propitiation themselves but all behavior related to these "non-human agencies." Whatever its imperfections, this formulation provides, in Goody's opinion, "a focus for the comparative analysis of religious institutions which is of greater utility than the extensive definition preferred by Durkheim."[120] Furthermore, in his view, adoption of this definition by sociologists and anthropologists would only make *de jure* what is already *de facto,* for he maintains that this definition "is the one employed in practice by the majority of writers on this field."[121] Such scholars might, therefore, be more receptive to his call for "a return to the usages of earlier, pre-Durkheimian writers" than would appear likely at first sight.[122]

Like his British counterparts, the American anthropologist Melford Spiro also formulates a definition of religion inspired by a profound dissatisfaction with the Durkheimian rejection of gods or supernatural beings as legitimate referents of "religion."[123] Thus, while he disputes Durkheim's factual assessment of the atheistic character of Buddhism (so crucial to the attack on British anthropological substantivism), Spiro is much more concerned to expose and condemn the implicit methodological principle that universal applicability is a necessary characteristic of an acceptable definition of religion:

> Even if it were the case that Theravada Buddhism contained no belief in gods or supernatural beings, from what methodological principle does it follow that religion – or, for that matter, anything else – must be universal if it is to be studied comparatively? . . . Does the study of religion become any the less significant or fascinating – indeed, it would be even more fascinating – if in terms of a consensual ostensive definition it were discovered that one or seven or sixteen societies did not possess religion? If it indeed be the case that Theravada Buddhism is atheistic and that, by a theistic definition of religion, it is not therefore a religion, why can we not face, rather than shrink from this consequence?[124]

Unless value judgments are involved, he argues, "there is reason neither for dismay nor for elation concerning the empirical distribution of religion attendant upon our definition."[125] However, greater awareness of this elementary truth might have prevented the confusion created by the widespread abandonment of substantive definitions in favor of enticingly vague functional formulations.

In Spiro's estimation, functional definitions make it "virtually impossible to set any substantive boundary to religion and, thus, to distinguish it from other sociocultural phenomena."[126] Disregarding the fact that, for many functionalists, this is precisely their virtue, he asserts:

> In sum, any comparative study of religion requires, as an operation antecedent to inquiry, an ostensive or substantive definition that stipulates unambiguously those phenomenal variables which are designated by the term.[127]

Noting that while definition cannot replace inquiry and that inquiry cannot proceed without definition, Spiro also suggests that the absence of an explicit definition implies the existence of an implicit one. Substantive definition is, then, a necessity even though aspects of any particular definition will appear arbitrary to other scholars. "Religion," therefore, is not removed "from the arena of definitional controversy" but is transferred "from the context of fruitless controversy over what religion 'really is' to the context of the formulation of empirically testable hypotheses susceptible to cross-cultural testing."[128]

In forging such a definition of his own, Spiro insists that since "religion" is a term laden with "historically rooted meanings" its definition "must satisfy not only the criterion of cross-cultural applicability but also . . . of intra-cultural intuivity; at the least, it should not be counter-intuitive."[129] For him, any definition of religion that does not include the belief in superhuman beings as a crucial component ranks as counter-intuitive:

> I would argue that the belief in superhuman beings and in their power to assist or to harm man approaches universal distribution, and this belief – I would insist – *is the core variable which ought to be designated by any definition of religion.*[130]

Thus, in a formula very similar to those of Horton and Goody, he defines religion as "an institution consisting of culturally patterned interaction with culturally postulated superhuman beings."[131] Parenthetically, it may be observed that detection of the spirit of Tylor in this context requires no special psychic ability.

The articles by Horton, Goody and Spiro just discussed may be regarded as the frequently cited classics of the Anglo-American substantivist reaction of the 1960s. Quicker to regain an intellectual foothold in the United Kingdom than in North America, substantive definitions were being promoted in texts by the early 1970s. Thus, Roland Robertson formulated a definition resting upon "the substantive cultural content of religious phenomena" that defined "religious culture" as a "set of beliefs and symbols (and values deriving directly therefrom) pertaining to a distinction between an empirical and a super-empirical transcendent reality; the affairs of the empirical being subordinated in significance to the non-empirical."[132] In similar vein, Michael Hill defined religion in terms of a set of beliefs "that postulate and seek to regulate the distinction between an empirical reality and a related and significant supra-empirical segment of reality."[133] Shortly before these British sociologists offered their substantive definitions as considered alternatives to the usual functionalist fare, a broad substantivism found an eminent and eloquent American spokesman in the widely read sociologist Peter L. Berger, whose conception of religion as "the human enterprise by which a sacred cosmos is established" is indebted chiefly to Rudolf Otto.[134]

With these definitions, it may be argued, sociological substantivism began to regain a certain legitimacy and ceased to be generally regarded merely as an outmoded, intellectually disreputable or crankish aberration. From the early 1970s, therefore, substantivism has appeared to some students of religion as an idea whose time has come – again. Naturally, it has not been universally welcomed and its critics have not been reluctant to indicate its deficiencies. Thus, while on the one hand a broad substantive definition of religion is open to charges of vagueness and over-inclusiveness, a narrow one may be accused of arbitrariness, exclusivism and parochialism, as the price paid for the preservation of common sense. Even among substantivists, the merits of the somewhat specific content of formulations like those of Horton, Goody and Spiro must be weighed against those of the rather vaguer substances revealed, for example, by Berger, Robertson and Hill.

While the debate between substantivism and functionalism is by no means the only important dispute among those seeking to define religion, it is certainly the pre-eminent conflict in a social-scientific context. As Thomas Luckmann has noted, however, the battle lines are frequently obscure, and "functionalism" and "substantivism" must, to some extent, be regarded as labels of convenience:

A great amount of internecine warfare goes on in the two camps, if they can be called that. They do not constitute theoretical "schools" – nor are they exclusive clubs, as is shown by several cases of double membership. There are as many similarities as there are differences in the "functional" positions of, e.g. Marx, Durkheim, Yinger, Parsons, Herberg, Bellah and Geertz. And Rudolf Otto, Van der Leeuw, Eliade, the French scholars in the *sociologie religieuse* and Peter Berger, as representative adherents of "substantivism", are as mixed a bag as any.[135]

The general accompaniments, consequences and ramifications of explicit commitment to either perspective are subject to a wide range of interpretation. Luckmann, for example, detects a preference among functionalists for grand theories (or terrible simplifications) of a global evolutionary kind and perceives a predilection on the part of substantivists for "middle-to-short-range analyses of specific processes involving religious institutions . . . in relation to other institutions."[136] In a brief consideration of the sources of broad, inclusive and narrow, exclusive definitions, Robertson draws a number of conclusions relevant to the crosscutting distinction between functionalism and substantivism. Extrapolation from his suggestions might indicate therefore, that inclusive functional definitions will be held not only by those concerned with the structure and process of total societies, but also by those preoccupied with "more detailed and closely circumscribed problems, such as the study of particular religious organizations." For the latter abstract theoretical debate is largely irrelevant; there is "little intellectual incentive to use precise definitions," and lukewarm espousal of an inclusive functionism appears to offer the best of all possible definitional worlds.[137] Exclusive, substantive definitions, however, seem liable to attract those who stress the presence of conflict rather than consensus in social life, and who exhibit suspicion of religion in an all-embracing, integrative guise. Similarly, those whose precise concern is with the connection, contrast or conflict between religious and other aspects of society, for example in the context of "secularization," are likely to regard an exclusive, substantive definition as of most utility.[138]

It should be noted that in the heat of definitional debate, scholars are prone to discover increasingly undesirable aspects of their opponents' formulations in direct proportion to the growing evidence of the virtues of their own viewpoint. Any perspective may, therefore, suffer condemnation on a variety of grounds that can even be mutually contradictory. Thus, for example, functional definitions have occasionally been criticized for exhibiting a theological or poetic rather than a scientific sensitivity.[139] Yet it is for a diametrically opposed reason that Peter Berger is warlike in his opposition to them. Perceiving the functional approach to religion as increasingly implicated in an ideologically partisan justification of a secularized world view and a "quasi-scientific legitimation of the avoidance of transcendence," he argues:

> It achieves this purpose by an essentially simple cognitive procedure. The specificity of the religious phenomenon is avoided by equating it with other phenomena. The religious phenomenon is "flattened out". Finally, it is no longer perceived. Religion is absorbed into a night in which all cats are grey. The greyness is the secularized view of reality in which any manifestations of transcendence are, strictly speaking, meaningless and *therefore* can only be dealt with in terms of social or psychological functions that can be understood without reference to transcendence.[140]

Depending upon the point of view of the critic, therefore, functionalism may be condemned either as a party to mystification or as a means of disenchantment, a state of affairs in which it cannot fail to be in the wrong. In fairness, however, it must be noted that its fate is no worse than that suffered by substantivism at the hands of its functionalist detractors.

Emphasis upon a single intellectual debate is often the most useful (and least painful) way of initiating the novice into the theoretical battleground of a particular field of scholarship. In the present context, close scrutiny of the arguments and counter-arguments of able proponents of both functional and substantive definitions of religion provides a rough path through the definitional forest. Its twists and turns reveal the good faith and good sense of most of those on either side of the functional-substantive divide, the plausibility of both approaches, and the impossibility of any easy resolution of this intellectual conflict. Exposure to both sides of the definitional debate in no way precludes or discourages eventual partisan commitment. It would be a pity, however, if it did not induce sensitivity and tolerance even into the heat of intellectual hostilities.

Whichever metaphor is used, it is undeniable that the excursion through the definitional forest or the conceptual labyrinth of the study of religion is a harrowing one even if undertaken more than once. Occasionally assuming the character of an intellectual *Pilgrim's Progress* or a quest for a definitional Holy Grail, its rewards lie in the journey itself rather than in reaching an ultimate destination. Thus, the student who regards this journey as merely an unpleasant *rite de passage* to be suffered in anticipation of its eventual culmination in the warm embrace of conceptual certainty will be sadly disappointed. No single, clear, unambiguous, useful and widely accepted definition of religion awaits the weary traveller at the end of this expedition for the simple reason that none exists, whether in the general field of religious studies, in the domain of the social-scientific study of religion, or even within the narrower sub-disciplinary confines of the sociology, anthropology or psychology of religion.[141] To recognize this fact is not to abandon hope of meaningful communication regarding religion, nor is it to resign oneself to working within a perpetual state of conceptual chaos, but it is to acknowledge a contemporary intellectual reality. While lack of a clear, widespread consensus may be regrettable, it is also inevitable under present circumstances. This intellectual fact of life is far better revealed openly than camouflaged under an empty verbal formula calculated to conceal more than to enlighten.

Though it is, of course, impossible to predict the likelihood of enhanced agreement regarding a definition of religion, the auspices appear generally unfavourable. The short-term outlook seems decidedly unpromising, and it is doubtful whether, even in the long run, the marked differences between disciplinary, theoretical or ideological perspectives can or ought to be reconciled.[142] If, therefore, the goal of a single, all-purpose formal definition of religion is chimerical, it is necessary for the student to possess some general principles for evaluating and choosing between rival definitions. It would be presumptuous and absurd to suggest that there is any simple formula by which, for example, the superiority of substantive over functional or inclusive over exclusive definitions might be demonstrated. From the preceding discussion, it should be obvious that logic, eloquence, insight and persuasiveness are not confined to any particular perspective, and that the task of determining the relative merits of conflicting viewpoints is an unenviable one. Yet, in such circumstances, a number of assumptions, perhaps almost too obvious to deserve reiteration, may prove of incalculable value.

In the first place, the social scientist in search of a definition should abandon the search for the real meaning or essence of religion as being, from his point of view, an irrelevant and fruitless task. While such a quest may be meaningful for the philosopher, theologian or student of *religionswissenschaft,* the appropriate pursuit for a social scientist is to identify the most useful definition available for purposes of social research and analysis. Prosaic though it may seem, the social scientist's concern is with utility rather than reality in this context.[143] Concern with the formulation or evaluation of scientific conceptualizations of religion (whether in a positivistic or humanistic sense) also assumes that a good (or useful) definition will be epistemologically neutral and rooted in methodological atheism (or, perhaps better, methodological agnosticism). Peter Berger expresses this sentiment convincingly:

> The *scientific* study of religion must bracket the ultimate truth claims implied by its subject. This is so regardless of one's particular conceptions as to scientific methodology. . . . If science means anything at all, as distinguished from other types of mental activity, it means the application of logical canons of verification to empirically available phenomena. And whatever else they may be or not be, the gods are not empirically available, and neither their nature nor their existence can be verified through the very limited procedures given to the scientist. What is available to him is a complex of human experience and thought that purports to refer to the gods. Put differently, within the framework of science the gods will always appear in quotation marks, and nothing done within this framework permits the removal of these quotation marks. Anyone engaged in the scientific study of religion will have to resign himself to this intrinsic limitation - regardless of whether, in his extrascientific existence, he is a believer, an atheist or a skeptic.[144]

Naturally, objectivity and ethical neutrality must be understood as aims rather than as automatic accomplishments in a definitional context, and the student must maintain sensitivity to ideological or political bias in the guise of impartial scientific assertion manifested in either the formulations of others or in his own reasoning. No attempt at formal definition of any sort is immune to the possibility of such extra-scientific bias, but in the sphere of religion the problem is acute.[145] Eternal vigilance must, therefore, be exercised regarding each and every definitional proposal to ensure that conscious or unconscious emotional, political, cultural or sectarian preferences are not confused with necessary, objective, scientific premises or propositions. Fortunately, from this point of view, the lack of definitional consensus is itself extremely useful. No proposal remains long without severe criticism, keenly attuned to evidence of ideological bias and watchful of attempts to project the world views of certain Western intellectuals onto the rest of the human race. Alert to the biases of others, the student of religion wishing to adopt a social-scientific perspective needs to practise a certain reflexivity with regard to his own thinking and to bear in mind that inclusive and functional formulae are subject to ideological subversion no less than exclusive and substantive definitions framed specifically with the intention of remaining down-to-earth and reflecting the usage of ordinary language.

The price of commitment to a social-scientific perspective on religion is an undertaking to apply the rules of logic and the principles of scientific verification in determining the merits of any definitional strategy, one's own included. The student who thus commits himself must be on guard against the predilections, affections and animosities that may, so often, lurk behind an apparent neutrality. He must, likewise, be harsh in his rejection of illogical argument, sentimental suasion, inappropriate evidence, illegitimate inference, confused categories and trivial truisms. In short, when the utility of a definition is being appraised, rhetoric must never be mistaken for logic. Finally, faced with a number of apparently useful definitions, the student bent upon social-scientific investigation of religion, must pick and choose among them on grounds of their specific utility (or potential utility) in the context of particular research topics or stages of the research process. In this sense, all useful definitions are operational in kind, and their utility is dependent upon an appropriateness to the task in hand. Such definitions will be as explicit, clear, unambiguous and objective as befits the enterprise of social science.

This final point may, perhaps, be made more simply and clearly by adoption of the metaphor proposed by an American philosopher, J.E. Barnhart:

> In some ways a definition is like a map. It marks off boundaries and "locates" different factors. It would be as foolish to boast that one has the definitive definition of "religion" as to claim that one has drawn up the final and absolute map of an area. Better definitions arise . . . just as better maps arise according to appropriate needs. A map maker has to observe and study his territory, and whoever attempts to develop useful verbal definitions must be alert to the interchange of communication in the appropriate field of inquiry . . . one map is better than another only to the extent that it satisfies a particular interest.[146]

The evidence presented in this chapter indicates the wide range of definitions of religion generated within the social sciences, and bounded intellectually as well as chronologically by the century-old substantivism of Tylor and the recent radical functionalism of Luckmann. Such definitional diversity, even within the confines of a single discipline, though disillusioning to some students, may be viewed in a positive light if the criterion of relative or differential utility is kept firmly in mind. Of course, the extent of definitional multiplicity need not be defended, and neither is every formulation justifiable in intellectual and utilitarian terms. As human creations, social-scientific definitions may bear the imprint of extra-scientific influences, just as their popularity may be determined by disciplinary politics rather than by their intellectual worth. While this is undeniable, it must be stressed again that lack of a clear definitional consensus is by no means the worst of all possible theoretical worlds and that, despite the understandable sense of frustration exhibited by their advocates, precipitate schemes to induce such a state of intellectual uniformity might well prove scientifically counterproductive or, as William James would express it, "more misleading than enlightening."[147]

To perceive attempts to secure widespread definitional agreement, at the present time, as almost as misplaced as the search for the real meaning of religion in a social-scientific context is not to deny the need for useful definitions of the phenomenon. In a similar way, sensitivity to the danger of contracting "clarity neurosis" and appreciation of the insightful, if excessive, sentiment that "clarity is the last refuge of those who have nothing to say"[148] should not deter the student from demanding clarity, precision and objectivity in definition and, *a fortiori,* should not tempt him into surrender to "the inarticulate mumbo jumbo which substitutes awe for inquiry."[149]

Though frequently appreciated, the complexity of the definitional task in a religious context has perhaps nowhere been better expressed than in William James' classic *The Varieties of Religious Experience*. Referring, in 1901, to an already evident plethora of definitions of religion, James observes, in terms prophetically pertinent to the contemporary social-scientific study of religion:

> . . . the very fact that they are so many and so different from one another is enough to prove that the word "religion" cannot stand for any single principle or essence, but is rather a collective name. The theorizing mind tends always to the over-simplification of its materials. This is the root of all that absolutism and one-sided dogmatism by which both philosophy and religion have been infested. Let us not fall immediately into a one-sided view of our subject, but let us rather admit freely at the outset that we may very likely find no one essence, but many characters which may alternately be equally important in religion.[150]

In the chapters that follow, the task of describing the nature of the sociology of religion will be undertaken, as far as possible, in the spirit of this exhortation.

Footnotes to Chapter Two

[1] A concern with the analysis of language is associated with both Oxford and Cambridge philosophy and their transatlantic offspring. The literature is copious, although the central figures in what might be termed this philosophical "movement" are undoubtedly Wittgenstein and Austin. For a critique, see Ernest Gellner, *Words and Things,* Hammondsworth: Penguin Books, 1968.

[2] Of course, the degree of conceptual uniformity in the physical sciences is often exaggerated by outsiders and the co-existence of rival "paradigms" is sometimes naïvely assumed to be merely a characteristic of the infantile nature of the social sciences. See Thomas S. Kuhn, *The Nature of Scientific Revolutions,* Chicago: University of Chicago Press, 1962 and the vast literature generated by this treatise.

[3] This is revealed by a cursory investigation of any good text in contemporary sociological theory. Howard S. Becker has expressed the point well in his declaration that "it is not one world in sociology any more," "What's Happening to Sociology?" in *Society,* vol. 16, No. 5, 1979, p. 24. It is tempting to add "if it ever was."

[4] This sentiment is capable of provoking a long philosophical debate on the nature of science, "positivism" and the relative merits of "nominal" versus "real" definitions. Though the approach advocated here would be perceived by some as an espousal of a "nominalist" position, the variation in understandings of the nature of "real" and "nominal" definitions seems so great that a discreet avoidance of the terms in the present context appears to be the most advisable strategy. For discussion of the distinction, however, see Carl G. Hempel, *Fundamentals of Concept Formation in Empirical Science,* Chicago: University of Chicago Press, 1952; Roland Robertson, *The Sociological Interpretation of Religion,* New York: Schocken Books, 1970, p. 36; Abraham Kaplan, *The Conduct of Inquiry,* San Francisco: Chandler Publishing

Co., 1964; and Peter L. Sissons, "The Sociological Definition of Religion," *The Expository Times,* Vol. 82, No. 5, 1971, p. 135. See also the discussions in the works of Spiro and Dagenais cited here.

[5] Discussion here suggests the lack of enthusiasm that greets, for example, the infusion of theological definitions into social-scientific constructs.

[6] It is arguable that sociologists, anthropologists and historians could quite conceivably operate with a common definition of religion, whereas psychologists would find it difficult to co-operate. (See, for example, W.G. Runciman, "The Sociological Explanation of 'Religious' Beliefs," *Archives Européennes de Sociologie,* Vol. 10, No. 2, 1969, p. 172). On the other hand, many anthropologists and sociologists frequently stray into psychological territory in formulating definitions. (See some of the discussions of functionalism in the notes following.)

[7] Max Weber, *The Sociology of Religion* (trans. E. Fischoff), Boston: Beacon Press, 1963 (first published 1922), p. 1.

[8] Emile Durkheim, *The Elementary Forms of the Religious Life* (trans. J.W. Swain), New York: Collier Books, 1961 (first published 1912). For other writings see W.S.F. Pickering (ed.), *Durkheim on Religion,* London: Routledge & Kegan Paul, 1975.

[9] Runciman, *op. cit.,* p. 181.

[10] Smith's best known work is *Lectures on the Religion of the Semites,* first published 1889. For Smith's influence on Durkheim and others, see T.O. Beidelman, *W. Robertson Smith & the Sociological Study of Religion,* Chicago: University of Chicago Press, 1974.

[11] Sir Edward Tylor, *Primitive Culture,* London: John Murray, 1871, Vol. I, p. 383.

[12] Durkheim, *Elementary Forms* (cited above), pp. 44-48. For criticism of Durkheim on this point see Melford E. Spiro, "Religion: Problems of Definition & Explanation," in Michael Banton (ed.), *Anthropological Approaches to the Study of Religion,* London: Tavistock Publications, 1966, pp. 91-94.

[13] Durkheim, *Elementary Forms,* p. 62.

[14] See Jack Goody, "Religion and Ritual: The Definitional Problem," *British Journal of Sociology,* Vol. 12, 1961, pp. 148-149.

[15] Durkheim, *Elementary Forms,* p. 237.

[16] *Ibid,* p. 257.

[17] *Ibid,* pp. 464-465 and pp. 14-15. See also Runciman, *op. cit.,* p. 197.

[18] See Talcott Parsons, "The Theoretical Development of the Sociology of Religion: A Chapter in the History of Modern Social Science," *Journal of the History of Ideas,* Vol. 5, 1944, pp. 184-185. See also Parsons' *The Structure of Social Action,* Glencoe: The Free Press, 1937, p. 427, and his "Durkheim on Religion Revisited: Another Look at The Elementary Forms of the Religious Life" in C.Y. Glock and P.E. Hammond (eds.), *Beyond the Classics? Essays in the Scientific Study of Religion,* New York: Harper and Row, 1973, pp. 156-180.

[19] Runciman, *op. cit.,* pp. 190 and 187.

[20] Spiro doubts whether the universality of "religion" is intellectually desirable. (*op. cit.,* p. 88.) The most explicit form of this thesis may be seen in Thomas Luckmann, *The Invisible Religion: The Problem of Religion in Modern Society,* New York: The Macmillan Company, 1967 (first published in German in 1963). Elsewhere Luckmann has noted that opponents of such an inclusive definition "usually overstate their case by saying that the definition is all-inclusive and therefore without heuristic value." See Thomas Luckmann, "Theories of Religion and Social Change," *Annual Review of the Social Sciences of Religion,* Vol. 1, 1977, p. 9. See also Luckmann's "On Religion in Modern Society: Individual Consciousness, World View, Institution," *Journal for the Scientific Study of Religion.* Vol. 2, 1963, pp. 147-162.

[21] Jane E. Harrison, *Themis: A Study of the Social Origins of Greek Religion,* Cambridge: Cambridge University Press, 1912. (Cited by both Goody and Runciman, noted in previous footnotes to this chapter.)

[22] *Ibid,* p. 29.

[23] S.F. Nadel, *Nupe Religion*, London: Routledge & Kegan Paul, 1954, pp. 7-8. Compare the similar strategy proposed by the eminent British anthropologist Evans-Pritchard, who asserts that general conclusions must be built up from particular ones. Rather than asking "What is Religion?" we should, says Evans-Pritchard, inquire into "the main features of . . . the religion of one Melanesian people." See E.E. Evans-Pritchard, *The Institutions of Primitive Society*, Oxford: Basil Blackwell, 1954, p. 9.

[24] See the comments on Evans-Pritchard in Spiro, *op. cit.*, p. 90. See also the remarks on Weber's non-definition of religion in Peter L. Berger, *The Sacred Canopy: Elements of a Sociological Theory of Religion*, New York: Doubleday & Co., 1967, Appendix I, p. 176.

[25] Goody, *op. cit.*, p. 142.

[26] Robin Horton, "A Definition of Religion and its Uses," *Journal of the Royal Anthropological Institute*, Vol. 90, 1960, p. 201.

[27] Peter L. Berger, *op. cit.*, pp. 175-176. See also Robertson, *op. cit.*, pp. 34-35.

[28] Consider, for example, Runciman's indictment of Durkheim's definitional enterprise. Runciman, *op. cit.*, pp. 187-190.

[29] James J. Dagenais, "The Scientific Study of Myth and Ritual: A Lost Cause," *The Human Context*, Vol. 6, No. 3, 1974, pp. 586-620. See also Hans H. Penner, "Lost Causes: A Reply to James Dagenais," *The Human Context*, Vol. 7, No. 1, 1975, pp. 136-141.

[30] Dagenais, *op. cit.*, p. 611. One possible source of such a procedure, according to Dagenais, might be found in Bernard Lonergan's "much despised 'heuristic structure'," by which one names the unknown, works out its properties, and uses the properties to direct, order and guide the inquiry. (This seems akin to what social scientists would term an "operational definition" or "working definition," though Dagenais would probably disagree.) See Dagenais, *op. cit.*, pp. 594-595 and Bernard J.F. Lonergan, *Insight: A Study of Human Understanding*, New York: Harper & Row, 1978 (first published 1958), pp. 3-69. See also the approach taken in Karel Dobbelaere and Jan Lauwers, "Definition of Religion: A Sociological Critique," *Social Compass*, Vol. 20, 1973-74, pp. 535-551.

[31] Dagenais, *op. cit.*, p. 611.

[32] For use of this term, see Goody, *op. cit.*, p. 143.

[33] As Berger notes, Durkheim "begins with a substantive description of religious phenomena, particularly in terms of the sacred/profane dichotomy, but ends with a definition in terms of the general social functionality of religion." Peter L. Berger, *The Sacred Canopy* (cited above), p. 176. That Durkheim was sensitive to the relative claims of "form" and "content" in the definition of religion is evident from the footnote he appends to his own definition. See *Elementary Forms*, p. 63, footnote 68.

[34] Parsons, "The Theoretical Development of the Sociology of Religion," cited above, p. 185.

[35] *Ibid*, p. 186.

[36] The classic "textbooks" of this perspective are Talcott Parsons, *The Social System*, Glencoe: The Free Press, 1951; Kingsley Davis, *Human Society*, New York: The Macmillan Co., 1948; Harry M. Johnson, *Sociology: An Introduction*, New York: Harcourt, Brace and World, 1960. See also N.J. Demerath and R.A. Petersen (eds.), *System, Change and Conflict*, New York: The Free Press, 1967; Mark Abrahamson, *Functionalism*, Englewood Cliffs, N.J.: Prentice-Hall, Inc., 1978; and Robert W. Friedrichs, *The Sociology of Sociology*, New York: The Free Press, 1970.

[37] General sociological textbooks treated religion in this manner. See, for example, Davis, *op. cit.*, pp. 509-548. This was also true of the leading textbooks in the sociology of religion. See, for example, the works by O'Dea, Yinger and Nottingham cited in subsequent notes.

[38] Thomas F. O'Dea, *The Sociology of Religion*, Englewood Cliffs, N.J.: Prentice-Hall, Inc., 1966, p. 2.

[39] *Ibid,* p. 4. This seems to come perilously close to an unwarranted assumption of what Merton calls "indispensability." See Robert K. Merton, "Manifest and Latent Functions," in *Social Theory and Social Structure* (revised edition), Glencoe, Illinois: The Free Press, 1957, pp. 27-38. See also Spiro, *op. cit.,* pp. 119-120; and J.M. Yinger, *Religion, Society and The Individual,* New York: The Macmillan Co., 1957, pp. 58-59.

[40] This refers primarily to Sir Edward Tylor and Sir James Frazer. The emergence of neo-Tylorian and neo-Frazerian viewpoints stirred up heated controversy in anthropological circles. For some insight into the debate see the works of Runciman, Horton, Spiro and Goody (cited previously in this chapter) and consult Robin Horton, "Neo-Tylorianism: Sound Sense or Sinister Prejudice?" *Man: The Journal of the Royal Anthropological Institute,* Vol. 3, 1968, pp. 625-634; Ian C. Jarvie, *The Revolution in Anthropology,* London: Routledge & Kegan Paul, 1964; Edmund R. Leach, "Golden Bough or Gilded Twig?" *Daedalus,* Vol. 90, 1961, pp. 371-387. Tylor's best-known work, *Primitive Culture,* I have already cited. Frazer is best known for *The Golden Bough,* a multi-volume work first published in 1890. An accessible modern abridgement is *The New Golden Bough,* edited by T.H. Gaster, Garden City, N.Y.: Doubleday and Co., 1961.

[41] See, for example, works by Merton, Abrahamson, and Demerath and Petersen cited previously.

[42] Elizabeth K. Nottingham, *Religion and Society,* New York: Random House, 1954, p. 12.

[43] Robertson, *op. cit.,* p. 38. See also p. 18.

[44] Nottingham, *op. cit.,* p. 13.

[45] *Ibid,* p. 15.

[46] *Ibid,* p. 16. Luckmann notes that the "common element of the various 'social- functional' approaches" (including his own) is integration. See Thomas Luckmann, "Theories of Religion and Social Change," p. 7. It is interesting that Nottingham, like some other functionalists, claims linguistic legitimation for the integrative or binding character of religion when she refers to the "literal sense of the word" (p. 16). It is true that the Latin *religare* is often taken as the root of the word, but, in fact, "religion" is of "doubtful etymology." See *Oxford English Dictionary* (On Historical Principles), edited by James A.H. Murray *et. al.,* Oxford: The Clarendon Press, 1933; as well as Yinger, *op. cit.,* p. 13.

[47] T.F. O'Dea, *op. cit.,* p. 13.

[48] *Ibid,* p. 5.

[49] *Ibid,* p. 6.

[40] *Ibid,* pp. 6-7.

[51] Talcott Parsons, in the introduction to Weber's *The Sociology of Religion,* pp. xlvii.

[52] *Ibid,* pp. xlvii-xlviii.

[53] *Ibid,* p. xxxiii.

[54] Robertson, *op. cit.,* p. 35.

[55] This dual influence is clearly evident in the numerous writings of both scholars.

[56] Robertson, *op. cit.,* p. 40; and see, for example, Talcott Parsons' introduction to the section on culture and the social system in Parsons *et al* (eds.), *Theories of Society,* Glencoe: The Free Press, 1961, pp. 967-993; and Robert N. Bellah, *Tokugawa Religion,* Glencoe: The Free Press, 1957. See also footnotes 68 and 98 of this chapter.

[57] Parsons, "Introduction" (cited above), xxviii.

[58] See Paul Tillich, *Biblical Religion & the Search for Ultimate Reality,* Chicago: University of Chicago Press, 1955; *The Courage To Be,* New Haven, Conn: Yale University Press, 1959; and *The Protestant Era,* Chicago: University of Chicago Press, 1948. It is interesting, and not too fanciful, to link the concern with ultimacy to the concern with grounds of meaning investigated above. Thus, in *Biblical Religion & The Search for Ultimate Reality,* Tillich declares: "We are driven from one level to another to a point where we cannot speak of level

anymore, where we must ask for that which is the ground of all levels, giving them their structure and their power of being" (pp. 12-13, footnote 50). The influence of Tillich on O'Dea's thinking is apparent. See O'Dea, *op. cit.*, pp. 27-28.

[59] Yinger, *op. cit.*, p. 9. Religion, says Tillich, "deals with what concerns us inescapably, ultimately, unconditionally." See *The Protestant Era, p. 87.*

[60] *Yinger, op. cit.*, p. 9.

[61] *Ibid*, p. 9.

[62] *Ibid*, p. 10. It should be noted that sociological borrowing from the prescriptive writings of theologians such as Neibuhr and Tillich is not without its dangers. This issue is raised again in this chapter.

[63] Thomas Luckmann, *The Invisible Religion* (cited above).

[64] Luckmann's sociological background is phenomenological and owes more to Alfred Schutz than to Talcott Parsons. *The Invisible Religion* is inspired directly by the classic tradition in sociology, and specifically by the "convergence in the thinking of Durkheim and Weber" on "the fate of the person in the structure of modern society," *Ibid*, pp. 12-13.

[65] *Ibid*, pp. 48-49.

[66] *Ibid*, p. 49.

[67] See Bronislaw Malinowski, *Magic, Science & Religion & Other Essays*, Glencoe, Illinois: The Free Press, 1948. It should be stressed that Malinowski's functionalism is social as well as psychological, but it is important to note that, in his view, both "magic and religion arise and function in situations of emotional stress" (p. 67). For further discussion see George C. Homans, "Anxiety and Ritual: The Theories of Malinowski and Radcliffe-Brown," *American Anthropologist*, Vol. 43, 1941, pp. 164-172; and Spiro, *op. cit.*, pp. 107-112.

[68] See, for example, Talcott Parsons, "Religion in a Modern Pluralistic Society," *Review of Religious Research*, Vol. 7, 1966, pp. 125-146; *The Social System*, pp. 1-55; Introduction to "Culture & the Social System" in Parsons *et al* (eds.), *Theories of Society*, pp. 967-993; "Christianity & Modern Industrial Society," in E.A. Tiryakian, *Sociological Theory, Values and Sociocultural Change*, Glencoe: The Free Press, 1963, pp. 33-70; and *Structure and Process in Modern Societies*, Glencoe: The Free Press, 1960, pp. 295-321. See also Robert N. Bellah, *Tokugawa Religion* (cited above) and R.N. Bellah (ed.), *Religion and Progress in Modern Asia*, New York: The Free Press, 1965. Goody notes that "it is perhaps significant that in their pragmatic treatment of religious phenomena [Parsons and Bellah] adhere much more closely to the 'traditional' sphere of discourse" (*op. cit.*, p. 154); while Robertson remarks that this "is not an approach which is sustained rigorously by its proponents" (*op. cit.*, p. 40). The possibility of overlap between a functional definition based upon a conception of religion as the highest level of culture and one rooted in a notion of ultimacy is evident in Bellah's statement: "Ultimate concern has to do with what is ultimately valuable and meaningful, what we might call ultimate value; and with the ultimate threats to value and meaning. What we might call ultimate frustration. It is one of the social functions of religion to provide a meaningful set of ultimate values on which the morality of a society can be based. Such values when institutionalized can be spoken of as the central values of a society." (*Tokugawa Religion*, p. 153.) For the overlap between the ideas of ultimacy and grounds of meaning, see footnote 58.

If the drift into conventionalism and substantivism is one danger of ambitious theoretical intentions, another is, according to Luckmann, a "predilection for rather grand schemes of 'evolutionary' or 'universal-historical' transformations of religion [and as] their opponents are quick to point out, the borderline between such grand schemes and terrible simplifications is often so faint as to be invisible to the naked eye." Luckmann, "Theories of Religion & Social Change," cited above, p. 9.

[69] As Luckmann notes ("Theories of Religion and Social Change" p. 9): "In the end, [functionalists] must identify historical *forms* of religion in which the presumably universal religious 'function' becomes a datum for the social scientists." In *The Invisible Religion*,

Luckmann distinguishes between the "universal yet specific anthropological condition of religion" and the "historically differentiated social forms of religion" that have, as their source, the universal condition (p. 49).

[70] The resort to such usage parallels the drift noted in footnote 68, though notions such as "political religion" and "secular religion" clearly violate conventional usage of the term "religion," as Parsons is aware. Again, from this perspective, the work of Parsons and Bellah merits careful examination. See Goody, *op. cit.*, p. 154.

[71] See Yinger, *op. cit.*, pp. 13-15. The great totalitarian movements of the present century have frequently been labelled "religious" in this sense, particularly where they may be seen to constitute "state religions." Likewise scientific and even avowedly "anti-religious" organizations may be perceived as performing "religious" functions. See, for example, Donald Macrae, "The Bolshevik Ideology" in his *Ideology and Society,* London: Heinemann, 1961, pp. 181-197- and Sally F. Moore and Barbara G. Myerhoff (eds.) *Secular Religion,* Assen/Amsterdam: Van Gorcum, 1977. On the religion of "Americanism" see Will Herberg, *Protestant-Catholic-Jew: An Essay in American Religious Sociology,* Garden City, N.Y.: Doubleday Anchor Books, revised edition, 1960; and Herberg's "America's Civil Religion: What It Is and Whence it Comes" in Russell E. Richey and Donald G. Jones (eds.), *American Civil Religion,* New York: Harper and Row, 1974, pp. 76-78. See also R.N. Bellah, "Civil Religion in America" in R.E. Richey and D.G. Jones, *op. cit.* (originally published in *Daedalus,* 1967). In lighter vein, see Morris R. Cohen, "Baseball as a National Religion" in his *The Faith of a Liberal,* New York: Henry Holt, 1946, pp. 334-336 (originally published in 1919); and Tom Sinclair- Faulkner, "A Puckish Reflection on Religion in Canada" in Peter Slater (ed.), *Religion and Culture in Canada/Religion et Culture au Canada,* Canadian Corporation for Studies in Religion, 1977, pp. 407-420. See chapter six of this book.

[72] Spiro, for example, questions the virtue of universality and asks: "from what methodological principle does it follow that religion - or for that matter, anything else - must be universal if it is to be studied comparatively?" Spiro, *op. cit.*, p. 88. See also the discussion in Spiro, pp. 86-87.

[73] See, for example, the sceptical view of the anthropologist Edward Sapir, *Culture, Language and Personality: Selected Essays,* Berkeley: University of California Press, 1964, p. 122. See also Goody, *op. cit.*, p. 154.

[74] J.M. Yinger, *op. cit.*, p. 10.

[75] See footnote 71. The difficulties of transposing the theological notion of "ultimacy" are noted by Robertson, *op. cit.*, pp. 39-40 and by Gregory Baum, "Definitions of Religion in Sociology," in Mircea Eliade and David Tracy (eds.), *What is Religion? An Inquiry for Christian Theology* (Concilium No. 136), New York: Seabury Press, 1980, pp. 25-32. Similarly, confusion might well occur in use of the terms "grounds of meaning," "grounds of levels" or "grounds of being" in the different contexts of social science and theology. See the discussion in notes 57-62 of this chapter. See also John A.T. Robinson, *Honest to God,* London: SCM Press, 1963, pp. 45-63. On the problem of clear communication between social scientists and theologians, see Gregory Baum, "Liberation Theology and the 'Supernatural'," *The Ecumenist,* Vol. 19, No. 6, 1981, pp. 81-87. Baum observes that "it is difficult for sociologists to understand theological language, just as it is often difficult for theologians to know what sociologists are talking about" (p. 81). See also David Martin, John Orme Mills, and W.S.F. Pickering, (eds.), *Sociology and Theology: Alliance and Conflict,* New York: St. Martin's Press, 1980.

[76] See the discussion in Yinger, *op. cit.*, pp. 58-60; and Merton, *op. cit.*, pp. 19-84. For insightful discussion of the actor's versus the observer's point of view, see Goody, *op. cit.*, pp. 152-162.

[77] Major credit (or blame) for the revival of interest in Herbert Spencer must go to Talcott Parsons and Robert Bellah, despite the fact that Parsons had begun his first book by echoing Crane Brinton's question, "Who now reads Spencer?" See Talcott Parsons, *The Structure of*

Social Action (cited above). See also his introduction to the reprinting of Jay Rumney, *Herbert Spencer's Sociology,* New York: Atherton Press, 1966, and his article "Evolutionary Universals in Society," *American Sociological Review,* Vol. 29, 1964, pp. 339-357. Consult also Robert Bellah's article "Religious Evolution" in the same issue, pp. 358-374. For the revival of Tylor and Frazer, see Runciman, Goody, Horton and Spiro, previously cited in the notes to this chapter.

[78] This minimal definition occurs in Tylor's *Primitive Culture* (cited above), first published in 1871. Almost any discussion of substantivism in the definition of religion (for or against) begins with his definition.

[79] See, for example, Spiro, Horton and Goody, cited previously. Goody advocates a "return to the usages of earlier, pre-Durkheimian writers in this field" (p. 160) and cites the recent use of Tylorian definitions by Evans-Pritchard and Raymond Firth. Horton confesses that the definition he puts forward is so close to Tylor's that he hesitates to call it new (p. 204), while the same could certainly be said of Spiro's. See also Anthony F.C. Wallace, *Religion: An Anthropological View,* New York: Random House, 1966, p. 52, and more discussion in this chapter.

[80] Luckmann, "Theories of Religion and Social Change," cited above, p. 6.

[81] Robert H. Lowie, *Primitive Religion,* New York: Liveright Publishing Company, revised edition, 1948, first published in 1924, p. v and pp. 338-347.

[82] See footnote 67, and Yinger's discussion of "Religion and Personality," *op. cit.,* pp. 73-124 and the sources cited therein.

Psychological views of religion are as varied as anthropological or sociological ones and any attempt at a brief summary of them is bound to be inadequate. A student might, however, begin with classic works by Freud and Jung reprinted in many editions (Freud's *The Future of an Illusion, Civilization and its Discontents, Totem and Taboo;* and Jung's *Psychology and Religion*); and then consult Robert H. Thouless, *An Introduction to the Psychology of Religion,* Cambridge: Cambridge University Press, 1961 (first published in 1923); G. Stephens Spinks, *Psychology & Religion: An Introduction to Contemporary Views,* London: Methuen & Co., 1963; Michael Argyle and Benjamin Beit-Hallahmi, *The Social Psychology of Religion,* London: Routledge and Kegan Paul, 1975; Paul W. Pruyser, *A Dynamic Psychology of Religion,* New York: Harper and Row, 1968; and L.B. Brown (ed.), *Psychology & Religion,* Harmondsworth: Penguin Books, 1973.

[83] Durkheim, *Elementary Forms of the Religious Life* (cited above), pp. 248-251.

[84] Rudolf Otto, *The Idea of the Holy: An Inquiry into the Non-Rational Factor in the Idea of the Divine & its Relation to the Rational* (trans. John W. Harvey), London: Humphrey Milford and Oxford University Press, 1926 (first published in German, 1917).

[85] See footnote 82.

[86] See footnote 59.

[87] See footnote 58.

[88] Sapir, *op. cit.,* pp. 122-123; see also footnote 73.

[89] *Ibid,* pp. 122-123.

[90] William James, *The Varieties of Religious Experience: A Study in Human Nature,* London: Collins, 1960, first published in 1902.

[91] *Ibid,* p. 47.

[92] *Ibid,* p. 47.

[93] *Ibid,* p. 47.

[94] *Ibid,* p. 47.

[95] *Ibid,* pp. 47-48.

[96] Georg Simmel, "A Contribution to the Sociology of Religion," *American Journal of Sociology,* Vol. 10, 1905, p. 360. This article, translated by W.W. Elwang, was reprinted in *American Journal of Sociology,* Vol. 60, 1955 and in abridged form in Yinger, *op. cit.,* pp.

332-344. See also Georg Simmel, *Sociology of Religion* (trans. Curt Rosenthal), New York: The Philosophical Library, 1959, first published in 1905.

[97] Simmel, "A Contribution to the Sociology of Religion," p. 360; and *Sociology of Religion*, p. 29.

[98] There is great overlap between functional and substantive definitions rooted in ultimacy. Robert Bellah observes, for example, "It is one of the social functions of religion to provide a meaningful set of ultimate values on which the morality of a society can be based. Such values when institutionalized can be spoken of as the central values of a society." (*Tokugawa Religion*, cited above, p. 6.) Obviously wishing to define religion in functional terms, Bellah none the less seems to imply that "central values" might serve, at least partially, as substantive referents for religion. The same might, therefore, be argued with respect to Parsons' "common ultimate-value attitudes" and Lessa and Vogt's view that "religion is concerned with the explanation and expression of the ultimate values of a society." (Parsons, *The Structure of Social Action*, cited above, pp. 433-434; and William A. Lessa and Evon Z. Vogt, *Reader in Comparative Religion*, Evanston, Illinois: Row, Peterson and Company, 1958, p. 1.) Of the latter definition, Goody notes: "The utility of so vague and general a formulation is open to doubt. Quite apart from the question of the operation involved in specifying 'ultimate' or 'central' values, this definition would include all purely 'rational' pursuits in the economic or political sphere that were of major interest to the members of a particular society." Goody, *op. cit.*, p. 154. It might be stressed that Goody's criticism would apply whether Lessa and Vogt regarded their definition as functional or substantive. See footnotes 56, 58 and 68 of this chapter.

[99] Sapir, *op. cit.*, p. 22.

[100] This point is stressed by Runciman, *op. cit.*, pp. 149-150, but its importance is also evident in the works of Horton, Goody and Spiro, cited previously.

[101] See Runciman, *op. cit.*, pp. 163-166; and see footnote 7 of this chapter.

[102] *Ibid*, p. 165.

[103] They combine the "factual" with the "ethical." *Ibid*, p. 115.

[104] *Ibid*, p. 166.

[105] *Ibid*, p. 152.

[106] Horton, *op. cit.*, p. 204.

[107] *Ibid*, p. 204.

[108] *Ibid*, p. 204.

[109] *Ibid*, pp. 204-205.

[110] *Ibid*, p. 207. Horton notes that "we can point to no single ontological or epistemological category which accommodates all religious entities [and] we find that every major ontological and epistemological category we can devise contains religious as well as secular entities" (p. 205).

[111] *Ibid*, p. 206. For further discussion of science and religion, see Chapter Three. For a useful recent analysis, see Ian G. Barbour, *Myths, Models and Paradigms: A Comparative Study in Science and Religion*, New York: Harper & Row, 1974.

[112] *Ibid*, p. 205. See also E.E. Evans-Pritchard, *Nuer Religion*, Oxford: Oxford University Press, 1956, pp. 315-320.

[113] Horton, *op. cit.*, p. 206. Horton relies for this analysis on W.C. Kneale, *Probability and Induction*, Oxford: Oxford University Press, 1952, pp. 89-113.

[114] Horton, *op. cit.*, p. 211.

[115] *Ibid*, p. 211.

[116] *Ibid*, p. 211.

[117] Goody, *op. cit.*, p. 157.

[118] *Ibid*, p. 157 and Evans-Pritchard, *Nuer Religion*.

[119] Horton, *op. cit.*, p. 157.

[120] *Ibid,* p. 158.

[121] *Ibid,* p. 158.

[122] *Ibid,* p. 160.

[123] Spiro, *op. cit.,* pp. 85-96.

[124] *Ibid,* p. 88.

[125] *Ibid,* p. 89.

[126] *Ibid,* pp. 89-90.

[127] *Ibid,* p. 91.

[128] *Ibid,* p. 91.

[129] *Ibid,* p. 91.

[130] *Ibid,* p. 94.

[131] *Ibid,* p. 96.

[132] Robertson, *op. cit.,* pp. 46-47.

[133] Michael Hill, *A Sociology of Religion,* London: Heinemann Educational Books, 1973, p. 43. It is interesting that in formulating definitions based on a distinction between the "empirical" and the "super-" or "supra-empirical," both Robertson and Hill tread again the treacherous ground of a natural-supernatural dichotomy abandoned by many scholars in favour of the vaguer division between the sacred and profane. For discussion of the difficulties of such distinctions, particularly in the context of the social-anthropological work of Frazer, Malinowski and Evans-Pritchard, see Goody, *op. cit.,* pp. 149-151; Horton, *op. cit.,* pp. 205-206; Spiro, *op. cit.,* pp. 88-96; and Durkheim, *Elementary Forms of the Religious Life* (cited above), pp. 39-43. See footnotes 110 and 111, of this chapter.

[134] Peter L. Berger, *The Sacred Canopy* (cited above), p. 25. Berger (p. 177) notes his indebtedness to Otto's *The Idea of the Holy* (cited above).

[135] Thomas Luckmann, "Theories of Religion and Social Change" (cited above), p. 8.

[136] *Ibid,* p. 8.

[137] Robertson, *op. cit.,* p. 37. Compare Luckmann's discussion in "Theories of Religion and Social Change," pp. 8-9.

[138] See Luckmann, pp. 8-9, and Robertson, p. 37.

[139] This is true, for example, where notions like "ultimacy" or "grounds of meaning" are an integral part of functionalist analysis. Spiro hints at such an interpretation of functionalism. See Spiro, *op. cit.,* p. 89.

[140] Peter L. Berger, "Some Second Thoughts on Substantive versus Functional Definitions of Religion," *Journal for the Scientific Study of Religion,* Vol. 13, 1974, pp. 128-129. See also Dobbelaere and Lauwers, *op. cit.,* on this point.

[141] Sociologists and anthropologists are divided among themselves along functional-substantive and other lines, while theologians and historians of religion debate the admissability of social-scientific definition without attaining any agreement on a useful definition. See the plea for consensus in Frederick Ferré, "The Definition of Religion," *Journal of the American Academy of Religion,* Vol. 38, 1970, pp. 3-16.

[142] As I have noted, it is by no means clear that any common interdisciplinary definition is either possible or desirable. Runciman's assertion that a common definition is possible for the disciplines of sociology, anthropology and history makes good sense, as does the view that many such definitions might not be useful to psychologists. Some students of comparative religion and the history of religions and even theologians have been tempted by social-scientific perspectives and are willing to espouse sociological or anthropological definitions. Other scholars from these disciplines are less than enthusiastic about the adoption of such perspectives or definitions. For an early case of the receptivity of theological and religious scholarship to social science, see L.L. Bernard, "The Sociological Interpretation of Religion," *The Journal of Religion,* Vol. 18, 1938, pp. 1-18, and for a more recent discussion of religion and the methodology of the social sciences, see Hans H. Penner and Edward A. Yonan, "Is a Science of

Religion Possible?" *The Journal of Religion*, Vol. 52, 1972, pp. 107-133. For a recent rejection of social science, see Dagenais, *op. cit.*, pp. 591-596, and pp. 601-614. For Dagenais, all the social sciences, including the social-scientific study of religion, represent "pseudo-knowledge" and the search for adequate definitions is merely a symptom of their inadequacy. Dagenais pleads with all students of *Religionswissenschaft* to resist "making common cause with the social scientist whose cause is lost" (p. 596).

[143] Weber, of course, decisively rejected the "essence of religion" as a concern of social science. (*Sociology of Religion*, p. 1.) The connection between "real definitions" and those "necessarily vague" definitions that stipulate the "essential nature" of religion are noted by Spiro (*op. cit.*, p. 86 and p. 89). See also William James, *op. cit.*, p. 46.

[144] Berger, *Some Second Thoughts. . .* "(cited above), pp. 125-126.

[145] The heavily value-laden and emotional content of "religion" in European and North American society is noted in chapter one. Thus, religion and politics were long avoided with good reason, as "polite" topics of discussion on "social" occasions, at least in Anglo-American etiquette. The topic of "religion" is still capable of generating considerable heat even in scientific contexts.

[146] J.E. Barnhart, "Is One's Definition of 'Religion' always Circular?" *International Yearbook for the Sociology of Knowledge & Religion*, Vol. 9, 1975, p. 122.

[147] James, *op. cit.*, p. 46.

[148] Friedrich Waismann, "How I See Philosophy," in A.J. Ayer (ed.), *Logical Positivism*, New York: The Free Press, 1959, pp. 360-361, cited in Barnhart, *op. cit.*, p. 122.

[149]Barnhart, *op. cit.*, p. 122.

[150] James, *op. cit.*, p. 46. It is interesting to note that as early as 1901 a multiplicity of dogmatic and oversimplified definitions already "infested" theoretical discussion of religion. See James, p. 46 and especially the reference to Professor James H. Leuba's article in *The Monist* for January 1901 (pp. 46-47n).

CHAPTER THREE
THE ORIGINS OF THE SOCIOLOGY OF RELIGION

The term "religion" may not quite imply all things to all men but, as evidenced by the discussion in the previous chapter, it has many connotations and several major variants even within the confines of organized scholarship. Within the disciplinary boundaries of sociology, its scope and referents vary greatly, vascillating mainly between the poles of functionalism and substantivism, on one hand, and inclusivism and exclusivism, on the other. While such a state of affairs demands considerable caution and circumspection on the part of neophyte students and experienced scholars alike, it need only be entirely bemoaned to the extent that scholars persist in regarding the problem of the "ambiguity which surrounds the origin and nature of religion" as one for which, in the words of Georg Simmel, "a single word will be the 'open sesame.'"[1] Indeed, the emphasis already placed upon definitional utility, the relative nature of such utility, and the necessarily partial or incomplete character of useful definition is pithily expressed in Simmel's observation that "a theory is only . . . entirely erroneous when it assumes to be the sole explanation, and . . . only correct when it claims to point out merely one of the sources of religion."[2]

As Peter Berger notes, definitions "slice up" reality in different ways[3] and sociologists engage in the process of slicing up "religion" beside colleagues and rivals from within and without their own discipline.[4] The particular ways in which sociologists of religion slice up reality, together with their conceptions of reality itself, provide the main foci of interest in this chapter.

It is perhaps misleading at the outset to refer to "the" sociology of religion in such a monolithic and definitive manner. This is so for two reasons: in the first place, as will be apparent from the definitional discussion in Chapter Two, this subdiscipline is not characterized by a benign consensus on even the most fundamental matters; and secondly, what is true of the subdiscipline in this regard is writ large in the discipline of sociology as a whole.[5] It might, therefore, be more accurate to follow the lead of an eminent French sociologist of religion and speak of "sociologies" of religion, regarding a sociology of religion as an aim rather than an accomplishment.[6] For reasons of convenience, the phrase "sociology of religion" will be used throughout the present chapter, but it cannot be stressed too strongly that the terms "sociology" and "religion" are vague, problematic and contentious in the extreme, even as used by those who are proud to combine them in the designation of their subdisciplinary commitment.[7]

More positively, however, it may be remarked that the very existence of the subdiscipline itself attests to a primordial commonality of intellectual concern which, despite its mutations, is embedded in what C. Wright Mills has termed the "classic tradition" of social science.[8] Any serious examination of the sociology of religion must, therefore, begin by tracing its roots in the work of the social-scientific founding fathers.[9]

Nature, Progress, Evolution and the Study of Religion

Like sociology itself, the sociology of religion has its origins in the atmosphere of enlightenment, rationalism and optimism that permeated intellectual circles in the eighteenth century. Under the cold gaze of the Scottish philosopher, the English historian, the American radical and the French social thinker, traditional religion, especially in its European Christian forms, was subjected to an unprecedented process of demystification, even iconoclasm. Engendered in a climate of scientific scepticism, secularism and anti-clericalism, the sociological study of religion emerged to pronounce an immediate death-sentence upon its subject matter at the same time as it toppled theology from its lofty intellectual throne. If the beginnings of sociology proper are perceived in the works of Saint-Simon and Comte, the genesis of the sociology of religion must surely be discerned in their writings also. Whether viewed substantively - as an erroneous and pernicious means of understanding the natural world through the doings of supernatural or super-empirical beings - or functionally - as an ideational basis for social harmony - the topic of religion is undoubtedly of paramount importance in their thought.[10]

For Auguste Comte, traditional religion represented a relic from an age of fetishism and superstition; a way of thinking and behaving that was totally inappropriate to the stage of development attained by the human mind in the first half of the nineteenth century. In an age of science or positivism, this primitive mode of thought had no place, and "religion" deserved to survive only in a functional sense as a socially integrative body of doctrines and rituals derived from the scientific analysis of nature and society.

Comte's "Religion of Humanity," like its predecessor, Saint-Simon's "New Christianity," was viewed by its founder as the only form of religion destined to sustain humanity in the final stage of its intellectual ascent. In these earliest sociological discussions one may discern an intellectual bias that regards religion as essentially cognitive in nature,[11] although in its hitherto existing forms it has necessarily offered only an inadequate and mistaken view of reality. However, oddly coupled with this emphatic bias, an uncertainty regarding its appropriate conceptualization is already apparent in the theorizing of those who sought immortality not merely as the architects of a new science but as founders of a new religion, as well.

Inspired by doctrines of social evolution, British sociologists, anthropologists, ethnographers and comparative religionists of the second half of the nineteenth century desired less to become prophets of a new religion than to discover the origins of religion in the life of humankind.[12] Working in a Victorian cultural climate that was in many ways inhospitable to disinterested and dispassionate probing of cherished customs and beliefs, these scholars nonetheless succeeded in laying the foundations of the scientific study of religion, whatever damaging criticisms may subsequently have been levelled at their enterprise. Like their continental predecessors, these British writers formulated an intellectualist interpretation of religious phenomena. Reinforced by, if not actually rooted in, Britain's rôle as the hub of a worldwide empire, this perspective led, at its best, to an awareness of Western man's links with his "rude forebears" and with contemporary "primitives" and "savages." At its worst, however, it exhibited a paternalistic and contemptuous racism.[13]

In what may be loosely termed the "British anthropological tradition" of the last century, the central figure, especially from the standpoint of research on religion, is undoubtedly Sir Edward Tylor, whose celebrated "minimum definition" of the phenomenon was encountered in Chapter Two.[14] Deriving a term from the word "anima" meaning "soul," Tylor perceived the origin of religion in "animism." Denoting, in its original formulation, the belief that human beings, creatures, plants and natural objects all possess life, personalities and souls, animistic theory was to remain influential in various guises for many years. In an imaginative reconstruction of the mind of primitive man, Tylor conjectured that religion emerged as a result of the spectacle of death and the experiences of trances, ecstatic visions and, especially, dreams. These occurrences generated belief in an immaterial "apparitional soul," separable from the body and mobile in inclination. This conception, confined initially to human contexts, was subsequently applied, through the inevitable logic of "lower psychology," to animals and plants, and ultimately to inorganic objects as well. Furthermore, in the primitive mentality, the idea of the soul underwent a natural transformation, evolving first into a belief in spiritual beings (Tylor's minimum definition of religion) and developing finally into a belief in gods, beings to whom human beings were subordinate.

Despite its protracted popularity,[15] the theory of animism appears, to most modern scholars, to reveal less about the savage mind than about the mind of Sir Edward Tylor. Evans-Pritchard nicely expresses this attitude when he remarks:

> In the absence of any possible means of knowing how the idea of soul and spirit originated and how they might have developed, a logical construction of the scholar's mind is posited on primitive man and put forward as the explanation of his beliefs.[16]

For this reason, Tylor's "savage" has something of the character of "a primitive philosopher struggling to solve the problems of existence." He is treated, from a point of view that Parsons terms "rationalistic positivism," as though he were "a rational, scientific investigator acting 'reasonably' in the light of the knowledge available to him."[17]

Tylor's viewpoint was shared, and indeed arrived at independently, by the great English sociologist Herbert Spencer, in whose opinion primitive man was rational though mistaken.[18] Given his limited knowledge, Spencer's "savage" made reasonable, if invalid, inferences so that, for example, observation of the natural world led him to posit a duality between the visible and invisible. Furthermore, observation of states of temporary human insensibility, coupled with his own dream experiences, encouraged belief in his own dual nature. Like his reflection and his shadow, his dream-self attained great importance in the world-view of primitive man and culminated in the belief in a soul, not merely as a human possession but as an attribute also of animals, plants and even material objects. Unlike Tylor, however, Spencer discovered the origin of religion in the belief in ghosts rather than simply in souls. From a perceived duality of human nature, his hypothetical savage inferred the survival of the soul after death (for a time, at least), a view that was reinforced by the reappearance of the dead in the dreams of the living. As "spiritual beings" (in Tylor's terminology), these ghosts are the evolutionary prototypes of the gods. In Spencer's view, the gods are the spirits of the remote dead, hallowed and divinized by tradition. Spencer concludes that the root of all religion is, therefore, to be found in ancestor-worship.

To the modern reader, the enquiries of both Spencer and Tylor reveal more about the procedures and biases of Victorian social science than they do about the roots of religion. Embedded in highly unreliable ethnographic sources classified according to a selectively anecdotal, comparative method, the theory of animism caricatures the "primitive mind."[19] In seeking the origins of religion in man's remote past while at the same time drawing inferences from the activities of contemporary "savages," Tylor and Spencer enter the realm of fantasy rather than history. While religion may have originated and developed in the way they describe, there is no evidence that it did. The elaborate cognitive, evolutionary schemes of both authors remain no more than the purest speculation: mere accounts of how Tylor and Spencer would think (or thought they would think) if they were savages. Thus, there is no proof that dreams generate belief in a soul, that ghosts or spirits are derivations of this belief, or that gods are the logical offspring of such a progressive development. The "inevitable" progressions discerned and the "obvious" inferences drawn by Tylor and Spencer are inevitable and obvious only by virtue of an imaginative leap that grossly underestimates the propensity of primitives for perfectly ordinary "natural" explanations, and that confuses speculation with certitude.[20]

Much the same may be said of the main contemporaneous rival of animistic theory, the German-inspired "nature-myth" perspective. The main proponent of this theory in Britain was the distinguished Oxford linguist Max Müller. Promulgated somewhat earlier than the animistic orientation of evolutionist sociology and anthropology, the nature-myth theory fared ill at the hands of Tylor's and Spencer's followers, who were intent on the irradication of outmoded scientific doctrines. At least in British intellectual circles, the theory was disdained and disregarded even before Müller's career had reached its end, and that demise accentuated the temporary triumph of Tylorianism.

To a modern scholar, privy through hindsight to the transcience of the evolutionist social-scientific hegemony, the similarities between the approach of Müller and that of Tylor and Spencer appear far more striking than they did to those embroiled in the scholarly skirmishes of the late nineteenth century. Both approaches now appear unfounded and far-fetched, rooted in a speculative intellectualism that substitutes shaky inference for hard evidence. Thus, while it is tempting to applaud with amusement Spencerian or Tylorian criticism (and even ridicule) of the worst excesses of Müller and his disciples, it is salutary to recall the speed and thoroughness with which social-scientific knowledge evolved inexorably beyond sociological and anthropological evolutionism.[21]

Müller was a brilliant linguist and distinguished Sanskrit scholar; his chief interest lay in the gods of India and classical antiquity rather than in primitive or savage religion in the anthropological sense. Bearing the distinct imprint of the eighteenth-century enlightenment, his explanation of the origin of religion posits a "Natural Religion" common to the whole of mankind and views the history of religion as a process of decline from this pure form into the depths of mythology, priestcraft and institutionalism. Müller argues that religion universally originates in man's perception of the infinite as implicit in all his perceptions of finite reality. But religion proper only appears when this sense of the infinite, divined mainly from the encounter with the forces of nature, is combined with a moral sense that constrains man in his actions. This portrayal of *Homo Religiosus* in his natural state is, in a sense, remarkably "proto-Durkheimian" in character.[22] Understandably, however, it has been accorded less attention than its author's account of man's bondage in language and mythology, the primary target of his critics' wrath.

To Müller, the religion of Vedic India most nearly approximated pure, natural religion, and its literature offered the best means of appreciating man's original state of sensuous contact with the infinite. In the Vedic hymns is documented "the first discovery that behind this visible and perishable world there must be something invisible, imperishable, eternal or divine."[23] But these sacred writings reveal to Müller something more about the earliest forms of religion and mythology; a fact of apparent universal significance in the history of religious and mythological thought, and one that comprises the central insight of the nature-myth school:

> No one who has read the hymns of the Rig-Veda can doubt any longer as to what was the origin of the earliest Aryan religion and mythology. Nearly all the leading deities of the Veda bear the unmistakeable traces of their physical character. Their very names tell us that they were all in the beginning names of the great phenomena of nature, of fire, water, rain and storm, of sun and moon, of heaven and earth.[24]

Herein lies the key to Müller's interpretation of the further history of religion and mythology; tracing the development of deities back to man's apprehension of natural phenomena the great linguist, appropriately enough, perceives their genesis in an elementary linguistic confusion. In Müller's view, man had been "noble and pure from the very beginning" and "the divine gift of a sound and sober intellect belonged to him from the very first." Thought is inextricably and interdependently linked with language so that, as symptoms of a "period of temporary insanity" in the human mind, historical religion and mythology are the unhealthy effects of a "disease of language," a condition that casts grave doubt upon the evolutionary assumption of the inevitable progress of the human intellect.[25] Thus, as expressed concisely by Evans-Pritchard, Müller's thesis was:

> . . . that the infinite, once the idea had arisen, could only be thought of in metaphor and symbol, which could only be taken from what seemed majestic in the known world, such as the heavenly bodies, or rather their attributes. But these attributes then lost their original metaphorical sense and achieved autonomy by becoming personified as deities in their own right. The *nomina* became *numina*.[26]

In one important aspect of this process, for example, gender is attributed to "nature-nouns" in ancient languages, and sun and moon, day and night, seasons and storms inevitably acquire "something of an individual, active, sexual, and at last, personal character."[27] Müller therefore infers a process by which purely figurative expressions become reified and attain concreteness. *Nomina* become *numina* in a kind of linguistic estrangement, and thus the meaning of ancient religion can only be discovered (or recovered) through philology or etymology. By such means, the degenerate expressions of obscured truth may be penetrated and explored to reveal the perception of the infinite hidden deep within them. From this point of view, for example, belief in souls, ghosts and an invisible world beyond death is traced to a linguistic confusion, while the Greek myth of Daphne freeing Apollo and being transformed into a laurel tree is deciphered into an account of the sun chasing away the dawn.

Müller's penchant for uncovering solar myths in the unlikeliest places brought him, at times, to the point of self-caricature, and his reputation was by no means enhanced by fellow nature-mythologists, who extolled with equal enthusiasm the unrivalled religious significance of the moon, the stars and many other natural phenomena. Largely discredited even in Max Müller's own lifetime, the theory of nature-mythology itself acquired something of the character of a myth. It depicted pure, noble, rational Man falling from grace and losing contact with the infinite as a result of a linguistic original sin: the objectification of metaphor in the realm of nature. At its worst it was outrageously fanciful; more often it was merely implausible; but even at its best it could never be anything more than ingenious speculation. In all this, however, it was not notably different from those theories of religious origins that were somewhat smugly espoused by its late-nineteenth-century detractors.[28]

Sir James George Frazer is still perhaps the most famous anthropologist in the world and his reputation rests largely on his monumental contribution to the search for the origins of religion. Like Müller, Frazer outlived his own reputation; his vast literary legacy is largely ignored by modern anthropologists. But his multi-volume enterprise, *The Golden Bough,* "a work of immense industry and erudition," though deeply flawed, remains an imposing intellectual landmark in the investigation of primitive religion.[29]

A classicist by training, Frazer was encouraged in his initial anthropological explorations by his friend and colleague, the brilliant and controversial Robertson Smith; his early investigations of totemism and taboo bear the strong imprint of Smith.[30] His great, monolithic *Golden Bough,* dedicated to Smith, began as an attempt to explain the legend of the "golden bough," which grew in the sacred grove of the goddess Diana at Aricia on the shores of Lake Nemi; the work was offered, finally, "as a contribution to that still youthful science which seeks to trace the growth of human thought and institutions in those dark ages which lie beyond the range of history."[31] Indeed, as one commentator notes, from a "relatively simple beginning," Frazer "followed one promising trail after another, and left his original purpose farther and farther behind, until it was almost entirely lost sight of," so that the final result was "a vast compendium of data concerning religious belief and practice."[32]

From a theoretical viewpoint, the "youthful science" of evolutionary anthropology that Frazer built upon was essentially the Tylorian theory of animism. His own distinct contribution to evolutionism, however, appears indebted to Auguste Comte, and introduces further strain into an already shaky intellectual framework. Utilizing Tylor's distinction between religion and magic, and arguing that religion proper is always preceded by magic, Frazer postulates a three-stage process of human intellectual development in which religion appears to occupy the least admirable position. Rooted in problematic, pre-historical intellectual conjecture and dubious inferences from the evidence provided by contemporary primitive "survivals," Frazer's evolutionary scheme combines pseudo-history with pseudo-psychology in a theory that attempts to chart the progress of mankind from childhood to maturity. His "epic of humanity" affirms the developmental priority of magic over religion on both logical and ethnological grounds since, in his view, the Australian Aborigines, "the rudest savages as to whom we possess accurate information," are adept practitioners of magic but nearly complete strangers to religion.[33]

In Frazer's opinion, therefore, the origins of religion must first be sought in magic, the characteristics and roots of which are treated in a famous passage at the beginning of *The Golden Bough:*

> Analysis shows that magic rests everywhere on two fundamental principles: first that *like produces like,* effect resembling cause; second, that *things which have once been in contact continue ever afterwards to act on each other.* The former principle may be called the Law of Similarity; the latter that of Contact or Contagion. From the one the magician infers that he can produce any effect he desires merely by imitating it in advance; from the other, that whatever he does to a material object will automatically affect the person with whom it was once in contact. Practices based on the Law of Similarity may be termed Homeopathic Magic; those based on the Law of Contact or Contagion, Contagious Magic. Both derive, in the final analysis, from a false conception of natural law. The primitive magician, however, never analyzes the mental assumptions on which his performance is based, never reflects on the abstract principles involved. With him, as with the vast majority of men, logic is implicit, not explicit; he knows magic only as a practical thing, and to him it is always an art, never a science, the very idea of science being foreign to his thinking.[34]

At first glance, Frazer's attitude to magic appears completely deprecatory. Its "principles" are regarded as unwarranted and confused misapplications of the association of ideas grounded in a spurious system of natural law, and are portrayed as practically misleading and artistically abortive, as well as scientifically absurd. Yet, though "the very idea of science" may be foreign to savage thought, magic nonetheless seems to Frazer to be a sort of fallacious science, by virtue of its attempt to establish laws of cause and effect on the basis of a "fundamental conception identical with that of modern science," its faith in the "order and uniformity of nature."[35] Like science, therefore, magic assumes that man may exercise direct control over his circumstances on the basis of a presumed knowledge of Natural Law, however misguided. It is through the failure of magic to achieve its ends that religion arises.

Man's eventual awareness of the futility of his magical efforts at manipulating his environment leads him to think not in empirical, scientific terms, but in terms of religion, according to Frazer:

In magic man depends on his own strength to meet the difficulties and dangers that beset him on every side. He believes in a certain established order of nature on which he can surely count, and which he can manipulate for his own ends. When he discovers his mistake, when he recognizes sadly that both the order of nature which he had assumed and the control which he had believed himself to exercise over it were purely imaginary, he ceases to rely on his own intelligence and his own unaided efforts, and throws himself humbly on the mercy of certain great invisible beings behind the veil of nature, to whom he now ascribes all those far-reaching powers which he once arrogated to himself. Thus in the acuter minds magic is gradually superseded by religion, which explains the succession of natural phenomena as regulated by the will, the passion, or the caprice of spiritual beings like man in kind, though vastly superior to him in power.[36]

Thus, an "Age of Magic" evolves into an "Age of Religion" as an attitude of confidence is replaced by one of awe and fear.

In a formula that at least partially anticipates a number of the recent "Neo-Tylorian" substantive enunciations discussed in the previous chapter,[37] Frazer defines religion as "a propitiation or conciliation of powers superior to man which are believed to direct and control the course of nature and of human life."[38] As such, religion is no less illusory than magic, and inevitably the shrewder savages come to appreciate the inadequacy of their religious interpretation of reality:

. . . as time goes on this [religious] explanation in turn proves to be unsatisfactory. For it assumes that the succession of natural events is not determined by immutable laws, but is to some extent variable and irregular, and this assumption is not borne out by closer observation. On the contrary, the more we scrutinize that succession the more we are struck by the rigid uniformity, the punctual precision with which . . . the operations of nature are carried on. Every great advance in knowledge has extended the sphere of order and correspondingly restricted the sphere of apparent disorder in the world. . . . Thus the keener minds, still pressing forward to a deeper solution of the mysteries of the universe, come to reject the religious theory of nature as inadequate, and to revert in a measure to the older standpoint of magic by postulating explicitly, what in magic had only been implicitly assumed, to wit, an inflexible regularity in the order of natural events, which, if carefully observed, enables us to foresee their course with certainty and to act accordingly. In short, religion, regarded as an explanation of nature, is displaced by science.[39]

That Frazer's sympathies lie with science and magic rather than with religion is readily apparent. Strange bedfellows though they might appear, magic and experimental science are perceived as sharing more than either shares with religion. Both "rest on a faith in order as the underlying principle of all things," although, as Frazer is at pains to emphasize, "the order presupposed by magic differs widely from that which forms the basis of science."[40] Yet, though the former is merely "an extension, by false analogy, of the order in which ideas present themselves to our minds" and the latter "is derived from patient and exact observation," both genuine science and magical pseudo-science exhibit, in this portrayal, an intellectual integrity and dignity that is absent in the religious world-view.[41]

While both magic and religion might, therefore, appear inevitably and inescapably doomed to extinction in the evolution and advance of human knowledge, that "infinite progression towards a goal that for ever recedes,"[42] Frazer nonetheless displays a stubborn reluctance to weave an unconditional obituary to religion into the famed final metaphor of his epic work:

> . . . we may illustrate the course which thought has hitherto run by likening it to a web woven of three different threads – the black thread of magic, the red thread of religion, and the white thread of science, if under science we may include those simple truths drawn from observation of nature, of which men in all ages have possessed a store. Could we then survey the web of thought from the beginning, we should probably perceive it to be at first a chequer of black and white, a patchwork of true and false notions, hardly tinged as yet by the red thread of religion. But carry your eye further along the fabric and you will remark that, while the black and white chequer still runs through it, there rests on the middle portion of the web, where religion has entered most deeply into its texture, a dark crimson stain, which shades off insensibly into a lighter tint as the white thread of science is woven more and more into the tissue. To a web thus chequered and stained, thus shot with threads of diverse hues, but gradually changing colour the farther it is unrolled, the state of modern thought, with all its divergent aims and conflicting tendencies may be compared. Will the great movement which for centuries has been slowly altering the complexion of thought be continued in the near future? Or will a reaction set in which may arrest progress and even undo much that has been done? To keep up our parable, what will be the colour of the web which the fates are now weaving on the humming loom of time? Will it be white or red? We cannot tell. A faint glimmering light illumines the backward portion of the web. Clouds and thick darkness hide the other end.[43]

As an explanation of the origin of religion, Frazer's perspective is essentially an elaboration of the general thesis propounded by Tylor and Spencer. Most notable, perhaps, for its provocative though problematic elucidation of the distinction between religion and magic; and for its suggestive, if overdrawn, parallel between magic and science, his approach has been subjected to devastating criticism at the same time as it has laid the foundation for more sophisticated exploration and analysis.[44] To the modern reader, Frazer's patronizing treatment of "our rude forebears" and the living representatives of "the lower races" appears distastefully smug and ethnocentric even by comparison with the discussions of his Victorian predecessors. In particular, the implicit contempt in his assumption of the simple, childish mental constitution of primitive man, whether prehistoric or contemporary, is in sharp contrast to the standpoint of contemporary social science. Yet, though his hypothetical savage lacks that dignity that is always retained by Tylor's primitive man, Frazer shares with both Tylor and Spencer a fundamentally intellectualist view of the genesis of magic and religion.

From this perspective, primitive man is seen painfully formulating his first crude philosophies of life as he struggles to solve the problems of existence. As embryonic natural philosophies, therefore, magic and religion are characterized by a rationality grounded in observation and logical deduction. Indeed, this characteristic transcends all the precise and shameful details of observational inadequacy, faulty logic and erroneous belief on the part of primitive man; seeming to imply the possibility of his ultimate redemption from the absurdity, nonsense, fantasy and superstition in which he is steeped.

Frazer's work is open to criticism similar to that which has been applied to the evolutionary perspectives of Tylor and Spencer; his account of the origins of religion is equally unacceptable to modern scientific scholarship. The "faint glimmering light" by which Frazer discerns man's early, deluded attempts to understand and control his environment provides insufficient illumination for contemporary research.[45] Thus, Frazer's vision, like that of his immediate predecessors, is now generally regarded as indebted more to creative speculation and imaginative reconstruction than to reliable scientific observation.

Although the social-scientific study of religion may undoubtedly be said to have evolved beyond the insights both of British anthropological evolutionism and the Germanic school of nature-mythology, their intellectualistic viewpoint, with its interpretation of religion and magic as cognitive means of making sense of the world, exerts an understandable and recurrent attraction for scholars. The revival of Tylorianism discussed in Chapter Two provides a perfect illustration of the truth of this assertion.[46] Moreover, while the psychological orientation of both the evolutionary and nature-myth schools was to suffer condemnation and ridicule at the hands of later functionalist critics, it has, none the less, never been bereft of advocates, even within the ranks of sociological and anthropological structural-functionalism.[47] Finally, the quest for the origins of religion, so enthusiastically undertaken by Victorian scholarly explorers and so vigorously denounced by a succeeding generation of social scientists, continues in its various reincarnations to attract and intrigue sociological and anthropological investigators, however inhospitable the prevailing intellectual climate.[48]

Feuerbach, Marx and the Criticism of Religion

Few commentators on the nineteenth-century intellectual scene would be likely to speak of Karl Marx and Max Müller in the same scholarly breath or, even less, to accord them any categorization in common. Yet, exhibiting greater similarity than might initially be supposed, both of these thinkers must be enrolled in the pantheon of pioneers in the sociology of religion.[49] Despite the long-established disrepute of his solar-myth theory, Müller is none the less widely regarded as the father of the comparative study of religion; Marx's credentials as a student of religion are less readily acknowledged. Contemporaries in the German university system in the turbulent years of the eighteen-forties, both Marx and Müller were profoundly influenced in their youth, as was most of their generation, by German romantic idealism and post-Hegelian philosophy.[50] Thus, notwithstanding their very different subsequent careers as British residents, it is not far-fetched to discern a slight affinity in their work.

Müller's attempt to assist in the birth of a new "true religion of humanity" that would comprise 'the fulfillment of all the religions of the past"[51] echoes a theme of the enlightenment, but it also echoes the aspirations of Hegelian and post-Hegelian German philosophy. Indeed, his attempt to uncover and recover the authentic core of "natural religion," man's common encounter with the infinite, from the elaborate and varied priestly perversions, mythological mystifications and institutionalized illusions time has hallowed, has a decidedly Hegelian ring. More particularly, Müller's conviction that the roots of mythology lie in a "disease of language" that compels man to create a fantastic world populated by conceptions possessing "an individual, active, sexual, and at last, personal character" vividly recalls the neo-Hegelianism of Ludwig Feuerbach.[52] Dominated and imprisoned by mythical entities of his own making, Müller's *Homo Religiosus* is alienated or estranged no less than is the hypothetical human being portrayed in the writings of Feuerbach or the early writings of Marx.

The ideas of Feuerbach are the "brook of fire"[53] through which it is necessary to pass to comprehend Marx's analysis of religion. Feuerbach's thesis may be briefly summarized in the statement that metaphysics is esoteric psychology and in the injunction that theology must be transposed into anthropology. In his best-known work, *The Essence of Christianity,*[54] Feuerbach asserts that the objects of religious belief and veneration, whether circumscribed spiritual beings or an omnipotent and omnipresent God, are in essence nothing more than the projections, reifications or objectifications of man's own needs, desires and aspirations. Thus, in the act of religious belief or worship, man is self-alienated or self-estranged:

And here may be applied, without any limitation, the proposition: the object of any subject is nothing else than the subject's own nature taken objectively. Such as are a man's thoughts and dispositions, such is his God; so much worth as a man has, so much and no more has his God. Consciousness of God is self-consciousness, knowledge of God is self-knowledge. By his God thou knowest the man, and by the man his God; the two are identical. Whatever is God to a man, that is his heart and soul; and conversely, God is the manifested inward nature, the expressed self of a man – religion the solemn unveiling of a man's hidden treasures, the revelation of his intimate thoughts, the open confession of his love-secrets.[55]

In an exercise in psychological speculation akin to those examined earlier, Feuerbach suggests that religion is man's earliest form of self-knowledge, preceding philosophy in the course of human intellectual development as childhood precedes maturity:

Man first of all sees his nature as if *out of* himself, before he finds it in himself. His own nature is in the first instance contemplated by him as that of another being. Religion is the childlike condition of humanity; but the child sees his nature – man – out of himself; in childhood a man is an object to himself, under the form of another man.[56]

In a historical hypothesis later to find its echo in Müller's diagnosis of religion as a "disease of language," Feuerbach conjectures that the origin of religion is "lost sight of" as it is forgotten "that what the activity of the reflective power has converted into a predicate distinguishable or separable from the subject, was originally the true subject."[57] States of mind are thereby metamorphosed into independent beings, and religious man exists in sublime ignorance of the fact that God is merely an externalization of the self, his own anthropomorphic creation:

Man – this is the mystery of religion – projects his being into objectivity, and then again makes himself an object to this projected image of himself thus converted into a subject; he thinks of himself, is an object to himself, but as the object of an object, of another being than himself.[58]

Man's self-estrangement involves, as the "very core of religion,"[59] the depreciation of the human as the price of denial of the identity of the human and divine. In Feuerbach's view, the chasm that separates man from God diminishes man as it widens:

. . . as what is positive in the conception of divine being can only be human, the conception of man, as an object of consciousness can only be negative. To enrich God, man must become poor; that God may be all, man must be nothing.[60]

Yet, accompanying the progressive development of the human intellect, Feuerbach detects a healthy, continuous process of religious de-mystification:

. . . the historical progress of religion consists in this: that what by an earlier religion was regarded as objective is now recognized as subjective; that is, what was formerly contemplated and worshipped as God is now perceived to be something *human*. What was at first religion becomes at a later period idolatry; man is seen to have adored his own nature. Man has given objectivity to himself, but has not recognized the object as his own nature; a later religion takes this forward step; every advance in religion is therefore a deeper self-knowledge.[61]

In proceeding to de-mythologize and expose the essence of religion, therefore, his concern is to perfect rather than debunk; to preach atheism in the interest of a more authentic religion that will survive the death of God:

Not the attribute of the divinity, but the divineness or deity of the attribute, is the first true Divine Being. Thus what theology and philosophy have held to be God, the Absolute, the Infinite, is not God; but that which they have held not to be God, is God: namely, the attribute, the quality, whatever has reality. . . .

The fact is not that a quality is divine because God has it, but that God has it because it is in itself divine; because without it God would be a defective being. Justice, wisdom, in general every quality which constitutes the divinity of God, is determined and known by itself, independently, but the idea of God is determined by qualities which have thus been previously judged to be worthy of the divine nature. . . . But if God as a subject is the determined, while the quality, the predicate is the determining, then in truth the rank of the godhead is due not to the subject, but to the predicate.[62]

As the "highest subjectivity of man abstracted from himself,"[63] God must die in order that man may become truly, self-consciously human. Thus, the course of religious development outlined by Feuerbach consists specifically in an evolutionary process by which "man abstracts more and more from God, and attributes more and more to himself."[64] The erosion of God's omnipotence lessens the external constraints on man and fosters the growth of criticism and freedom: God's ultimate demise will signify man's coming-of-age and imply the possibility of a genuine religion of humanity:

Thus do things change. What yesterday was still religion is no longer such today; and what today is atheism, tomorrow will be religion.[65]

Feuerbach thus sees the decline of traditional forms of religious belief as implicit in man's intellectual development. It is important to stress, however, that in his view religion is by no means a purely cognitive phenomenon. The replacement of a God-centred theology with a man-centred philosophy is the final act in a drama of emotional and moral as well as intellectual progress. The future promises "man in communion with man, the unity of the I and Thou. . . ."[66]

Karl Marx's view of religion can only be appreciated if it is understood as a revision and extension of Feuerbach's radical overturning of Hegelian theology. Indeed, paradoxical as it may seem, Marxism itself, whether viewed as a scientific doctrine or as a dramatic myth, has its genesis in the analysis of religion just as it echoes Feuerbach's comment that "Man is what he eats."[67] Observing that "the criticism of religion is the premise of all criticism,"[68] Marx follows Feuerbach in regarding the goal of history as man's ultimate humanization and credits him with performing a truly Copernican intellectual feat:

The criticism of religion disillusions man so that he will think, act and fashion his reality as a man who has lost his illusions and regained his reason; so that he will revolve about himself as his own true sun. Religion is only the illusory sun about which man revolves so long as he does not revolve about himself.[69]

In a more critical vein, however, Marx is impatient with a view that prescribes a critical cognitive act, a reorientation of human thinking as a sufficient cure for human enslavement. In his view, it is not enough that man is awakened from his religious dream merely to apprehend and come to terms with the world as it already exists:

Feuerbach's whole deduction with regard to the relation of men to one another goes only so far as to prove that men need and *always have needed* each other. He wants to establish consciousness of this fact, that is to say . . . merely to produce a correct consciousness about an *existing* fact; whereas . . . it is a question of overthrowing the existing state of things.[70]

For Marx, liberation is "a historical and not a mental act, and it is brought about by historical conditions"; it is a matter of "revolutionizing the existing world, of practically attacking and changing existing things."[71]

Nonetheless, Feuerbach's achievement in revealing the true latent meaning of Hegelian theology is indisputable and irreversible:

Man, who looked for a superman in the fantastic reality of heaven and found nothing there but the *reflection* of himself, will no longer be disposed to find but the *semblance* of himself, the non-human (Unmensch) where he seeks and must seek his true reality.[72]

Thus, in "resolving the religious world into its secular basis,"[73] Feuerbach must be credited with breaking the spell that Hegelianism had exercised over Marx's mind, enabling him to formulate his own revolutionary critique of religion as a prelude to his political and economic explorations.

Marx parts company with Feuerbach because Feuerbach fails to appreciate the necessity of changing the world subsequent to its release from religious illusion, and also because (as a modern scholar might express it) this failure is rooted in a philosophical and psychological rather than sociological conception of man:

The basis of irreligious criticism is: Man makes religion, religion does not make man. In other words, religion is the self-consciousness and self-feeling of man who has either not yet found himself or has already lost himself again. But *man* is no abstract being squatting outside the world. Man is the *world of man*, the state, society. This state, this society, produce religion, *a reversed world-consciousness* because they are *a reversed world*. Religion is the general theory of that world, its encyclopaedic compendium, its logic in a popular form, its spiritualistic *point d'honneur*, its enthusiasm, its moral sanction, its solemn completion, its universal ground for consolation and justification.[74]

Although Feuerbach has successfully resolved the "religious essence" into the "human essence," he fails to see "that the 'religious sentiment' is itself a *social product* and that the abstract individual whom he analyzed belongs in reality to a particular form of society."[75] It is Marx's task, therefore, to expose the human essence as, in reality, "the ensemble of the social relations," and to reveal religion as their "fantastic realization":

The struggle against religion is therefore mediately the fight against *the other world* of which religion is the spiritual *aroma*.

Religious distress is at the same time the expression of real distress and the *protest* against real distress. Religion is the sigh of the oppressed creature, the heart of a heartless world, just as it is the spirit of a spiritless situation. It is the *opium* of the people.[76]

For Marx, therefore, it is impossible to extinguish the illusions of religion without first eradicating the social conditions that give rise to them:

The abolition of religion as the *illusory* happiness of the people is required for their *real* happiness. The demand to give up the illusions about its condition is the *demand to give up a condition which needs illusions*. The criticism of religion is therefore *in embryo the criticism of the vale of woe*, the *halo* of which is religion.[77]

Marx regards religion as epiphenomenal and ideological, indicating man's alienation and false consciousness at the same time as it reflects his economic and social misery. Religion functions as pie-in-the-sky for the hungry, as hope for the hopeless and as a universal tranquilizer to soothe the agony of living. Life determines consciousness, not consciousness life; and thus religion may be reduced, for purposes of explanation, to the social conditions that give it birth.[78]

From a Marxian evolutionary point of view, religion and the social orders that sustain it belong to "pre-history" and are doomed to imminent extinction.[79] Yet, until the death knell of private property sounds and the expropriators are expropriated, the conditions for the creation and persistence of religion remain in existence.[80] Specifically, the "rule of ideas or illusions in history" may only be understood from the standpoint of class, and the enduring character of religion is explicable in terms of the interests of a ruling class:

The ideas of the ruling class are in every epoch the ruling ideas: i.e., the class which is the ruling *material* force of society, is at the same time its ruling *intellectual* force. The class which has the means of material production at its disposal, has control at the same time over the means of mental production, so that thereby, generally speaking, the ideas of those who lack the means of mental production are subject to it. The ruling ideas are nothing more than the ideal expression of the dominant material relationships.[81]

In this sense, religious ideas function to maintain the status quo in a given society. They are tools in the domination of one class by another despite their deceptive appearance as consensual expressions of a common moral sentiment. Religion is thus an important tool by which those who control the means of mental production maintain in subjection those who do not.

Though intellectually erroneous, religious conceptions are socially functional in suppressing class-conflict, and psychologically functional in dulling the pain and quelling the rage of the oppressed.[82]

From this point of view, religion would seem destined to be always a reactionary or conservative force, a conclusion sustained and reinforced by an interminable repetition, generally out of context, of the phrase "opium of the people" both by self-styled Marxists and by their opponents. There is, however, another side to Marx's analysis of religion which, although frequently neglected, is none the less crucial to a complete understanding of the role of religion in society. Thus, in a major variation from this main theme, Marx acknowledges the revolutionary potential of religion under certain circumstances and at particular stages of historical development. In contrast to the reactionary nature of contemporary Christianity, for example, early Christianity may be perceived as representing the revolutionary aspirations of the disinherited of the Roman Empire, just as the millenarian sects of the German Peasants' War and the English Civil War express the political yearnings of the dispossessed and downtrodden through the medium of Holy Writ.[83]

It should be emphasized, however, that this occasionally redeeming aspect of religion in no way controverts its essentially alienating and reactionary nature. From his evolutionary vantage point, Marx insists that the cognitive and emotional hold of religion on the minds and hearts of human beings will weaken as capitalistic society undergoes its inevitable transformation to a new stage of development. By the same token, the emergence of a new society will ensure the extinction of religion by eliminating the social conditions that generate it. No less than Comte or Saint-Simon, therefore, Marx pens an epitaph to religion in its traditional forms, arguing that its functions will be redundant in the classless, truly human society whose herald he is.

Marx provides an interpretation of religion that attempts to combine philosophical, psychological and sociological analysis in the interest of a general "scientific" understanding of the phenomenon. Implicitly utilizing an ordinary-language definition, in keeping with the substantivism of British anthropology and German naturism, he invokes both evolutionary and functional explanation. Stressing the role of religion in repressing dissent and stifling social conflict, Marx nonetheless hints at its capacity to alter social relationships fundamentally. Emphasizing its contributions to social order rather than to social change, to statics rather than dynamics, he adopts an essentially functionalist viewpoint while repudiating a consensualist solution to the problem of order. Though viewing emancipation from religion as an important aspect of the intellectual progress of humanity, Marx by no means approaches religion entirely in cognitive terms. Thus, the existence and persistence of religion are explained as much in terms of man's suffering as on the basis of his ignorance. It is, incidentally, consistent with Marx's conception of social science that religion should be explicitly condemned at the same time as it is analyzed.

Karl Marx is rarely accorded a place among the pioneers of the sociology of religion. This is understandable given the minimal interest in religion shown in his mature work; and, until recently, his relative lack of influence upon practising sociologists of religion. To what extent this is explicable purely in terms of such scholarly factors as the obscure, unsystematic, fragmentary and limited character of his reflections on religion is of less interest in the present context than the undoubted fact that, until recently, Marx's intellectual influence upon sociologists of religion has been relatively small. Nonetheless, a widening subdisciplinary consensus now claims him as a patron and proclaims the relevance of his ideas for current theory and research in a specialized setting.[84]

Marx was no mere academic specialist; his interpretation of religion is inseparable from his radical humanism, his theory of historical materialism and his revolutionary conception of social progress. Thus, although his "account of the facts and sequences of religious history" in terms of successive modes of production differs "in no significant respect" from the prevailing wisdom of evolutionary anthropology, it is distinguished, as Birnbaum observes, by the "interpretive context" in which it is placed: his analysis of "the inner structure of religion and its relationship to society."[85] Marx's contention that religion is the spiritual response to the condition of alienation might initially appear more theological than sociological; but the fascination of Marxism does not lie solely in its own arguable status as a religion of secular humanism.[86] On the contrary, some representatives of a new generation of social scientists have enthusiastically adopted such emotive humanistic formulations to affirm the scientific truth of Marx's proposition that religion is the truth of a false condition. Portraying religion as "a demand at once for dignity and consolation, for explanation and moral coherence,"[87] the writings of Marx offer an intellectual resource for political revolutionaries and a spiritual treasury for radical theologians without forfeiting their fascination for some social scientists.

Thus, while the thought of Karl Marx has been accorded a mixed reception by sociologists of religion, and the goal of a Marxist sociology of religion is shared only by a few, fewer still within the subdisciplinary ranks would, any longer, deem the circumvention of Marxian views intellectually advisable.

Footnotes to Chapter Three

[1] Georg Simmel, "A Contribution to the Sociology of Religion," trans. W.W. Elwang, *American Journal of Sociology,* Vol. 60, 1955, p. 2. (Originally published in Vol. 10, 1905, pp. 359-376.)

[2] *Ibid,* p. 2.

[3] Peter L. Berger, "Second Thoughts on Defining Religion," *Journal for The Scientific Study of Religion,* Vol. 1, 1974, p. 127.

[4] In this, their most consistent companions have been anthropologists, though theologians and historians of religion are also busily engaged in defining religion (see Chapter Two). It should be noted that to some scholars, such definitional "slicing up" appears as nothing less than sheer butchery in the name of science; see, for example, James J. Dagenais, "The Scientific Study of Myth and Ritual: A Lost Cause," *The Human Context,* Vol. 6, 1974, pp. 586-620.

[5] A glimpse of the lack of consensus within the subdiscipline may be obtained by referring to the definitional debates in chapter two. Further evidence will be provided later in this text. For an indication of the lack of consensus in sociology in general, see the remarks by Howard S. Becker, in "What's Happening to Sociology?" *Society,* Vol. 16, No. 5, 1979, pp. 19-24; and Peter David, in *The Times Higher Education Supplement,* 12th September, 1980. For overviews of the multifarious contending perspectives, fads and sects that comprise contemporary sociology, see Pitirim A. Sorokin, *Fads and Foibles in Modern Sociology,* Chicago: Henry Regnery Co., 1956; and Nicholas C. Mullins, *Theory and Theory Groups in Contemporary American Sociology,* New York: Harper and Row, 1973.

[6] Henri Desroche, *Jacob and the Angel: An Essay in Sociologies of Religion* (Trans. J.K. Savacool), Amherst: The University of Massachusetts Press, 1973. (Originally published as *Sociologies Religieuses,* Paris, 1968.) Desroche entitles his first chapter "From Sociologies of Religion to a Sociology of Religions," which gives an added twist to the argument.

[7] It would be fruitless to plead for a definitional armistice among sociologists similar to that proposed by Ferré for the field of Religious Studies. See Frederick Ferré, "The Definition of Religion," *Journal of the American Academy of Religion,* Vol. 38, 1970, pp. 14-16. Indeed, Ferré's own proposal was not widely endorsed. See Dagenais, *op. cit.*, p. 617n.

[8] On the notion that the sociology of religion is what it does, and on the role of the subdiscipline in defining implicitly what may be regarded as "religious," see Karel Dobbelaere and Jan Lauwers, "Definition of Religion: A Sociological Critique," *Social Compass,* Vol. 20, 1973-74, p. 550. These authors assert: "The sociologist of religion deals with an area which is fixed by his own socially shaped interest or situation; by division of labour within his university or department; by whatever other 'sociologists of religion' are doing or not doing; by whatever is submitted to him (possibly by his sponsor) as a problem. Thus, to the sociologist, the delimitation of his area of investigation is a matter of social involvement with a problem, indirect though it may be and whatever may have led to it."

On the "classic tradition," see C. Wright Mills, *The Sociological Imagination,* New York: Oxford University Press, 1959, pp. 3-24; and C.W. Mills (ed.), *Images of Man,* New York: George Braziller, 1960, pp. 1-17.

[9] The term is used loosely. See, for example, Timothy Raison (ed.), *The Founding Fathers of Social Science,* Harmondsworth: Penguin Books, 1969.

[10] See, for example, Henri de Saint-Simon, *Social Organization, the Science of Man and Other Writings,* translated and edited by Felix Markham, New York: Harper and Row, 1964, especially pp. 81-116; Georg G. Iggers, translator and editor of *The Doctrine of Saint-Simon: An Exposition,* New York: Schocken Books, 1972, pp. 201-213 and 244-276; Auguste Comte, *A General View of Positivism,* New York: Robert Speller and Sons, 1957, pp. 355-444; George Simpson, *Auguste Comte: Sire of Sociology,* New York: Thomas Y. Crowell Company, 1969, pp. 143-144; Frank Manuel, *The Prophets of Paris,* New York: Basic Books, 1965, pp. 59-105; and Gertrud Lenzer (ed.), *Auguste Comte and Positivism,* New York: Harper and Row, 1975, especially pp. 393-398 and 461-476.

[11] A distinction between "intellectualist" and "emotionalist" psychological theories of religion was made by the German scholar Wilhelm Schmidt and adopted by the British anthropologist E.E. Evans-Pritchard. See E.E. Evans-Pritchard, *Theories of Primitive Religion,* Oxford: The Clarendon Press, 1965, p. 4 and p. 29n.

[12] Although their search for origins was not without a certain "debunking" aspect. See E.E. Evans-Pritchard, *op. cit.*, pp. 15-16.

[13] *Ibid,* p. 8 and pp. 15-16. Of course, such a view reflected the predominant Victorian view of the contemporary "savage" in need of "civilization." See also Edmund Leach, "Golden Bough or Gilded Twig?" *Daedalus,* Vol. 90, Spring 1961, pp. 376 and 378.

[14] Sir Edward Tylor's minimum definition in terms of belief in spiritual beings is to be found in Volume One of his *Primitive Culture,* London: John Murray, 1871. See also Robin Horton, "A Definition of Religion and its Uses," *Journal of the Royal Anthropological Institute,* Vol. 90, 1960, p. 204; and Jack Goody, "Religion and Ritual: The Definitional Problem," *British Journal of Sociology,* Vol. 12, 1961, p. 143. For discussions of Tylor, see works by Dorson and Sharpe, cited in footnote 21 of this chapter.

[15] In broad terms, this explanation appears to retain a hold on the minds of contributors of popular accounts, much as the work of Sir James Frazer retains a surprising degree of popularity. Evans-Pritchard comments on the extent to which outmoded "explanations" of religion are "still trotted out." *op. cit.,* p. 4 and pp. 29-30.

[16] *Ibid,* p. 25.

[17] See Leach, *op. cit.,* p. 378; and Talcott Parsons, "The Theoretical Development of the Sociology of Religion," *Journal of the History of Ideas,* Vol. 5, 1944, p. 178.

[18] For Spencer's view of religion see Herbert Spencer, *The Principles of Sociology* (2 volumes), New York: D. Appleton and Company, 1892, third edition, pp. 53-423 and pp. 671-843. The view of religious evolution in Spencer's *Principles* pre-dated Tylor's and, although very similar, was arrived at completely independently. See also H. Spencer, *The Study of Sociology,* Ann Arbor: University of Michigan Press, 1961, pp. 266-285 (originally published in 1873); and Jay Rumney, *Herbert Spencer's Sociology,* New York: Atherton Press, 1966, pp. 187-210 (first published in 1937). For recent general appraisals of Spencer, see Stanislav Andreski (ed.), *Herbert Spencer: Structure, Function and Evolution,* London: Nelson, 1971; J.D.Y. Peel, *Herbert Spencer: The Evolution of a Sociologist,* London: Heinemann, 1971; and David Wiltshire, *The Social and Political Thought of Herbert Spencer,* Oxford: Oxford University Press, 1978.

[19] Arguments concerning the portrayal of the "savage mind" have continued to be important in anthropology. In this regard, the work of the French anthropologists Lucien Lévy-Bruhl and Claude Lévi-Strauss is important. See, for example, Lucien Lévy-Bruhl, *Primitive Mentality,* translated by L.A. Clare, London: Allen and Unwin, 1923; L. Lévy-Bruhl, *How Natives Think* translated by L.A. Clare, New York: Washington Square Press, 1966; and Claude Lévi-Strauss, *The Savage Mind,* London: Weidenfeld and Nicolson, 1966.

[20] In the view of Evans-Pritchard, such inferences have the quality of "just-so" stories, like "How the Leopard got his Spots." He notes that the "ideas of soul and spirit could have arisen in the way Tylor supposed, but there is no evidence that they did." *op. cit.,* pp. 25-26. For a theoretical defence of the "just-so" story, see Robert Towler, *Homo Religiosus,* New York: St. Martin's Press, 1974, pp. 71-72.

[21] Consider the famous opening passage of Talcott Parsons' *The Structure of Social Action,* New York: The Free Press, 1959 (first published 1937), p. 3. Quoting Crane Brinton, Parsons refers to the death of Spencer at the hands of his God of Evolution. Of course, Spencer and evolutionism were later to be resurrected by Parsons himself, among others. Useful material on Victorian social-scientific interpretations of religion is to be found in Eric J. Sharpe, *Comparative Religion: A History,* London: Duckworth, 1975; and Richard M. Dorson, *The British Folklorists: A History,* Chicago: University of Chicago Press, 1968. Also useful from a more philosophical point of view is B.M.G. Reardon, *Religious Thought in the Nineteenth Century,* Cambridge: Cambridge University Press, 1966.

[22] See the discussion of Durkheim in chapter four of this text, and consult Emile Durkheim, *The Elementary Forms of the Religious Life* (trans. J.W. Swain), New York: Collier Books, 1961, pp. 216-232 for an account of the overpowering force apprehended by man. On Müller, see Max Müller, *Anthropological Religion,* (1892), *Chips from a German Workshop* (4

Vols, 1867-1875); *Contributions to the Science of Mythology* (2 Vols, 1897); *Introduction to the Science of Religion* (1873); *Natural Religion* (1889); and *My Autobiography: A Fragment* (1901). See also Georgiana A. Müller (ed.), *The Life and Letters of the Right Honourable Friedrich Max Müller,* (2 Vols, 1902); Sharpe, *op. cit.*, pp. 35-46; and Dorson, *op. cit.*, pp. 160-171.

[23] Max Müller, *Three Lectures on the Vedanta Philosophy,* quoted in Sharpe, *op. cit.*, pp. 39-40. See also Dorson, *op. cit.*, p. 161.

[24] *Ibid,* p. 40.

[25] Max Müller, *Selected Essays,* (Vol. 1, 1881), pp. 306 and 308, quoted in Sharpe, p. 41. Evans-Pritchard describes the phrase "disease of language" as "a pithy but unfortunate expression which later Müller tried to explain away but never quite lived down." *op. cit.*, p. 22.

[26] Evans-Pritchard, *op. cit.*, p. 21.

[27] Max Müller, *Comparative Mythology* (1856), quoted in Sharpe, *op. cit.*, p. 42.

[28] In Evans-Pritchard's terms, Müller's theories were no more "just-so" stories than were those of his critics. On Müller's advice to "Be not afraid of Solar Myths" offered in *India: What Can it Teach Us?* (1883), see the quotation in Dorson, *op. cit.*, p. 163.

[29] Unlike the works of Tylor, Spencer or Müller, Sir James Frazer's magnum opus is still readily available in cheap, abridged form and retains a place in popular bibliographies of magic and the occult. Its theme was evident in, for example, the film *Apocalypse Now* and it enjoyed a vogue in the "counter-culture" of the late 1960s and early 1970s. Few modern readers, even among professional anthropologists, are prepared to tackle the full thirteen-volume edition of *The Golden Bough* but useful selections are to be found in Sir James George Frazer, *The New Golden Bough,* Theodor H. Gaster (ed.), Garden City, N.Y.: Doubleday and Co., Inc., 1961; and Sir James George Frazer, *The Illustrated Golden Bough* (Abridged by Sabine MacCormack with an introduction by Mary Douglas), London: Macmillan, 1978. For critical appraisals of Frazer and his work, see Leach, *op. cit.*; Evans-Pritchard, *op. cit.*, pp. 27-29; Edmund Leach, "Frazer and Malinowski," *Encounter,* Vol. 25, No. 5, 1965, pp. 24-36; Herbert Weisinger, "The Branch That Grew Full Straight," *Daedalus,* Vol. 90, Spring 1961, pp. 388-399; Bronislaw Malinowski, "Sir James George Frazer: A Biographical Appreciation" in *A Scientific Theory of Culture,* Chapel Hill: University of North Carolina Press, 1944, pp. 177-221; and Sharpe, *op. cit.*, pp. 87-94. The reference to Frazer's industry and erudition is from Evans-Pritchard, *op. cit.*, p. 27.

[30] See Leach, "Golden Bough or Gilded Twig?" (cited above), pp. 372-374. W. Robertson Smith also exercised an influence on Durkheim, a fact noted by Evans-Pritchard, *op. cit.*, p. 56; and Jack Goody, *op. cit.*, p. 144. Robertson Smith's most famous work is *Lectures on the Religion of the Semites,* London: A and C. Black, 1889. For summaries of the contributions of Robertson-Smith see Sharpe, *op. cit.*, pp. 77-82; and T.O. Beidelman, *W. Robertson Smith and the Sociological Study of Religion,* Chicago: University of Chicago Press, 1974.

[31] Frazer, *The New Golden Bough,* p. xix.

[32] Sharpe, *op. cit.*, p. 90.

[33] This is Frazer's own description of his major work. See Sharpe, *op. cit.*, p. 92.

[34] *The New Golden Bough,* p. 5.

[35] *Ibid,* p. 371.

[36] *Ibid,* p. 371.

[37] See, for example, the works of Horton and Goody cited above.

[38] Compare footnote 36 and the neo-Tylorian definitions of Horton and Goody. See Sharpe, *op. cit.*, p. 92.

[39] *Ibid,* p. 371.

[40] *Ibid,* p. 371.

[41] Frazer apparently perceived religion as more intellectually degrading than magic, though he courted ecclesiastical sympathy for his ideas.

[42] *The New Golden Bough*, p. 372.

[43] *Ibid*, p. 372.

[44] See, for example, Bronislaw Malinowski, *Magic, Science and Religion and Other Essays*, Glencoe: The Free Press, 1948. Consult also Edmund Leach, "Frazer and Malinowski," cited in footnote 29.

[45] See, for example, the appraisals by Leach cited in footnotes 13 and 29.

[46] See, for example, Robin Horton, "Neo-Tylorianism: Sound Sense or Sinister Prejudice?" in *Man: The Journal of the Royal Anthropological Institute* (new series), Vol. 3, 1968, pp. 625-634.

[47] See, for example, Malinowski's emphasis upon "anxiety" and emotion in *Magic, Science and Religion*, pp. 59-65; and J. Milton Yinger, *Religion, Society and the Individual*, New York: The Macmillan Company, pp. 73-124.

[48] See, for example, Thomas H. Grafton, "Religious Origins and Sociological Theory," *American Sociological Review*, Vol. 10, 1945, pp. 726-739. On the closely linked question of religious evolution, see Robert N. Bellah, "Religious Evolution," *American Sociological Review*, Vol. 29, 1964, pp. 358-374; and George Pepper, "Religion and Evolution," *Sociological Analysis*, Vol. 31, 1970, pp. 78-91.

[49] Both were German emigrés resident in England, though under very different circumstances.

[50] In this context see Reardon, *op. cit.*; Sidney Hook, *From Hegel to Marx*, Ann Arbor: University of Michigan Press, 1962; Robert Tucker, *Philosophy and Myth in Karl Marx*, Cambridge: Cambridge University Press, 1961; and G.W.F. Hegel, *On Art, Religion, Philosophy* (ed. J.G. Gray), New York: Harper & Row, 1970.

[51] G. Müller (ed.), *Life and Letters*, Volume 2, p. 135.

[52] See discussions of Feuerbach in works by Hook, Reardon and Tucker, cited in footnotes 21 and 50. See also Ludwig Feuerbach, *The Essence of Christianity* (trans. George Eliot), New York: Harper and Row, 1957 (first published 1841).

[53] This is Marx's phrase; a pun on the German meaning of Feuerbach's name, which translates as "brook of fire." He thus describes Feuerbach as being "the *purgatory* of our time." See Karl Marx, "Feuerbach," in Karl Marx and Frederick Engels, *The German Ideology*, London: Lawrence and Wishart 1965, pp. 27-85 (written 1845-6); and Karl Marx, "Theses on Feuerbach," in Marx and Engels, *On Religion*, Moscow: Foreign Languages Publishing House, 1958, pp. 69-72 (written 1845). For scholarly explorations of Marx's link with Feuerbach see Hook *op. cit.*, pp. 220-307; and Tucker, *op. cit.*, pp. 80-105. See also Engels, "Ludwig Feuerbach and the End of Classical German Philosophy," in *On Religion*, pp. 213-268.

[54] Feuerbach, *Essence of Christianity*.

[55] *Ibid*, pp. 12-13.

[56] *Ibid*, p. 13.

[57] *Ibid*, p. 22.

[58] *Ibid*, pp. 29-30.

[59] *Ibid*, pp. 25-26.

[60] *Ibid*, p. 26.

[61] *Ibid*, p. 13.

[62] *Ibid*, pp. 21-22.

[63] *Ibid*, p. 31.

[64] *Ibid*, p. 31.

[65] *Ibid*, p. 32.

[66] In viewing the religion of the future in these terms, Feuerbach has greatly influenced twentieth-century theology. See Martin Buber, *I and Thou* (trans. Walter Kaufman), New York: Charles Scribner's Sons, 1970. See also the introduction to Feuerbach's *Essence of Christianity*, by the celebrated protestant theologian Karl Barth, which draws attention to Feuerbach's formula "Man and man, the unity of I and Thou is God," p. xvi.

[67] *"Der Mensch ist was er isst"* is probably Feuerbach's best-known epithet. In the same vein might be quoted: ". . . we are no abstract beings, but creatures of flesh and blood"; the somewhat Protagorean "Man, especially the religious man, is to himself the measure of all things, of all reality"; and "The beginning middle and end of religion is MAN." See Feuerbach, *op. cit.*, pp. 49, 22 and 184.

[68] Marx, "Contribution to The Critique of Hegel's Philosophy of Right," in *Karl Marx, Early Writings* (Trans. and ed. T.B. Bottomore), New York: McGraw-Hill, 1964, p. 43 (written 1844).

[69] *Ibid,* p. 44.

[70] Marx, *The German Ideology,* p. 54.

[71] *Ibid,* p. 56.

[72] Marx, "Contribution to the Critique of Hegel's Philosophy of Right" in Marx and Engels, *On Religion,* p. 41.

[73] Marx, "Theses on Feuerbach" in *On Religion,* p. 70.

[74] Marx, "Contribution to the Critique of Hegel's Philosophy of Right" in *On Religion,* p. 41.

[75] Marx, "Theses on Feuerbach" in *On Religion,* p. 71.

[76] Marx, "Contribution to the Critique of Hegel's Philosophy of Right" in *On Religion,* p. 42.

[77] *Ibid,* p. 42.

[78] See Marx, *The German Ideology,* p. 38. This insight is fundamental to the perspective of historical materialism. Later, in his preface to *A Contribution to the Critique of Political Economy* (1859), Marx was to state: "It is not the consciousness of men that determines their being but, on the contrary, their social being which determines their consciousness."

[79] Their death sentence is proclaimed most eloquently in Marx and Engels, *The Manifesto of the Communist Party,* 1848.

[80] See the sketch of the "conditions of oppression" in modern bourgeois society to be found in the *Manifesto.*

[81] Marx, *The German Ideology,* p. 63 and p. 60. The notion of the "ruling class" imposing a dominant ideology on the whole of society is a central one to Marxism, and one that is presented in simple but effective polemical terms in the *Manifesto*. For a sophisticated, recent discussion of this question see Nicholas Abercrombie, Stephen Hill and Bryan S. Turner, *The Dominant Ideology Thesis,* London: Allen & Unwin, 1980.

[82] From this point of view, Marx's analysis of religion might certainly be described as a variant of functionalism in a broad sense.

[83] It seems true to say that it was Engels who best developed this perspective. See, for example, Engels, *The Peasant War in Germany,* Moscow: Foreign Languages Publishing House, 1958; "On the History of Early Christianity" in Marx and Engels, *On Religion,* pp. 316-347; and "The Book of Revelation," in *On Religion,* pp. 205-212. See also Marx and Engels, *On Britain,* Moscow: Foreign Languages Publishing House, 1953, pp. 515-516, 528, 536-538; *Selected Correspondence,* Moscow: Foreign Languages Publishing House, 1956, pp. 257-258; *Selected Works* (2 Vols), Moscow: Foreign Languages Publishing House, 1948, Vol. 2, pp. 205-206, 465, 476-477. Investigation of the revolutionary potential of religious ideology was conducted by the collaborators and immediate heirs of Marx and Engels. See, for example, Eduard Bernstein, *Cromwell and Communism,* New York: Schocken Books, 1963 (first published 1895); Karl Kautsky, *Foundations of Christianity* (trans. M.F. Mims), New York: Russell and Russell, 1953; Karl Kautsky, *Communism in Central Europe at the Time of the Reformation,* London: T. Fisher Unwin, 1897; E. Belfort Bax, *The Social Side of the Reformation in Germany* (3 Vols), London: Swan Sonnenschein & Co., 1894-1903; and Max Beer, *Social Struggles and Socialist Forerunners,* New York: International Publishers, 1929. For a general overview of the classic Marxian analysis of religion, consult Delos B. McKown, *The*

Classical Marxist Critique of Religion: Marx, Engels, Lenin, Kautsky, The Hague: Martinus Nijhoff, 1975.

[84] See, for example, Henri Desroche, *op. cit.,* and Norman Birnbaum, "Beyond Marx in the Sociology of Religion?" in Charles Y. Glock and Phillip E. Hammond (eds.), *Beyond the Classics? Essays in the Scientific Study of Religion,* New York: Harper & Row, 1973, pp. 3-70. Consult also articles and bibliography in *Social Compass,* Vol. 22, Nos. 3-4, 1975, a special issue on Marxism and religion edited by Otto Maduro; and chapter six of this text.

[85] Birnbaum, *op. cit.,* pp. 13 - 14.

[86] It is certainly true that Marxism exerts a contemporary fascination for theologians for many reasons, not the least of which is its origin in a critique of German theology. On the religious or mythical aspects of Marxism itself, see Birnbaum, *op. cit.,* p. 10; Tucker, *op. cit.*; H.B. Mayo, "Marxism and Religion," *The Hibbert Journal,* Vol. 51, 1953, pp. 226-233; Herbert Weisinger, *op. cit.,* pp. 391-392; Louis J. Halle, "Marx's Religious Drama," *Encounter,* Vol. 25, No. 4, 1965, pp. 29-37; and Donald G. MacRae, "The Bolshevik Ideology," in his *Ideology and Society: Papers in Sociology and Politics,* London: Heinemann, 1961. On the "dialogue" or *rapprochement* between Christian theology and Marxism, see, for example, Roger Garaudy, *From Anathema to Dialogue,* New York: Vintage Books, 1968; and A. Van der Bent, *The Christian Marxist Dialogue,* Geneva: World Council of Churches, 1969. Consult also the bibliographies provided by Maduro and Birnbaum, cited above, and see Birnbaum, pp. 60-63.

[87] Birnbaum, *op. cit.,* p. 14. As Birnbaum states, "Religion was a response to people's homelessness in the world, an effort to construct an imaginary home - a moral universe in which humanity could find repose - and an ideal image of itself," p. 14; phrased differently, it was "a spiritual response to a condition of alienation," p. 12. It is quite clear that, in Birnbaum's words, "The Marxist Sociology of Religion is inseparable from the radical humanism of Marx and Engels," p. 10.

CHAPTER FOUR

EMILE DURKHEIM: RELIGION AND SOCIAL INTEGRATION

More than any other thinker, the French sociologist Emile Durkheim qualifies for recognition as the founder of the sociology of religion. Though his work has been variously interpreted, widely criticized and hotly debated, its impact has been lasting and profound. In the field of sociology in general and in the subdiscipline of the sociology of religion in particular, Durkheim is frequently honoured as the greatest of all sociologists, even by those whose disagreements with him are intense.[1]

Though a concern with religion is evident in his earlier writings, Durkheim's towering contribution to the understanding of religion is his book *The Elementary Forms of the Religious Life,* which first appeared in 1912.[2] In this *tour de force* he propounds a provocative thesis that is "brilliant and imaginative, almost poetical,"[3] though also, according to certain critics, seriously flawed and fundamentally misconceived.[4]

In his attempt to provide a distinctly sociological or "sociologistic" account of religious origins, Durkheim is impatient to dismiss the futile psychological speculations of his predecessors among British evolutionists and German naturists. The accuracy with which he diagnoses the weaknesses of these viewpoints, however, has frequently obscured the fact that such theorizing was already largely outmoded among professional anthropologists, at least by the time *The Elementary Forms* appeared. Furthermore, his critical artistry has tended to camouflage two elements in his own thinking that link him intellectually to those he condemns, at least in the opinion of some commentators. These elements may, for the present, merely be noted as an underlying evolutionism and (much more provocatively) a tendency toward a psychological mode of explanation.[5]

In discussing Durkheim's thesis, it is easier to report what its author says then to explain what he *means*, for when and where he is to be taken at his word is a profound and complex problem in the sociology of knowledge as much as in sociological theory.[6] Nonetheless, in the present context, brief textual commentary is called for, so that at the very least some of the strengths as well as the ambiguities and difficulties of Durkheim's analysis may be more readily apparent.

As already observed, Durkheim's concern with religion clearly precedes his preoccupation with the subject in *The Elementary Forms,* his last major work. In both *The Division of Labour* and *Suicide* as well as in other writings, he exhibits deep concern with morality, social solidarity and the link between them, and this leads inevitably to consideration of "religion" in the colloquial sense of the term.[7] In *The Elementary Forms,* however, Durkheim devotes his undivided attention to the tasks of defining and explaining the phenomenon of religion in sociological terms. He does so, moreover, on the basis of a case-study of primitive religion; an exotic "crucial experiment" conducted in the intellectual lair of evolutionary anthropology.

In the light of the arguments I presented in Chapter Two, it is rewarding to retrace the process by which Durkheim arrives at his definition of religion. In direct contrast to Weber, he is convinced that the "prejudicial question" of definition "must be treated before all others":

> It is not that we dream of arriving at once at the profound characteristics which really explain religion: these can be determined only at the end of our study. But that which is necessary and possible, is to indicate a certain number of external and easily recognizable signs, which will enable us to recognize religious phenomena whenever they are met with, and which will deter us from confounding them with others.[8]

Religious phenomena will be recognized by the sociologist only "by freeing the mind of every preconceived idea" and transcending ethnocentric, everyday *societal* conceptions of what religion is:

> Men have been obliged to make for themselves a notion of what religion is, long before the science of religions started its methodical comparisons. The necessities of existence force all of us, believers and non-believers, to represent in some way these things in the midst of which we live, upon which we must pass judgment constantly, and which we must take into account in all our conduct. However, since these preconceived ideas are formed without any method, according to the circumstances and chances of life, they have no right to any credit whatsoever, and must be rigorously set aside. . . . It is not from our prejudices, passions or habits that we should demand the elements of the definition that we must have; it is from the reality itself that we are going to define.[9]

It will be immediately apparent to the reader of the previous chapters that Durkheim's definitional stance, particularly in its exclusion of societal conceptions and its invocation of "reality," is highly contentious. Equally so, however, is the actual definition he formulates only after repudiating the two main forms of substantive definition current in his own day; forms that are, incidentally, still very much in intellectual circulation.[10]

Thus, rejecting a definition of religion in terms of a broad, substantive conception of the "supernatural" with all its connotations of mystery, the unknown, the unutterable and the infinite; and dismissing a narrower definition based upon belief in gods or spiritual beings, Durkheim espouses a definition that combines a broadly substantive component with a strongly functionalist ingredient:

Thus we arrive at the following definition: *A religion is a unified system of beliefs and practices relative to sacred things, that is to say, things set apart and forbidden – beliefs and practices which unite into one single moral community called a Church, all those who adhere to them.* The second element which thus finds a place in our definition is no less essential than the first; for by showing that the idea of religion is inseparable from that of the Church, it makes it clear that religion should be an eminently collective thing.[11]

This formula is composed of a number of explicit categories and distinctions, which must be treated briefly.

Firstly, Durkheim distinguishes between beliefs and rites:

The first are states of opinion, and consist in representations; the second are determined modes of action. Between these two classes of facts there is all the difference which separates thought from action.[12]

Rites may only be distinguished from other human practices by the "special nature of their object" which is, in turn, expressed only in a *belief*. Consideration of the nature of beliefs, therefore, necessitates the explication of Durkheim's second pair of categories:

All known religious beliefs, whether simple or complex, present one common characteristic: they presuppose a classification of all the things, real and ideal, of which men think, into two classes or opposed groups, generally designated by two distinct terms which are translated well enough by the words *profane* and *sacred*. This division of the world into two domains . . . is the distinctive trait of religious thought; the beliefs, myths, dogmas and legends are either representations or systems of representations which express the nature of sacred things, the virtues and powers which are attributed to them, or their relations with each other and with profane things.[13]

No matter how its particular forms may vary, this dichotomy is universal, and in all the history of human thought, maintains Durkheim, no other case may be found of "two categories of things so profoundly differenciated or so radically opposed to one another."[14] Furthermore, the main characteristic of religious phenomena is that they always assume such a "bipartite division of the whole universe."[15] Thus, from the twin dichotomies of beliefs and rituals, and the sacred and profane, Durkheim is able to forge the substantive aspect of his definition of religion:

When a certain number of sacred things sustain relations of co-ordination and subordination with each other in such a way as to form a system having a certain unity, but which is not comprised within any other system of the same sort, the totality of these beliefs and their corresponding rites constitutes a religion.[16]

The incompleteness of this formulation necessitates scrutiny of the distinction between the categories of "religion" and "magic," thereby underlining the vital importance of the last major component in the final definition, the concept of the Church.

Like religion, magic is composed of beliefs and rites; it embraces myths and dogmas; conducts ceremonies, prayers and dances; and invokes similar, if not the same, forces. Detecting an inherent opposition between magic and religion, however, Durkheim is reluctant to combine them into a unified category. He therefore traces "a line of demarcation" between these two domains:

The really religious beliefs are always common to a determined group, which makes profession of adhering to them and of practising the rites connected with them. They are not merely received individually by all the members of this group; they are something belonging to the group, and they make its unity. The individuals which compose it feel themselves united to each other by the simple fact that they have a common faith. A society whose members are unified by the fact that they think in the same way in regard to the sacred world and its relations with the profane world, and by the fact that they translate these common ideas into common practices, is what is called a Church. In all history, we do not find a single religion without a Church.[17]

By contrast, magic is an essentially individual matter, for while its beliefs may be widely diffused, it neither binds together its adherents nor unites them into "a group leading a common life." The magician has clients but no congregation, for there is no Church of magic, and religion alone functions as "an eminently collective thing." While open to severe criticism, this assertion is basic to Durkheim's investigation, analysis and explanation of the fundamental forms of religion.[18]

To explain religion in general, Durkheim analyzes the phenomenon of religion in what he conceives to be its "most primitive and simple" particular form.[19] Through a much disputed investigation and description of totemism, he attempts to gain "an understanding of the religious nature of man" and thereby to display "an essential and permanent aspect of humanity."[20] Thus, by means of an analysis greatly indebted to the work of Robertson Smith, Durkheim identifies himself with those who perceive in totemism the origin, or at least the earliest discernible form, of religion.[21]

By devoting special attention to the totemic cults of the Australian Aborigines, Durkheim attempts to take advantage of the most recent developments in ethnography against a general background of more familiar comparative material dealing with totemism in North America and elsewhere. In his view, the primal form of religion is a cult linked to the social unit of the clan, which is totemic in nature. The clan "holds a preponderating place in the collective life" of the Australian tribes, and those who compose it "consider themselves united by a bond of kinship . . . of a very special nature."[22] Sharing the name of "a determined species of material things" the members of a clan believe they have "very particular relations" with this species:

The species of things which serves to designate the clan collectively is called its *totem*. The totem of the clan is also that of each of its members.[23]

The totem is thus a "coat-of-arms," a heraldic emblem that identifies a clan and its members.[24] But it is more than either a name or an emblem, as revealed by its employment in religious ceremonies:

While the totem is a collective label, it also has a religious character. In fact, it is in connection with it, that things are classified as sacred or profane. It is the very type of sacred thing.[25]

Set apart as something "special," the totemic animal or plant is surrounded by prohibitions, interdictions and taboos. Even more remarkably, however, Durkheim notes that representations of the totem are also considered sacred and that regulations concerning them are more strictly and severely enforced than those referring to the totem itself. Thus, he asserts:

Since the number and importance of the interdictions which isolate a sacred thing, and keep it apart, correspond to the degree of sacredness with which it is invested, we arrive at the remarkable conclusion that *the images of totemic beings are more sacred than the beings themselves*.[26]

Experiencing a strong need to represent the idea of the totem "by means of material and external signs," the Australian Aborigine consequently looks upon such representations with adoration and regards them as "more actively powerful than the totem itself."[27]

But the quality of sacredness is not confined to the totem and its images, for it even touches man himself:

Every member of the clan is invested with a sacred character which is not materially inferior to that . . . in the animal. This personal sacredness is due to the fact that the man believes that while he is a man in the usual sense of the word, he is also an animal or plant of the totemic species . . . he bears its name; this identity of name is therefore supposed to imply an identity of nature.[28]

There is thus a duality in man's nature. The profane and mundane human organism "conceals within its depths a sacred principle, which visibly comes to the surface in certain determined cases" and does not differ "from that which causes the religious character of the totem." Possessing a "religious power," it "holds profane things at a distance."[29]

If specific plants or animals, their representations and the human beings who create such representations are all sacred, their religious character cannot therefore, according to Durkheim, be due to "the special attachments distinguishing them from each other":

The similar sentiments inspired by these different sorts of things in the mind of the believer, which give them their sacred character, can evidently come only from some common principle partaken of alike by the totemic emblems, the men of the clan and the individuals of the species serving as a totem.[30]

In reality, argues Durkheim, the cult is addressed to this common principle:

In other words, totemism is the religion, not of such and such animals or men or images, but of an anonymous and impersonal force, found in each of these beings but not to be confounded with any of them. No one possesses it entirely and all participate in it. It is so completely independent of the particular subjects in whom it incarnates itself, that it precedes them and survives them. Individuals die, generations pass and are replaced by others; but this force always remains actual, living and the same. It animates the generations of today as it animated those of yesterday and as it will animate those of tomorrow. Taking the words in a large sense, we may say that it is the god adored by each totemic cult. Yet it is an impersonal god, without name or history, immanent in the world and diffused in an innumerable multitude of things.[31]

This impersonal force is not, however, represented in an abstract manner by the Aborigine, but rather in the form of a familiar, visible and concrete object:

This is what the totem really consists in: it is only the material form under which the imagination represents this immaterial substance, this energy diffused through all sorts of heterogeneous things, which alone is the real object of the cult.[32]

Identifying the anonymous and impersonal force underlying totemism with the *wakan* of the Sioux, the *orenda* of the Iroquois, the *pokunt* of the Shoshone, the *manitou* of the Algonquin, the *nauala* of the Kwakiutl, the *yek* of the Tlinkit and the *sgâna* of the Haida; Durkheim also recognizes it in the *mana* of the peoples of Melanesia. Is this not, he asks, "the same notion of an anonymous and diffused force, the germs of which we recently found in the totemism of Australia?" Though abstracted and generalized to a higher degree, the ubiquitous forces that characterize the religious systems of the North American Indians and the Melanesians are, in Durkheim's view, "obviously related" to the more primitive and restricted forces that permeate Australian totemism.[33]

For the Aborigines, the universe is "filled and animated" by a number of forces that their imagination objectifies mostly in animal or vegetable form. These totems are the means by which individuals are put in touch with these sources of energy. There are as many forces as there are clans in the tribe and each is embodied in a particular category of visible things as its "essence and vital principle."[34] In his discussion of the nature of the totemic force, Durkheim insists that the word is not used metaphorically, either in a physical or moral context:

In one sense, they are even material forces which mechanically engender physical effects. Does an individual come in contact with them without having taken proper precautions? He receives a shock which might be compared to the effect of an electric discharge. . . . But in addition to this physical aspect, they also have a moral character. When someone asks a native why he observes his rites, he replies that his ancestors always have observed them, and he ought to follow their example. So if he acts in a certain way towards the totemic beings, it is not only because the forces resident in them are physically redoubtable but because he feels himself morally obliged to act thus.[35]

The sacred totemic beings are thus both feared and respected by the Aborigines. The totemic force is an awesome moral power and all beings partaking of the same totemic principle are morally bound together by the ties and duties of kinship.

Totemism is therefore, for Durkheim, not merely a form of animal worship, but a much more complex phenomenon than is at first apparent. Far from being just a collection of fragmentary beliefs relating to special objects, it is, on the contrary, a system of ideas that provides a conception of the universe in both physical and moral terms. The totem is a symbol, the "outward and visible form" of what Durkheim calls "the totemic principle or god"; but it also symbolizes something more:

. . . it is also the symbol of the determined society called the clan. It is its flag; it is the sign by which each clan distinguishes itself from the others, the visible mark of its personality, a mark borne by everything which is a part of the clan under any title whatsoever, men, beasts or things.[36]

But this dual symbolization has a deeper meaning, according to Durkheim:

. . . if it is at once the symbol of the god and of the society, is that not because the god and the society are only one? How could the emblem of the group have been able to become the figure of this quasi-divinity, if the group and the divinity were two distinct realities? The god of the clan, the totemic principle, can therefore be nothing else than the clan itself, personified and represented to the imagination under the visible form of the animal or vegetable which serves as totem.[37]

In attempting to explain the "apotheosis" of the clan, Durkheim provides both general and specific arguments. Firstly, by a general consideration of the character of any society, he tries to demonstrate that "it has all that is necessary to arouse the sensation of the divine" in human minds merely by virtue of the power that it exerts over them. To its members, he maintains, a society is "what a god is to his worshipers . . . a being whom men think of as superior to themselves, and upon whom they feel that they depend."[38] In a classic sociologistic statement, Durkheim therefore describes the collective reality of society in terms of its external and constraining character:

Since it has a nature which is peculiar to itself and different from our individual nature, it pursues ends which are likewise special to it; but, as it cannot attain them except through our intermediacy, it imperiously demands our aid. It requires that, forgetful of our own interest, we make ourselves its servitors, and it submits us to every sort of inconvenience, privation and sacrifice, without which social life would be impossible. It is because of this that at every instant we are obliged to submit ourselves to rules of conduct and of thought which we have neither made nor desired, and which are sometimes even contrary to our most fundamental inclinations and instincts. . . . [The] empire which it holds over consciences is due much less to the physical supremacy of which it has the privilege than the moral authority with which it is invested. If we yield to its orders, it is not merely because it is strong enough to triumph over our resistance; it is primarily because it is the object of a venerable respect.[39]

Though possessing a reality external to individuals, society may also be said to live in the hearts of men. It is thus both transcendent and immanent. Its precepts are internalized in the individual moral conscience and, in Durkheim's opinion, "respect is the emotion which we experience when we feel this interior and wholly spiritual pressure operating upon us."[40]

But why does this experience assume a totemic or mythological character? Durkheim answers this question:

Since it is in spiritual ways that social pressure exercises itself, it could not fail to give men the idea that outside themselves there exist one or several powers, both moral and, at the same time, efficacious, upon which they depend. They must think of these powers, at least in part, as outside themselves, for these address them in a tone of command and sometimes even order them to do violence to their most natural inclinations.[41]

Because the influence of society is exerted in "ways that are too circuitous and obscure," and because it involves "psychical mechanisms that are too complex" to allow an "ordinary observer" to trace its source, men know only that they are acted upon but do not know by whom. They therefore "invent by themselves the idea of these powers," representing them "under forms that are really foreign to their nature."[42]

In attempting to formulate a specific explanation of the transfiguration of the clan, Durkheim turns his attention to complex "physical mechanisms" and invokes the insights of the newly emerging field of crowd psychology. Focussing upon the collective ceremonials of the Australian Aborigines, he discerns in their fiery, unrestrained, noisy and violent savagery the origins of the religious impulse.[43] Generating "the wildest excitement," these periodic gatherings display a "general effervescence," which reaches its climax in scenes of passionate abandon wholly alien to the "civilized" Western observer:

The very fact of the concentration acts as an exceptionally powerful stimulant. When they are once come together, a sort of electricity is formed by their collecting which quickly transports them to an extraordinary degree of exaltation. Every sentiment expressed finds a place without resistance in all the minds, which are very open to outside impressions; each re-echoes the others and is re-echoed by the others. The initial impulse thus proceeds, growing as it does, as an avalanche grows in its advance. And as such active passions so free from all control could not fail to burst out, on every side one sees nothing but violent gestures, cries, veritable howls, and deafening noises of every sort, which aid in intensifying still more the state of mind which they manifest.[44]

In developing a more rhythmic and regular aspect, such occasions, according to Durkheim, "lose nothing of their natural violence" and continue to release passions "of such an impetuosity that they can be restrained by nothing" and result in "unheard of actions." Thus, for example, participants "are so far removed from their ordinary conditions of life, and they are so thoroughly conscious of it, that they feel that they must set themselves outside of and above their ordinary morals" by engaging in orgiastic or incestuous sexual behaviour.[45]

For Durkheim, the effect of such ceremonies on the minds of those involved can be easily imagined. It is to produce a "violent super-excitation of the whole physical and mental life."[46] Thus:

One can readily conceive how, when arrived at this state of exaltation, a man does not recognize himself any longer. Feeling himself dominated and carried away by some sort of an external power which makes him think and act differently than in normal times, he naturally has the impression of being himself no longer. . . . And as at the same time all his companions feel themselves transformed in the same way and express their sentiment by their cries, their gestures and their general attitude, everything is just as though he really were transformed into a special world, entirely different from the one where he ordinarily lives, and into an environment filled with exceptionally intense forces that take hold of him and metamorphose him. How could such experiences . . . fail to leave in him the conviction that there really exist two heterogeneous and mutually incomparable worlds? One is that where his daily life drags wearily along; but he cannot penetrate into the other without at once entering into relations with extraordinary powers that excite him to the point of frenzy. The first is the profane world, the second that of sacred things.[47]

Religion is born, therefore, "in the midst of these effervescent social environments and out of this effervescence itself," a view Durkheim regards as confirmed by the fact that in Australia "the really religious activity" is largely confined to such assemblies.[48] In such circumstances, the clan is transfigured in the form of a totem, or, more generally, society is represented in the form of a god:

Since religious force is nothing other than the collective and anonymous force of the clan, and since this can be represented in the mind only in the form of the totem, the totemic emblem is like the visible body of the god. . . . This is the explanation of why it holds the first place in the series of sacred things.[49]

Of course, the Aborigine is completely unaware of this sociological truth, just as, according to Durkheim, the soldier who dies defending his flag accords first place in his consciousness to flag rather than country:

Whether one isolated standard remains in the hands of the enemy or not does not determine the fate of the country, yet the soldier allows himself to be killed to regain it. He loses sight of the fact that the flag is only a sign, and that it has no value in itself, but only brings to mind the reality that it represents; it is treated as if it were this reality itself.[50]

The totem is "the flag of the clan," and because social organization is "too complex a reality to be represented clearly in all its complex unity by such rudimentary intelligences," the Aborigines naturally trace their sense of dependence and increased vitality to the totem rather than to the clan, thereby directing their sentiments toward a representation rather than a reality.[51] Thus, though in reality they are worshipping their own society, reaffirming their social solidarity and reinforcing individual commitment to the collectivity, those engaged in totemic rites are unaware of the latent meaning of their actions. Ignorant of the process by which "new energies" are generated by "the coming together of a number of men associated in the same life," the Australian Aborigines fail to perceive that the god of the clan is nothing more or less than the clan itself.[52]

In their inability to detect the true identity of their "god," the Aborigines are by no means unique. Indeed, it might be argued somewhat crudely that if religion is rooted in "alienation" for Marx and in "a disease of language" for Müller, then for Durkheim its roots lie in mistaken identity:

It is undoubtedly true that if [men] were able to see that these influences which they feel emanate from society, then the mythological system of interpretations would never be born. But social action follows ways that are too circuitous and obscure, and employs psychical mechanisms that are too complex to allow the ordinary observer to see whence it comes. As long as scientific analysis does not come to teach it to them, men know well that they are acted upon, but they do not know by whom. So they must invent by themselves the idea of these powers with which they feel themselves in connection. . . .[53]

Though Durkheim clearly espouses an undiluted positivism in his conception of "scientific analysis" as the single source of truth, it would be incorrect to regard him simply as an intellectualist observer of the mistaken notions implicit in a religious world view.[54] In fact, any attempt to characterize religion in terms of an illusion is anathema to him: "Our entire study rests upon this postulate that the unanimous sentiment of the believers of all times cannot be purely illusory."[55]

Declaring his agreement with William James, Durkheim maintains that "religious beliefs rest upon a specific experience whose demonstrative value is, in one sense, not one bit inferior to that of scientific experiments":

We, too, think that "a tree is known by its fruits," and that fertility is the best proof of what the roots are worth. But from the fact that a "religious experience," if we choose to call it this, does exist and that it has a certain foundation . . . it does not follow that the reality which is its foundation conforms objectively to the idea which believers have of it. The very fact that the fashion in which it has been conceived has varied infinitely in different times is enough to prove that none of these conceptions express it adequately.[56]

Resorting, appropriately enough, to an analogy from the physical sciences, Durkheim argues:

If a scientist states it as an axiom that the sensations of heat and light which we feel correspond to some objective cause, he does not conclude that this is what it appears to the senses to be. Likewise, even if the impressions which the faithful feel are not imaginary, still they are in no way privileged intuitions; there is no reason for believing that they inform us better upon the nature of their object than do ordinary sensations upon the nature of bodies and their properties.[57]

Believing that this object or reality "which mythologies have represented under so many different forms, but which is the universal and eternal objective cause of these sensations *sui generis* out of which religious experience is made" has been revealed through scientific analysis as society, Durkheim proclaims the truth of all religion in a sociological sense:

. . . it is an essential postulate of sociology that a human institution cannot rest upon an error and a lie, without which it could not exist. If it were not founded in the nature of things, it would have encountered in the facts a resistance over which it could never have triumphed. So when we commence the study of primitive religions, it is with the assurance that they hold to reality and express it. . . .[58]

In a classic, sweeping statement, he proceeds to summarize the sociological reasoning behind the promulgation of his new social-scientific doctrine:

When only the letter of the formulae is considered . . . religious beliefs and practices undoubtedly seem disconcerting at times and one is tempted to attribute them to some sort of a deep-rooted error. But one must know how to go underneath the symbol to the reality which it represents and which gives it its meaning. The most barbarous and the most fantastic rites and the strangest myths translate some human need, some aspect of life, either individual or social. The reasons with which the faithful justify them may be, and generally are, erroneous; but the true reasons do not cease to exist, and it is the duty of science to discover them.

In reality then, there are no religions which are false. All are true in their own fashion; all answer, though in different ways, to the given conditions of human existence.[59]

Durkheim's account of religion is characteristically sociological in the extreme, for not only does it identify God with society by means of a form of "structuralist" reduction;[60] it also asserts an inextricable connection between religion and society:

The general conclusion . . . is that religion is something eminently social. Religious representations are collective representations which express collective realities; the rites are a manner of acting which take rise in the midst of the assembled group and which are destined to excite, maintain or recreate certain mental states in these groups.[61]

Indeed, so intertwined in his analysis are religion and society that it may well be argued that if religion is a social phenomenon, then it is equally true that society is a religious phenomenon.[62]

Thus, despite its iconoclastic thesis, Durkheim's argument has implications of a politically conservative kind. Its emphasis upon the socially integrative function of collective ritual as well as the role of ceremony in securing individual commitment to the existing social order suggests a concern with social statics rather than social dymanics, which is well expressed in the following observation:

> There are occasions when [the] strengthening and vivifying action of society is especially apparent. In the midst of an assembly animated by a common passion, we become susceptible of acts and sentiments of which we are incapable when reduced to our own forces. . . . This is why all parties political, economic or confessional are careful to have periodic reunions where their members may revivify their common faith by manifesting it in common.[63]

Yet, although it is arguable that Durkheim is less concerned with social change than with the solidarity, continuity and persistence of society; and though scrutiny of his analysis of religion bears out such an interpretation, it would, nonetheless, be inaccurate to maintain that he is unaware of or uninterested in any possible link between religion and changes in society. Though it has received little attention from commentators, Durkheim's treatment of the role of religion in social change undoubtedly merits comment here.[64]

Just as he perceives religion emerging from the intense, electrically charged and effervescent atmosphere of concentrated collective activity, so also he discerns an explosive nucleus of social transformation in the spontaneity, excitement, passion and enthusiasm of mass gatherings. Thus, in a discussion that appears to echo the controversial work of Gustave Le Bon and that anticipates later work in the field of "Collective Behaviour,"[65] Durkheim indicates the "religious" character of uninstitutionalized crowd activity:

> This aptitude of society for setting itself up as a god or for creating gods was never more apparent than during the first years of the French Revolution. At this time . . . under the influence of the general enthusiasm, things purely laical by nature were transformed by public opinion into sacred things: these were the Fatherland, Liberty, Reason. A religion tended to become established which had its dogmas, symbols, altars and feasts. It was to these spontaneous aspirations that the cult of Reason and the Supreme Being attempted to give a sort of official satisfaction. It is true that this religious renovation had only an ephemeral duration. But that was because the patriotic enthusiasm which at first transported the masses soon relaxed. The cause being gone, the effect could not remain.[66]

Returning to this theme in the conclusion to his great work on religion, Durkheim diagnoses the ills of modern society and, much like Marx or Weber, dons the garb of the prophet. Arguing that no society can dispense with the need for regular reaffirmation of its collective sentiments, he maintains that such "moral remaking" requires reunions, assemblies and meetings of its members. Thus there emerge ceremonies "which do not differ from regular religious ceremonies, either in their object, the results which they produce, or the processes employed to attain these results."[67]

Affirming that "there is something eternal in religion which is destined to survive all the particular symbols in which religious thought has successively enveloped itself," Durkheim believes that he lives in a time of "transition and moral mediocrity" when "the old gods are growing old or already dead, and others are not yet born":[68]

> The great things of the past which filled our fathers with enthusiasm do not excite the same ardour in us, either because they have come into common usage to such an extent that we are unconscious of them, or else because they no longer answer to our actual aspirations; but as yet there is nothing to replace them.[69]

While in such circumstances the emergence of some form of "secular religion," combining science with patriotism in appropriate ceremony, might present a distinct possibility, any attempt to "artificially" construct such a humanistic rite by reviving "old historic souvenirs" in the manner of Auguste Comte is doomed to failure.[70]

In Durkheim's judgment, only "life itself, and not a dead past . . . can produce a living cult."[71] In spite of the death agonies of the old gods, life still goes on, and thus the contemporary condition of "incertitude and confused agitation" that Durkheim discerns must inevitably run its course and be replaced:

> A day will come when our societies will know again those hours of creative effervescence, in the course of which new ideas arise and new formulae are found which serve for a while as a guide to humanity. . . .[72]

"Collective effervescence" and, by implication, crowd or "mob" activities are crucial both to Durkheim's understanding of social change and to his essentially cyclical conception of religion's "eternal" nature. The spontaneous character of such mass excitement renders precise prediction of its outcome difficult, however, and therefore Durkheim's certainty regarding recurrent religious renovation is qualified by a reluctance to forecast the imminent future, which recalls Sir James Frazer peering blindly into the "clouds and thick darkness" that obscure what is to come:[73]

> There are no gospels which are immortal, but neither is there any reason for believing that humanity is incapable of inventing new ones. As to the question of what symbols this new faith will express itself with, whether they will resemble those of the past or not, and whether or not they will be more adequate for the reality which they seek to translate, that is something which surpasses the human faculty of foresight. . . .[74]

Durkheim's work on religion constitutes a provocative, controversial and ambiguous legacy, and although it has undoubtedly been the greatest single intellectual influence in the sociology of religion, it has been accorded a less than enthusiastic reception in other quarters.[75] The comparative religionist

Eric J. Sharpe, for example, sums up Durkheim's failings in terms that essentially typify the non-sociological reception of the latter's interpretation of religion:

Although widely read, Durkheim was so dominated by the desire to explain away the phenomenon of religion that his theories about the origins of religion are of little consequence. His failure to accept mankind's belief in the actual existence of an unseen supernatural order – a failure in which he was to have many followers – led him into serious errors of interpretation. . . . The student of comparative religion will, perhaps, read him less in order to acquire a knowledge of either the nature of religion or the thorny problem of the origins of religion, than to learn something of the standing of these theories in turn-of-the-century France.[76]

In thus consigning the Durheimian enterprise to a place among the curios of the history of ideas, Sharpe is less concerned that "many of the anthropological theories and assumptions on which [Durkheim] built have since been shown to have been unreliable" than with the fact that his attempt to "explain away" religious phenomena is essentially misguided.[77]

A more sympathetic though no less critical commentator, the British social anthropologist Evans-Pritchard also remains unconvinced that Durkheim has successfully explained or explained away the phenomenon of religion by sociological means. Perceiving Durkheim as having been "misled" by the influence of Robertson Smith, and regarding many aspects of his work on religion as "unconvincing," "questionable," doubtful or invalid, he maintains that the great sociologist's "brilliant," "imaginative" and even "poetical" thesis is a noble failure, not least because it violates its author's own carefully formulated and loudly promulgated rules of sociological method.[78]

To acknowledge the unprecedented and unrivalled impact of Durkheim's writings upon sociologists of religion is not to suggest, however, that they have been greeted with universal acclaim in this context. Indeed, even in this specific scholarly circle, they have been accorded a decidedly mixed reception, having initially encountered, according to Talcott Parsons, an "overwhelmingly unfavourable" response on the part of "the social science community," especially in the English-speaking world.[79] Thus, although so eminent a figure as Parsons is able to proclaim, in a recent reappraisal, that Durkheim has been widely misunderstood to the extent that his ideas were "too far ahead of his time," this view in no way provokes universal assent from his fellow sociologists.[80] While some would, no doubt, concur that social scientists, who have been, after all, "the only ones who have paid serious attention to Durkheim's work," have perhaps "simply not been ready to appreciate the importance of the kinds of considerations which Durkheim put forward," few would be inclined to conclude thereby that hostility to the Durkheimian thesis stems solely from misunderstanding, misinterpretation or misinformation.[81] If, in Parsons' assessment, even the most distinguished and "culturally sophisticated" of contemporary sociologists can sink to caricature rather than interpretation of Durkheim's view of religion, this may surely be in part because the contention that sacred things are symbols of society comes "very close to being nonsense" in the context of "the usual received senses of the concept 'society'."[82] Thus, while Parsons' reading may indeed be the most sensitive and accurate one, it is as well to remember that the undoubted complexity and ambiguity of Durkheim's thought combined with its frequently unfortunate manner of expression contrive to render a definitive interpretation difficult, if not impossible.[83]

Durkheim's impact upon the sociology of religion has perhaps been the more profound because his deceptively simple sociological equation of society and god has generated intense controversy rather than uncritical celebration. With a confidence at least equalling that of Professor Parsons, sociological critics of Durkheim endeavour to indicate his errors and undermine his arguments often in the most fundamental way at the same time as they acknowledge and enhance his stature as a classic thinker and a great founding father of the sociology of religion. It might, indeed, be asserted that Emile Durkheim's singular intellectual status is recognized even by those sociologists of religion who reject his main thesis as essentially tautological.[84]

Numerous and severe anthropological criticisms of his interpretation of "totemism" and Aborigine ritual suggest that Durkheim was wholly mistaken in regarding this work as a comparative and evolutionary "crucial experiment" that revealed religion in its barest elementary forms.[85] None the less, the contention that his general thesis does not rest solely on the accuracy of the evidence provided in his case-study is widely accepted both by Durkheim's defenders and detractors, and has the effect of broadening the terms in which it is debated.[86]

Thus, whatever the merits or defects of its ethnological underpinnings, Durkheim's indentification or equation of "religion" and "society" may simultaneously appear self-evidently valid, demonstrably false, tautologically true or nonsensically misleading, depending upon the commentator's particular point of view.[87] Despite his fierce protests that his theory of religion is not a variant of historical materialism, some observers have seen Durkheim as an advocate of some form of materialistic reductionism.[88] For, by perceiving the chief purpose (or function) of religious symbolism as the representation or reproduction of "society," he is led, as even so sympathetic an interpreter as Robert Bellah admits, to adopt "what appears to be a straightforward representational or objective theory of religious symbols: religious symbols stand for society; particular symbols stand for particular groups."[89] But such a perspective makes most sense if society is conceived in physical terms as a group inhabiting a precise territory; Durkheim is, therefore, frequently perceived as harbouring such a conception despite his shrill denials.[90]

The Durkheimian socio-religious equation appears most sophisticated and tantalizing in the terms in which it has been formulated by Parsons and Bellah as a "fundamental reference point" for contemporary understanding of society, personality, symbolism and their interpenetration.[91] This is not to suggest, however, that this interpretation does not itself entail serious theoretical difficulties, some of which will shortly be indicated. Though he treads precariously close to an objective representationalism at times, Durkheim essentially espouses the view, according to Bellah, that "religious symbols do not merely give an intellectual conception of society" but that, on the contrary, they create it and continually make it possible.[92] Thus, in distinguishing between judgements of reality and judgements of value, Durkheim observes:

> If all judgements involve ideals we have different species of ideals. The function of some is to express the reality to which they adhere. These are properly called concepts. The function of others is, on the contrary, to transfigure the realities to which they relate, and these are the ideals of value. In the first instance the ideal is a symbol of a thing and makes it an object of understanding. In the second the thing itself symbolizes the ideal and acts as the medium through which the ideal becomes capable of being understood.[93]

This passage appears to indicate a "more active, forming, imaginative role" for religious symbolism than Durkheim is often perceived as assigning, and thus Bellah seems justified in speculating that its author at least comes close to adopting the perspective of "symbolic realism," which asserts the "autonomous creative function of religious symbolism operating in a different way from the cognitive symbolism of science."[94] Such a viewpoint, it may be observed, places Durkheim at some considerable distance from most varieties of historical materialism, and very far indeed from any simplistic sociological determinism or reductionism, a fact astutely recognized by at least one distinguished Marxian sociologist:

> From a Marxist standpoint Durkheim inverts the real relationships in society; he takes no account of the material basis – the mode of production – and explains social phenomena by the movement of ideas.[95]

Thus characterizing Durkheim as an idealist rather than as a materialist, Tom Bottomore aptly observes:

> . . . in his later studies it is evident that he came to attribute an ever greater importance to the role of moral ideas expressed in collective representations. For Durkheim it *is* "the consciousness of men that determines their being," and not, as Marx argued, "social being [that] determines their consciousness."[96]

But if society is not to be defined, in Durkheim's equation, in physical terms, and if, as Parsons suggests, the notion of God as a symbolic representation of a concrete empirical entity is "substantively unacceptable to most modern social scientists,"[97] how exactly is the concept "society" to be understood? In his youthful consideration of this problem in *The Structure of Social Action,* Parsons offers the following solution:

Looked at from the point of view of the observer the identification of society with the object of reference of religious ideas retains a certain degree of plausibility. . . . Moreover, of the factors which bear upon *concrete* social life, it is those which are in Durkheim's sense the distinctively social, the common ultimate-value attitudes which are in closest relation to religious ideas. . . . but even looked at in these "objective" terms it is clear that the fundamental significance of Durkheim's "equation" (which cannot be accepted as a simple equation with one variable on each side, but rather as a much more complex function) is not in the relating of religious ideas to a known "material" entity but rather the reverse - it is his proof of the great extent to which the empirical, observable entity "society" is understandable only in terms of men's ideas of and active attitudes toward the non-empirical. If the "equation" is to be accepted at all the significant way of putting it is not "religion is a social phenomenon" so much as "society is a religious phenomenon."[98]

Thus, according to Parsons, Durkheim regards society not as a "concrete phenomenon" but rather as an "abstract social factor" defined as a system of common ultimate-value attitudes that is "inseparable from religious ideas."[99] He concludes:

Thus the charge of "materialism" is not justified. Durkheim arrives at the equation of religion and society by emphasizing not the material aspect of religion, but rather the ideal aspect of society.[100]

In reappraising Durkheim's treatment of religion and society more than thirty years after his original exegesis, Parsons draws essentially the same conclusion, though he expresses it in somewhat different terms:

Durkheim's assertion that sacred things are symbols, the meanings of which should not be interpreted in terms of their intrinsic properties . . . was one of the main points of his . . . devastating critiques of the theories of animism and naturism concerning religion. When, however, the question arose: symbols of what, Durkheim's tendency, disturbing to so many including myself, was to say symbols of society. In the usual received senses of the concept "society," this seemed very close to being nonsense. If, however, one . . . speaks of symbols of the grounding of human existence, which is always inherently, at least in major part, social, it seems a much more reasonable formula.[101]

In suggesting that Durkheim's symbolic referent is correctly understood as the "grounding of human existence," Parsons has in mind the basic framework of order that must be assumed, in both cognitive and moral contexts, "in order to make the phenomena of human life, with special emphasis on its social aspect, intelligible."[102] No great difficulty is involved in relating this to his earlier conception of common ultimate-value attitudes.

In the sphere of Durkheimian textual explication, the sophisticated and insightful interpretations of Parsons and Bellah have gained wide acceptance from sociologists of religion, particularly among those who regard themselves, in some sense, as "functionalists."[103] Yet even the briefest consideration of these interpretations indicates their difficulties and suggests why some social scientists, particularly anthropologists, may have preferred to interpret Durkheim rather more concretely. In Chapter Two it was suggested that broad, functional definitions of religion in terms of "ultimate values" or "grounds of meaning" risk meaninglessness as the price of comprehensiveness and inclusiveness.[104] In the present context it may be intimated that the Parsons-Bellah intepretation of Durkheim comes perilously close to tautology so that everything social is religious, just as in Luckmann's unashamedly explicit view the religious is identical to the human.[105]

But even if the Durkheimian equation is meaningful in the sense in which Parsons and Bellah understand it, does it provide an accurate formulation of the manner in which societies, personalities and symbols actually interpenetrate? It would certainly be maintained by many sociologists that consensualist accounts, whether reported by Durkheim, Parsons or Bellah, fail to depict the real nature of human society and merely point the way down an intellectual blind alley. From this critical angle of vision, belief in the existence of commonly held "ultimate-value attitudes" and shared "grounds of meaning" is completely unwarranted, being rooted in a static and conservative ideological world-view. For such critics, therefore, the very foundation of the Durkheimian or Parsonian conception of religion is nothing more than a utopian illusion.[106]

None the less, rooted in a primary concern with social order as the basis not merely of a sociology of religion but of a general sociological perspective, the work of Durkheim, Parsons and Bellah exhibits an explicit obsession with questions of consensus, integration, solidarity and community. Noting that the main clue to Durkheim's insight into the social relation of religious ideas is "the identity of the attitude of respect held toward them with that held toward moral rules" and that this is "perhaps the most fundamental substantive sociological proposition of Durkheim's theory of religion,"[107] Parsons underlines the importance of morality as a socially binding force:

> . . . those who profess the same beliefs and practice the same rites may be regarded by virtue of these facts as possessing a common system of ultimate-value attitudes, that is, as constituting a "moral community."[108]

Thus he maintains on the basis of Durkheim's definition of religion and because of the spirit of Durkheim's whole theoretical argument that those who have a common religion constitute a moral community, and that the reverse also holds true:

. . . every true moral community, that is, every "society," is characterized to a certain degree by the possession of a common "religion". For without a system of common values, of which a religion is in part a manifestation, a system adhered to in a significant degree, there can be no such thing as a society.[109]

Regarding Durkheim's view that "every religion pertains to a moral community" and its converse that "every community is in one aspect a religious unit" as "entirely acceptable," Parsons baulks only at using the term "church" as synonymous with such a moral community, regarding Durkheimian usage in this respect as too open to misinterpretation.[110]

In appearing to promulgate the related propositions that religion is a societal universal and that society is impossible without religion, the writings of both Durkheim and Parsons antagonize not only the opponents of a conception of social order founded on the sharing of core-values, but also those who perceive use of the term "religion" in this sense as too vague and inclusive to be of any possible utility as a tool of social-scientific analysis.[111]

Sociologists need not be committed to Marxism or any other variant of "conflict theory" in order to question seriously whether Durkheim's conception of the relation between religion and society may be transposed from a relatively undifferentiated "simple" or "primitive" setting into a modern key. If, indeed, it is applicable in the former case, its utility in more complex, though by no means necessarily contemporary, societal contexts is highly questionable. To the reader of his earlier work, *The Division of Labour in Society* (1893),[112] Durkheim's subsequent deduction of sweeping socio-religious propositions from the evidence of a single, simple society is a surprise that is only explicable in terms of a major break or profound discontinuity in his intellectual enterprise. That such a "break" does occur in Durkheim's work is an argument that has been advanced by a number of scholars and that appears to be substantiated by Durkheim's own assessment:

It was only in 1895 that I had a clear sense of the capital role played by religion in social life. . . . It was for me a revelation.[113]

Referring to the first university course in the sociology of religion that he taught at Bordeaux in 1895, he asserts:

This . . . marks a line of demarcation in the development of my thought, so that all my earlier researches had to be revised anew in order to be put in harmony with these new views.[114]

Robert Bellah has noted that *The Division of Labour* was "the last unadulterated celebration of the glories of progress in Durkheim's writing" and the last occasion on which he would "unambiguously applaud the decline of the common conscience and of religion."[115] After 1895, the notion of *conscience collective* became the central element in Durkheim's understanding of society, just as *representations collectives* were the key to understanding religion. Doubtful of "many aspects of modern society" and concerned increasingly with discovering "a new moral basis which would allow it to rise from its malaise," Durkheim became obsessed with the problem of normative order rooted in a set of common-value attitudes. Thus, as Bellah observes:

It is therefore not surprising that Durkheim would return imaginatively, especially in the years after 1900, to the profound depths of social life expressed in primitive society, where the common conscience was vividly, disturbingly alive.[116]

While to some sociologists the transition in Durkheim's thought from the *Division of Labour* to the *Elementary Forms* is perceived as a brilliant intellectual advance, to others it appears, for a variety of reasons, to represent a lamentable course of intellectual regression in which the identification of "society" and "church" reduces either or both concepts to absurdity and leads logically and irrevokably to a generic "anthropological" conception of religion such as that advocated by Thomas Luckmann in his famous "Invisible Religion" thesis.[117] Moreover, some critics of the Durkheimian socio-religious equation resent a perspective, whether propounded by Durkheim or his contemporary disciples, in which "religion" appears to integrate, legitimate and reproduce the societal status quo and to resist and inhibit social change by definition, however large or small the social unit in question. To such commentators, this analytic framework seems calculated to avoid discerning the most important aspects of both religion and society by portraying (or assuming) an orderly and static world in which everything is persuaded to run smoothly by definition.[118]

As will now be apparent, sociologists argue interminably over the general and specific accuracy and utility of Durkheim's attempt to provide a distinctively sociological explanation of religion. Such arguments range from ethnographic disputes concerning his treatment of totemism through to examination of the crowd-psychological basis of his theory as well as its consensualist and functionalist premises. His audacious enterprise may, however, be examined at an even more fundamental level by questioning whether it is possible to explain, or rather explain away religion by sociological means. Not surprisingly, students of religion from outside the social sciences, particularly those with personal "religious" commitments, have been quick to challenge Durkheim's neat iconoclasm.[119] The fundamental importance of their query has, however, rightly been acknowledged by the most eminent sociologists and anthropologists.[120] Thus, Evans-Pritchard argues that while, in a nutshell, for Freud God is really the father, for Durkheim God is really society. Of such a reductionist formula, however, he maintains:

It can be allowed that religious conceptions must bear some relation to the social order, and be in some degree in accord with economic, political, moral and other social facts, and even that they are a product of social life, in the sense that there could be no religion without society . . . but Durkheim is asserting more than that. He is claiming that spirit, soul, and other religious ideas and images are projections of society, or of its segments, and originate in conditions bringing about a state of effervescence.[121]

Evans-Pritchard is unconvinced that Durkheim successfully justifies his claim any more than his predecessors who also believed that they had discovered the answer in the quest for the origins of religion. In this regard, Parsons too raises a pertinent question and indicates a "serious weakness" in Durkheim's argument, of which the latter was apparently unaware. Considering the forms taken by collective representations, the totems, gods, spirits and forces familiar to investigators of religion, Parsons inquires quite simply:

If the reality underlying religion is an empirical reality, why should religious ideas take symbolic form in a way in which scientific ideas do not? Why could that reality not be represented directly by the theory of sociological science?"[122]

As an heir of Comte, Durkheim was well aware that such direct representation was indeed possible, particularly in the modern era, in various forms of humanistic and nationalistic cult.[123] Yet, in Parsons' view, he was unable to explain satisfactorily why "society" should, almost universally, be transmogrified into such myriad and unlikely guises by a process reminiscent of Feuerbach's account of religious projection and alienation.[124] It might plausibly be argued that Durkheim was "so dominated by the desire to explain away the phenomenon of religion" and so anxious to interpret the objects of religious belief and ritual as collective representations of something else that he failed to give due consideration to the rather obvious and elementary problem Parsons was later to unearth.[125] Moreover, this matter may be pressed even further and Durkheim's exposé called into question more sharply by contemplating why, after all, the worship of society is "any more readily explicable than the worship of gods."[126]

It is thus clearly unnecessary to be committed to the belief that religion may only be understood or explained in religious terms in order to regard with scepticism Durkheim's sociological revelation of the real nature of religious activity, especially in the sweeping and extravagant terms in which it is articulated and proclaimed. If Bellah is justified in discerning in Durkheim's work "significant parallels with Freud" (in much the same way as Evans-Pritchard), then it is useful to compare Durkheim's "extended imaginative sojourn among the primitive Australians" with Freud's research into dreams. Such comparison suggests that Freud's attempt to understand "the unconscious sources of personal existence" is paralleled by Durkheim's effort to comprehend the unconscious roots of social existence.[127] Both Durkheim and Freud envisioned the scientist de-coding symbols: the psychoanalyst interpreting dream symbolism and the sociologist of religion translating religious symbolism into social terms. Understood in such terms, Durkheim's enterprise provokes criticism, not merely in the form of an understandable scepticism toward grandiose formulae that lay claim to the means of revealing the real meaning of human activities by reducing them to some other terms. More fundamentally, Durkheim's perspective is calculated to incite the animosity of those who regard the claim of positivistic science to be "man's sole significant cognitive relation to external reality" as dubious, and who detect no inherent superiority in external or internal accounts of the meaning of beliefs and rituals.[128] From this standpoint, Durkheim's strategy for understanding or explaining religion is misconceived because it seeks to "explain away" religion by decreeing its latent rather than manifest meaning; and to "justify" its existence by an Olympian conception of objective societal needs.[129] Indeed, such a note of imperiousness and finality is struck by Durkheim's formula that it even seems legitimate to draw the conclusion that specific forms of religion, as opposed to religion in general, ought not to hold interest for the sociologist and that, therefore, any concern with the content of beliefs is misplaced.[130] In this regard, Parsons observes that "Durkheim is inclined to depreciate the importance of particular religious doctrines" that refer, after all, "to symbols and 'mere' symbols are not intrinsically important – that is, the particular symbol, however important the role of symbolism in general may be."[131] To most sociologists of religion, such a deduction would seem misguided to the point of folly, though it might well gain assent from some "functionalists" within their subdiscipline.[132]

Despite Durkheim's devastating critique of both animism and naturism, it is possible to discern in his work on religion rather more intellectual parallels with the formulations of his predecessors than he himself would have preferred to admit. Thus, though he stresses the authenticity and "truth" of religion in a sociological sense, it seems clear that intellectually no less than Tylor, Frazer, Müller, Feuerbach or Marx, Durkheim regards the content of religious beliefs as erroneous and implicitly, if not formally, debunked by science. While his view of the genesis of religion in the highly charged context of crowd behaviour may therefore, perhaps, be interpreted as "anti-intellectualist" or "emotionalist" in comparison with the previously discussed "intellectualist" speculations of Tylor, Spencer or Frazer, his evaluation of the intellectual worth of religious ideas is essentially not dissimilar to theirs.[133] Religious symbols are certainly, for Durkheim, much more than symptoms of a disease of language; and yet it is not too far-fetched to suggest, paraphrasing Feuerbach, that for him religion is esoteric sociology and is to be deciphered accordingly.[134]

The knowledge that Durkheim's theory is not "intellectualist" in the same sense as the perspectives of anthropological evolutionism and the nature-myth school does not mean, therefore, that it should be regarded as entirely "emotionalist." While its emphasis upon value, motivational commitment, social solidarity and moral community is manifest, this should not lead to the conclusion that the purely cognitive holds no interest for Durkheim. Although he does not attempt to trace the origin of religion to the earliest intellectual gropings of mankind, it is clear that the cognitive aspect of religion is by no means overlooked in his work. His concern with epistemology and sociology of knowledge is, as Parsons notes, not gratuitously "dragged in" but is, in fact, an integral part of the theme of the *Elementary Forms.*[135] Convinced that it is common knowledge "that the first systems of representations with which men have pictured to themselves the world and themselves were of religious origin," Durkheim observes that there is no religion that is not a cosmology at the same time that it is a speculation upon divine things."[136] Perceiving philosophy and even science itself as "born of religion," he regards this as a consequence of the fact that "religion began by taking the place of the sciences and philosophy."[137] Moreover, in an important though frequently overlooked passage, he presses the point even further:

> But it has been less frequently noticed that religion has not confined itself to enriching the human intellect, formed beforehand with a certain number of ideas; it has contributed to forming the intellect itself. Men owe to it not only a good part of the substance of their knowledge, but also the form in which this knowledge has been elaborated.[138]

Thus, while Durkheim may have recognized, as Bellah asserts, that "the speculative side of religion . . . which produced the great cosmologies and world classifications" is always secondary to its societal aspect, he was certainly not indifferent to its "speculative" role.[139] Just as the French term *conscience collective* may be translated to stress either consciousness or conscience, the cognitive or the moral, so Durkheim may be seen as concerned with the cognitive as well as the cathectic nature of religion.

While the validity of his general theorem does not, in fact, depend upon the accuracy of the Australian case-study from which it is ostensibly derived, Durkheim's utilitization of the popular nineteeth-century methodological tool of the primitive social "survival" provides an important link with anthropological evolutionism.[140] Thus, despite the disdain in which he holds the futile quest for the origins of religion, Durkheim no less than his British rivals finds himself drawn down the treacherous path of psychological speculation. As Evans-Pritchard comments on his thesis:

> I am afraid that we must once more say that it is also a just-so story. Totemism could have arisen through gregariousness, but there is no evidence that it did; and other forms of religion could have developed, as it is implicit in Durkheim's theory that they did, from totemism . . . but again there is no evidence that they did.[141]

More specifically, it may be argued that even the most persuasive evidence of what Alpert terms the "disciplinary, cohesive, vitalizing and euphoric" aspects of functions of ritual and ceremony and their role in the "remaking" of individuals and groups reveals nothing about the origins of such beliefs and rites.[142] Thus, Durkheim's discernment of the strengthening and revivifying action of groups, as well as the susceptibility in act and sentiment of the individual in "the midst of an assembly animated by a common passion" by no means provides sufficient justification for discovering the emergence of religion in a state of effervescence characteristic of occasions of intense collective behaviour.[143] This fact, which the usually perceptive Parsons appears to overlook, is nonetheless seized upon by Evans-Pritchard:

> It was all very well for him to pour contempt on others for deriving religion from motor hallucination, but I contend that this is precisely what he does himself. No amount of juggling with words like "intensity" and "effervescence" can hide the fact that he derives the totemic religion of the [Aborigines] from the emotional excitement of individuals brought together in a small crowd, from what is a sort of crowd hysteria.[144]

Denials that Durkheim's thesis is indeed rooted in a variant of "crowd psychology" are less than convincing. Yet as it proceeds, Evans-Pritchard's argument becomes, on logical grounds, even more damaging to one of the central propositions of *The Elementary Forms of the Religious Life:*

> What is the evidence that the [Aborigines] are in any particular emotional state during the performance of their ceremonies? And if they are, then it is evident that the emotion is produced, as Durkheim himself claimed, by the rites and the beliefs which occasion them, so the rites and the beliefs which occasion them cannot convincingly be adduced as a product of the emotions. Therefore heightened emotion, whatever it may be, and if there is any particular emotional state associated with the ritual, could indeed be an important element in the rites, giving them a deeper significance for the individual, but it can hardly be an adequate causal explanation of them as a social phenomenon. The argument, like so many sociological arguments, is a circular one - the chicken and the egg. The rites create the effervescence, which creates the beliefs, which cause the rites to be performed; or does the mere coming together generate them?"[145]

To the sociology of religion Durkheim bequeaths a confused legacy. Though his work has attained classic status and constitutes required reading in the subdiscipline, it is understood and interpreted in a variety of ways. As I have indicated, Talcott Parsons attributes an insufficient appreciation of Durkheim's insights to the fact that they were so far ahead of their time as to guarantee a scholarly rediscovery of their merits in "the relatively near future."[146] Such a sentiment provokes the earnest dissent and dismay of some scholars quite as effectively as it elicits the fervent assent and enthusiasm of others. Thus, for example, although they do not simply disregard his work, Marxian and Weberian scholars remain highly critical of Durkheimianism in its treatment of religion no less than in other respects and exhibit little elation at the prospect of its "coming into its own fairly soon."[147] In this respect, one Weberian partisan perceives the "fundamental defect" of

Durkheim's sociology or religion as that it is misconceived "whatever its incidental merits or subsequent influence," and views *The Elementary Forms* "for all its merits" as "a warning both of how not to try to explain beliefs and also of how not to classify them, no matter how ingenious or suggestive" its particular arguments.[148]

Scholarly appraisal of his analysis of religion reveals, depending on the source, that Durkheim was both a materialist and an idealist, a determinist and a voluntarist, as well as a covert psychologist and an unrepentant and undiluted sociologist. He is perceived, therefore, as postulating both that social being determines consciousness and that consciousness determines social being. Paraphrasing Henri Bergson, the eminent French sociologist Raymond Aron has suggested that, in Durkheim's view, societies are "machines for the making of gods." It might also be contended, with equal justification, that he reveals religion as a machine for the making of society.[149]

Despite - indeed, because of - the violent controversy that has always surrounded its complex contribution, the work of Emile Durkheim stands as one of the main foundations of the modern sociology of religion. As a sociologistic or ultra-sociological interpretation and explanation of the phenomenon of religion, it retains its powers of attraction and repulsion, challenging a new generation of scholars nearly three-quarters of a century after its first appearance. Whatever else his feelings may be, it is as impossible for a sociologist of religion to be indifferent to the Durkheimian equation as it is to be unaware of it.

Footnotes to Chapter Four

[1] Viewed by many as the sociologist *par excellence,* Durkheim still provokes adulation, animosity and controversy more than half a century after his death. A recent issue of a scholarly journal was devoted, under the editorship of Edward A. Tiryakian, to the theme "Durkheim Lives." See *Social Forces,* Vol. 59, No. 4, June 1981. The literature on Durkheim in English is immense, but the following titles are of special importance: Harry Alpert, *Emile Durkheim & His Sociology,* New York: Columbia University Press, 1961 (first published 1939); R.A. Nisbet, *The Sociology of Emile Durkheim,* New York: Oxford University Press, 1974; R.A. Nisbet (ed.), *Emile Durkheim,* Englewood Cliffs, N.J.: Prentice-Hall, Inc., 1965; K.H. Wolff (ed.), *Emile Durkheim: Essays on Sociology and Philosophy,* New York: Harper and Row, 1964; E.A. Tiryakian, *Sociologism and Existentialism,* Englewood Cliffs, N.J.: Prentice-Hall, Inc., 1962; R.N. Bellah (ed.), *Emile Durkheim: On Morality and Society,* Chicago: University of Chicago Press, 1973; E. Wallwork, *Durkheim: Morality and Milieu,* Cambridge, Mass.: Harvard University Press, 1972; T. Parsons, *The Structure of Social Action,* New York: The Free Press, 1949 (first published 1937), pp. 301-470. The most comprehensive treatment of Durkheim is Steven Lukes, *Emile Durkheim: His Life and Work,* Harmondsworth: Penguin Books, 1975; this work also contains the most comprehensive bibliography. The most recent study is K. Thompson, *Emile Durkheim,* London: Tavistock Publications, 1982.

[2] Emile Durkheim, *The Elementary Forms of the Religious Life* (trans. J.W. Swain), New York: Collier Books, 1961 (first published 1912). A useful collection of writings is W.S.F. Pickering (ed.), *Durkheim on Religion,* London: Routledge & Kegan Paul, 1975.

[3] It is so described by E.E. Evans-Pritchard in his *Theories of Primitive Religion,* Oxford: The Clarendon Press, 1965, p. 64.

[4] Scholars have not been slow to pounce upon Durkheim's thesis from the moment of its appearance. Its provocative nature has ensured a heated reaction. See, for example, the following early critiques: A.A. Goldenweiser, "Review of *Elementary Forms,*" *American Anthropologist,* Vol. 17, 1915, pp. 719-735; A. Van Gennep, "Review of *Elementary Forms*" (trans. J. Redding and W.S.F. Pickering) in Pickering, *op. cit.,* pp. 205-208 (first published in French, 1913); G. Richard, "Dogmatic Atheism In the Sociology of Religion" (trans. J. Redding and W.S.F. Pickering) in Pickering, *op. cit.,* pp. 228-276 (first published in French 1923). For more recent criticism see, for example, Ivan Oliver, "The Limits of the Sociology of Religion: A Critique of the Durkheimian Approach," *British Journal of Sociology,* Vol. 27, 1976, pp. 461-473; and W.G. Runciman, "The Sociological Explanation of 'Religious' Beliefs," *Archives Européennes de Sociologie,* Vol. 10, 1969, pp. 149-191. Runciman considers the "fundamental defect of Durkheim's sociology of religion" to be that it is *misconceived,* "whatever its incidental merits or subsequent influence" (p. 187).

[5] These characteristics that are generally perceived in the British anthropological tradition and German nature-myth theory (see chapter three) have been discerned in Durkheim's approach to religion. See, for example, Evans-Pritchard, pp. 67-69; K. Thompson, op. cit., p. 124; and Lukes, op. cit., p. 456. It is arguable that Durkheim's thesis is more evolutionary and psychologistic than he himself believed. There is more of this discussion in subsequent notes.

[6] It is, therefore, as difficult a task to read Durkheim as it is to read Marx or Weber and different readings result in very different "Durkheims." One writer has referred to the difficulty of unravelling and evaluating Durkheim's conceptions with regard to "an explanation of social phenomena in terms of moral and religious beliefs and the associated practices and [an explanation] in terms of underlying social conditions." See Tom Bottomore, "A Marxist Consideration of Durkheim," *Social Forces,* Vol. 59, 1981, pp. 902-917. This is a difficulty of profound importance, as will be evident from the discussion in this chapter.

[7] Emile Durkheim, *The Division of Labour in Society* (trans. G. Simpson), Glencoe: The Free Press, 1933 (first published 1893); and Emile Durkheim, *Suicide: A Study in Sociology* (trans. J.A. Spaulding and G. Simpson), Glencoe: The Free Press, 1951 (first published 1897).

[8] Durkheim, *Elementary Forms,* pp. 37-38. As one commentator notes: "Durkheim . . . set out quite explicitly to say what religion *is* and to put forward a general theory of its origin. Weber, equally explicitly, did not. . . ." See Runciman, *op. cit.,* pp. 181-182.

[9] Durkheim, *Elementary Forms,* p. 38.

[10] See, for example, the neo-Tylorian definitions of Jack Goody, "Religion and Ritual: The Definitional Problem," *British Journal of Sociology,* Vol. 12, 1961, pp. 142-164; and Robin Horton, "A Definition of Religion, and its Uses," *Journal of the Royal Anthropological Institute,* Vol. 90, 1960, pp. 201-226. See also definitions in terms of the "super-empirical" or "supra-empirical" in Roland Robertson, *The Sociological Interpretation of Religion,* New York: Schocken Books, 1970; and Michael Hill, *A Sociology of Religion,* London: Heinemann, 1973. For more detailed discussion see chapter two.

[11] Durkheim, *Elementary Forms,* pp. 62-63. For an earlier attempt by Durkheim to formulate a definition of religion, see "Concerning the Definition of Religious Phenomena" in Pickering, *op. cit.,* pp. 74-99 (originally published in *L'Année sociologique,* 1899). See Durkheim's discussion of this earlier definition in the footnote on p. 63 of *Elementary Forms.*

[12] *Elementary Forms,* p. 51.

[13] *Ibid,* p. 52.

[14] *Ibid,* p. 53.

[15] *Ibid,* p. 56.

[16] *Ibid,* p. 56.

[17] *Ibid,* p. 59.

[18] In thus distinguishing religion from magic, Durkheim, like Frazer, is explicitly adopting the viewpoint of the Scottish scholar W. Robertson Smith. In a footnote in *Elementary*

Forms, p. 61, he observes that "Robertson Smith has already pointed out that magic is opposed to religion, as the individual to the social." See W. Robertson Smith, *The Religion of the Semites,* New York: Schocken Books, 1972 (first published 1889). See also *Elementary Forms,* pp. 59-60. Many sociologists, of course, question the validity of a distinction between "religion" and "magic" in the terms Durkheim uses; some assert the collective aspect of magic, while others question the utility of any such distinction. Malinowski refers to "the famous dictum of Robertson Smith, that primitive religion is the concern of the community rather than of the individual" but asserts, in contradiction, that "in primitive societies religion arises to a great extent from purely individual sources." See Bronislaw Malinowski, *Magic, Science and Religion and Other Essays,* Glencoe: The Free Press, 1948, pp. 37 and 41. It is worth noting that Max Weber shared Durkheim's belief that a distinction between religion and magic was useful. See chapter five.

[19] *Elementary Forms,* p. 37. Durkheim's affinity with British anthropological evolutionism is manifest here in general and specific terms: a general concern with the primitive, and a specific recognition of the most primitive human society in Australian Aboriginal life. Sir James Frazer, for example, regarded the Australian Aborigines as "the rudest savages as to whom we possess accurate information" and - significantly, in the context of the magic-religion distinction adopted by Durkheim - denied that they possessed religion. Acknowledging that among them "magic is universally practised" he claims that religion "in the sense of a propitiation or conciliation of the higher powers" seems to be unknown. See footnote 18. On Frazer, consult chapter three and also J.Z. Smith, "When the Bough Breaks," *History of Religions,* Vol. 12, 1973, pp. 342-371. See also Eric J. Sharpe, *Comparative Religion: A History,* London: Duckworth, 1975, p. 92; and Lukes, *op. cit.,* pp. 455-457 and p. 244.

[20] Durkheim, *Elementary Forms,* p. 13; Lukes, *op. cit.,* pp. 244, 450-459. In concentrating his analysis upon totemism and the Australian Aborigines, Durkheim acknowledged himself indebted to Robertson Smith in particular, and to British and American ethnography in general. As Lukes notes, he accepted Smith's sociological analysis of religion, which asserted that it was "a relation of all the members of a community to the power that has the good of the community at heart," and that it "did not exist for the saving of souls but for the preservation and welfare of society." He also accepted Smith's view of clan totemism as "the earliest known form of religion, involving the idealization and divinization of the clan, personified by the god and materially represented by the totemic animal." See Lukes, *op. cit.,* p. 450 and Robertson Smith, *op. cit.*

[21] See footnote 20. In *Elementary Forms,* p. 20, Durkheim notes that "in the primitive religions, the religious fact still visibly carries the mark of its origins: it would have been well-nigh impossible to infer them merely from the study of the more developed religions." In his analysis of totemism, Durkheim is clearly saturated in the Anglo-American ethnographical literature on the topic and merits the description "veteran in Australian ethnology," albeit at a distance. See W.E.H. Stanner, "Reflections on Durkheim and Aboriginal Religion" in Maurice Freedman (ed.), *Social Organization: Essays Presented to Raymond Firth,* London: Cass, 1967, pp. 217-240 (reprinted in Pickering, *op. cit.,* pp. 277-303). The literature on totemism was already immense in Durkheim's time, as is apparent from *Elementary Forms,* pp. 121-215, and Durkheim's work was not slow in provoking highly critical comment. See Stanner, *op. cit.*; Goldenweiser, *op. cit.*; A.A. Goldenweiser, "Religion and Society: A Critique of Durkheim's Theory of The Origin and Nature of Religion," *Journal of Philosophy, Psychology and Scientific Methods,* Vol. 12, 1917; and W.D. Wallis, "Durkheim's View of Religion," *Journal of Religious Psychology,* Vol. 7, 1914, pp. 252-267. Though not taken seriously by Durkheim and his circle, the criticisms of A. Van Gennep were particularly devastating. See A. Van Gennep, *L'État actuel du problème totemique,* Paris, 1920; and the review in *Mercure de France,* Vol. 101, pp. 389-391 (translated in Pickering, *op. cit.*); and Evans-Pritchard, *op. cit.,* pp. 64-68. Recent important anthropological works on totemism are Claude Lévi-Strauss, *Totemism,* London: Merlin Press, 1964; and Edmund Leach (ed.), *The Structural Study of Myth and*

Totemism, London: Tavistock Publications, 1967. It is worth noting that Freud shared with Durkheim a fascination with totemism. See Sigmund Freud, *Totem and Taboo* (trans. J. Strachey), London: Hogarth Press, 1950. Evans-Pritchard notes that, at the time Durkheim embarked on *Elementary Forms,* "the attention of anthropological writers was particularly engaged by recent discoveries made in Australia by the researches of Spencer and Gillen, Strehlow, and others. However, Durkheim's choice of that religion for his experiment was unfortunate, for the literature on its aboriginals was, by modern standards, poor and confused, and it still is" (*op. cit.,* p. 58). Stanner observes that Durkheim succeeded in finding what he sought among the Aborigines because a "freakish, passing state of affairs in Australian ethnography gave some of the central Australian material the appearance of satisfying the requirement" (*op. cit.,* p. 240). For a recent overview of Aborigine society, see Kenneth Maddock, *The Australian Aborigines: A Portrait of their Society,* Harmondsworth: Penguin Books, 1972; for recent sociological critiques of Durkheim's analysis of Aborigine religion, see Hans Mol, "The Origin and Function of Religion: A Critique of, and Alternative to, Durkheim's Interpretation of the Religion of the Australian Aborigines," *Journal for the Scientific Study of Religion,* Vol. 18, 1979, pp. 379-389; and Hans Mol, *The Firm and the Formless: Religion and Identity in Aboriginal Australia,* Waterloo: Wilfred Laurier University Press, 1982. An excellent overview and bibliography of the literature about Durkheim's work on religion and totemism is provided in Lukes, *op. cit.*, pp. 237-244, 450-484, 506-529.

[22] *Elementary Forms,* p. 122.

[23] *Ibid,* p. 123.

[24] *Ibid,* p. 134.

[25] *Ibid,* p. 140.

[26] *Ibid,* p. 156.

[27] *Ibid,* p. 156.

[28] *Ibid,* pp. 156-157.

[29] *Ibid,* p. 161.

[30] *Ibid,* pp. 215-217.

[31] *Ibid,* p. 217.

[32] *Ibid,* p. 217.

[33] *Ibid,* pp. 223-224.

[34] *Ibid,* p. 218.

[35] *Ibid,* p. 218.

[36] *Ibid,* pp. 217 and 236.

[37] *Ibid,* p. 236.

[38] *Ibid,* p. 237.

[39] *Ibid,* p. 237.

[40] *Ibid,* pp. 237-238.

[41] *Ibid,* p. 239.

[42] *Ibid,* pp. 239-240.

[43] *Ibid,* pp. 239, 245-253. In his view of the uninhibited and exotic ritual practices of contemporary "primitives," Durkheim appears to have shared the combined repulsion and fascination of some of the Victorian British anthropologists and their readers among the general public. In the context of a discussion of the prolonged impact of Sir James Frazer on the popular imagination, Leach offers some insights into this phenomenon. See Edmund Leach, "Golden Bough or Gilded Twig?" *Daedalus,* Vol. 90, Spring 1961, pp. 383-384. See also Bellah, *op. cit.*, pp. xlv-xlvi.

[44] *Elementary Forms,* pp. 246-247.

[45] *Ibid,* p. 247.

[46] *Ibid,* p. 248.

[47] *Ibid,* pp. 249-250.

[48] *Ibid,* p. 250.

[49] *Ibid,* p. 253.

[50] *Ibid,* pp. 251-252.

[51] *Ibid,* p. 252.

[52] *Ibid,* pp. 251-252.

[53] *Ibid,* pp. 239-240. See the discussions of Feuerbach, Marx and Müller in chapter three.

[54] As noted in chapter three, Wilhelm Schmidt's distinction between "intellectualist" and "emotionalist" psychological theories of religion was adopted in Evans-Pritchard (*op. cit.,* p. 4). A parallel distinction is sometimes made between "cognitive" and "expressive" (or "affective") orientations. The theories of Tylor and Frazer, for example, may justly be regarded as intellectualistic in their attempt to explain the origins of religion in primitive man's fumbling efforts to make sense of the world. Even the fact that Durkheim is able to accuse Frazer of presupposing "a thorough-going idiocy on the part of the primitive" (*Elementary Forms,* p. 203) underlines this view. So also does Leach's ability to state that if "Tylor's 'savage' sometimes seems to be a primitive philosopher struggling to solve the problems of existence, Frazer's 'savage' is a lunatic at large - a child of nature, whose ignorance evokes our amusement rather than our sympathy." (Leach, "Golden Bough or Gilded Twig?" cited in footnote 43, p. 378.) The Oxford anthropologist R.R. Marett, himself a disciple of Tylor, was none the less to deliver, in his consideration of "pre-animistic" religion, a powerful argument against the intellectualistic position. Convinced that what primitive men thought was of less interest and importance than what they did, Marett argued that Tylor and Frazer had concentrated upon the "savage" as a reasoning being (however deficient) and had neglected to consider him as an emotional being. In Marett's view, such an emphasis was completely misguided for, among primitives, actions give rise to ideas and not vice versa. In a famous phrase, he summed up his view by observing that "savage religion is something not so much thought out as danced out." (The phrase appears in his work *The Threshold of Religion.*) See Evans-Pritchard, *op. cit.,* pp. 32-33; and Sharpe, *op. cit.,* p. 70. Writers vary in their appraisal of whether Durkheim's theory is primarily cognitive or emotional. Thus, for example, Runciman regards the view that religious thought and ritual express, symbolize and dramatize social actions and relationships as "neo-Durkheimian," whereas Lukes believes that it is the cognitive role of religion that is central in Durkheim's thinking. See Runciman, *op. cit.,* p. 153; and Lukes, *op. cit.,* p. 483. On the "expressive side," Robert Bellah argues that Durkheim "recognized that the speculative side of religion, that which produced the great cosmologies and world classifications, is always secondary. The chief aim of religious symbolism is to reproduce society-social forces, not the cosmos." See Bellah, *op. cit.,* p. li. Similarly Talcott Parsons maintains that, for Durkheim, "the central importance of religion lies in its relation to action, not to thought" (*Structure of Social Action,* p. 441). Thus, although in his view the cognitive aspect of religion was extremely important in Durkheim's analysis, Parsons concludes that Durkheim "contributed notably to the beginning elucidation of a very general code of ritual symbolism, which is culturally expressive rather than primarily cognitive or moral, which is intimately concerned with the maintenance of levels of motivation in the individual, but which is also connected with social solidarity." See Parsons, "Durkheim on Religion Revisited: Another Look at the Elementary Forms of the Religious Life" in Charles Y. Glock and Phillip E. Hammond (eds.), *Beyond the Classics? Essays in the Scientific Study of Religion,* New York: Harper and Row, 1973, pp. 171-172.

[55] *Elementary Forms,* pp. 464-465. This, of course, implies a criticism of Marx, Tylor, Frazer and Müller, among others.

[56] *Ibid,* p. 465. See also William James, *The Varieties of Religious Experience,* London: Collins, 1960 (first published 1902); note especially the first two lectures.

[57] *Elementary Forms,* p. 465.

[58] *Ibid,* p. 14.

[59] *Ibid,* pp. 14-15.

[60] In the sense in which Bottomore uses the term in "A Marxist Consideration of Durkheim," pp. 908-909, drawing on the work both of Lévi-Strauss and the Marxist structuralists.

[61] *Elementary Forms,* p. 22.

[62] See Parsons, *Structure of Social Action,* p. 427; and Talcott Parsons, "The Theoretical Development of the Sociology of Religion," *Journal of the History of Ideas,* Vol. 5, 1944, pp. 185-186.

[63] *Elementary Forms,* p. 240.

[64] Durkheim's preoccupation with the themes of social order and social solidarity is generally considered to be at the expense of a concern with social conflict or social change. Parsons notes in *Structure of Social Action* (p. 448), as an "issue of great importance," the fact that "any theory of social change" is "conspicuous by its absence" from Durkheim's thought. In Parsons' view, the problem of social change is, almost without exception, "outside his field of interest" (p. 448). See also the comments in Bottomore, "A Marxist Consideration of Durkheim." Parsons briefly alludes to an embryonic Durkheimian perspective on social change (pp. 449-450), noting that while "Durkheim's approach was inherently unfavourable to the solution of these problems," he none the less "accomplished a great deal of the fundamental spade work which is an indispensable preliminary to the construction of a theory of social change" by clarifying "what it is that changes" (p. 450). The single "hypothesis in this field" contributed by Durkheim occurs, according to Parsons, "at the very end of his work" (p. 450). This is the hypothesis under consideration in chapter four. See also Bellah, *op. cit.,* pp. xlvi-xlviii.

[65] There is no documentary evidence that Durkheim was influenced by the "voguish" work of Le Bon but there can be little doubt that Durkheim would have been familiar with Le Bon's ideas among those of the other "crowd psychologists" whose works achieved popularity at the end of the nineteenth century. See Lukes' rebuttal of Mary Douglas' suggestion that Durkheim "seems to have freely drawn upon" Le Bon, in Lukes, *Emile Durkheim,* p. 462n. Consult Mary Douglas, *Purity and Danger,* Hamondsworth: Penguin Books, 1966, p. 20; and Gustave Le Bon, *The Crowd: A Study of the Popular Mind,* New York: Viking Press, 1960 (first published in French 1895); Scipio Sighele, *Psychologie des Sectes,* Paris: Giard et Brière, 1898. On "collective behaviour" in general consult Robert E. Park and Ernest W. Burgess, *Introduction to the Science of Sociology,* Chicago: University of Chicago Press, 1924; and R.E. Park, *On Social Control and Collective Behaviour* (ed. R.H. Turner), Chicago: University of Chicago Press, 1967. The literature on crowd psychology and the "aristocratic" critique of the crowd is discussed in L. Bramson, *The Political Context of Sociology,* Princeton, N.J.: Princeton University Press, 1961, pp. 52-57.

[66] *Elementary Forms,* pp. 244-245.

[67] *Ibid,* pp. 474-475.

[68] *Ibid,* pp. 474-475.

[69] *Ibid,* p. 475.

[70] *Ibid,* p. 475.

[71] *Ibid,* p. 475.

[72] *Ibid,* p. 475. Eventually, such enthusiasm and creativity will lose its momentum and the novel ideas and formulas will tarnish with institutionalization, yet "men will spontaneously feel the need of reliving them from time to time in thought, that is to say, of keeping alive their memory by means of celebrations which regularly reproduce their fruits" (*Elementary Forms,* p. 275). That Durkheim's view is possibly a cyclical one is asserted by Parsons. See *Structure of Social Action,* p. 450.

[73] See Sir James George Frazer, *The New Golden Bough* (ed. T.H. Gaster), Garden City, N.Y.: Doubleday & Co., 1961, p. 372. (The first volumes of this work were published in 1890.) See also chapter three. To compare Durkheim's ruminations on the future with those of Weber, consult Max Weber, *The Protestant Ethic and the Spirit of Capitalism* (trans. T. Parsons), London: George Allen & Unwin, 1930 (first published in German in 1904-05), pp. 180-182.

[74] *Elementary Forms,* p. 476. To study Durkheim's predictions regarding religious evolution, see Frances Westley, "'The Cult of Man': Durkheim's Predictions and New Religious Movements," *Sociological Analysis,* Vol. 39, 1978, pp. 135-145.

[75] Parsons doubts that Durkheim has been the greatest influence on the sociology of religion, believing that this honour belongs to Weber. He observes that "Weber's influence has been the most important of any scholar of his generation in that branch of the study of religion which connected closely with sociological problems," and considers that "by comparison, the impact of Durkheim strictly in this field seems to have been rather meagre." See Talcott Parsons, "Durkheim on Religion Revisited," p. 174. Although it is true that Durkheim is sometimes thought of, especially in the context of religion, as the anthropologist's sociologist, whereas Weber is regarded as the sociologist's sociologist, it is hard to agree with the Parsonian view if the influence of Weber's "Protestant Ethic" thesis is discounted. Thus, MacIntyre notes that "there has been no systematic development of Weber's approach to religion, while Durkheim's influence by contrast has been the basis of a series of brilliant enquiries. . . ." Likewise, Runciman asserts that it is "undeniable that Durkheim's positive influence has been the greater of the two." See Alasdair MacIntyre, "Weber at His Weakest," *Encounter,* Vol. 25, No. 5, 1965, p. 87; and Runciman, *op. cit.,* pp. 180-181.

[76] Sharpe, *op. cit.,* p. 86.

[77] *Ibid,* p. 86.

[78] Evans-Pritchard, *op. cit.,* pp. 64-86. Evans-Pritchard believes that Durkheim offers what is fundamentally "a psychological explanation of social facts, and he himself has laid it down that such explanations are invariably wrong" (pp. 67-88). Similar criticism is to be found in Bronislaw Malinowski's review of *Elementary Forms* in *Folklore,* Vol. 24, 1913, pp. 525-53. See Lukes, *op. cit.,* pp. 523-524. For a defence of Durkheim see Parsons, *Structure of Social Action,* pp. 436-438. Consult Emile Durkheim, *The Rules of Sociological Method* (trans. S.A. Solovay and J.H. Mueller), Glencoe: The Free Press, 1950 (first published 1895).

[79] Parsons, "Durkheim on Religion Revisited," p. 162.

[80] *Ibid,* p. 174. See, for example, the works by Runciman, Bottomore and Oliver cited above.

[81] Parsons, "Durkheim on Religion Revisited," pp. 174-175. Although Durkheim's work is open to more than one interpretation and is ambiguous in certain respects, much criticism of Durkheim has been too profound and sophisticated to be dismissed as rooted in misinterpretation. See the range of criticism discussed in Lukes, *op. cit.,* pp. 506-529.

[82] Parsons, "Durkheim on Religion Revisited," pp. 159, 177, and 174-175. See Reinhard Bendix and Guenther Roth, *Scholarship and Partisanship: Essays on Max Weber,* Berkeley: University of California Press, 1971, pp. 291-297.

[83] See Bottomore, *op. cit.,* p. 908. It is possible, for example, to make a case for both a "materialist" and an "idealist" Durkheim. Thus Evans-Pritchard considers that Durkheim "might well have written Marx's famous aphorism, that it is not the consciousness of men that determines their being but their social being which determines their consciousness," whereas Bottomore asserts that for Durkheim "it *is* 'the consciousness of men that determines their being', and not, as Marx argued, social being [that] determines their consciousness." See Evans-Pritchard, *op. cit.,* p. 77; and Bottomore, *op. cit.,* p. 913.

[84] See, for example, the acknowledgement of Durkheim's brilliance and originality by such critics as Goldenweiser, Malinowski and Stanner.

[85] Malinowski, in his review of Durkheim, cited in footnote 78, questioned the scientific appropriateness of basing so sweeping a theory on an "analysis of a single tribe, as described in practically a single ethnographical work." See also Evans-Pritchard's and Stanner's comments quoted in footnote 21. In addition to the critiques cited therein, see Robert H. Lowie, *Primitive Religion,* London: Routledge, 1925.

[86] See Runciman, *op. cit.,* pp. 187-189.

[87] Compare, for example, the contradictory appraisals of Durkheim by Runciman and MacIntyre.

[88] See Evans-Pritchard, *op. cit.*, p. 77. On the "materialist" interpretation of Durkheim, see, for example, Guy Swanson, *The Birth of The Gods*, Ann Arbor: University of Michigan Press, 1960; J. Alan Winter, "The Metaphoric Parallelist Approach to the Sociology of Theistic Beliefs: Theme, Variations and Implications," *Sociological Analysis*, Vol. 34, 1973, pp. 212-229; and John H. Simpson, "Sovereign Groups, Subsistence Activities, and the Presence of a High God in Primitive Societies," in Robert Wuthnow (ed.), *The Religious Dimension: New Directions in Quantitative Research*, New York: Academic Press, Inc., 1979, pp. 299-310.

[89] See R.N. Bellah, *op. cit.*, p. 1. See also footnote 88.

[90] Durkheim disclaims a materialist position in the *Elementary Forms* when he states that "it is necessary to avoid seeing in this theory of religion a simple re-statement of historical materialism: that would be misunderstanding our thought to an extreme degree. In showing that religion is something essentially social, we do not mean to say that it confines itself to translating into another language the material forms of society and its immediate vital necessities. It is true that we take it as evident that social life depends upon its material foundation and bears its mark, just as the mental life of an individual depends upon his nervous system and in fact his whole organism. But collective consciousness is something more than a mere epiphenomenon of its morphological basis, just as individual consciousness is something more than a simple efflorescence of the nervous system" (p. 471). Durkheim is primarily dissociating his views from Marxian materialism, but he may also be interpreted as rejecting materialism in whatever form. Parsons, for example, believes that the view that Durkheim is a "religious materialist" cannot be justified (*Structure of Social Action*, pp. 417-421 and 427); while Evans-Pritchard comments that he was "not nearly so deterministic and materialistic as some have made him out to be" and is more suitably regarded "as a voluntarist and idealist" (*op. cit.*, p. 55). See also Bellah, *op. cit.*, pp. l-lii; and David E. Greenwald, "Durkheim on Society, Thought and Ritual," *Sociological Analysis*, Vol. 34, 1973, pp. 157-168.

[91] See Bellah, *op. cit.*, p. xlviii.

[92] *Ibid*, pp. l-li.

[93] Emile Durkheim, "Value Judgments and Judgments of Reality" in *Sociology and Philosophy* (trans. D.F. Pocock), Glencoe: The Free Press, 1953, p. 96. (The essay was first published 1911.)

[94] Bellah, *op. cit.*, p. lii.

[95] Bottomore, *op. cit.*, p. 912.

[96] *Ibid*, p. 913. See the discussion of Marx in chapter three.

[97] Parsons, "Durkheim on Religion Revisited," p. 174.

[98] Parsons, *Structure of Social Action*, pp. 426-427.

[99] *Ibid*, p. 427.

[100] *Ibid*, p. 427.

[101] Parsons, "Durkheim on Religion Revisited," p. 159.

[102] *Ibid*, p. 159.

[103] Parsons and his disciples are generally included among American "structural-functionalists," although in his last years Parsons denied that he could accurately be categorized under this rubric.

[104] See the discussion of the relative merits of substantive and functional definitions in chapter two.

[105] See Thomas Luckmann, *The Invisible Religion: The Problem of Religion in Modern Society*, New York: The Macmillan Company, 1967, pp. 49-53.

[106] For some critics, Durkheim is thus an archetypically conservative social theorist who stresses consensus rather than conflict and statics rather than dynamics. Parsons has na-

turally been subjected to a similar portrayal. See Lewis Coser, "Durkheim's Conservatism and its Implications for his Sociological Theory" in Wolff, *op. cit.*, pp. 211-232; Robert A. Nisbet, "Conservatism and Sociology," *American Journal of Sociology,* Vol. 58, 1952, pp. 167-175; and Bellah, *op. cit.*, pp. xvi-xvii. Greenwald notes that a "number of Durkheim's interpreters have charged him with an almost obsessive interest in order and cohesion to the neglect of conflict and strife" (*op. cit.*, p. 167n). See, for example, Raymond Aron, *Main Currents in Sociological Thought,* Vol. 2 (trans. R. Howard and H. Weaver), New York: Basic Books, 1967, p. 90; Don Martindale, *The Nature and Types of Sociological Theory,* London: Routledge & Kegan Paul, 1960, p. 128; and Bottomore, *op. cit.*, pp. 906-907. On the general issue of conflict versus consensual views of society, see John Rex, *Key Problems of Sociological Theory,* London: Routledge & Kegan Paul, 1961; Irving Louis Horowitz, "Consensus, Conflict and Co-operation: A Sociological Inventory," *Social Forces,* Vol. 41, 1962, pp. 177-188; N.J. Demerath and R.A. Peterson (eds.), *System, Change and Conflict,* New York: The Free Press, 1967; and L. McDonald, *The Sociology of Law and Order,* Toronto: Methuen, 1979. For Parsons' views on the Durkheimian account of social solidarity, see *Structure of Social Action,* and "Durkheim's Contribution to the Theory of Integration of Social Systems" in Wolff, *op. cit.*, pp. 118-153.

[107] Parsons, *Structure of Social Action,* p. 428.

[108] *Ibid,* p. 434.

[109] *Ibid,* p. 434.

[110] *Ibid,* p. 435.

[111] In one such criticism, Stanner (in Pickering, *op. cit.*, p. 301) attacks the view, which he terms "potted Durkheim" and which involves "an impression that the function of religion is simply to be there, to support the structure and process of society as and when needed," a perspective that "transforms a theory of transcended selves into a theory of public conveniences." Conceptions of "religion" open to similar attacks on grounds of over-inclusiveness are to be found in Luckmann, *The Invisible Religion*; and Hans Mol, *Identity and the Sacred: A Sketch for a New Social-Scientific Theory of Religion,* Agincourt: The Book Society, 1976. See the discussion of the relative merits of inclusive and exclusive definitions of religion in chapter two.

[112] Durkheim, *Division of Labour.* See Parsons, "Durkheim on Religion Revisited," p. 156; *Structure of Social Action,* pp. 308-324; and Bellah, *op. cit.*, pp. xxxi-xlvi.

[113] Durkheim, Lettres au directeur de la *Revue neo-scolastique,* Vol. 14, 1907. Quoted in Bellah, *op. cit.*, p. xlv and (in a different translation) in Lukes, *op. cit.*, p. 237.

[114] Durkheim, in Bellah, *op. cit.*, p. xlv. On the notion of a decisive break in Durkheim's thought, see Parsons, *Structure of Social Action,* pp. 460-468, 407-408; and Bellah, *op. cit.*, pp. xliii-xlvi. The importance attributed in *Division of Labour* to the transition from mechanical to organic solidarity is forgotten and in *Elementary Forms* Durkheim generalizes from the evidence of a small-scale society that exhibits organic solidarity and a strong conscience collective. This would be unthinkable in the framework of the earlier work, which posited a breakdown in conscience collective in modern, highly differentiated society.

[115] Durkheim, in Bellah, *op. cit.*, p. xlvi.

[116] *Ibid,* p. xlvi.

[117] See Luckmann, *op. cit.*

[118] Thus, utopia is constructed by definitional fiat. See Ralph Dahrendorf, "Out of Utopia: Toward a Reorientation of Sociological Analysis," *American Journal of Sociology,* Vol. 64, 1958, pp. 115-127.

[119] Sharpe, for example, speaks of many. See footnotes 76 and 77.

[120] See, for example, Oliver, *op. cit.*, and Runciman, *op. cit.*, and works referred to in footnote 21.

[121] Evans-Pritchard, *op. cit.*, p. 64.

[122] Parsons, *Structure of Social Action,* p. 429. In fact, Durkheim seems to suggest that

direct representation *may* occur. In discussing the "aptitude of society for setting itself up as a god or for creating gods" that was demonstrated during the early years of the French Revolution, he remarks that "in one determined case we have seen society and its essential ideas become, directly and with no transfiguration of any sort, the object of a veritable cult" (*Elementary Forms,* pp. 244-245). Parsons might, however, regard this as the exception that proves the rule. On the roots of the need for "transfiguration," see *Elementary Forms,* pp. 239-240.

[123] See Durkheim, *Elementary Forms,* pp. 474-479; Lukes, *op. cit.,* pp. 477, 516-517; Westley, *op. cit.*; and Evans-Pritchard, *op. cit.,* pp. 63-64.

[124] For discussion of Feuerbach, see chapter three. For Durkheim's explanation of the need for social forces to be represented in "forms foreign to their nature" see *Elementary Forms,* pp. 239-240.

[125] Sharpe, *op. cit.,* p. 86.

[126] Runciman, *op. cit.,* p. 188.

[127] Bellah, *op. cit.,* pp. liv-lv.

[128] See Parsons, *Structure of Social Action,* p. 421. For insight into external and internal accounts of religion see the discussion of Durkheim and Weber in Runciman, *op. cit.*

[129] Parsons notes that "in his positivistic vein" Durkheim is undoubtedly seeking for "the 'reality' underlying religious ideas" and that this amounts to "making of religion a worship of the flesh, of what is merely human" (*Structure of Social Action,* pp. 417-418). See Robert K. Merton, "Manifest and Latent Functions" in his *Social Theory and Social Structure,* Glencoe: The Free Press, 1957, pp. 19-84.

[130] On the grounds that since the functions of religion are universal, its particular forms are of little consequence for the sociological theorist.

[131] Parsons, *Structure of Social Action,* p. 437.

[132] From such a perspective, sociological and anthropological work concerned with the relations of specific doctrines, liturgies, rituals and beliefs to other aspects of particular societies would have to be viewed as misguided. It is worth noting that, in this regard, Weber's explanation of the links between specific theological beliefs and certain forms of worldly activity in *The Protestant Ethic and the Spirit of Capitalism* would be precluded. See chapter five.

[133] Religion, for Durkheim, cannot be founded upon illusion, error or lies, but its truth is of a sociological nature. The contents of its beliefs and the objects of its reverence are "true" only symbolically, that is, in the sense that they are "an expression of something else" (*Structure of Social Action,* p. 236). Durkheim personally shared the agnosticism of many of the post-Darwinian British anthropologists. On emotionalist versus intellectualist perspectives, see footnote 54. For Durkheim's discussion of the genesis of religion in the effervescence of crowd activity, see *Elementary Forms,* pp. 245-251; and see also footnote 65. Evans-Pritchard argues that Durkheim breaks his own rules of sociological method by putting forward a psychologistic rather than sociologistic explanation in this regard (Evans-Pritchard, *op. cit.,* pp. 67-68). This parallels the accusation that Durkheim's ultimate explanation of the division of labour is biologistic rather than sociological. (See Parsons, *Structure of Social Action,* p. 323.)

[134] It may be recalled that Feuerbach regarded religion as "esoteric psychology." See chapter three.

[135] Parsons, "Durkheim on Religion Revisited," pp. 157-158.

[136] Durkheim, *Elementary Forms,* p. 21.

[137] *Ibid,* p. 21.

[138] *Ibid,* p. 21.

[139] Bellah, *op. cit.,* p.1.

[140] Lukes, *op. cit.,* pp. 244, 455-457 and works cited in footnote 19.

[141] Evans-Pritchard, *op. cit.,* p. 64.

[142] Alpert, *op. cit.,* p. 202.

[143] Durkheim, *Elementary Forms,* p. 240. On the notion of "collective behaviour" in the specialized sociological sense of the term see Park, *op. cit.*, and Park and Burgess, *op. cit.*

[144] Evans-Pritchard, *op. cit.* p. 68.

[145] *Ibid,* p. 68.

[146] Parsons, "Durkheim on Religion Revisited," p. 174. For an attempt to view Durkheim's *Elementary Forms* in a manner that accords it proper recognition as a sociological classic while also treating it in a novel and original manner, see Edward A. Tiryakian, "Durkheim's 'Elementary Forms' as 'Revelation'" in Buford Rhea (ed.), *The Future of the Sociological Classics,* London: George Allen & Unwin, 1981, pp. 114-135.

[147] *Ibid,* p. 177. See, for example, Bottomore, *op. cit.*, and Runciman, *op. cit.*, for Marxian and Weberian views respectively.

[148] Runciman, *op. cit.*, pp. 187, 190-191.

[149] See Aron, *op. cit.*, p. 53.

CHAPTER FIVE

MAX WEBER: RELIGION AND SOCIAL CHANGE

In its impact on the sociology of religion, the work of Max Weber is the only intellectual enterprise that might be considered to rival the contribution of Emile Durkheim. Thus, while some scholars regard Weber's influence as unquestionably greater and others perceive Durkheim's pre-eminence as clear, it appears undeniable that together these two sociological founding fathers have erected the main pillars supporting the intellectual structure of the subdiscipline throughout its construction.[1]

One perceptive commentator, by no means unsympathetic to Weber, has suggested that "the best advice to those who wish to read Weber on religion would perhaps be 'Read Durkheim instead!'"[2] As refreshingly blunt and honest as this judgment is, it should be readily apparent from the discussion in chapter four that it is unlikely to be universally applauded by readers of Durkheim's work. Indeed, some scholars believe that Durkheim's contribution is methodologically misconceived, substantively mistaken and intellectually misleading, and that Weber's writings provide an incomparably sound basis for the sociological study of religion.[3] While it is possible to argue that the ideas of Durkheim and Weber are more alike than is initially apparent, it seems unwise to exaggerate such similarities when, even in their most elementary conceptions of the task of the sociology of religion, the two writers appear committed to completely contradictory strategies.[4] In commencing an assessment of Max Weber's work, therefore, it seems appropriate to begin by comparing and contrasting his approach with that of his illustrious French contemporary.

W.G. Runciman has rightly observed that Durkheim "set out quite explicitly to say what religion *is* and to put forward a general theory of religion" whereas Weber "equally explicitly did not . . . ."[5] As I noted in chapter two, Weber declines the opportunity of formulating a definition of religion at the outset of his researches in a now famous statement:

> To define "religion", to say what it *is,* is not possible at the start of a presentation such as this. Definition can be attempted, if at all, only at the conclusion of the study. The essence of religion is not even our concern, as we make it our task to study the conditions and effects of a particular type of social behaviour.[6]

Durkheim, it will be recalled, exhibited no such reluctance in approaching the problem of definition and in promulgating his own sociological formula.[7]

The clue to Weber's caution is immediately apparent in the second paragraph of his treatise, *The Sociology of Religion;* advocating what is now generally known as the method of *Verstehen,* he asserts:

> The external courses of religious behaviour are so diverse that an understanding of this behaviour can only be achieved from the viewpoint of the subjective experiences, ideas, and purposes of the individuals concerned - in short, from the viewpoint of the religious behaviour's "meaning."[8]

In contrast to Durkheim, Weber is unwilling to impose an arbitrary definition from the outside; he emphasizes the necessity of interpreting action through a "subjective" understanding of the motives of the actor. This strategy thus involves an observer or investigator in the attempt to imagine himself in the actor's place, with all the obvious difficulties so entailed. Durkheim is prepared to begin with a formulation of the nature of religion from the point of view of the social scientist and, on that basis, to deduce the objective meaning of the beliefs and behaviour of "religious" actors. Weber, by comparison, envisions the inductive derivation of a definition from the subjective meanings of those engaged in religious activity and resorts to implicit definition; that is the price he pays for his refusal to adopt an explicit formula. This has already been noted and will be considered again. For the present, however, it is important to stress that Weber's definitional caution is deeply rooted in his fundamental conception of the nature of sociological explanation.[9]

By far the most striking contrast between the work of Weber and Durkheim is apparent in the former's pronounced emphasis upon the role of religion in social change. Although both thinkers may be perceived as embracing evolutionary perspectives, in a broad sense, Weber's work has a dynamic aspect that is almost entirely alien to the thought of his great French contemporary.[10] Thus, while Durkheim offers the germ of a cyclical view of social change in his discussion of the birth of new values in the collective effervescence generated by great common rituals, Parsons is undoubtedly correct in asserting that a "clear-cut theory of social change" is conspicuous by its absence from his work.[11] More than this, however, it may be suggested that the Durkheimian perspective is essentially unconcerned with social change, and is thereby characterized by a concentration upon substance rather than process, on order rather than change.[12] Weber's approach is entirely different; as Thomas Luckmann has noted, his "far-ranging investigations of Ancient Judaism, Hinduism, Confucianism and modern Protestantism were not ends in themselves but means to one end: an understanding of what in modern parlance is called social change."[13] Thus, though Weber's readers will search in vain for an explicit or "clear-cut" theory of social change in his writings, the reason for its absence is obvious and, it may be added, in no way derived from a static conception of society:

> For Weber, social change was not a specific kind of process requiring a special theory. He took it for granted that the explanation of 'social change' was *the* business of general social theory and he would have been reluctant to consider as social theory any propositions about social reality that did not try to explain its transformations.[14]

Embedded in a single, static case-study and utilizing a minimum of comparative material, Durkheim's analysis of religion and society could provide no greater contrast to Weber's sweeping and staggeringly encyclopaedic "wide-ranging, non-parochial comparative approach in the study of both religion and social change."[15]

More specifically, it may be observed that Weber's detailed investigations of religion in historical and cultural contexts of extreme diversity were crucial to his attempt "to account theoretically for those historical processes that led to the emergence of modern society."[16] Therefore, while "Weber would have been the last to maintain that religion is generally and necessarily the source of historical change" it clearly held for him "the key to a fascinating and fateful puzzle: how did it come about that one particular line of historical development assumed such global importance that it appears retrospectively as the central thread in the history of mankind"?[17]

The contrast between the Durkheimian and Weberian approaches having been indicated at its most fundamental level, more specific comparisons may be noted as they emerge. It will already be apparent, however, that Weber's contribution to the sociology of religion is very different in form, content and intent from the analysis undertaken in *The Elementary Forms of the Religious Life*.[18]

Any attempt to segregate Max Weber's contribution to the sociology of religion from his broad intellectual legacy is an impossible task, which is at the same time entirely misconceived. The study of "religion," however the term may be defined, is not for Weber a discrete, circumscribed and hermetic subdisciplinary activity that may be conveniently divorced from more mundane concerns. It is, on the contrary, a central component of his life's work and an absolutely indispensable element in his understanding of the nature of social order, historical change and the perplexities of human existence. Indeed, notwithstanding the range of Weber's insights into the human condition, it is by no means an exaggeration to perceive his central concern as "the influence of the religious ethics of the historic world religions on men's action and institutions," and the "unifying thread" or "nucleus," at least of his later writings, as a process of rationalization in the sphere of religion that advances according to its own distinct inner logic.[19] Thus, Weber's claim that he was tone-deaf to the music of religion can in no way subvert the supreme significance of religion in his general sociology; nor can it diminish the brilliance and magnitude of his achievement in the comparative analysis of religious phenomena.

In a few brief pages it is impossible to do more than sketch a few of the primary themes in Weber's vast undertaking in the context of the sociology of religion. A literary output pertinent to this venture comprising a part of Weber's major work *Economy and Society,* full-length volumes on the religion of India, China and Ancient Judaism, the well-known work translated under the title *The Protestant Ethic and the Spirit of Capitalism,* together with a number of other essays on religious themes presents a considerable obstacle to any simple, systematic summary.[20] In charting a course through this scholarly labyrinth with its wealth of imaginative ideas, its overpowering historical grasp, its shrewd observations and painstaking detail, it may perhaps be best to gain our bearings by beginning with Weber at his most familiar. It is sometimes lamented by Weberian scholars that for so long Max Weber was known to English-speaking readers only through the work translated by Talcott Parsons as *The Protestant Ethic and the Spirit of Capitalism;* a fact that is perceived as a continuing impediment to an accurate assessment of the nature of his intellectual contribution.[21] Certainly, no one would seek merit in a fragmentary evaluation of Weber rooted in what Parsons himself has described as "a nearly complete dissociation, at least in the English- speaking world, between the reputation of Weber as the author of the *Protestant Ethic* and as the author of the comparative studies in the sociology of religion and of the relations of economy and society."[22] None the less, it must not be forgotten that while the *Protestant Ethic* is only a fragment, "it is a fragment which is in many ways of central significance for Weber's philosophy of history, as well as being of very great and very general interest for the thesis it advances to explain some of the most important aspects of modern culture."[23] It might also be added that, in terms of the present discussion, this work is unquestionably of "central significance" in what might be artificially isolated as Weber's sociology of religion. Like the scriptures of the great world religions, the *Protestant Ethic* is potentially misleading if read out of context. When interpreted as a fragment of a much larger, though sadly unfinished project, however, it assumes its correct proportions as an indispensable key component of an intellectual structure of breathtaking scholarly audacity; an edifice whose "most central focus . . . lay in the field of religion."[24]

Subject to constant interpretation, reinterpretation and misinterpretation since its appearance in 1904–05, Weber's renowned and controversial Protestant Ethic thesis has been the focus of a disproportionate attention, on the part of scholars and publishers, that has by no means been confined to the English-speaking world. As a fragment that, in a sense, "stands on its own as a classical analysis of a specific problem," this provocative essay "must certainly count as one of the major landmarks of recent Western intellectual history."[25] Perceived initially as an attempt at a complete explanation of the origins of the modern world, it was both hailed and reviled as a general "counterattack against the Marxist assertion of the predominance of 'material' interests in the historical process," at the same time, its specific historical assertions were critically scrutinized by theologians and historians.[26] Having by now attained the status of a classic, the *Protestant Ethic* is still read as a "positive critique of historical materialism" and still provokes intense methodological, meta-theoretical and ideological debate among sociologists.[27] Furthermore, after three-quarters of a century it remains capable of generating specific and detailed research into the merits of its historical and theological interpretations and propositions.[28] Happily, however, it has slowly become more widely understood that "in Weber's broad plan of work the book was intended as no more than an essay in historical-sociological interpretation," and that it represents "a point of departure, not a culmination, for his main contributions to the sociology of religion."[29]

Herbert Luethy has commented that the "study of Weber's work is an invaluable school of distrust against all clear-cut formulas, including those he himself, though reluctantly, could not avoid formulating."[30] This observation is acutely pertinent in the context of the link Weber posits between the "ethic" of Protestantism and the "spirit" of capitalism, and provides a useful caveat for the scholar who seeks, by unravelling the complexities of Weber's thought, to arrive at a definitive interpretation of this connection. If it is true that today Weber's Protestant Ethic thesis is better known among scholars as "an intimation of a program, a provocative sketch" of extreme intricacy and sophistication, its calculated ambiguities remain no less perplexing.[31] Thus, though it is intellectually indefensible to maintain any longer the vulgar notion that Weber construes a simple causal connection between Calvinism and capitalism, it is inevitable, given the present state of publication, translation and critical editing of his works, that his exact intentions remain the subject of profound scholarly disagreement and that the intellectual significance of his seminal essay continues to be hotly debated. For the present, it may briefly be noted that while the *Protestant Ethic* does indeed provide an occasion for a timely rebuttal of a vulgar Marxism, this is by no means its sole or even primary purpose.[32] Neither does it appear that the essay is adequately understood merely as a component, however strategic, in the "exploration of the origins and workings of the Western institutions and Western form of capitalism," a venture that is nearly universally regarded as "the centre, heart and unique concern of Weber's great efforts."[33] In fact, though the full scope of the claims made in the *Protestant Ethic* does not appear to have been immediately apparent even to Weber himself, the work may be read as nothing less than a sketch or intimation of what Benjamin Nelson has termed a "comparative historical differential sociology of sociocultural process and of civilizational complexes."[34]

In merely contemplating the possible impact of Calvinistic theological ideas upon economic activity in seventeenth-century Europe Weber was far from being an intellectual pioneer. His brilliance lay not in postulating a link between Protestantism and capitalism, for such a connection had long been perceived both in scholarship and folklore, but rather in the manner in which he analyzed the plausibility of such a bond in terms of its causal and meaningful adequacy. Weber was well aware that such writers as Baron Montesquieu and Henry Thomas Buckle had intuited an affinity between Protestantism and the rise of commerce. He knew well that the militaristic Frederick William I had been prepared to tolerate the pacifism of Mennonite settlers in East Prussia for the soundest economic reasons and that the wealth of some Protestant sects was a legendary ingredient of popular wisdom. In addition, he believed that Catholics (for example in England, Holland and Germany) had, in comparison with other religious minorities, failed notably to compensate for their exclusion from the national political and social life by intensified and concerted economic activity. Indeed, far from promoting industriousness, their marginality appeared to be associated with an aversion to industrial pursuits that had persisted until Weber's own time.[35]

Yet, while these insights strongly suggest the independent effect of religious ideas in capitalist development, they do not really go beyond restatement of an already widely accepted correlation. Weber, however, offers something more:

> The point is that Weber saw a major issue in what everyone else had taken for granted. It seemed plausible that during the sixteenth century the wealthiest regions and cities had turned to Protestantism if the latter had really facilitated the pursuit of economic gain. However, in Weber's view this was a great paradox, because intense religiosity and intense economic activity involved mutually incompatible tendencies. According to all experience, religious devotion was usually accompanied by a rejection of mundane affairs, while men who were engrossed in economic pursuits tended toward religious indifference. Why, then, had the rising commercial classes

embraced Protestantism when the medieval Church's control over daily life had been so notoriously lax that few real obstacles had been put in the way of the rising capitalist economy?[36]

Weber notes that to discover why, during the sixteenth century, "districts of highest economic development [were] at the same time particularly favourable to a revolution in the church" is "by no means as simple as one might think."[37] He stresses the complexity of the issue and the superficial implausibility of any link between Protestantism and capitalism:

The emancipation from economic traditionalism appears, no doubt to be a factor which would greatly strengthen the tendency to doubt the sanctity of the religious tradition, as of all traditional authorities. But it is necessary to note, what has often been forgotten, that the Reformation meant not the elimination of the Church's control over everyday life, but rather the substitution of a new form of control for the previous one. It meant the repudiation of a control which was very lax, at that time scarcely perceptible in practice, and hardly more than formal, in favour of a regulation of the whole of conduct which, penetrating to all departments of private and public life, was infinitely burdensome and earnestly enforced.[38]

Why, asks Weber, did the bourgeois classes of Europe trade the relatively benign indulgence of the Roman Catholic Church for what, from a modern standpoint, appears as "the most absolutely unbearable form of ecclesiastrical control of the individual which could possibly exist"? Why, moreover, did they attain unparalleled heights of heroism in the defence of this "unexampled tyranny," thus deviating significantly from what Reinhard Bendix terms "the simple acquisitiveness, religious indifference and more or less outright hedonism usually characteristic of social groups engaged in the development of economic enterprises"?[39] Thus *The Protestant Ethic and the Spirit of Capitalism* is an attempt to explain a paradox and not, as it is sometimes perceived, an explication of a relationship that is, *prima facie,* obvious. Weber's task is, therefore, the unenviable one of demonstrating how, apparently against all the odds, "certain types of Protestantism became a fountainhead of incentives that favoured the rational pursuit of economic gain."[40]

Noting that, during the Reformation period, "worldy" activities appear to have acquired an unprecedentedly positive spiritual and moral meaning, Weber regards analysis of the theological doctrines of the Reformation as absolutely essential to an appreciation of how this "new wordly orientation," and in particular its secular ethical aspect, was related to the purely religious ideas of the era.[41] Aware of the difficulties experienced by modern men attempting "to visualize the power and the torment of those metaphysical conceptions," Weber none the less affirms his general conviction that "historical reality just cannot be pushed around" and expresses his specific persuasion that such ideas played a vital part in the process of social change at this time:[42]

The people of that period had after all very specific ideas of what awaited them in the life after death, of the means by which they could improve their chances in this respect, and they adjusted their conduct in accordance with these ideas. The orientation of their conduct varied with the different ideas [that were developed] concerning the conditions which [the individual] must fulfil in order to be sure of his salvation. And these different ideas became significant for the development of culture.[43]

Wary of the trite oversimplifications, artificial parallels and multiform "pushing around" of historical reality that have frequently infused discussions of the origins and development of progress, liberty and enlightenment, Weber is at pains to avoid any easy association of Protestantism with human emancipation and happiness in a secular sense:

. . . the spirit of hard work, of progress, or whatever else it may be called, the awakening of which one is inclined to ascribe to Protestantism, must not be understood, as there is a tendency to do, as joy of living nor in any other sense as connected with the Enlightenment. The old Protestantism of Luther, Calvin, Knox, Voet, had precious little to do with what today is called progress. To whole aspects of modern life which the most extreme religionist would not wish to suppress today, it was directly hostile. If any inner relationship between certain expressions of the old Protestant spirit and modern capitalistic culture is to be found, we must attempt to find it, for better or worse, not in its alleged more or less materialistic or at least anti-ascetic joy of living, but in its purely religious characteristics.[44]

In turning, then, to the "purely religious characteristics" of Protestantism and their role in social change, Weber evidences an incomparable originality of insight by focussing attention upon the Lutheran theological notion of "the calling" and the Calvinist doctrine of predestination. Thus, in a scholarly argument that combines the utmost theological sensitivity with a brilliant and sophisticated psychological reconstruction of the Puritan mind, he endeavours to uncover the causal and meaningful connection between the ethic of Protestantism and the spirit of capitalism.

No short summation of Weber's deductive reasoning in this context can do justice to the intellectual subtlety of his own account, and to present a bare synopsis is to risk misinterpretation. In the interest of a general appreciation of Weberian sociology of religion, however, a minimal résumé is an unavoidable necessity. Briefly: it is clear that Weber perceives development of the "spirit of capitalism" as an unintended consequence of the emergence of specific theological ideas. Nothing could have been further from the thoughts of the great figures of the Reformation than the promotion of anything resembling a spirit of capitalistic enterprise. Yet, Weber maintains, some of their doctrines none the less contain what Bendix terms "implicit incentives in this direction."[45] Martin Luther's conception of "the calling" (*Beruf*) may in this sense be regarded as a necessary though insufficient element in the genesis of the capitalistic spirit within the Protestant milieu.

The concept of a "calling" in the sense of a life-task or a definite field in which to work is one that "has existed for all predominantly Protestant peoples" although in Weber's opinion "it appears that neither the predominantly Catholic peoples nor those of classical antiquity have possessed any expression of similar connotation."[46] Originating, in its modern sense, in Luther's translation of the scriptures, "it speedily took on its present meaning in the everyday speech of all Protestant peoples, while earlier not even a suggestion of such a meaning could be found in the secular literature of any of them."[47] Like the meaning of the word, observes Weber, the idea is new; it is a distinctive product of the Reformation:

. . . at least one thing was unquestionably new: the valuation of the fulfilment of duty in worldly affairs as the highest form which the moral activity of the individual could assume. This it was which inevitably gave everyday worldly activity a religious significance, and which first created the conception of a calling in this sense.[48]

The concept of "the calling," in Weber's view, "thus brings out that central dogma of all Protestant denominations which the Catholic division of ethical precepts . . . discards."[49] It indicates that it is not necessary to "surpass worldly morality in monastic ascetism" and that, on the contrary, the "only way of living acceptably to God" is "solely through the fulfilment of the obligations imposed upon the individual by his position in the world."[50]

If the fulfilment of worldly duties is, without exception, the only way of pleasing God, it follows that "every legitimate calling has exactly the same worth in the sight of God."[51] Such a view involves a moral justification of worldly activity that is, according to Weber, without doubt "one of the most important results of the Reformation, especially of Luther's part in it," though the detailed practical significance of this achievement is "dimly felt rather than clearly perceived:"[52]

But it is unnecessary to go into detail. For, above all, the consequences of the conception of the calling in the religious sense for worldly conduct were susceptible to quite different interpretations. *The effect of the Reformation as such was only that, as compared with the Catholic attitude, the moral emphasis on and the religious sanction of organized worldly labour in a calling was mightily increased.* The way in which the concept of the calling, which expressed this change, should develop further depended upon the religious evolution which now took place in the different Protestant Churches."[53]

The conception of the calling is something held in common by Protestant denominations; the doctrine of predestination is specific to Protestantism in its Calvinistic form. Acknowledging the "conspicuous part" played by Calvinism and the "ascetic" Protestant sects in the rise of capitalism, Weber perceives this particular theological doctrine to have been crucial to the creation of a capitalistic spirit despite its apparent remoteness from worldy, practical and every-day concerns.[54] Moreover, with profound intellectual insight and psychological sensitivity, he proceeds to trace and examine this unlikely nexus between eternal human destiny and a particular form of economic enterprise.

Considered by Weber to be the most characteristic dogma of Calvinism, the belief in predestination is, in his view, most authoritatively and eloquently expressed in the words of the *Westminster Confession* of 1647:

> Man, by his fall into a state of sin, hath wholly lost all ability of will to any spiritual good accompanying salvation. So that a natural man, being altogether adverse from that Good, and dead in sin, is not able, by his own strength to convert himself, or to prepare himself thereunto. . . . By the decree of God, for the manifestation of His glory, some men and angels are predestined unto everlasting life, and others foreordained to everlasting death. . . .
>
> Those of mankind that are predestinated unto life, God before the foundation of the world was laid, according to His eternal and immutable purpose, and the secret counsel and good pleasure of His will, hath chosen in Christ unto everlasting glory, out of His mere free grace and love, without any foresight of faith and good works, or perseverance in either of them, or any other thing in the creature as conditions, or causes moving him thereunto. . . .
>
> The rest of mankind God was pleased, according to the unsearchable counsel of His own will, whereby He extendeth, or with-holdeth mercy, as He pleaseth, for the glory of His sovereign power over His creatures, to pass by, and to ordain them to dishonour and wrath for their sin, to the praise of His glorious justice.[55]

This bleak and apparently fatalistic doctrine is lodged as the keystone of a system of theological propositions that Talcott Parsons has called "one of the few logically consistent solutions of the problem of evil in history," and which he has schematized as follows:

> (1) There is a single, absolutely, transcendental God, creator and governor of the world, whose attributes and grounds of action are, apart from Revelation, completely beyond the reach of finite human understanding. (2) This God has predestined all human souls, for reasons totally beyond possible human comprehension, either to eternal salvation or to "eternal sin and death." This decree stands from and for eternity and human will or faith can have no influence on it. (3) God for His own inscrutable reasons has created the world and placed man in it solely for the increase of His glory. (4) To this end He has decreed that man, regardless of whether predestined to salvation or damnation shall labour to establish the Kingdom of God on Earth, and shall be subject to His revealed law in doing so. (5) The things of this world, human nature and the flesh, are, left to themselves, irreparably lost in "sin and death" from which there is no escape by divine grace.[56]

In Weber's view, the "dark and dangerous teaching" of predestination, so repugnant to Lutheranism, increased its significance in Calvinist doctrine with every improvement in the logical consistency of a form of religious thought interested not in man but only in God.[57] If God exists not for man, but purely for His own sake, all creation is merely a means of glorifying Him and any attempt to apply earthly standards of justice to His decisions is both meaningless and insulting:

His decrees can only be understood by or even known to us in so far as it has been His pleasure to reveal them. We can only hold to these fragments of eternal truth. Everything else, including the meaning of our individual destiny, is hidden in dark mystery which it would be both impossible to pierce and presumptuous to question.

For the damned to complain of their lot would be much the same as for animals to bemoan the fact they were not born as men. . . . We know only that a part of humanity is saved, the rest damned. To assume that human merit or guilt play a part in determining this destiny would be to think of God's absolutely free decrees, which have been settled from eternity, as subject to change by human influence, an impossible contradiction.[58]

Thus, the God of the New Testament who rejoices over the repentant sinner and the rescue of the lost sheep has been superseded by "a transcendental being, beyond the reach of human understanding," whose incomprehensible decrees have "decided the fate of every individual and regulated the tiniest details of the cosmos from eternity."[59]

But what, asks Weber, were the practical consequences in the lives of believers, of the awesome doctrines of Calvinism? And how, specifically, were they related to the notion of "organized worldly labour in a calling"? Firstly, he argues that the utter transcendence of a divine law-giver who had, according to Calvinist precept, predestined human fates by irrevokable decree and whose will had to be done, reduced man to a mere instrument of his creator and thereby directed religious energies along an active, ascetic rather than passive, mystical route:

Deep-lying differences of the most important conditions of salvation which apply to the classification of all practical religious activity appear here. The religious believer can make himself sure of his state of grace either in that he feels himself to be the vessel of the Holy Spirit or the tool of the divine will. In the former case his religious life tends to mysticism and emotionalism, in the latter to ascetic action; Luther stood close to the former type, Calvinism belonged definitely to the latter.[60]

Mystical union with or absorption in the divine spirit is precluded by the fundamental dualism implied by God's complete transcendence; such a God cannot be embraced or even approached, but only served. In Weber's view, such service could only be rendered by the Calvinist through control over the flesh; by subjecting it entirely to a discipline applied *omnia in majorem dei gloriam*. Yet if the essence of ascetism for Weber lies in control, its locale was, for the Calvinist, no longer the cloister but the workplace.

Perceiving that the Calvinistic conception of a divine order entailed both a faith in the natural order which was highly conducive to modern scientific development, and an abhorrence of ritual practices as being magical, superstitious and idolatrous, Weber asserts that the ascetic activity of the Calvinist believer was, of necessity, "diverted away from ritual channels of expression into active control over the intrinsic relations of the world."[61] Utilizing the earlier doctrine of "the calling" and reiterating the general Protestant rejection of monasticism, this compulsion toward ethical control over the world in the service of an ideal thus succeeded in replacing a monkish other-worldly ascetism with the worldly ascetism of the man of the world. In a sense, every Christian now had to be a monk all his life:

The drain of ascetism from everyday worldly life had now been stopped by a dam, and those passionately spiritual natures which had formerly supplied the highest type of monk were now forced to pursue their ascetic ideals within mundane occupations.

But in the course of its development Calvinism added something positive to this, the idea of the necessity of proving one's faith in worldly activity. Therein it gave the broader groups of religiously inclined people a positive incentive to ascetism.[62]

Rooted in the terrifying doctrine of predestination, the ethic of Calvinism "substituted for the spiritual aristocracy of monks outside of and above the world the spiritual aristocracy of the predestined saints of God within the world."[63] Indeed, as Weber wryly observes, this new spiritual elite was segregated from the doomed remainder of the human race "by a more impassable and in its invisibility more terrifying gulf, than separated the monk of the Middle Ages from the rest of the world about him, a gulf which penetrated all social relations with its sharp brutality."[64]

But, in Weber's analysis, the link between the doctrine of predestination and the compulsion to unremitting work in a calling is by no means simply a logical one. Involving a perceptive psychological twist, its account of the specific consequence for human conduct of a belief in predestination has been accorded a mixed scholarly reception. Regarded, on the one hand, as a *tour de force* of social-psychological and historical reconstruction, it has also been perceived as a thesis that weakens, to the point of circularity, the very causal connection it seeks to establish. Thus, its introduction of a subjective, intervening variable between Calvinist doctrine and ascetic activity may be interpreted as a strategy of infinite sensitivity and subtlety or, less kindly, as a misguided exercise in unwarranted speculation.[65]

Weber argues that the doctrine of predestination made its greatest impact upon patterns of worldly activity precisely at the point at which the early Calvinists experienced the greatest strain in adhering to it. Contrasting the "bitter seriousness" of Calvinism with "the very human Catholic cycle of sin, repentance, atonement, release, followed by renewed sin," he indicates the "tremendous tension to which the Calvinist was doomed by an inexorable fate, admitting of no mitigation" as a consequence of the "rationalization of the world" or "the elimination of magic as a means to salvation" required by his church:[66]

For him such friendly and human comforts did not exist. He could not hope to atone for hours of weakness or of thoughtlessness by increased good will at other times, as the Catholic or even the Lutheran could. The God of Calvinism demanded of his believers not single good works, but a life of good works combined into a unified system.

The moral conduct of the average man was thus deprived of its planless and unsystematic character and subjected to a consistent method for conduct as a whole.[67]

In Weber's view, the life of the Calvinist "saint" was, therefore, directed solely toward the transcendental end of salvation, and for that reason was "thoroughly rationalized" and "dominated entirely by the aim to add to the glory of God on earth." Only a life "guided by constant thought" could conquer the state of nature, and such rationalization gave Calvinism its peculiarly ascetic character.[68]

But how precisely is the harsh doctrine of predestination linked to this worldly ascetic tendency of Calvinism? Weber suggests that the ordinary individual was bound to feel, as Bendix summarizes it, "profoundly troubled by a doctrine that did not permit any outward signs of his state of grace and that imparted to the image of God such terrifying majesty that He transcended all human entreaty and comprehension."[69] Standing alone before such an awesome deity and entitled to no external sign of his own election or damnation, the Calvinist believer could only regard himself humbly as God's instrument and place himself at the Lord's disposal in the work of establishing the kingdom of God on earth through ascetic activity. By throwing himself into ceaseless work in a calling, however, the ordinary believer was able to attempt to overcome the psychological tension created by what Parsons has termed "the strict construction of the doctrine of predestination."[70]

Calvin had taught that one must find solace solely on the basis of the true faith. Each man was duty-bound to consider himself chosen and to reject all doubt as a temptation of the devil, for a lack of self-confidence was interpreted as a sign of insufficient faith. To attain that self-confidence, unceasing work in a calling was recommended. By his increasing activity in the service of God, the believer strengthened his self-confidence as the active tool of the divine will.[71]

Even immersed in the daily activity of his calling, could the ordinary believer in predestination ward off doubt and submit to his predestined fate in the manner prescribed by Calvin? Though Calvin himself may have been convinced of his own election and certain of salvation as the chosen agent of God's purpose, Weber believes that such assurance was by no means universally experienced by rank-and-file members of Calvin's church. For these, the twin torments of ignorance and doubt were a constant accompaniment to all rumination on their individual states of grace and ultimate eternal destinies, according to Weber:

For us the decisive problem is: How was this doctrine [of predestination] borne in an age to which the after-life was not only more important, but in many ways also more certain, than all the interests of life in this world? The question, Am I one of the elect? must sooner or later have arisen for every believer and have forced all other interests into the background.[72]

Thus, as Parsons notes, in as much as this religious question was undoubtedly taken most seriously and believers' interest in salvation was strong, the individual must have endured psychological agony. Impotent to influence his eternal destiny, "the whole pressure of his religious interest was to *know* whether he was saved or damned."[73]

For Calvin, the elect always remained an invisible church. It was impossible, therefore, to learn from the lives or conduct of others, or even from subjective introspection, whether a soul was saved or damned and any attempt to do so constituted "an unjustifiable attempt to force God's secrets." Quite naturally, observes Weber, "this attitude was impossible for his followers . . . and, above all, for the broad mass of ordinary men for whom the *certitudo salutis* in the sense of the recognizability of the state of grace necessarily became of absolutely dominant importance."[74] Therefore, whenever there was commitment to the doctrine of predestination, it proved impossible, in Weber's reckoning, to suppress the question of "whether there were any infallible criteria by which membership in the *electi* could be known."[75]

It is here, argues Parsons, that "the 'psychological' as distinct from the purely logical consequences" of belief in predestination emerge in Weber's analysis:

Given a serious interest, he holds the pressure was too great for the mass of men. Under this pressure it was the first doctrine which gradually gave way. It gradually came to be held that good works, while they could not influence salvation, could be interpreted as signs of grace. A good tree could not bear evil fruit. Then gradually the elect came to be identified with the "righteous", those who did the will of God, and the damned with "sinners", those who failed to obey His will.[76]

Although not formally abandoned, Calvin's orthodox conception of predestination proved psychologically and pastorally unpalatable to many Calvinists, so that where it was not subjected to reinterpretation or "toned down" for popular consumption, it was at least placed in a context in which divine intimations of personal salvation might indeed be discerned by the anxious Calvinist believer. The pastoral attempt to reduce the suffering caused among the faithful by the doctrine thus involved, as noted above, an insistence upon the "absolute duty to consider oneself chosen, and to combat all doubts as temptations of the devil," and an injunction to engage in intense worldly activity as the most suitable means of acquiring such self-confidence and of "counteracting feelings of religious anxiety."[77] More than this, however, it encouraged the belief that "true faith" might be recognized "by a type of Christian conduct which served to increase the glory of God." Genuine good works are therefore the monopoly of the elect and the sign by which they may be identified. Though they are of no assistance in the attainment of salvation, they are the "technical means" of overcoming the fear of damnation and generating the conviction of salvation in the individual.[78] It is by no means unreasonable to suggest, as does Weber, that the notion that "God helps those who help themselves" is implicit in this belief, and to detect, furthermore, the beginnings of the idea that possession of God's grace might be indicated by success in a worldly calling.[79]

Weber's interest in the psychology of the single human being faced with the doctrine of predestination is by no means accidental, for it reflects the fact that Calvinism represented a highly individualistic form of religion. Painting a chilling picture of the individual in this disenchanted setting, he observes:

> In its extreme inhumanity this doctrine must above all have had one consequence for the life of a generation which surrendered to its magnificant consistency. That was a feeling of unprecedented inner loneliness of the single individual. In what was for the man of the age of the Reformation the most important thing in his life, his eternal salvation, he was forced to follow his path alone to meet a destiny which had been decreed for him from eternity. No one could help him. No priest. . . . No sacraments. . . . No Church. . . . Finally, even no God.[80]

The Calvinist overcame his anxiety and attained self-confidence in complete spiritual isolation from his fellow men. Incapable of placing any trust in the friendship and goodwill of humankind, his only possible confidant was God himself, a state of affairs which, by Weber's estimation:

> . . . forms one of the roots of that disillusioned and pessimistically inclined individualism which can even today be identified in the national characters and the institutions of the peoples with a Puritan past, in such a striking contrast to the quite different spectacles through which the Enlightenment later looked upon men.[81]

Moreover, he maintains, the combination of this inner isolation of the individual with "the harsh doctrines of the absolute transcendality of God and the corruption of everything pertaining to the flesh" leads to an entirely negative attitude toward "all the sensuous and emotional elements in culture and in religion," providing the basis for a fundamental antagonism to sensuous culture of all kinds." Thus the "humble sinners to whom Luther promised grace" in return for trust and persistent faith in a loving God were superseded by a new breed of Christians: those cold-blooded, austere and "self-confident saints" whom Weber rediscovers "in the hard Puritan merchants of the heroic age of capitalism."[82]

As Parsons expresses it, the Calvinist sense of inner isolation, in combination with the other aspects of the doctrine of predestination, had "an extremely important implication for the rationalization of conduct."[83] Thus, Weber maintains that the "moral conduct of the average man" was "deprived of its planless and unsystematic character and subjected to a consistent method for conduct as a whole." Engaged in "systematic self-control," the Calvinist endeavoured to live "a life of good works combined into a unified system"[84] for reasons well articulated by Parsons:

> . . . since individual good works could not affect grace, and outward conduct could at most be a sign of grace, the conduct enjoined could be judged only as a *total coherent system,* as the expression of the *kind of man* one was, not as a plurality of disconnected acts.[85]

Unlike the Catholic, for whom absolution from sins and the spiritual rewards of good deeds were ever present and immediate facts of life, the Calvinist experienced no relief from intense spiritual and psychological pressure, developing in consequence "an incomparably greater drive to the rational systematization of conduct."[86]

Practically, as has already been observed, the energy of the Calvinist was thus diverted into those pursuits (or "callings") in which he could labour soberly, rationally and systematically throughout his earthly life. From this point of view, "independent, solid, honest business" was an especially appropriate field of activity; one whose potential material rewards were accompanied by a special spiritual bonus. Moreover, the stern Calvinistic condemnation of self-indulgence in the consumption of worldly goods and satisfaction of sensual appetites generated what Weber terms an "ascetic compulsion to save" whose most obvious and "inevitable practical result" was the accumulation of capital. The release of acquisition "from the bonds of traditionalist ethics" provided the Calvinist, therefore, with an unprecedented opportunity for securing objective as well as subjective evidence of his own salvation.[87]

As a technique for controlling the flesh, stifling spiritual doubt, dominating nature and preparing the kingdom of God on earth, the novel ascetic approach to labour was crucial, in Weber's estimation, to the emergence of a hitherto unknown spirit of capitalism. Thus, restless, continuous and systematic hard work in a useful calling was perceived by the Calvinist not as a negative consequence of Adam's original sin, but as a positive means of doing God's will. Such worldly activity was the primary means by which the Calvinist's religious duty might be performed and not merely an unpleasant legacy of man's fall from grace. Doing a good job was "the highest fulfilment of his own deep religious interests" and the means to subjective assurance of salvation.[88] But if such righteous conduct could be interpreted as a legitimate sign of divine grace, was it not likely, the ordinary believer asked, that God would favour his elect in this world as well as in the next? Did it not make sense, therefore, to hold that honestly attained success in a calling should itself be regarded as a mark of the elect? Though remote from Calvin's own view of predestination, this perception of a convenient objective means by which God's intentions might be inferred undoubtedly armed the successful businessman with a spiritual rationale for his worldly success. Instilling a smug self-righteousness concerning profit-making, it encouraged a cold-bloodedness toward the less fortunate that was mitigated only by a chilling charity of severe, rational, disciplined and ruthless character.

With acute ingenuity, Weber investigates the ethic of Protestantism through the sermons of Puritan divines, discerns the spirit of capitalism within the tracts of Benjamin Franklin, and asserts a close connection:

> One of the fundamental elements of the spirit of modern capitalism, and not only of that but of all modern cultures: rational conduct on the basis of the idea of the calling, was born . . . from the spirit of Christian ascetism. . . . the essential elements of the attitude [which Franklin calls] the spirit of capitalism are the same as . . . the content of the Puritan worldly ascetism, only without the religious basis, which by Franklin's time had died away.[89]

Finally, Weber bemoans a culture in which ceaseless activity, profit-seeking and the expansion of rational bureaucratic organization appear to have become ends in themselves; the horrifying, unintended and mutated bequests of ascetic Protestantism:

> The Puritan wanted to work in a calling; we are forced to do so. For when ascetism was carried out of monastic cells into everyday life, and began to dominate worldly morality, it did its part in building the tremendous cosmos of the modern economic order. This order is now bound to the technical and economic conditions of machine production which today determine the lives of all the individuals who are born into this mechanism, not only those directly concerned with economic acquisition, with irresistible force. Perhaps it will so determine them until the last ton of fossilized coal is burnt. In Baxter's view the care for external goods should only lie on the shoulders of the "saint like a light cloak, which can be thrown aside at any moment." But fate decreed that the cloak should become an iron cage.[90]

Thus, in a world in which "material goods have gained an increasing and finally an inexorable power over the lives of men as at no previous period in history," the "rosy blush" of the Enlightenment seems to fade irretrievably while "the idea of duty in one's calling prowls about in our lives like the ghost of dead religious beliefs."[91]

Weber does not proceed substantially beyond the analysis of theological doctrines and pastoral writings; nor, by establishing a "congruence" or "elective affinity" between the Protestant ethic and the spirit of capitalism, does he prove that religion was "an important factor in the genesis of the capitalistic attitude and through it of rational bourgeois capitalism."[92] In seeking to show that the inherent logic of Calvinist doctrines and the pastoral advice derived from them "both directly and indirectly encouraged planning and self-denial in the pursuit of economic gain,"[93] Weber was quite clear about the precise limits of his scholarly probings:

In view of the tremendous confusion of interdependent influences between the material basis, the forms of social and political organization, and the ideas current in the time of the Reformation, we can only proceed by investigating whether and at what points certain correlations between forms of religious belief and practical ethics can be worked out. At the same time we shall as far as possible clarify the manner and the general direction in which, by virtue of those relationships, the religious movements have influenced the development of material culture. Only when this has been determined with reasonable accuracy can the attempt be made to estimate to what extent the historical development of modern culture can be attributed to those religious forces and to what extent to others.[94]

Weber's attempts to investigate "the influence of those psychological sanctions which, originating in religious belief and the practice of religion, gave a direction to practical conduct and held the individual to it," were thus the necessary preliminaries to any such estimation.[95]

Whether Weber is indeed successful in his illustrious attempt to link Protestantism with capitalism logically and psychologically is, of course, a matter of bitter scholarly dispute. Talcott Parsons is, however, unequivocal in his endorsement of the intent and execution of this enterprise:

There can be no doubt that in his treatment of the ethics of ascetic Protestantism Weber has in general succeeded in his task of finding a system of ultimate-value ideas "adequate" to the spirit of capitalism as he himself formulated the latter conception. All its leading traits find their counterpart in the Protestant attitude properly interpreted. Above all the "irrational" element in which the peculiar capitalistic "rationalism" is centred, so incomprehensible from any hedonistic point of view, has found a meaning. What other explanation of it has accomplished this fundamental thing?[96]

But, if Weber's achievement is acknowledged in this way, it is also necessary to consider briefly the manner in which he combines this meaningful interpretation of the Protestant-capitalist nexus with a causally adequate account of it. In this regard, it must be noted that cause and meaning, in Weber's analysis, hinge finally upon a comparative sociology of religion.[97]

Observing that in any country of mixed religious composition "business leaders and owners of capital, as well as the higher grades of skilled labour, and even more the higher technically and commercially trained personnel of modern enterprises, are overwhelmingly Protestant,"[98] Weber notes that statistical evidence suggests a pertinent connection between religious affiliation and location in the social structure. Thus, in his view, "the greater participation of Protestants in the positions of ownership and management in modern economic life" hints at a causal connection between Protestantism and capitalism, a hypothesis that is strengthened by the fact that the Protestant ethic appears to have chronologically preceded the spirit of capitalism in the geographical areas and social strata under scrutiny.[99]

Combined with the crucial insight that the development of the Protestant ethic, especially in the context of the sect, was no mere process of accommodation to the secular world, but rather the result of following positive religious interests, this view depicts "one side of the causal chain"[100] in an argument that has been conveniently summarized by Parsons:

The gist of Weber's causal argument may be put as follows: The empirical material [the writings of Protestant leaders down through the seventeenth century] shows a process of development toward the stronger and stronger sanction of individualistic acquisitive activities. Is this accommodation or is it an independent development of the religious ethic for *religious* reasons? Weber argues for the importance of the latter element on the ground that such a development is meaningful within the framework of the system of religious ideas; it is not only possible in the sense of not conflicting with essential elements of it, but it is in accord with strong religious motives inherent in the system of religious ideas itself in relation to the world. Furthermore the element of concrete capitalism in which Weber is interested is not at odds with this later ethic; it may on the contrary to a large extent be interpreted as the direct expression of these motives in practical conduct.[101]

Concentrating solely upon that side of the causal chain that treats "the influence of certain religious ideas on the development of an economic spirit, or the *ethos* of an economic system," Weber utilizes "the method of agreement" with unparalleled ingenuity.[102] Yet a convincing causal case for "the connection of the spirit of modern economic life with the rational ethics of ascetic Protestantism" can only be made, Weber suggests, by investigations that employ "the method of difference."[103] It is upon this insight, therefore, that his subsequent great comparative studies in the sociology of religion are predicated. Noting that the "specific and peculiar rationalism of Western culture which permeates its scientific, artistic, political and economic development" has had no counterpart in the civilizations of India and China, Weber considers why this has been the case.[104] Thus, instead of "continuing to ask directly what specific forces account for the appearance of rational bourgeois capitalism in the modern West, he asks inversely, why did anything like it *fail* to appear in any of the other great civilizations of the world?"[105] Pondering the difficulties involved in providing a causally adequate answer to this question, Weber observes:

It is . . . our first concern to work out and to explain genetically the special peculiarity of Occidental rationalism, and within this field that of the modern Occidental form. Every such attempt at explanation must, recognizing the fundamental importance of the economic factor, above all take account of the economic conditions. But at the same time the opposite correlation must not be left out of consideration. For though the development of economic rationalism is partly dependent on rational technique and law, it is at the same time determined by the ability and disposition of men to adopt certain types of practical rational conduct. When these types have been obstructed by spiritual obstacles, the development of rational economic conduct has also met serious inner resistance. The magical and religious forces, and the ethical ideas of duty based upon them, have in the past always been among the most important formative influences on conduct.[106]

The Protestant Ethic and the Spirit of Capitalism focuses upon only one side of the causal chain; the later studies of the "Economic Ethics of the World Religions" attempt investigation of both sides by means of a review of "the relations of the most important religions to economic life and to the social stratification of their environment."[107]

The causal relationships implied when either the economic or the religious factor is viewed as the "independent variable" in the investigation are thereby pursued as far as necessary in order that "points of comparison with the Occidental development" may be discerned:

> For only in this way is it possible to attempt a causal evaluation of those elements of the economic ethics of the Western religions which differentiate them from others, with a hope of attaining even a tolerable degree of approximation.[108]

Intended originally as an examination of Confucianism, Buddhism, Hinduism, Judaism, early Christianity and Islam, this particular awesome enterprise remained incomplete at Weber's death. Even in its fragmented form, however, its focal concern is clearly with the foundations of modern capitalism, for it constitutes "a comparative study of the ethics of other religions in respects relevant to the spirit of capitalism and the ethics of ascetic Protestantism" rather than a general outline of the sociology of religion.[109] Thus, in comparing the ethics of several major religions, Weber focuses upon their accelerating or retarding effect upon the rationality of economic life; and, in each case he investigates, "Weber succeeds in demonstrating that the economic ethic associated with the religion in question is fundamentally different from that of ascetic Protestantism in its implications for economic activities."[110] Noting, furthermore, that in areas where the ethic under scrutiny has predominated, "no development has taken place which is at all comparable with that of Western rational bourgeois capitalism," he establishes a connection between the lack of capitalistic development and the character of the ethic itself.[111] By contrast with the ethic of ascetic Protestantism, therefore, the ethics of the other world religions have, in his judgement, inhibited rather than encouraged the emergence of a capitalistic spirit. In both India and China, for example, Weber maintains that, at the crucial time, the combination of non-religious factors was as favourable to capitalistic development as in Western Europe; a solution that suggests that "the religious element of the economic ethic" was a crucial differentiating factor in determining the likelihood of such development.[112] Hence, through a comparative survey of religious ethics, Weber attains a deeper understanding of the peculiarly rational character and "*universal* significance and value" of Western culture.[113] Implicit in this understanding, of course, is a perception of the central importance of specific religious ideas and interests in the unique line of development and "progress" in the Occident.

Central though it is to an appreciation of Weber's work as a whole, *The Protestant Ethic and the Spirit of Capitalism* has been examined in the preceding pages for a precise reason: to offer a framework for discerning in its arguments the fundamental assumptions of Weber's sociology of religion. What, then, are the characteristics of a Weberian approach to religion that may be derived from an examination of the *Protestant Ethic* thesis?

It is obvious, firstly, that the phenomenon of religion looms large in Weber's general historical and comparative understanding of society; indeed, it is no exaggeration to suggest that Weber's analysis of religion provides the key to understanding the nature of his whole sociological life's work.[114] Secondly, expressed in contemporary terminology, the extent to which Weber is concerned with religion as culture is manifest.[115] Fascinated by religious ideas, beliefs, values and ethics, and intrigued by their relationship to secular attitudes and activities, Weber explores their relevance for a wide range of human behaviour, leaving no doubt that his interest is not in religion *per se:*

> When he turned his studies toward religion, his focus was not upon religion "as such", as the theologian or church historian conceives it, but upon *the relations between* religious ideas and commitments and other aspects of human conduct. . . . Weber's concern with religion was thus focussed upon the *sociology* of religion.[116]

In Parsons' opinion, Weber thereby "inaugurated a new phase in the understanding of the relations between religious aspects and other aspects of human behaviour" by his treatment of the interplay between religious ideas and economic activity in the specific context of the genesis of modern rational capitalism.[117]

Thus, as Thomas Luckmann observes, "Weber's detailed investigations of religion in the most diverse historical and cultural contexts were not motivated by any pronounced personal or ideological interest in religion." Rather, they were "a necessary step in his effort to account theoretically for those historical processes that led to the emergence of modern society."[118]

Thirdly, Weber's formulation of what Parsons has termed the ultimate-value attitudes and ideas of ascetic Protestantism is a particularly important clue to his fundamental, though implicit, conception of religion in terms of a search for grounds of meaning and ultimate reference points. It thus helps to reveal a "working definition" of subject matter that Weber himself never attempted to make explicit, but that strongly implies the universality of religion in human society.[119]

Fourthly, Weber's quest for the ultimate-value attitudes of ascetic Protestantism and his concern with systems of meaning in *The Protestant Ethic and the Spirit of Capitalism* underscore his commitment to *Verstehen* as the most appropriate social-scientific method for understanding religious phenomena. Involving a methodologically individualistic attempt to interpret action through imaginative empathy, this research procedure attempts to interpret action and reconstruct meaning by an understanding of an actor's motives from the subjective point of view. Thus, Weber's effort to imagine himself in the place of the ordinary rank-and-file Puritan of the seventeenth century as a means of understanding the nature of the latter's situation, interests and motives, provides a paradigmatic case of interpretive analysis in the sociology of religion, one that points the way to further reconstructions of systems of meaning in a variety of religious contexts and that stresses the social-psychological aspect of such endeavours.[120]

Fifthly, Weber's analysis of the link between ascetic Protestantism and the spirit of capitalistic enterprise perfectly illustrates the fact that his "primary interest is in religion as a source of the dynamics of social change, not religion as a reinforcement of the stability of societies."[121] In contrast to Durkheim, who viewed religion primarily in terms of its contribution to societal stability and the integration of individuals within the existing social order, Weber perceives the social role of religion in dynamic terms.[122] His analysis of religion, therefore, is not undertaken on the basis of a static concern with social order, but rather in the context of general sociological assumptions that the explanation of social change is "the business of a general social theory" and that propositions about society that make no attempt to explain its transformations ought not to be classified as genuine social theory.[123]

Sixthly, the caution, circumspection, sensitivity and sophistication with which Weber handles the religious "variable" in his attempt to trace a link between the ideas of ascetic Protestantism and the character of modern, rational capitalism is a model for his undogmatic and undeterministic treatment of religion in subsequent writings. Though he sees religion as "the key to a fascinating and fateful puzzle" of world-historical importance, he does not assert "that religion is generally and necessarily the source of historical change."[124] Though offering a positive critique of a monistic, historical materialism, Weber has no intention of advancing the claims of a form of religious idealism, for he notes the necessity of investigating "how Protestant Ascetism was in turn influenced in its development and its character by the totality of social conditions, especially economic."[125] In his view, this is absolutely essential to any attempt to make a comprehensive assessment of "the quantitative cultural significance of ascetic Protestantism in its relation to the other plastic elements of modern culture:"[126]

> The modern man is in general, even with the best will, unable to give religious ideas a significance for culture and rational character which they deserve. But it is, of course, not my aim to substitute for a one-sided materialistic an equally one-sided spiritualistic causal interpretation of culture and of history. Each is equally possible, but each, if it does not serve as the preparation, but as the conclusion of an investigation, accomplishes equally little in the interest of historical truth.[127]

Thus, while rejecting idealism, Weber is nonetheless able to deny the merely epiphenomenal status of religious phenomena and to posit the relative autonomy of religious ideas at the same time as he acknowledges the relevance of social and economic factors in the shaping of religious life.

Finally, *The Protestant Ethic and the Spirit of Capitalism* deals with such matters as the internal logic of systems of ideas, the evolutionary process of rationalization and the role of religious ideas in the provision of individual and collective systems of meaning. More specifically, it is concerned with such topics as salvation, theodicy, the importance of the sectarian form of religious organization, the nature of breakthroughs into a higher, more systematized cultural order, and the discrepancy between the formally defined doctrinal creations of intellectuals and the convictions of popular religiosity.[128]

No attempt to condense Weber's sociology of religion into a short summary of a few pages can do more than indicate some of its main themes and hint at the brilliance of Weber's treatment of them. It cannot hope to capture the excitement of Weber's "rich empirical studies of the world's great historical religions" or his "extraordinary combination of erudition in the social sciences, disinterested and impartial observation, and poignant yet scientifically cautious nostalgia toward religious phenomena of the past."[129] In contrast to Durkheim's more direct and circumscribed "case-study" approach to the explanation of religion, Weber's work appears rambling, fragmentary and perhaps too rich in detail. As it investigates and compares the esoteric, the exotic and the familiar in the light of a formidable range of scholarship, the student may become lost in the wealth of detail, failing to see the theoretical wood for the factual trees. As Parsons has noted, "Weber's was the type of mind which, in an often baffling way, combined enormous sensitivity to the most complex detail with certain not only very broad, but very precisely conceived main lines of analysis."[130] In his writings, however, these main lines of analysis are frequently obscured by the very facts marshalled to reveal them:

> The peculiar circumstances under which Weber's work on the relations of Protestantism and capitalism has come to the attention of English scholarship have given rise to a widespread but erroneous impression of his intellectual character. This association with what has been widely interpreted as a dramatic and radical thesis in historical interpretation has favoured the view that he was the type that takes a simple idea and drives it to extremes, concerned only with bold outlines and showing a sovereign disdain of meticulous detailed factual study. He has often been interpreted as a "philosopher" or "theorist" in the derogatory sense of one who makes the facts fit his theories rather than the reverse.[131]

Such a view could hardly be further from the truth, however. For while it is evident that Weber formulates his views very sharply at times (particularly in polemical contexts), none the less his customary mode of expression is very different in kind:

Anyone who attempts to understand his sociological work in its completeness to any degree cannot fail to be impressed and to a great extent bewildered, by the enormous mass of detailed historical material which Weber commanded. Indeed, so vast is this mass, and much of it so highly technical in the various fields from which it is drawn, that an ordinary human being is under very serious difficulties in any sort of critical analysis, since a real factual check on Weber's work as a whole would probably be well beyond the powers of any single living scholar. Weber's was, what is exceedingly rare in the modern age, an encyclopaedic mind.[132]

By contrast, in its concentration upon "a small body of crucial facts rather than a vast body of information," and in its concern with "relatively simple bold outlines and clear-cut alternatives," Durkheim's mind was what Parsons has described as almost purely theoretical, with an interest "mainly intensive rather than extensive, of the order of the crucial experiment." In this regard, Durkheim in fact clearly exhibited the pattern of thought that is sometimes wrongly associated with Weber.[133]

In Weber's mind, the theoretical component, immensely important though it was, "co-existed with an omnivorous appetite for detail and for piling up masses of fact." Thus, the "bold outlines of a theoretical system stand out clearly above the mass of detail" only at "certain crucial points" and, indeed, only after they have been painfully extracted "by following his interest from a clearly defined starting point step by step."[134] In the present context it is Weber's main lines of analysis that are of paramount concern.

Weber's work in the sociology of religion may be regarded as "the strategically central part of a general evolutionary view of the development of human society."[135] In forging this general perspective, Weber explicitly and unashamedly accords a primary causal significance to "religious orientation," viewing it (as Parsons puts it) both as an initiating and as a differentiating factor in this evolutionary process. Yet this factor is never regarded as entirely independent in its operation. It is, on the contrary, "nowhere treated as automatically unfolding or 'actualizing itself' except through highly complex processes of interaction with other factors." Thus, major social changes are always the result of such interaction and may never be attributed to "any one factor alone."[136]

Furthermore, Weber is acutely sensitive to the importance of material factors in the process of social change; to deny this is to badly misinterpret his intentions. As Talcott Parsons has rightly observed:

Weber clearly insisted on the independent significance of the ideas which originated as solutions of the problems of meaning, independent significance of the "religious interests" which operate within this framework. But at the same time he made as great a single contribution to the understanding of the role of "material" factors in the process of social development as did any scholar, at least up to his time – including . . . Karl Marx."[137]

Within this broad framework, Weber clearly regards the development of modern Western civilization, and particularly those aspects of it that were influenced by the ideas of ascetic Protestantism, as the spearhead of the most important and uniquely significant world-historical evolutionary trend. Decisively influenced by religious phenomena (with the qualifications already noted), the Western world has created an industrial form of society whose rational modes of economic and political organization have provided models of "modernity" and "progress" for the rest of the world. Imitated and diffused with varying degrees of success, the bureaucratic society founded upon modern capitalism is thus the unprecedented and unparalleled creation of Western civilization and is, in part at least, the unlikely, unforeseen and unintended consequence of Puritan pietism.

Weber's sociology of religion is concerned, in Donald MacRae's phrase, with "the working of religion on everyday life, on political, administrative, economic, and moral behaviour in different historical situations that he tries to understand and reduce to order."[138] In this regard, it is "profoundly ironical," as Thomas Luckmann has noted, that Weber should perceive the historical role of religion as generally that of an "agent of rationalization" that has "contributed involuntarily but decisively to a de-sacralization of the world and thereby perhaps also to its own demise." The irony lies in the fact that, for Weber, religion appears to originate ultimately in the irrationality of what Luckmann terms "the purely subjective, personal dimension of individual existence" although even in its "earliest manifestations" it undoubtedly involves what Weber himself regards as "relatively rational behaviour."[139]

Before discussing his exposition of the complex and multifaceted role of religion in this "working of everyday life," however, it seems advisable to engage in that fundamental preparatory task of definition that Weber so conspicuously succeeded in postponing and avoiding.

Investigation of Weber's writings reveals two main implicit definitions of the term "religion." The first, which may be encountered in his discussion of the "rise of religions," combines a more-or-less "every-day" societal sense of the phenomenon with a substantive scientific conception entirely in line with the usage of Tylorian, Spencerian or Frazerian anthropological evolutionism.[140] Concerned with the development of the idea of the soul and the emergence of the belief in spirits and other supernatural phenomena, Weber is, like Durkheim, intrigued by "the diversity of possible relationships between a spiritual being and the object behind which it lurks and with which it is somehow connected."[141] In the context of the immediate discussion, his most important observation is that the ordering of the relations to men of "gods," "demons" and "supernatural powers" may be said to constitute "the realm of religious behaviour."[142]

Weber's second definition departs considerably from the first formulation and may justifiably be regarded as more distinctively and characteristically Weberian in tone. Its nature may only be indirectly inferred, but in terms of Weber's broad framework for the analysis of religion its greater importance is not in doubt; a point underscored by Theodore M. Steeman's laudable attempt to outline its main features:

What is religion for Weber? I think that a definition of religion in Weber's thought would run something like this: Religion is man's continuous effort to deal rationally with the irrationalities of life. Religion rises out of the *Not* (needs) of existence, its ambiguities and conflicts, and gives the necessary *Begeisterung* (enthusiasm) to live. It promises freedom and salvation from life's precariousness, however it be understood in the concrete situation, and gives a reason to live with enthusiasm. Thus, it is concerned with the problems of ultimate meaning and with the promise of the fullness of life. It makes life's precariousness acceptable, gives life preciousness and prescribes a way of life that makes living worthwhile. It formulates, in short, man's basic understanding, at any moment in history of himself, of the world in which he lives, and of how life should be lived.[143]

As a number of commentators have observed, this is essentially a functional definition of religion. With considerable eloquence Steeman elaborates this insight:

Religion rises out of the dialogue between man and nature, or between man and his experience of life, and plays an indispensable role in man's dealings with nature and himself, because it is the way life is defined as a task. In its concrete forms religion is therefore dependent on the way man finds his life as a task and on his capacity, intellectual and practical, to deal with this task.[144]

In some cases the central problem of life may be the simple struggle for physical survival, while in circumstances of material adequacy or abundance, the struggle for life may give way to the struggle for the good life as, broadly speaking, ideal interests outweigh material interests. In such a context, as Steeman notes, "ethical considerations may supersede considerations of utility and need."[145] But, however man's basic problems and needs are perceived, religion is always "the outcome of the attempt to live meaningfully" and its function is to make meaningful man's existence in his natural and social environment.[146] It is thus an integral and essential aspect of human life, whose inextricability from the human condition clearly underlies Weber's theoretical and methodological reluctance to identify final causes in sociocultural settings:

. . . man is never wholly the product of his natural environment and his primitive nature, but at the same time he is never able completely to transcend these. This means that if we cannot understand man's life apart from his religion, we cannot understand his religion apart from the larger picture of his whole life. As part of life, religion is both exponent and forming force. It is therefore that Weber rejects every kind of unilateral causal explanation.[147]

The product, in Weber's view, of an innate human "drive" for meaning, religion provides the ultimate "grounds of meaning" (in Parsons' phrase) for individuals and organized social groups, and it is this basic function that is its defining characteristic and primary focus of sociological interest:[148]

It is a consequence of this emphasis on the central function of religion in the interpretation of the task of living, that Weber stresses so much the conditions under which religions can function, and, on the other hand, the consequences of a religious orientation for the conduct of life. This is but another way of saying that Weber is less concerned about the religious institutions in themselves than about religious life.[149]

Thus, Weber's concern with the details of religion in its specific historical and contemporary manifestations is subservient to his sociological obsession with religion in general, and this generic interest in the problems of meaning and ultimate commitment reverberates throughout his work.[150]

If the problem of meaning is indeed a ubiquitous aspect of the human condition, and if ultimate grounds of meaning are a functional requisite of any social order, then "religion," in Max Weber's sense of the term, must be regarded as a universal element in human society. Like Durkheim, Weber propounds the thesis of the universality of religion in a functional sense, if not also in the substantive sense indicated earlier.

Given Weber's failure to define terms and his tendency to intertwine functional and substantive usage of terms, it is extremely difficult, if not completely impossible, to determine the precise boundaries of his concept of religion. Hence, while it is apparent that all religion attempts to "deal rationally with the irrationalities of life," to define and make sense of reality, and to endow life with meaning, it is unclear whether Weber is prepared to pursue his implicit functional argument to its logical extremity by regarding any effort to perform these "tasks" as religious, whatever its substantive character.[151] Certainly, a radical-functionalist interpretation of Weber inevitably points in this inclusivist direction, as does much of the mainstream structural-functional literature. On the other hand, the reluctance of many sociologists to go the whole way with an undiluted functional analysis, and their resorting to the face-saving formula of the "functional alternative," may equally derive justification from Weber's own ambivalence about definitions.[152]

An appreciation of Weber's implicit functional definition of religion helps elucidate the connection that has already been noted between religion and rationality. If religion indeed represents, for Weber, "Man's continuous effort to deal rationally with the irrationalities of life," then its perceived contribution to the broad, historical processes of rationalization of human life is hardly surprising. Luckmann's analysis makes this quite clear:

Religion contributes to the historical processes of rationalization of human life on different levels. The inherent predisposition to "rational" organization of individual conduct that is rooted in the requirements of survival in a natural environment is *generally* supported by religion inasmuch as *all* religion provides a socially stabilized interpretation of reality. All religions systematize solutions of everyday problems and critical situations in life; all religions interpret the world and make it meaningful to the individual by providing a stable framework of orientation for the unstructured "irrational" subjectivities of individual existence. All religions thus tend to "rationalize" individual biographies; they contribute more or less significantly to the cognitive integration and affective structuring of life and, thereby, to the calculability of conduct.[153]

Rationalization is thus conceived by Weber as a universal process in the history of mankind, and one that has its roots in "the ecological and anthropological conditions of life." It is a process, however, that "assumes varied forms in history and . . . differs significantly in its potency and consequences." Thus, while Weber "very definitely assigns to religion, this product of the irrational dimension of human existence, the paradoxical function to initiate and to reinforce the process of rationalization,"[154] he is well aware that, in specific social and historical contexts, particular religions have performed this function in widely differing ways.

In the West, as has been noted, the process of rationalization has involved, according to Weber, a historically unique line of development culminating in a modern social, economic and political order characterized above all by its rationality. This does not mean that he espouses any simplistic enlightenment, positivist or evolutionary anthropological notion that "the exercise of reason [has] significantly improved over the ages or that a scientific stage [has] succeeded inferior stages of mental development."[155] It means, rather, that in modern society may be discerned "the prevalence of a highly systematic, anonymous and calculable form of law . . . an economy guided by its own principles of calculability and means ends rationality," a "trend to an anonymous, calculable and bureaucratic system of political administration," and a reliance upon an objective science that dominates nature by rendering it "technically calculable."[156] The emergence of such a social order "consisting of interconnected yet relatively autonomous institutional sub-systems determined by functionally specific criteria of rational organization and action"[157] was, in Weber's view, clearly not the inevitable result of any evolutionary law or inescapable process of differentiation. On the contrary, it was a specific and unique outcome of a complex of factors and circumstances in which religious motives and religious legitimations played a central part, most strikingly but by no means exclusively in Puritan form:

According to Weber, the forms of rationality that characterize the various segments of the social structure of modern societies presupposed genetically a highly rationalized pattern of life; the rationality of modern capitalism, in particular, presupposed forms of conduct and of biographical discipline that derive, again according to Weber, from certain elements in the Protestant view of the world. But the roots of modern "rationality" he traced farther back, to constellations of structural and cultural elements in which religion again played an important role: to the *Entzauberung* of the world-view that was initiated by the single-minded prophets of Jahwist monotheism and continued and "compromised" by competing groups of priests engaged in everyday pastoral care for an urban, petit-bourgeois clientele.[158]

In this crucial line of historical development, therefore, rationalization has implied the progressive disenchantment, de-mystification or de-magification of the world, and religion has, in a sense, acted as its own grave digger.[159] In other circumstances, however, as Weber is at pains to emphasize, religion has contributed to the process of rationalization with very different consequences.

The necessary general connection between religion and rationalization, in Weber's conception of society and culture, is perhaps best expressed by Talcott Parsons:

Rationalization is the master conception through which cultures define their religious situations and through which the sociology of religion must understand such cultural definitions of the situation.[160]

In Parsons' view, rationalization involves, in the first instance, the "intellectual classification, specification and systematization of ideas," ideas that are generated, according to Weber, by "the teleological *meanings* of man's conceptions of himself and his place in the universe, conceptions which legitimize man's orientations in and to the world and which give *meaning* to man's various goals." These ideas imply "metaphysical and theological conceptions of cosmic and moral orders" and define man's position in relation to them.[161] But, while Weber perceives the process of rationalization as intellectual in its concern with existential (though non-empirical) ideas, he is also, according to Parsons, aware of its normative aspect. In seeking to discover the meaning of life, men are inevitably led to ask what constitutes "the good life" and thereby to lay the foundation for a normative order and system of sanctions that imposes demands upon them and controls their actions. Thus, any attempt to rationalize the problem of "the meaning of life" involves inquiry into the normative aspect of culture and entails change in the conception of right conduct:

. . . men's conception of the nature of . . . normative order is not a constant; rather there is a differentiated variety of possible normative orders, and even a single society's conceptions of normative order change in the course of history. Weber's primary concern is the exploration of these different possible natures and the directions these natures may take when attempting to answer by rationalizing the problems of the meaning of life.[162]

Finally, in Parsons' view, the Weberian process of rationalization involves a "motivation of commitment" both in terms of belief in the validity of ideas concerning life's meaning and in a practical willingness to "put one's own interests at stake" on behalf of these intellectual and normative ideas. Thus, by a fusion of theory and practice, this third aspect of rationalization makes possible "the systematization of a pattern or programme for life as a whole, which is given meaning by an existential conception of the universe, and within it the human condition in which this action is to be carried out."[163]

If, therefore (as may be argued), the process of rationalization represents the unifying theme of Max Weber's sociological enterprise,[164] the study of religion is its most central concern. Recognizing the "central function of religion in the task of living," Weber perceives religion as belonging at "the very heart of a culture" and as operating "where the culture is most alive, where it is lived."[165] He offers, then, in Steeman's view:

> . . . an approach . . . that views religion at the same time as a fundamental fact of human existence, as the central feature of a culture, and as the prime moving force in social evolution.[166]

If rationality is "always related to man's ability to take account of his situation, to stand over against himself and nature and to order his own life," religion surely comprises the broadest attempt to achieve these ends.[167] Thus, in a Weberian context, the symbiotic connection between the process of rationalization and the primary function of religion is readily apparent, not least in its decidedly ambiguous aspect. Related to the fact of "living as a continuous enterprise . . . to the necessities of life, to the economy and the established order," rationality possesses, at the same time, "the power to transcend this level of immediate involvement" in the day-to-day tasks of living, and the ability to "engage in the quest for meaning and in the formulation of life's ends."[168] In a similar manner, religion is heavily concerned with the basic needs and routines of mundane existence while offering the opportunity of transcending them in the search for meaning and the good life. Despite the disenchanted character of the line of development he discerns in Western civilization, it seems clear that Weber by no means universally identifies the general process of rationalization with the specific process of secularization.[169] It is equally apparent that while the "organizing, regulating, preserving function" of rationality may be best perceived in religious contexts, the impetus that rationalization exerts toward a break with the established social and cultural order is also manifested primarily in religious form.[170]

Rooted in the individual human being's ability "to take account of his situation, to stand over against himself and nature and to order his own life," the fundamental concern with the "task of living" exhibited by religion has, for Weber, a decidedly dual aspect.[171] Thus, while religion may, in his view, be the means by which human beings adjust to their natural, social, economic, political and intellectual environments, it may also, *a fortiori,* be the means by which these are transcended or changed. Weber's chief interest, it may be noted, is primarily in this latter aspect.

Weber's sociology of religion is therefore characterized by tension, not only because the strategy of *verstehen* necessarily puts the sociological observer in "a curious position of suspense between a universal skepticism and an equally universal acceptance of thought-worlds other than his own,"[172] but because it acknowledges the dynamic as well as the static potential of religion, discerning its role in social change and conflict as well as in social consensus and cohesion. This tense ambivalence is, not surprisingly, expressed unambiguously in those dichotomous and dialectically opposed categories Weber generates in his attempt to grapple intellectually with the complexity and flux of religious reality. Thus, in such distinctions as those that oppose magic to religion, church to sect, priest to prophet and routine to charisma may be perceived the contrast between religion that adapts man to the world, "making tolerable by law and ritual the disorder of experience," and religion that repudiates the world in adventurous pursuit of a "transcendent other-worldly goal," shaking as it does so the very foundations of society.[173]

The part played by religion in the preservation of the status quo, particularly in the context of "traditional" societies, has already been noted in the earlier discussion of the Protestant Ethic thesis. Thus, while the general importance of religion in the legitimation or sanctification of social orders is a fundamental assumption of Weber's analysis of power and authority,[174] the specific role of religion in resisting or preventing the genesis of modern, rational capitalistic enterprise outside Western Europe is a crucial element in his grand historical and comparative attempt to "experimentally" assess the economic impact of ascetic Calvinist ideas.

A consciously "one-sided"[175] attempt to illustrate briefly the manner in which religion acts as a means of "adapting" human beings to their social environments must recall that, for Weber, the primary function of religion is the provision of "meaning" in both an intellectual and emotional sense. If religion is always the outcome of an attempt to live meaningfully, it involves, in his view, a fusion of ideas, ideals and interests, which gives it both a cognitive and cathectic character. From this point of view, therefore, the adjustment of human beings to given social structures, and the stability and persistence of such social arrangements, depend upon satisfactory societal solutions to the problem of meaning. Expressed more concretely, this means that sanctification or legitimation of a specific social order is accomplished and reinforced by an appropriate range of religious beliefs and practices, which enable the members of a society to come to terms with "the world."

In distinguishing between magic and religion proper, Weber seems to perceive the former as essentially adaptive in nature, due to its relatively *ad hoc* aims and its character as a "complex of heterogeneous prescriptions and prohibitions derived from the most diverse motives and occasions."[176] Claiming the ability to compel "demons" or magical forces to fulfil the human needs of his client, the magician invokes a normative order based upon "taboo," the prescription and prohibition of various specified activities. Thus, magic serves as a means of individual adjustment to an existing social structure and may be regarded as unconducive to social change.

This does not imply that religion may not be equally effective in maintaining a specific status quo through a normative order based on religious ethics rather than taboo, through gods rather than demons and through priests rather than sorcerers. For, as Weber admirably demonstrates, the worship and propitiation of divinities and the formulation of a generalized, systematic and universalistic ideal pattern of action is entirely consistent with extreme stability and inertia. In his view, the "most elementary" actions motivated by religion or magic are oriented to this world, and the reason for their performance is aptly expressed by the Biblical aspiration that "it may go well with thee . . . and that thou mayest prolong thy days upon the earth."[177] Moreover, the "pervasive and central theme" of such actions is summed up in the Latin *do ut des*, a general orientation that, as Weber observes, "clings to the routine and the mass religious behaviour of all peoples at all times and in all religions."[178]

> The normal situation is that the burden of all prayers, even in the most other worldly religions, is the aversion of the external evils of the world and the inducement of the external advantages of this world.[179]

Thus, perceiving religion as a universal social phenomenon, Weber sees its primary focus on "mundane, worldly concerns: health, long life, defeat of enemies, good relations with one's own people, and the like"[180] as by no means restricted to primitive societies. Indeed, as Parsons has commented, "Weber's insistence that the conception of a supernatural order does not imply any 'transcendental' goals or focus of interest for man" is particularly important.[181]

Like magic, religion is a means of resolving the tensions and strains of every-day life, but its essential function - of rendering rational the irrationalities of life through the provision of meaning - precludes that *ad hoc* orientation that is a defining characteristic of magical intercourse with the supernatural. Unlike magic, therefore, religion is potentially capable of transcending the mundane gains and losses of practical life through a cumulative rational systematization of ideas concerning the supernatural and on the basis of a progressive preoccupation with other-worldly goals. Thus, Weber perceives an inherent tendency of religious ideas toward incorporation into successively more integrated systems, and in this regard the role of a priesthood is crucial. Indeed, Weber states bluntly that the "full development" of a religious ethic and "metaphysical rationalization" requires "an independent and professionally trained priesthood, permanently occupied with the cult and with the practical problems involved in the cure of souls."[182]

If the "relationships of men to supernatural forces which take the forms of prayer, sacrifice and worship may be termed 'cult' and 'religion', as distinguished from 'sorcery'," then, in Weber's view, the "sociological aspect of this differentiation is the rise of the 'priesthood' as something distinct from 'practitioners of magic'."[183] Thus, although empirically this "contrast is fluid" as magical coercion shades into, and combines with, religious propitiation, in ideal-typical terms the intent of the distinction between priests and magicians is clear. If magicians are self-employed practitioners diverting their "individual and occasional efforts" to the coercion of supernatural entities, priests are, by contrast, organization men, "the functionaries of a regularly organized and permanent enterprise concerned with influencing the gods."[184] While there can be a cult without priests, there can be no priesthood without a cult, and it is within this group context that priests are disciplined and trained to preserve and impart a particular doctrinal revelation. It need not be stressed that the rational and systematic character of priestly, specialized knowledge concerning religious concepts and ethics stands in stark contrast to the individual, idiosyncratic and personal inspiration and revelation of the magician.

According to Weber, the sustained effort to provide more adequate solutions to the problem of meaning is the dynamic of religious evolution. Especially as it involves the existence of a class or stratum of priests, therefore, religion is concerned not merely with resolving those day-to-day problems that are also handled by magic, but with answering the larger or ultimate questions of suffering and evil, life and death through the development of an appropriate theodicy. Hence, to understand religion's role in the maintenance of social integration and stability, its efficacy in providing solutions to questions of both mundane and ultimate significance must be evaluated. Within this functional framework, it is also necessary to assess the role of any social groups that might be considered to hold a vested interest in perpetuation of the status quo.

Weber's clearest and most convincing portraits of religions that have adapted human beings to the world are to be found in his discussions of Confucianism and Hinduism.[185] The manner in which they facilitate such adjustment, thereby maintaining the existing social order, may be briefly noted. As Weber suggests, the toleration and, indeed, informal encouragement of magic was an important means by which Chinese Confucian officials maintained their power over their countrymen, accordingly perpetuating the status quo. More generally, though, the impact of Confucian religion in preserving the existing state of things was rooted in its fundamentally benign attitude to the world and humankind. Thus, accepting the world and man as inherently good, Confucianism emphasized their compatability, a state of affairs well summarized by Bendix:

> By adjusting to the requirements of the social order the Confucian man adjusted to the cosmic harmony of heaven and earth. His cardinal virtue was to fulfill the traditional obligations of family and office, to observe the proper ceremonies in all circumstances of life.[186]

In Weber's view, Confucianism was "a rational ethic which reduced tension with the world to an absolute minimum," which saw this world as "the best of all possible worlds" and which regarded human nature as "disposed to the ethically good."[187] As a religion that perceived insufficient education, government mismanagement and economic scarcity as the primary causes of human misery and the main means of disturbing and offending (magically conceived) spirits, Confucianism advocated a simple and practical rule of life:

> The right path to salvation consisted in adjustment to the eternal and supra-divine orders of the world . . . and hence to the requirements of social life, which followed from cosmic harmony. Pious conformism with the fixed order of secular powers reigned supreme. The corresponding individual ideal was the elaboration of the self as a universal and harmoniously balanced personality, in this sense a microcosm. For the Confucian ideal man, the gentleman, "grace and dignity" were expressed in fulfilling traditional obligations. Hence the cardinal virtue and goal in self-perfection meant ceremonial and ritualist propriety in all circumstances of life. The appropriate means to this goal were watchful and rational self-control and the repression of whatever irrational passions might cause poise to be shaken.[188]

Consisting of "lack of respect for traditional authorities and breaches of ceremonial and convention," evil was curable by re-education. Accordingly, as Bendix expresses them, the goals of the righteous man were "health, a comfortable income, a long life, and a good name after death – clearly ends of this world, not of the next."[189]

The extent to which Confucianism constituted a means of human adaptation to the world is most eloquently underlined by Weber's comparison of this religion with Puritanism. Examined in the light of that "tremendous and grandiose tension" that may be discerned in the Puritan attitude to the world, the character of Confucianism as a means of minimizing tension is most clearly visible.[190] Puritanism dynamically transformed a civilization by assuming "the absolute unholiness of tradition," and by taking upon itself the "truly endless task of ethically and rationally subduing and mastering the given world." This reminder throws into strong relief the Confucian emphasis on "the inviolability of tradition" and the perpetuation of "all bequeathed forms of life-conduct."[191]

Weber's analysis of Hinduism provides another case study of a religion that was engaged in adapting its adherents to the world rather than in attempting to change it. Here, as in his investigation of Chinese religion, Weber is conscious that, for the broad masses of the population, the systematic development of doctrine and the formulation of a rational theory of salvation were remote concerns. Exhibiting merely a "crude and this-worldly holy interest," they remained steeped in magic, albeit within the general framework of Hinduism.[192] Nonetheless, the religious ideas formulated by a priestly and administrative elite are crucial to an understanding of the traditional and unchanging character of Indian society. The interpenetration and integration of Hindu doctrine and the caste system of social stratification provides a classic case of the mutual support of culture and social structure in the interest of societal equilibrium. The caste system is legitimated, reinforced and reproduced by hegemonic religious doctrine while, in a practical sense, such doctrine is coherent and meaningful only within the rigid confines of the caste hierarchy. There is thus an appropriate circularity in the relations between Hindu ideas and Indian social structure.

As a sharply graded hierarchy that precludes individual social mobility, the caste system effectively maintains the status quo and successfully resists social change. It does so because, despite its flagrant inequities, it is accepted and upheld from within as being the best of all possible social worlds. Commitment to this stratification system throughout its main castes and myriad subcastes is, therefore, highly dependent upon the powerful and all-embracing ideological rationale supplied by Hindu religious doctrine.

On the basis of its central belief in the transmigration of souls and reincarnation, Hinduism preaches an attitude of passive acceptance of the world that is in stark contrast to the inner-worldly ascetism of Puritanism as Weber depicts it. The indifference to the world in the midst of mundane activity demanded by Hinduism is fundamentally at odds with any efforts to alter social circumstances, but thoroughly consistent with the logic of Hindu theology, especially its concepts of *samsara* ("transmigration") and *karma* ("compensation" or "retribution"). As Weber emphasizes:

> These alone are the truly "dogmatic" doctrines of all Hinduism, and in their very interrelatedness they represent the unique Hindu theodicy of the existing social, that is to say, caste system.[193]

In the Hindu view, death is the occasion for the reincarnation of an individual soul in a new existence, one that will appropriately reward or punish the conduct of the previous life. Weber suggests that belief in the transmigration of souls "grew directly out of universally diffused representations of the fate of the spirit after death."[194] The departed soul was not perceived as immortal, and the Brahmins eventually formulated the idea of another death "leading the dying spirit or god into another existence."[195]

Observing that the "connecting of the doctrine of transmigration of souls with that of compensation for good and evil deeds in the form of a more or less honourable rebirth" is not exclusive to India, Weber stresses that nowhere else was it systematized to the same degree:

. . . two principles are characteristic of Brahmin rationalism which determined the pervasive significance of the doctrinal turn (1) it was believed that each single ethically relevant act has inevitable consequences for the fate of the actor, hence that no consequence can be lost. (2) the idea of compensation was linked to the individual's social fate in the societal organization and thereby to the caste order. All (ritual or ethical) merits and faults of the individual formed a sort of ledger of accounts; the balance irrefutably determined the fate of the soul at rebirth, and this in exact proportion to the surplus of one or other side of the ledger.[196]

This theodicy provides both a justification for things as they are and a good reason for individuals to wish to leave them unchanged. The present state of things is the inevitable consequence of things as they were before. The place of an individual within the caste system is the direct result of his activities in previous incarnations:

The very caste situation of the individual is not accidental. In India the idea of the "accident of birth" so critical of society is almost completely absent. The Indian views the individual as born into the caste merited by conduct in a prior life. The individual Hindu is actually believed to have used or failed to use "foresight" in the choice of his caste, though not of his "parents" as the German joke has it. An orthodox Hindu confronted with the deplorable situation of a member of an impure caste would only think that he has a great many sins to redeem from his prior existence.[197]

In the caste system, individual social mobility occurs only through reincarnation; thus anyone seeking to retain or improve his position can do so only by living a good life in his present incarnation. But what is the "good life" in the context of Hinduism? Essentially, it involves making the most of one's circumstances. Righteousness consists in the conscientious performance of the ritual duties (*dharma*) of one's own caste, while evil consists in their neglect. The means of "salvation," then, are simple, practical and ritualistic; they also entirely rule out any attempt to change one's social position or to alter the social order that assigns statuses. Life must be endured, whatever one's position in the caste hierarchy, and it must be lived in the hope of better things to come. The world is unalterable. But by doing one's duty, one can attain a better position in it in the lives to come:

Karma doctrine transformed the world into a strictly rational ethically determined cosmos; it represents the most consistent theodicy ever produced by history. The devout Hindu was accursed to remain in a structure which made sense only in this intellectual context; its consequences burdened his conduct. The *Communist Manifesto* concludes with the phrase "they [the proletariat] have nothing to lose but their chains, they have a world to win." The same holds for the pious Hindu of low castes. He too can "win the world," even the heavenly world; he can become a Kashtriya, a Brahmin, he can gain Heaven and become a god - only not in his life, but in the life of the future after rebirth into the same world pattern.[198]

It is not difficult to appreciate that the inertia of Indian society, "this well-integrated, unique social system" as Weber calls it, is the product of the inextricable "combination of caste legitimacy with *karma* doctrine" that links social structure to Brahmin theodicy in "a stroke of genius."[199]

> Only the wedding of this thought product with the empirical social order through the promise of rebirth gave this order the irresistible power over thought and hope of members and furnished the fixed scheme for the religious and social integration of the various professional groups and pariah peoples.[200]

This holy alliance of caste system and *karma* doctrine locates the individual "within a clear circle of duties," offering him a well-rounded, metaphysically satisfying conception of the world.[201] Moreover, it offers a worldview that is intellectually and emotionally satisfying to those whose present circumstances might otherwise lead them to overthrow the prevailing system. The efficacy of Brahmin theodicy in the "domestication" of the lower orders cannot be underestimated:

> It is difficult to imagine more traditionalistic ideas of professional virtues than those of Hinduism. Estranged castes might stand beside one another with bitter hatred – for the idea that everybody had "deserved" his own fate, did not make the good fortune of the privileged more enjoyable to the underprivileged.[202]

However, so long as the doctrine of *karma* remained unshaken and continued to receive the assent of the masses, "revolutionary ideas or progressivism were inconceivable:"[203]

> The lowest castes, furthermore, had the most to win through ritual correctness and were least tempted to innovations. Hinduism's particularly strong traditionalism finds its explanation also in the great promises which indeed were at stake for the lowly caste whenever the members deviated from their caste.[204]

Knowing one's place and accepting it is thus the Hindu first rule of life, an orientation singularly undisposed to disturbing the universe or rocking the boat. Imprisoned in a virtually endless cycle of birth, death and rebirth, the devout Hindu represses any sacrilegious yearning to belong to another caste and immerses himself in the strict fulfilment of his caste obligations:

> Order and rank of the castes is eternal (according to doctrine) as the course of the stars and the difference between animal species and the human race. To overthrow them would be senseless. Rebirth can drag man down into the life of a "worm in the intestine of a dog", but, according to his conduct, it might raise and place him into the womb of a queen.[205]

No urgently felt desire for social change can emerge in such a context because there is no logical sense in it. In traditional Indian society, therefore, religion suppresses potential dissent and discourages social disequilibrium by a theodicy that utilizes a system of transcendental reward and punishment to induce commitment to the world as it is, rather than as it might be.

From a Durkheimian perspective, Hinduism provides a classic case of religion functioning, through its beliefs and rituals, to ensure the integration and stability of a specific society. In Marxian terms, however, the Hindu theodicy represents a prime example of an ideology formulated in the interests of a ruling elite and propagated among the wretched masses as a soporific. In relieving their pain by explaining and justifying it theologically, religion supplies them with fantastic compensatory delusions concerning their anticipated future lives. Inhaling such potent ideological opium, these unfortunates inevitably experience the pipe-dream of an utterly false consciousness in their commitment to Hindu beliefs and their loyalty to a social order that so blatantly exploits them.

It is worth commenting that either perspective, Durkheimian or Marxist, may be adopted without seriously undermining or challenging the main features of Weber's analysis of the role of Hindu religion in maintaining the Indian status quo and discountenancing even minor efforts at social change.

It has already been noted that "Weber's primary interest is in religion as a source of the dynamics of social change, not religion as a reinforcement of the stability of societies."[206] Nonetheless, an understanding of the ways in which religion contributes to the maintenance of social stability and participates in the prevention of social change is useful in exploring Weber's treatment of the "other side" of religion's relations with the social order.[207] Weber's discussions of Confucianism and Hinduism suggest that religion helps maintain the status quo by satisfying the cognitive and cathectic needs of members of a society. Religion is thus perceived as ensuring that the world is given meaning, and that suffering and evil are endured as natural, inevitable and just, whenever they cannot be overcome by crude and simple magic. Yet, more specifically, Weber's analysis also indicates the importance of religious sacralization or legitimation of an existing political order and system of social stratification. In this context, the vested interests of privileged status groups, the "domestication" of the relatively deprived or dispossessed, and the existence of any formally organized priesthood are all important issues for investigation. Thus, the failure of institutionalized religion to provide satisfactory solutions to ultimate human problems, its consequent inability to legitimate existing social structures, and its painful and provocative irrelevance for certain status groups are all matters of importance in Weber's exploration of the processes of social change.

Weber's primary concern with "the problem of religion as a force for dynamic social change"[208] is, as Parsons notes, best conceived as an attempt to grapple with a series of problems:

> Under what cultural definitions of the religious situation can processes of change and breakthrough take place? Through what agencies and forms of organizations can processes of change and breakthrough take place? In what situations are breakthroughs most probable?[209]

By combining the earlier discussion of rationalization with those insights gained from the appreciation of religion as a conservative force, it is possible to discern Weber's basic perspective on the connection between religion and social change. As noted earlier, rationality is concerned with "living as a continuous enterprise, and consequently [with] the necessities of life . . . the economy and . . . the established order," but it also has "the power to transcend this level of immediate involvement in the task of living" and the capacity to "engage in the quest for meaning, and in the formulation of life's ends."[210] Thus, if the general evolutionary drift of human society is in the direction of increasing rationality, the evolution of religion represents

> the story of how man ever rises again out of his involvement in the immediate necessities and habits of life, takes distance from life, returns to it with an evermore systematic interpretation of it, and attempts to implement what in moments of detachment and value apprehension he has seen as giving meaning to it.[211]

In this way, both religion and rationalization are rooted in an aspect of the problem of meaning that is especially crucial in Weber's conception of social change: the potential contrast between what is and what ought to be. In contemplating the "integrations and discrepancies between expectation systems [that] are institutionalized in normative orders and the actual experiences people undergo," Weber confronts the distinction between the world as it exists and the world as specific individuals or groups would like it to be.[212] In his view, no social order succeeds perfectly in satisfying all the needs of its members, although the tension between ideal and actual may be resolved in some contexts more easily than others. Thus, as suggested by the discussion of the distinction between magic and religion, circumstances characterized by a low level of rationalization are most conducive to "a piecemeal resolution of the tensions [that] arise from discrepancies between normative expectations and actual experiences:"[213]

> Weber takes the fundamental position that, regardless of the particular content of the normative order, a major element of discrepancy is inevitable. And the more highly rationalized an order, the greater the tension, the greater the exposure of major elements of a population to experiences [that] are frustrating in the very specific sense, not merely that things happen and contravene their "interests", but that things happen [that] are "meaningless" in the sense that they ought not to happen.[214]

In this context, tension is produced not by the mere existence of suffering and evil, but by the manner in which they are experienced. Discrepancies are perceived "when bad things happen to good people" and, as Parsons reminds us, human beings have perennially agonized over the question of why "the good die young and the wicked flourish as the green bay tree."[215]

Weber regards the human mind as "driven to reflect on ethical and religious questions," and he detects its "inner compulsion to understand the world as a meaningful cosmos and to take up a position toward it."[216] Postulating an innate human drive for meaning that involves a constant "metaphysical" need to resolve discrepancies, Weber views the problem of meaning as entailing progressively more comprehensive and abstracted attempts at solution.[217] Such proposed explanations, it should be stressed, are of the normative and motivational as well as the intellectual kind.[218] This evolutionary road of increasingly generalized explanation has forked, in his view, in two directions, the one leading to a static and passive view of the world and the other providing the path to a singularly dynamic and active world-view. Historically, the rationalization of religious ideas has culminated in the great theodicies, or fully consistent philosophies of moral meaning.[219] In one line of evolution, rooted in an immanent conception of the deity, the doctrine of *karma* emerges and effectively adapts human beings to the world. The other process of development, which assumes God's transcendence, achieves its ultimate logical expression in the Puritan doctrine of predestination, which, whatever its "dour bleakness," compelled men to mastery over the world.[220]

In Weber's view, an innate drive for meaning appears both to provoke dissatisfaction with the world and to be itself continuously reactivated by such dissatisfaction. In those unable or unwilling to come to terms with the world, there emerges a need for a personal, radical solution to the problem of meaning, which Weber terms the need for salvation, and which Parsons describes as

> the need for a basis of personal legitimation which is in accord with . . . ultimate standards, themselves conceived as standing in essential conflict with those of any institutionalized worldly order.[221]

Those "religions of salvation" generated by this need "have stored in them revolutionary and unpredictable potential," as Donald MacRae remarks:

> Invariably the relation between salvation religions and their social structures is one of tension, and where salvation is mediated by a redeemer then the tension is maximized; men desert their primordial bonds of kin and place, they question the economic order . . . and they call in doubt the political hierarchy because it is a hierarchy and a denial of the brotherhood of the saved in which there are neither bond nor free."[222]

The notion of salvation makes sense for Weber only in terms of a particular conception of "the world." It implies an attitude toward worldly things that characterizes them as inferior to supernatural ends at best, and the object of contempt, detestation or horror at worst. The tension between the quest for perfection and the constraint of the world is by no means always maximized, and the events sketched by MacRae do not inevitably occur. Thus, in his discussion of "an immense range of different modes and levels of conception of the problem of salvation," Weber attempts to trace "the balance between degrees of radicalism in the conception of the problem of salvation and the various devices by which radical implications can be mitigated."[223] Before he can do so, however, it is necessary for Weber to examine those fundamental reactions to the world that are exhibited by seekers of salvation. Accordingly, he discerns two basic answers to the problem of salvation:

These two generalized solutions are . . . resolution of tension by escape from the conflicts of worldly existence, and resolution by active agency attempting to bring the state of the "world" in this sense into accord with the normative requirements of a radical religious ethic.[224]

The need for salvation thus engenders, in the individual, either an attitude of resignation regarding the world or a compulsion to master it. The former orientation by which an adjustment to the world is effected is termed "mysticism." The latter strategy, which involves an attempt to control or alter conditions imposed by the world, is called "asceticism" by Weber. It is worth noting here that human collectivities as well as individuals may be regarded as predominantly mystical or ascetic in their conceptions of the world. For the seeker after salvation, a crucial decision involves remaining in the world or leaving it, in the sense of either tolerating or rejecting the established social, political, economic and cultural orders. Reviewing this dilemma as posing a choice between "inner-worldliness" and "other-worldliness," Weber regards both its options as open equally to the ascetic and the mystic. Thus, both mysticism and asceticism may take either an inner-worldly or other-worldly form.

In Weber's view the "distinctive content" of salvation is extremely varied. It may mean "freedom from the physical, psychological and social sufferings of terrestrial life" or its concern may be "liberation from the senseless treadmill and transitoriness of life as such:"[225]

Finally, it may be focussed primarily on the inevitable imperfection of the individual, whether this be regarded more as chronic contamination, acute inclination to sin, or more spiritually, as entanglement in the murky confusion of earthly ignorance.[226]

Whatever its particular form, however, Weber is interested in the desire for salvation "insofar as it [has] produced certain consequences for practical behaviour in the world."[227] From this point of view, he believes that "hope of salvation" may have the most decisive effect on the conduct of ordinary life when "salvation itself takes the form of a process that already casts a shadow before it in this life."[228] According to Weber, the search for salvation is most likely to have an impact upon mundane affairs when associated with "a pattern of life which is distinctively determined by religion and given coherence by some central meaning or positive goal."[229] More specifically, this insight is expressed in terms of the process of rationalization:

> . . . a quest for salvation in any religious group has the strongest chance of exerting practical influences when there has arisen, out of religious motivations, a systematization of practical conduct resulting from an orientation to certain integral values.[230]

Such religious systematization, Weber observes, has occurred "in exceedingly diverse fashions and in different degrees" even within a specific religion.[231]

Consideration of the four types of religious orientations he is able to derive from his two fundamental dichotomies suggests that the "innerworldly ascetic" combination is of the most profound importance in Weber's work, given his emphasis on the analysis of social change:

> Weber's primary concern is with the basis on which religious orientations can exert leverage toward evolutionary social change. . . . It is his clear view that only one of the four types does in fact provide powerful leverage, but that it is in the long run a more powerful factor than any elements of economic or political interest in the usual senses.[232]

By contrast, both other-worldly mysticism and other-worldly asceticism involve retreat from the world. The other-worldly mystic is obsessed with eliminating the desire for earthly things, while the other-worldly ascetic seeks the control that comes from victory over the flesh. The inner-worldly mystic, for his part, is in the world but not of it. Participating in a dance of shadows, his eyes are turned constantly to the light that casts them; he tolerates the world but is indifferent to its fate. From his perspective, the challenge of "mastering" the world is the ultimate absurdity.

If the purest other-worldly mysticism is realized in early Buddhism, inner-worldly ascetism finds its truest embodiment in ascetic Protestantism, a form of religion whose unique impact upon the world provides the theme of Weber's best-known argument. According to Weber, and as described in some detail above, Puritanism derives its powerful presence in the world from the theological doctrine of predestination. Although this belief "might logically be expected" to have resulted in a form of fatalism, it produced, in fact, "in its most consistent followers the strongest possible motives for acting in accordance with God's pattern."[233] Affecting the fate of the individual in the world beyond, it entailed, paradoxically, that "assurance of salvation was determined primarily by . . . maintenance of ethical integrity in the affairs of every-day life."[234] This belief generated followers who derived evidence of their salvation from mundane sources, and for whom the only significant human distinction was between the saved and the damned. The belief in predestination, as it evolved within Puritanism, necessarily posed a potential challenge to the existing order. As Weber notes:

> It is significant that the Puritan belief in predestination was regarded by authorities everywhere as dangerous to the state and as hostile to authority, because it made Puritans skeptical of the legitimacy of all secular power.[235]

More specifically, the Puritan belief in predestination was "an instrument for the greatest possible systematization and centralization of an ethic based on an inner religious mood and oriented to ultimate ends." As such, this doctrine of salvation made a crucial contribution to the "rationalized capitalistic temperment" by the "idea of the methodical demonstration of vocation in one's economic behaviour."[236] Thus, contends Weber, in a well-known though variously interpreted argument:

> The inner-worldly ascetism of Protestantism first produced a capitalistic state, although unintentionally, for it opened the way to a career in business, especially for the most devout and ethically rigorous people. Above all, Protestantism interpreted success in business as the fruit of a rational mode of life.[237]

In no other religion, observes Weber, was "the pride of the predestined aristocracy of salvation as closely associated with the man of vocation" and with the notion that "success in rationalized activity demonstrates God's blessing."[238] In no other religion, in short, was the "influence of ascetic motivation upon the attitude toward economic activity" so powerful.[239] It may also be added that the inherently favourable orientation of ascetism towards what Parsons calls "firm collectivity formation" was of some significance in determining the impact of Puritanism upon the world.[240] If asceticism in general is favourable to the development of the *Gemeinde,* or religious community, and if Christian other-worldly asceticism is associated with the growth of monasticism, the rise of ascetism in its inner-worldly form may be linked to the phenomenon of the sect. Thus, Weber emphasizes the role of the sect as an organizational weapon in the attempt of ascetic Protestantism to achieve mastery over the world.[241]

Dissatisfaction with the world, an inadequate sense of meaning and the need for salvation are experienced by individuals, but are by no means experienced in isolation. Weber's discussion of the links between specific religious ideas and the social circumstances of particular classes and status groups is therefore of the greatest importance to his sociology of religion as a whole. In analyzing the religious characteristics of various castes, estates and classes with his usual encyclopaedic comparative and historical flair, Weber's primary aim is to assess and understand the role of religion in evolutionary and even revolutionary social change. Intrigued with the part religion plays in the process of breakthrough to a more systematized and rationalized cultural order, he is necessarily concerned with tensions and disparities manifested in particular institutionalized orders. As Parsons expresses it, Weber is interested in the varieties and types of "soil" in which religious groups that threaten a break with the status quo may or may not be expected to grow.[242] Using Weber's own terminology, it might be suggested that his interest lies in discerning which groups, and under what conditions, are more or less likely to emerge as "carriers" of innovative religious and ethical movements. His concern is, therefore, to identify those social groups that have acted as agents of rationalization and breakthrough.

Examining first those groups least likely to respond to the stimulus of a religious movement calling for a break with the established order, Weber deals with social strata having what Parsons calls the lowest "propensity to alienation."[243] His initial concern is thus with groups that believe, rightly or wrongly, that their interests are inextricably tied up with the maintenance of things as they are, groups that fear things as they might be. With immense erudition, Weber devotes special attention, within this category, to the circumstances of the peasantry, feudal nobility, plutocrats and bureaucrats.[244] Distinguishing between those "sated" or privileged groups that are genuinely and deeply involved in the established order, and those strata whose societal commitment derives merely from prolonged immersion in custom and tradition, he emphasizes that in both cases the self-respect of the individual member is heavily invested in an identification with the status quo. In each kind of group, therefore, there exists a conservative vested interest in making the existing system work, and in ensuring its stability and persistence.

Turning from those social strata that exhibit a minimum of "alienation" and a maximum of resistance to religious calls for change, Weber proceeds to examine those groupings that do experience alienation, and whose members are thereby potentially available for mobilization in religious movements of reform. He explores in considerable detail the "specific importance of salvation religion for politically and economically disprivileged social groups."[245]

Noting, of privileged strata, that their "sense of self-esteem rests on their awareness that the perfection of their life pattern is an expression of their underived, ultimate, and qualitatively distinctive being," Weber offers his opinion that what the privileged classes require of religion, if anything at all, is the "psychological reassurance of legitimacy."[246] By contrast, the "sense of honour" of disprivileged classes "rests on some concealed promise for the future which implies the assignment of some function, mission or vocation to them:"[247]

> What they cannot claim to *be,* they replace by the worth of that which they will one day *become,* to which they will be called in some future life here or hereafter; or replace, very often concomitantly with the motivation just discussed, by their sense of what they signify and achieve in the world as seen from the point of view of providence. Their hunger for a worthiness that has not fallen to their lot, they and the world being what it is, produces this conception from which is derived the rationalistic idea of a providence, a significance in the eyes of some divine authority possessing a scale of values different from the one operating in the world of man.[248]

Since, in Weber's view, "every need for salvation is an expression of social distress," it is hardly surprising that, other things being equal, "classes with high social and economic privilege" have little use for the idea of salvation.[249] The situation of the disprivileged, however, is quite different.

According to Weber, their particular need is for "release from suffering," though they "do not always experience this need for salvation in a religious form."[250] Where it is manifested, their religious need for salvation assumes "diverse forms" and may be accompanied by "a need for just compensation envisaged in various ways but always involving reward for one's own good deeds and punishment for the unrighteousness of others."[251] Next to magic, this "hope for and expectation of just compensation" is, in Weber's estimate, "the most widely diffused form of mass religion all over the world."[252]

Weber is clearly well aware both that relatively underprivileged strata are by no means universally "available" for religious mobilization, and that salvation religion is far from constituting their monopoly. Nonetheless, while duly emphasizing the notorious conservatism of the peasantry and the equally noteworthy secularism of the modern urban proletariat, he does not hesitate to suggest that "social or economic oppression is an effective source of salvation beliefs, though by no means the exclusive source."[253] Noting that early Christianity was, from its beginnings, a religion of artisans, Weber considers the religious character of these "lower middle classes." Insisting that "uniform determinism of religion by economic forces" has never existed among artisans, he does discern among them, however, "in contrast to the peasantry, a definite tendency towards congregational religion, towards religious salvation, and finally towards rational ethical religion."[254] In Weber's opinion, it is the town rather than the countryside that is the breeding ground of salvation religion, though this is not necessarily the result of the distinctive economic patterns of urban life.[255] Thus, it is not surprising that early Christianity was profoundly urban in character and that, for its adherents, the terms "heathen" (*paganus*) and "rustic" converged. To Weber, the "religious glorification of the peasant and the belief in the special worth of his piety" appears as a relatively modern development, for in earlier times it was the city that was "regarded as the site of piety:"[256]

When one compares the life of a lower-middle-class person, particularly the urban artisan or the small trader, with the life of the peasant, it is clear that middle-class life has far less connection with nature. Consequently, dependence on magic for influencing the irrational forces of nature cannot play the same role for the urban dweller as for the farmer.[257]

According to Weber, such a state of affairs has important consequences:

. . . it is clear that the economic foundation of the urban man's life has a far more rational essential character, viz., calculability and capacity for purposive manipulation. Furthermore, the artisan and in certain circumstances even the merchant lead economic existences which influence them to entertain the view that honesty is the best policy, that faithful work and the performance of obligations will find their reward and are "deserving" of their just compensation.[258]

For these reasons, argues Weber, artisans and small traders are disposed to accept "a rational world view incorporating an ethic of compensation."[259] As noted earlier, he sees this as "the normal trend of thinking among all non-privileged classes" other than the magically inclined peasantry.[260]

Weber thus perceives a close link between the development of urban centres of craftsmanship and the process of religious rationalization:

> . . . whenever [a] magical frame of reference has once been broken through (this happens most readily in newly settled cities), the effect of the transformation may be that the artisan will learn to think about his labour and the small trader will learn to think about his enterprise much more rationally than any peasant thinks. The craftsman in particular will have time and opportunity for reflection during his work. . . . Consequently, the workers in occupations which are primarily of the indoor variety, e.g., in textile mills in our climate, are strongly infused with sectarian or religious trends.[261]

Hence, where magic no longer prevails, the tendency of "artisans, craftsmen and middle-class people" has been to "incline toward a rather primitively rationalistic, ethical and religious view of life," an inclination reinforced by "their very occupational specialization," which "makes them the bearers of an integrated pattern of life of a distinctive kind."[262]

At a slightly lower social level, handicraft apprentices have, in Weber's view, "at all times tended to share the characteristic religion of the lower middle classes."[263] Indeed, "in view of their workaday struggles with everyday needs, the fluctuations in the price of their daily bread, their quest for jobs, and their dependence on fraternal assistance," they have demonstrated a "conspicuous inclination toward various forms of unofficial religion of the sect type, which found particularly fertile soil among the lower occupational strata of the city."[264] Well represented in those "numerous secret or half-tolerated communities of 'poor folk' that espoused congregational religions which were by turn revolutionary, pacifistic-communistic and ethical-rational," wandering craft apprentices, freed of the constraints of the traditional fixed community, constitute, in Weber's opinion, "the available missionaries of every mass congregational religion."[265] By contrast, groups significantly lower on the social scale prove, on the whole, less likely carriers of mass religious movements. Thus, what Weber terms "the lowest and the most economically unstable strata of the proletariat" together with "the proletaroid or permanently impoverished lower middle-class groups who are in constant danger of sinking into the proletarian class" are "readily susceptible to influence by "religious missionary enterprise," especially the "soteriological orgies of the Methodist type, such as are engaged in by the Salvation Army."[266] If Weber is correct, however, such strata are unlikely to provide fertile soil for ethical and rational religion of a radical kind. In the rationalism of these groups, he argues, as in the wider sphere of proletarian rationalism, "religion is generally supplanted by . . . ideological surrogates" of a secular, political and economic kind.[267] From the point of view of the growth of rational and ethical salvation religion, the soil at the very bottom of the social hierarchy is even more barren. Thus, Weber comments that "the classes of the greatest economic disability, such as slaves and free day labourers, have hitherto never been the bearers of a distinctive type of religion."[268] By way of illustration he observes:

. . . the "talking inventory" of the ancient plantation, the lowest stratum of the slave class, was not the bearer of any congregational religion, or for that matter a fertile site for any sort of religious mission.[269]

So far, this brief sketch of Weber's treatment of religion in relation to various social strata has stressed that a primary source of the need for salvation and ethical religion is to be found in the social condition of the disprivileged, the rationalism of the middle classes and the practical way of life associated with both groups. There is, however, another important factor, which Weber calls "intellectualism as such,"[270] and which entails an examination of intellectuals as a social group in a variety of comparative historical contexts. Weber's interest in this topic is hardly surprising, given his firm belief that rationalization is "the single most crucial dynamic factor in the process of change" and his conviction that "the intellectually cognitive aspect is in turn central to rationalization."[271] Convinced that there is an "inherent dynamism in the intellectual function as such," Weber is conscious that its potential for radical innovation may be counteracted, to a greater or lesser degree, "by sufficiently high levels of identification with an established order."[272] The intellectualism of an official established priesthood, for example, may well be tempered in this manner.

Before considering the role of intellectualism in more detail, it is worth emphasizing that, while intellectuals as a distinct social group may well be recruited from, and affiliated with, the higher status groups in a society, such is by no means always the case. Indeed, in a religious context, intellectuals emerge from and act within a variety of social circumstances. As noted earlier, Weber conceives of the human mind as "driven to reflect on ethical and religious questions" not by any material need, but rather by an "inner compulsion to understand the world as a meaningful cosmos."[273] In the quest for meaning that is at the heart of religion, the intellectual clearly has an important part to play, especially as regards salvation:

The salvation sought by the intellectual is always based on inner need, and hence it is at once more remote from life, more theoretical and more systematic than salvation from external distress, the quest for which is characteristic of nonprivileged classes.[274]

Seeking to "endow his life with a pervasive meaning and thus to find unity with himself, with his fellow men, and with the cosmos," the intellectual transforms the concept of the world into the problem of meaning,"[275] thereby encouraging the process of rationalization:

As intellectualism suppresses belief in magic, the world's processes become disenchanted, lose their magical significance, and henceforth simply "are" and "happen" but no longer signify anything. As a consequence, there is a growing demand that the world and the total pattern of life be subject to an order that is significant and meaningful.[276]

The "philosophical intellectualism of those classes that are well provided for socially and economically" tends to generate religion possessing a distinctive "world-fleeing character."[277] Proletarian intellectualism, however, differs in "the character of its distinctive attitude."[278] Among the members of this class Weber includes

people at the edge of the minimum standard of living: small officials . . . equipped with what is regarded as an inferior education; scribes . . . elementary school teachers of all sorts; wandering poets; narrators; reciters; and practitioners of similar free proletarian callings. Above all . . . the self-taught intelligentsia of the disprivileged classes.[279]

Such groups, in Weber's view, play a critical part in the "attempt at religiously motivated mastery over the world,"[280] and to this general category of relatively non-privileged groups of intellectuals, he adds a number of specific and important examples:

the Dutch peasantry of the first half of the nineteenth century, who had an impressive knowledge of the Bible, the lower middle-class Puritans of seventeenth-century England, and handicraft apprentices, who are almost universally characterized by notable religious interests. Above all, there must be included the classical manifestations of the Jewish laity, including the Pharisees, the Chassidim, and the mass of pious Jews who daily studied the law.[281]

As Parsons observes, it is significant that both the Jews and the Puritans have gained fame or notoriety as "people of the Book."[282]

In summarizing the religious intellectualism of the disprivileged, Weber stresses the different circumstances of various kinds of non-privileged intellectuals, in accordance with his earlier observation that a "distinctive class religion of disprivileged social groups" may be said to exist only in a limited sense.[283] Thus, proletarian intellectualism "derives its intensity" from its location at the bottom of, or outside of, the social hierarchy, a vantage point that encourages a less-than-reverent attitude to social conventions and conventional opinions. Since they are "not bound by social conventions," proletarian intellectuals are "capable of an original attitude toward the meaning of the cosmos;" since material considerations do not impede them, "they are capable of intense ethical and religious emotion."[284] The needs of the "religiously self-taught lower middle-class groups" are viewed as tending to assume an "ethically rigorous or occult form," while the intellectualism of craft apprentices "stands midway between the privileged and proletarian manifestations of intellectualism," in Weber's estimate.[285]

It is impossible to conclude even the briefest sketch of Weber's sociology of intellectuals without noting that he unambiguously writes the epitaph to the role of the intellectual in the genesis of new forms of religion, at least within the context of modern societies. While acknowledging and, indeed, emphasizing the crucial role of intellectualism in salvation religion, rationalization and social change, Weber remarks of intellectually inspired religious movements:

> The practical importance of such movements for the sphere of culture was greater in the past than now. Many elements conspire to render unlikely any serious possibility of a new communal religion borne by intellectuals.[286]

As outlined by Weber, the "constellation of factors" includes the interest of privileged groups in maintaining existing religion as a means of social control; the hostility of such groups to mass education; their need to maintain social distance; their underlying scepticism regarding the possibility of a new mass religion; and the "scornful indifference of the privileged classes to religious problems and to the church."[287] In such circumstances, argues Weber, the "need of literary, academic, or cafe-society intellectuals to include religious feelings in the inventory of their sources of impressions and sensations, among their topics for discussion" carries little weight.[288] In a modern context, such a need has "never yet given rise to a new religion," nor can "a religious renaissance be generated by the need of authors to compose books or by the far more effective need of clever publishers to sell such books."[289] Regardless of "how much the appearance of a widespread religious interest may be simulated," maintains Weber, no new religion has ever resulted from the needs of contemporary intellectuals "or from their chatter."[290] Accordingly, he predicts that the "whirligig of fashion will presently remove this subject of conversation and journalism, which fashion has made popular," and that intellectuals will return to secular musings.[291]

Weber's discussion of religion, status groups and classes offers crucial insights into his conception of the link between ideas and social structure. This topic supplies the theme of his best-known work, *The Protestant Ethic and the Spirit of Capitalism,* and is of central importance in his general perspective on social change.

Though it is only partially true that Weber's work represents a dialogue with the ghost of Karl Marx, it is undeniable that the claims of Marxism loom large as Weber grapples with the complex connections between religious ideas and the circumstances of specific social strata.[292] One obvious and relevant conclusion may be drawn from Weber's treatment of religion and social stratification: any accusation that Weber embraces "a naive one-way conception of the development of human societies as the product of 'ideas'" is gravely inaccurate.[293] In concluding *The Protestant Ethic,* Weber observes:

The modern man is in general, even with the best will, unable to give religious ideas a significance for culture and rational character which they deserve. But it is, of course, not my aim to substitute for a one-sided materialistic an equally one-sided spiritualistic causal interpretation of culture and of history.[294]

In *The Protestant Ethic,* Weber quite deliberately treats "only one side of the causal chain" in dealing with the "connection of the spirit of modern economic life with the rational ethics of ascetic Protestantism."[295] He focusses on the impact religious ideas have had on practical economic activity, and challenges head-on a contemporary tendency toward "one-sided" materialistic determinism:

. . . though the development of economic rationalism is partly dependent on rational technique and law, it is at the same time determined by the ability and disposition of men to adopt certain types of practical rational conduct. When these types have been obstructed by spiritual obstacles, the development of rational economic conduct has also met serious inner resistance.[296]

At the same time, however, he makes abundantly clear his recognition of "the fundamental importance of the economic factor," and he acknowledges the necessity of taking economic conditions into account.[297]

If Weber deals only with "one side of the causal chain" in *The Protestant Ethic,* he is undoubtedly concerned with its other side in his studies of religion, class and status. Like his comparative work on the great world religions – which is "a survey of the relations of the most important religions to economic life and to the social stratification of their environment"[298] – these studies are undeniably concerned with the social and economic conditions favouring the development of certain kinds of religious ideas. Religion, however, is not portrayed as a purely epiphenomenal product of material circumstances; nor is its potential impact upon the world underestimated. In an understated and undramatic manner, Weber's investigation of religion and social stratification reveals his most basic assumptions regarding the structure of society and the process of social change. Thus, Weber notes the importance of both ideal and material interests in religious contexts and stresses his conviction that neither has primacy. This view is reflected, moreover, in the calculated ambivalence of his notion of the "elective affinity" by which particular religious ideas are linked with the religious and material interests of specific social groups.[299]

In Weber's perception, man is engaged in a struggle to live meaningfully. So, while "never wholly the product of his natural environment and his primitive nature," he is unable to transcend them completely:

This means that if we cannot understand man's life apart from his religion, we cannot understand his religion apart from the larger picture of his whole life. As part of life, religion is both exponent and forming force. It is therefore that Weber rejects every kind of unilateral causal explanation.[300]

Weber conceived of society essentially as "an arena of competing status groups, each with its own economic interests, status honour and orientation toward the world and man." He is understandably interested in the role such groups play as "carriers" of religious ideas.[301] Typically, however, he rejects any simplistic or one-sided interpretations of the link between religious ideas and the characteristics of various social strata. Instead, he espouses a multivariate perspective that, by its lack of dogmatism, appears admirably suited to cope with the complexity of the phenomena under scrutiny. In this specific context, therefore, the truth of Parsons' general appraisal is readily apparent:

> Weber attributes prime causal significance to the factor of "religious orientation." This factor is, however, nowhere treated as automatically unfolding or "actualizing itself" except through highly complex processes of interaction with other factors. . . . The outcomes are always resultant from and attributable to such interaction, never to any one factor alone.[302]

Weber insists on the independent significance of ideas that emerge as solutions to the problem of meaning, but he is none the less vitally concerned with exploring the material circumstances in which such ideas arise. In this respect, his analysis of the religious propensities of a wide range of social strata is at the very core of his sociology of religion.

The seeker of neat general formulas and simple social equations finds little attraction in the guarded complexities of Weber's sociology of religion. Unlike more doctrinaire formulations, Weber's analysis of the soil in which religious movements grow leads him to the conclusion that there is little relation between religious propensities and economic statuses as such.[303] He denies that radical religious movements are necessarily – or primarily – movements of economic protest originating within the most underprivileged social groups. By the same token, he emphasizes that a "whole range of 'bourgeois' classes, in the more generic sense, constitute a particularly important type of soil for the growth of religious radicalism."[304] Contrary to conventional wisdom and to the current wisdom of his Marxian contemporaries, Weber maintains that radical religion is, to a great extent, generated by various middle-class and artisan groups rather than by the poorest classes. These groups have, in an economic sense, frequently burdened rather than bettered themselves by their involvement in movements of a radically religious nature.

Weber's primary concern in the investigation of status groups and classes may be viewed metaphorically as the analysis of the "soil" in which religious movements grow. Extending the metaphor, we may say that this procedure by no means exhausts the range of his horticultural interests.

Weber is equally interested in the "seed" from which such movements are generated, and in the "sowers" of this seed. This involves him in a sociological consideration of the nature of prophecy, an enterprise of vital importance both in his sociology of religion and in his general conception of social change. For Weber, the prophet is

> above all the agent of the process of breakthrough to a higher, in the sense of more rationalized and systematized cultural order, an order at the level of religious ethics, which in turn has implications for the nature of the society in which it becomes institutionalized.[305]

As noted earlier, Weber's overriding interest is in the part played by religion in the dynamics of social change rather than its role in the reinforcement of social stability. From this point of view, therefore, his attempt to chart the evolution of religion and explore systematically those paths of development that have led to "breakthroughs" may be perceived as his central concern. By utilizing comparative and historical evidence, he traces the sources of those circumstances that have led to evolutionary or revolutionary change in the established order. He does so

> by searching back and forth between the "material" sphere of the conditions, structure and utilitarian interests of ordinary living, and the "ideal" sphere of the meanings of various conceptions of the supernatural and of other aspects of experience.[306]

In his quest for the sources of breakthrough into a more rationalized and systematized cultural order, Weber recognizes the absolute necessity of detailed investigation of a variety of classes and status groups. Equally indispensible from his point of view, however, is the serious sociological scrutiny of the individual agent of the process of breakthrough.

Beginning with a basic definition of "the prophet," Weber assesses the prophet's impact on the world and his role as a bringer of rationalization:

> We shall understand "prophet" to mean a purely individual bearer of charisma, who by virtue of his mission proclaims a religious doctrine or divine commandment. No radical distinction will be drawn between a "renewer of religion" who preaches an older revelation, actual or suppositious, and a "founder of religion" who claims to bring completely new deliverances.[307]

The religious prophet is, in Weber's view, the "charismatic leader" *par excellence*. His possession of the "gift of grace" marks him as the "prototype," though by no means the only example, of a leader whose authority flows from his "charisma."[308] But what exactly does Weber mean by this? Given the broad connotations of the term "charisma" in Weber's own writings, the answer to this question is by no means as easy as popular contemporary usage of the label would suggest. In the most fundamental sense, it is arguable that Weber's concept of "charisma" is virtually identical to Durkheim's conception of "the sacred":

Weber takes as his point of departure the contrast with routine (*Alltag*). Charisma is, then, a quality of things and persons by virtue of which they are specifically set apart from the ordinary, the everyday, the routine. . . This apartness is what characterizes charismatic things or persons.[309]

Noting that "extraordinary powers" are designated by "such special terms as 'mana', 'orenda', and the Iranian 'maga'," Weber applies the term "charisma" to these powers much as Durkheim employs his general category of "the sacred" in the context of such forces.[310] In this sense, therefore, it may be suggested that it is charisma that distinguishes the religious from the secular or profane, and, indeed, that it is "the name in Weber's system for the source of legitimacy in general."[311] The precise boundaries of Weber's concept of "charisma" are a matter of scholarly dispute that cannot be explored here. But whatever its more general sense, charisma is conceived in terms of a "specific theory of social change," a theory whose "most important empirical example" is the role of the prophet.[312]

Charisma transcends the ordinary routine of daily life, but it is, nonetheless, dependent upon recognition and acceptance by those engaged in mundane matters if it is to add "an area of new experience" to their lives:

New experiences do not function if they do not engender some active response. The specific power of charisma lies in the fact that it appeals to need and evokes enthusiasm. . . . Charisma has relevance, that is, insofar as it is an answer to specific questions in a culture, and insofar as it is an appeal strong enough to evoke some form of allegiance and to draw man out of the daily routine into a new perspective. These two characteristics make charisma a specifically revolutionary power that breaks through the established order.[313]

Thus, in Steeman's view, the concept of charisma highlights a basic Weberian social dichotomy or dialectic:

It formulates . . . the basic tension that exists between an established order of any kind on the one hand and the more spontaneous forces of human life and the inherent precariousness of social order on the other. . . . Charisma, as the presence of that which does not fit the ordinary routine of life, is the continuous challenge of the established order.[314]

Parsons notes that the "main context" of charisma is that of "a break in a traditional order," and that its anti-traditionalist and revolutionary character is combined with a "particularly close association with a specific person, a leader:"

The prophet is thus the leader who sets himself explicitly and consciously against the traditional order - or aspects of it - and who claims moral authority for his position, whatever the terms in which he expresses it, such as divine will. It is men's duty to listen to him and follow his commands or his example. . . . The prophet is one who feels himself to be reborn. He is qualitatively different from other men in that he is in touch with or the instrument of a source of authority higher than any which is established.[315]

A decisive break with tradition involves rationalization for, as Parsons comments, "the breaker of tradition is by his very act forced to define his attitudes toward that with which he has broken."[316] When such sharp breaks involve "religious elements," that is to say, when the breaker of tradition "claims charismatic authority," then the process is regarded by Weber as prophecy:

> The prophet is significant as the initiator of a great process of rationalization in the interpretation of the "meaning" of the world and the attitudes men should take toward it.[317]

What are the characteristics of charismatic authority in general? Weber applies the term charisma to "a certain quality of an individual personality by virtue of which he is set apart from ordinary men" and treated as the possessor of "supernatural, superhuman, or at least specifically exceptional powers or qualities," possibly of divine origin, which entitle the individual to be treated as a leader.[318] The "validity" of this charisma is always dependent upon the recognition of those subject to authority, and the "corporate group which is subject to charismatic authority is based on an emotional form of communal relationship."[319] The charismatic leader creates new precedents by his rulings, and these carry the authority of divine judgments or revelations:

> From a substantive point of view, every charismatic authority would have to subscribe to the proposition, "It is written . . . but I say unto you . . ." The genuine prophet, like the genuine military leader and every true leader in this sense, preaches, creates or demands new obligations.[320]

Charismatic authority is "specifically outside the realm of everyday routine and the profane sphere." It "repudiates the past" and is, therefore, a specifically revolutionary force. Spurning involvement in the business of everyday life, it is hostile to economic considerations. Finally, in what Weber calls "traditionally stereotyped periods," it is nothing less than "the greatest revolutionary force."[321] Charisma

> may involve a subjective or internal reorientation born out of suffering, conflicts or enthusiasm. It may then result in a model alteration of the central system of attitudes and directions of action with a completely new orientation of all attitudes toward the different problems and structures of the "world."[322]

Representing the extraordinary and the temporary against the every-day and routine, charisma may thus be encapsulated in a particular person who "takes the responsibility for announcing a break in the established normative order and declaring this break to be morally legitimate, thereby setting himself in significant respects in explicit opposition to the established order."[323] In this regard, the "essential criterion" of prophecy, according to Weber, is that "the message is a call to break with an established order."[324]

A close-up view of the prophet allows us to distinguish his activities from those of a number of overlapping roles. In this way the distinct general character of the historical contributions of such people as Jesus, Zoroaster, Muhammad, Buddha, Moses and the Israelite prophets may be differentiated and assessed in isolation from the doings of "the sundry purveyors of salvation, religious or otherwise."[325] Firstly, Weber is concerned to distinguish the prophet from the priest, and here the "personal call" experienced by the prophet is the key element:

The latter lays claim to authority by virtues of his service in a sacred tradition while the prophet's claim is based on personal revelation and charisma.[326]

It is not accidental, observes Weber, that so few prophets have emerged from the ranks of the priestly class, for whereas the priest dispenses salvation by virtue of his office in a "corporate enterprise of salvation," the prophet exercises his power simply "by virtue of his personal gifts."[327] Thus, as noted earlier, the task of a priesthood is to sustain and reinforce an established order rather than to break with it. Though the magician may also be said to exert power through his personal gifts, he claims no unique revelations, doctrines, commandments or mission. On the other hand, the "authentication" of charisma requires, in Weber's opinion, that prophets furnish proof of "possession of particular gifts of the spirit, of special magical or ecstatic abilities."[328] The prophet must also be distinguished from the legislator or law-giver, although in practice some prophets may also be legislators; Moses is the supreme example. Law-givers, in Weber's sense of the term, are engaged in systematic codification or reconstitution of laws and thus "in general what normally passes for prophecy does not belong to this category.[329]

Undoubtedly, the activities of the prophet overlap with those of the teacher, especially the teacher of ethics and more especially the teacher of social ethics:

Such a teacher, full of a new or recovered understanding of ancient wisdom, gathers disciples about him, counsels private individuals in personal matters and . . . in questions relating to public affairs, and purports to mould ethical ways of life, with the ultimate goal of influencing the crystallization of ethical regulations.[330]

Weber comments that the "most complete expression" of this master-disciple relationship is that of the Hindu guru. He stresses, however, that the guru is, "after all, only a teacher who transmits acquired, not revealed, knowledge, and this by virtue of a commission and not on his own authority."[331] In his view, philosophical ethicists, social reformers and even the founders of philosophical "schools" are not prophets in the sense in which he understands the term:

What primarily differentiates such figures from the prophets is their lack of that vital emotional preaching which is distinctive of prophecy, regardless of whether this is disseminated by the spoken word, the pamphlet, or any other type of literary composition. . . . The enterprise of the prophet is closer to that of the popular orator (*demagogue*) or political publicist than to that of the teacher.[332]

Though the teacher may sustain the established order, the prophet will always, by definition, challenge and seek to break with it. One role that involves such a break Weber terms the "mystagogue." Although he sometimes reveals "new ways of salvation," the mystagogue cannot, in Weber's view, be included among the prophets. Ethical doctrine plays no more than a minor part in his work and he is essentially a distributor of magical salvation.[333] Thus, rather than acting as an agent of rationalization, he counsels "escape from the problems of meaning which exert pressure to rationalize."[334] Furthermore, he normally makes a living from his art, a characteristic he shares with priests, magicians and teachers, among others. By contrast, the prophet is not remunerated. His service is gratuitous and his actions are free from economic constraints.

Among genuine prophets, Weber distinguishes two ideal types of prophecy, which he labels "ethical" and "exemplary:"

Thus, there remain only two kinds of prophets in our sense, one represented most clearly by the Buddha, the other with especial clarity by Zoroaster and Muhammad.[335]

As in the cases of Zoroaster and Muhammad, the prophet may be primarily "an instrument for the proclamation of a god and his will, be this a concrete command or an abstract norm:"

Preaching as one who has received a commission from God, he demands obedience as an ethical duty. This type we shall term the "ethical prophet."[336]

On the other hand, like the Buddha, the prophet may "by his personal example" demonstrate the way to salvation to others:

The preaching of this type of prophet says nothing about a divine mission or an ethical duty of obedience, but rather directs itself to the self-interest of those who crave salvation, recommending to them the same path as he himself traversed. Our designation for this second type of prophecy is "exemplary."[337]

The exemplary type of prophecy is, according to Weber, "particularly characteristic" of India, although it has also been manifested in China and the Near East. By contrast, the ethical type appears to have been confined to the Near East.[338] Whether a particular prophet is predominantly exemplary or ethical in character, however, his prophetic revelation involves, both for himself and his followers, "a unified view of the world derived from a consciously integrated and meaningful attitude" toward life as a whole.[339] Weber observes:

To the prophet, both the life of man and the world, both social and cosmic events, have a systematic and coherent meaning. To this meaning the conduct of mankind must be oriented if it is to bring salvation, for only in relation to this meaning does life obtain a unified and significant pattern.[340]

According to Weber, the structure of this meaning may take many forms and combine logically heterogeneous motives into a certain unity. Furthermore, the whole conception is dominated by practical assessments other than logical consistence:

> Yet it always denotes, regardless of any variations in scope and in measure of success, an effort to systematize all the manifestations of life; that is, to organize practical behaviour into a direction of life. . . . Moreover, it always contains the important religious conception of the world as a cosmos which is challenged to produce somehow a "meaningful" ordered totality, the particular manifestations of which are to be measured and evaluated according to this requirement.[341]

Though it is not alone in doing so, prophecy thus "produces the strongest tensions in man's inner life as well as in his external relationship to the world" by invoking a "conception of the world as a meaningful totality" and contrasting it with the reality of the world as it is.[342] The outcome of this tension is significant to the process of rationalization. If the concept of rationalization is the central theme of Weber's sociology as a whole, and if religion is crucial to the process of rationalization, it may also be suggested that the activity of prophecy is of special significance among the religious roots of rationalization.

It is characteristic of prophets, notes Weber, that "they do not receive their mission from any human agency," but on the contrary they "seize it."[343] In a sense, every prophet is a usurper, just as, in its pure form, his charismatic authority "has a character specifically foreign to everyday routine structures."[344] If his charisma is recognized and his prophecy is successful, the prophet will succeed in winning personal devotees and permanent helpers. But herein lies a fundamental tension:

> The social relationships directly involved are strictly personal, based on the validity and practice of charismatic personal qualities. If this is not to remain a purely transitory phenomenon, but to take on the character of a personal relationship forming a stable community of disciples or a band of followers or a party organization or any sort of political or hierocratic organization, it is necessary for the character of charismatic authority to become radically changed.[345]

Thus, in its pure revolutionary form, "charismatic authority may be said to exist only in the process of originating."[346] It cannot, therefore, remain stable but must become "either traditionalized or rationalized or a combination of both."[347] In discussing this process, and considering in particular the problem of succession faced by the religious "group" (*Gemeinde*) on the death or disappearance of the charismatic prophet, Weber introduces the notion of "routinization of charisma." Weber regards charisma as the antithesis of "routine" (*Alltag*), and a routinized charisma might seem to be a contradiction in terms.[348] However, in the more general sense of the term charisma, one in which it is virtually identical with Durkheim's concept of "the sacred," such notions as "lineage charisma" (*Gentilcharisma*), "heredity charisma" (*Erbcharisma*) and "charisma of office" (*Antscharisma*) make perfect sense.[349] Though Weber sees the possibility of charisma becoming "routine," he would undoubtedly view the notion of a "profane" charisma as a contradiction in terms.

Whatever form it takes, however, the institutionalization of charisma may be said to present the prophet with a parallel paradox to that discerned by John Wesley and remarked upon by Weber. In a famous passage quoted by Weber, Wesley laments:

> I fear, whenever riches have increased, the essence of religion has decreased in the same proportion. Therefore I do not see how it is possible, in the nature of things, for any revival of true religion to continue long. For religion must necessarily produce both industry and frugality, and these cannot but produce riches. But as riches increase, so will pride, anger and love of the world in all the branches.[350]

Pondering how Methodism, "a religion of the heart," can best retain its purity, Wesley is apprehensive regarding its evolutionary tendency:

> For the Methodists in every place grow diligent and frugal; consequently they increase in goods. Hence they proportionately increase in pride, in anger, in the desire of the flesh, the desire of the eyes, and the pride of life. So, although, the form of religion remains, the spirit is swiftly vanishing away. Is there no way to prevent this – this continual decay of pure religion?[351]

The "continual decay of pure religion" might serve from the point of view of revolutionary religious prophecy, as a terse description of the routinization of charisma and the institutionalization of a newly acclaimed doctrine of salvation. The "permanent revolution" is a goal that eludes political revolutionaries and religious radicals alike, so that, to the sociological observer, "revolution" appears to retain all its original connotations of an endless turning of the wheel of fate.[352] In this regard, Weber's overall perception of the evolutionary process of rationalization is tempered by a cyclical conception of religious revitalization and an appreciation of the charisma-routine dichotomy as perennial.

In the process of institutionalization, a radical creed becomes an orthodoxy and a revolutionary movement becomes an establishment. Through the routinization of charisma and the systematic codification of the way to salvation a new religious tradition is created. Thus, yesterday's new, extraordinary, spontaneous and mercurial revelation becomes today's stale, ordinary, rigid and seemingly permanent dogma. In this context, charisma "can be dealt with rationally for purposes of maintaining the established order" and "the extraordinary can be made subservient to the ordinary and to the interests vested in it."[353] Here, it may be said, charisma appears to have "lost its nerve."[354] Yet, in the midst of social stagnation and rigidity, it is through charisma that the individual may be spiritually reborn, the established order transformed, and the world made anew. Answering the needs, justifying the enthusiasm, dispelling the despair and fulfilling the hope of dissatisfied sections of society, new prophets may emerge bearing witness to new brands of salvation and demanding that their followers drastically and systematically re-order their lives according to the precepts of newly entrusted revelations. Only here, where it "leads to re-definition of social values, to a real change in the way of life" and where it provokes commitment, can charisma "fulfill its most proper function: to open the way for a break with the established order."[355]

The sociology of religion is central to Weber's work as a whole. But this intellectual focus in no way represents a whimsical bias on Weber's part. Quite simply, religion is of crucial interest for him because he perceives it to be of pivotal importance in human society. Claiming a religious "tone-deafness" or unmusicality, Weber is unconcerned with religion in its own terms or merely as part of the general cultural achievement of mankind.[356] Rather, his fascination with religion stems from his profound appreciation that something which, by definition, grapples with the problem of the meaning of life must inevitably play an important part in human affairs. He is interested in how man makes religion and how religion makes man. More precisely, he is intrigued both by the way society generates religion and by the way religion generates society. Durkheim perceives religion as a social phenomenon and society as a religious phenomenon; Weber appears equally preoccupied with the social aspects of religion and the religious aspects of society.[357]

It is clear that Weber perceives religion as a major force in human society, though one exerted in many different directions. As a key element in the process of rationalization and the generation of evolutionary and revolutionary social change, it is certainly no impotent epiphenomenon confined to a social superstructure. Yet, whatever its presumed divine origins, religion emerges and thrives within specific social structures, and it expresses, reflects or responds to the ideal and material interests of different sections of particular societies. In Weber's view, therefore, the mutual interaction of religion and society can only be analyzed in a context of conflicting social groups and changing social structures. Religion may merely be affected by such conflicts and changes, or it may play a part in initiating or maintaining them. Durkheim's analysis of religion emphasizes social stability and consensus; Weber's interpretation concentrates upon its role in the dynamics of social change and the uncertainties of social conflict. But it is as impossible to understand society, in Weber's terms, without understanding religion as it is to understand religion without understanding society.

Weber's intense concern with the "disenchantment" of the world has led some commentators to regard him as a proponent of a theory of inevitable secularization.[358] Such a view is only partly convincing, however, for while

Weber undoubtedly perceives the decline of magic and the irrelevence of religion as facts of overwhelming social importance, he does not seem to believe that the process of disenchantment is entirely irreversible. While Weber broods over the fate of the individual and laments the loss of community and "brotherhood" in a contemporary context of ever-increasing rationalization, he does not entirely dismiss the possibility of escape from the iron cage of economic acquisition, scientific calculation, bureaucratic organization and interpersonal instrumentalism.[359]

> No one knows who will live in this cage in the future, or whether at the end of this tremendous development entirely new prophets will arise, or there will be a great rebirth of old ideas and ideals, or, if neither, mechanized petrifaction, embellished with a sort of convulsive self-importance.[360]

Thus, in his gloomy vision of the future, the return of the sacred or the rebirth of the gods is at least a remote possibility. Weber's attempt to peer into the future bears a striking resemblance to the similar efforts of Durkheim and Frazer.[361]

In its comparative and historical range, its masses of detail, its variety of insights and its somewhat fragmented form, Weber's investigation of religion presents a stark contrast to Durkheim's neat, experimental case-study of a single society. It is not universally applauded: indeed, it is viewed by some commentators as misconceived.[362] Yet, for many sociologists of religion, Weber's work comprises the greatest single contribution to their field. For them it represents the "most crucial contribution of our century to the comparative and evolutionary understanding of the relations between religion and society, and even of society and culture generally."[363] We may question whether Weber's achievement can realistically serve as a model for contemporary sociologists of religion, but we cannot doubt that it is of far more than "anecdotal historical interest."[364] Its influence upon modern scholarship is widespread, profound and likely to increase.

Footnotes to Chapter Five

[1] In chapter four, the relative impact of the contributions of Durkheim and Weber was discussed. For a brief note on their shared feeling of "the intimate connection of religion and society" see Talcott Parsons, *The Structure of Social Action,* New York: The Free Press, 1949 (first published 1937), pp. 409-410.

[2] Alasdair MacIntyre, "Weber at His Weakest," *Encounter,* Vol. 25, No. 5, 1965, p. 87.

[3] See, for example, W.G. Runciman, "The Sociological Explanation of 'Religious' Beliefs," *Archives Européennes de Sociologie,* Vol. 10, 1969, pp. 180-187.

[4] The notion of a correspondence between the ideas of Weber and Durkheim is most often associated with Parsons. For a view that stresses the differences between these thinkers, see Reinhard Bendix, "Two Sociological Traditions," in Reinhard Bendix and Guenther Roth, *Scholarship and Partisanship: Essays on Max Weber,* Berkeley: University of California Press, 1971, pp. 291-298. For an attack on Bendix's position, see Talcott Parsons, "Durkheim on Religion Revisited: Another Look at the Elementary Forms of the Religious Life," in Charles Y.

Glock and Phillip E. Hammond (eds.), *Beyond the Classics? Essays in the Scientific Study of Religion,* New York: Harper and Row, 1973, p. 177n.

[5] Runciman, *op. cit.*, pp. 181-182. See also the view of Raymond Aron, *Main Currents in Sociological Thought,* Vol. 2 (translated by R. Howard and H. Weaver), New York: Basic Books, 1967.

[6] Max Weber, *The Sociology of Religion* (trans. E. Fischoff), Boston: Beacon Press, 1963, p. 1. (This is a translation of "*Religionssoziologie,*" a section of Weber's *Wirtschaft und Gesellschaft* [*Economy and Society*] published in German in 1922. This material is also included in Max Weber, *Economy and Society: An Outline of Interpretive Sociology* [Guenther Roth and Claus Wittich, eds.], New York: Bedminster Press, 1968, published in 3 volumes.)

[7] See chapter four. For Durkheim's definition, see Emile Durkheim, *The Elementary Forms of the Religious Life* (trans. J.W. Swain), New York: Collier Books, 1961 (first published 1912), pp. 56, 62-63.

[8] Weber, *Sociology of Religion,* p. 1.

[9] On Weber's methodology, see Max Weber, *The Methodology of the Social Sciences* (trans. and ed., E.A. Shils and H.A. Finch), Glencoe: The Free Press, 1949 (first published 1903-17); Parsons, *Structure of Social Action,* pp. 591-601; Raymond Aron, *German Sociology* (trans. T.B. Bottomore), Glencoe: The Free Press, 1957, pp. 68-82; Theodore Abel, "The Operation Called *Verstehen,*" *American Journal of Sociology,* Vol. 54, 1948, pp. 212-218; William Outhwaite, *Understanding Social Life: The Method Called Verstehen,* London: George Allen and Unwin, 1975; and W.G. Runciman, *A Critique of Max Weber's Philosophy of Social Science,* Cambridge: Cambridge University Press, 1972. In this context see also Max Weber, *The Theory of Social and Economic Organization* (trans. A.M. Henderson and T. Parsons), Glencoe: The Free Press, 1947, especially pp. 87-120. (This is the first part of Weber's *Economy and Society.*) On Weber's work in general an immense literature exists. Note especially Dennis H. Wrong (ed.), *Max Weber,* Englewood Cliffs, N.J.: Prentice-Hall, Inc., 1970; Reinhard Bendix, *Max Weber: An Intellectual Portrait,* London: Heinemann, 1960; Julien Freund, *The Sociology of Max Weber* (trans. M. Ilford), New York: Vintage Books, 1969; and Donald G. MacRae, *Weber,* London: Collins, 1974. The most recent overviews of Weber's work to appear in English are Frank Parkin, *Max Weber,* London: Tavistock Publications, 1982; and Franco Ferrarotti, *Max Weber and The Destiny of Reason* (trans. J. Fraser), Armonk, N.Y.: M.E. Sharpe, Inc., 1982 (first published in Italian in 1965). A useful anthology of Weber's writings is W.G. Runciman (ed.), *Weber: Selections in Translation* (trans. E. Matthews), Cambridge: Cambridge University Press, 1978.

[10] Parsons detects an evolutionary aspect to the work of both these scholars. See his introduction to Max Weber, *The Sociology of Religion,* p. xxvii, and "Durkheim on Religion Revisited," p. 157.

[11] See the discussion of Durkheim's "conservative" neglect of change and conflict in chapter four. See also Parsons, *Structure of Social Action,* p. 448.

[12] From this point of view, Durkheim's vision of society has been referred to as utopian; the suggestion was made in the previous chapter that his conception of society and religion creates a utopia by definition. See Ralf Dahrendorf, "Out of Utopia: Toward a Reorientation of Sociological Analysis," *American Journal of Sociology,* Vol. 64, 1958, pp. 115-127. The static emphasis of Durkheim is considered his main legacy to American structural-functionalism. On the general issue of statics versus dynamics, see N.J. Demerath and R.A. Peterson (eds.), *System, Change and Conflict,* New York: The Free Press, 1967.

[13] See Thomas Luckmann, "Theories of Religion and Social Change," *Annual Review of the Social Sciences of Religion,* Vol. 1, 1977, p. 11. For an appreciation of the scope of Weber's researches in the field of religion, see Max Weber, *The Protestant Ethic and the Spirit of Capitalism* (trans. T. Parsons), London: George Allen and Unwin, 1930 (first published 1904-05); *The Religion of China: Confucianism & Taoism* (trans. H.M. Gerth), Glencoe: The Free Press, 1951; *The Religion of India: The Sociology of Hinduism & Buddhism* (trans. and

ed. H.H. Gerth and D. Martindale), New York: The Free Press, 1952; and selected essays in H.H. Gerth and C.W. Mills (trans. & eds.), *From Max Weber: Essays in Sociology*, London: Routledge & Kegan Paul, 1948. (See especially "The Social Psychology of the World Religions," "The Protestant Sects and the Spirit of Capitalism," and "Religious Rejections of the World and their Directions.") For overviews of this aspect of Weber's work, see Bendix, *Max Weber* (cited above), pp. 103-264; Freund, *The Sociology of Max Weber* (cited above), pp. 176-217; and Parsons, *Structure of Social Action*, pp. 500-578.

[14] Luckmann, *op. cit.*, pp. 11-12.

[15] *Ibid*, p. 12.

[16] *Ibid*, p. 11.

[17] *Ibid*, p. 11.

[18] See Durkheim, *Elementary Forms* (cited above). This difference is acknowledged even by those who perceive an ultimate convergence of their thought. See, for example, Parsons, *Structure of Social Action*, pp. 409-410, 500-503; and his Introduction to Weber, *Sociology of Religion*, p. xx, where he refers to Durkheim approaching religion "from a very different point of view" from Weber.

[19] See Benjamin Nelson, "Review Article on Weber's *Sociology of Religion*," *American Sociological Review*, Vol. 30, 1965, p. 595; and Stephen Kalberg, "The Search for Thematic Orientations in a Fragmented Oeuvre: The Discussion of Max Weber in Recent German Sociological Literature," *Sociology*, Vol. 13, 1979, p. 127. Talcott Parsons also observes that the "most central focus of Weber's thought lay in the field of religion" (Introduction to Weber, *Sociology of Religion*, pp. xix-xx.)

[20] See footnote 19. On the difficulties of dealing with Weber's work on religion, see Nelson, *op. cit.*; Kalberg, *op. cit.*; and Constans Seyfarth, "The West German Discussion of Max Weber's Sociology of Religion Since the 1960s," *Social Compass*, Vol. 27, 1980-81, pp. 9-25. As Seyfarth suggests, the difficulties of assimilating, interpreting and summarizing Weber's massive published legacy in this area are by no means restricted to scholars in the English-speaking world. In this regard, see also Parsons, Introduction to Weber, *Sociology of Religion*, p. xix. Kalberg observes (p. 127) that "the sociologist who seeks to unmask the 'true' Weber confronts a maze set within a refined obstacle course."

[21] In this regard, see Talcott Parsons, "Preface to the New Edition" of Weber, *The Protestant Ethic*, xiii-xiv (1930). See also Benjamin Nelson, "Max Weber's 'Author's Introduction' (1920): A Master Clue to his Main Aims," *Sociological Inquiry*, Vol. 44, 1974, pp. 269-278; and "Weber's Protestant Ethic: Its Origins, Wanderings, and Foreseeable Futures" in C.Y. Glock and P.E. Hammond, *op. cit.*, pp. 71-130. Interestingly, the "disproportionate attention" devoted to *The Protestant Ethic* is not confined to the English-speaking world. See Seyfarth, *op. cit.*, p. 10; and Luckmann, *op. cit.*, p. 11.

[22] Parsons, "Preface to the New Edition," p. xiii.

[23] Parsons, "Translator's Preface," p. xi. On the fragmentary nature of Weber's work, see also Parsons, Introduction to Weber, *Sociology of Religion*, p. xx; and Kalberg, *op. cit.*

[24] Parsons, Introduction to Weber, *Sociology of Religion*, pp. xix-xx.

[25] See Kalberg, *op. cit.*, p. 127; and Parsons, Introduction to Weber, *The Sociology of Religion*, p. xx.

[26] Parsons, Introduction to Weber, *The Sociology of Religion*, p. xx.

[27] Weber entitled a series of lectures delivered in Vienna "A Positive Critique of Historical Materialism." See Bendix, *Max Weber*, p. 72n. Bendix notes that "Weber's essays on Protestantism gave rise to one of the great intellectual controversies of our time because he had challenged the Marxist interpretation of history." On the significance of *The Protestant Ethic* as an assault on Marxism, and on the relation of Marxist and Weberian perspectives in more general terms, see Luckmann, *op. cit.*, p. 13; Nelson, "Max Weber's 'Author's Introduction'" (cited above), p. 275; Parsons, *Structure of Social Action*, pp. 488-495, 509-510; Norman Birnbaum, "Conflicting Interpretations of the Rise of Capitalism: Marx and Weber,"

British Journal of Sociology, Vol. 4, 1953, pp. 125-141; Terry Lovell, "Weber, Goldmann and the Sociology of Beliefs," *European Journal of Sociology,* Vol. 14, 1973, pp. 304-323; Karl Löwith, *Max Weber and Karl Marx* (ed. T. Bottomore and W. Outhwaite, trans. H. Fantel), London: George Allen and Unwin, 1982 (first published in German in 1960); Anthony Giddens, "Marx, Weber and the Development of Capitalism," *Sociology,* Vol. 4, 1970, pp. 289-310; and Gordon Marshall, *In Search of the Spirit of Capitalism: An Essay on Max Weber's Protestant Ethic Thesis,* New York: Columbia University Press, 1982.

[28] The literature on Weber's Protestant Ethic thesis is immense, as is the volume of research inspired by it. For a sampling of such work, see Robert W. Green, (ed.), *Protestantism and Capitalism: The Weber Thesis and its Critics,* Boston: D.C. Heath and Co., 1959; S.N. Eisenstadt (ed.), *The Protestant Ethic and Modernization: A Comparative View,* New York: Basic Books, 1968; Robert N. Bellah, *Tokugawa Religion,* New York: The Free Press, 1957; S.N. Eisenstadt, "The Implications of Weber's Sociology of Religion for Understanding Processes of Change in Contemporary Non-European Societies and Civilizations" in Glock and Hammond, *op. cit.,* pp. 131-155; Robert K. Merton, *Science, Technology and Society in Seventeenth-Century England,* New York: Harper & Row, 1970 (first published 1938); R.K. Merton, *Social Theory and Social Structure,* Glencoe: The Free Press, 1957, pp. 574-627; and Hans Mol, "Marginality and Commitment as Hidden Variables in the Jellinek/Weber/Merton Theses on the Calvinist Ethic," *Current Sociology,* Vol. 22, 1974, pp. 279-297. See also the useful bibliographies in both works by Eisenstadt; in Nelson in Glock and Hammond (*op. cit.*) and in Marshall, *op. cit.*

[29] Parsons, Introduction to Weber, *Sociology of Religion,* p. xx.

[30] Herbert Luethy, "Once Again: Calvinism and Capitalism," *Encounter,* Vol. 22, No. 1, 1964, pp. 26-38; Benjamin Nelson, "In Defence of Max Weber," *Encounter,* Vol. 23, No. 2, 1964, pp. 94-95; and Herbert Luethy, "Max Weber - Luethy's Reply," *Encounter,* Vol. 24, No. 1, 1965, pp. 92-94. The quotation is taken from the reply, p. 94.

[31] Nelson, "Max Weber's 'Author's Introduction'," p. 271.

[32] See Marshall, *op. cit.* Nelson notes that in *The Protestant Ethic,* Weber's "main aim was neither to write an essay in economic history nor . . . to controvert historical materialism." See "Weber's Protestant Ethic . . ." in Glock and Hammond, *op. cit.,* p. 77.

[33] Nelson, "Max Weber's 'Author's Introduction'," p. 272.

[34] *Ibid,* pp. 271 and 273.

[35] Weber, *The Protestant Ethic,* pp. 39-40. On "marginality," see Mol, *op. cit.* Even so severe a critic of Weber as Hugh Trevor-Roper notes the contrasting economic influence, on their respective societies, of the French Huguenots and the English Catholics. See H.R. Trevor-Roper, *Religion, the Reformation and Social Change* (2nd edition), London: Macmillan, 1972, pp. 1-45; and H.R. Trevor-Roper, "Huguenots and Papists" in *Historical Essays,* London: Macmillan, 1957, pp. 227-232.

[36] Bendix, *Max Weber,* p. 78.

[37] Weber, *The Protestant Ethic,* p. 36.

[38] *Ibid,* p. 36.

[39] *Ibid,* pp. 36-37; and Bendix, *Max Weber,* p. 79.

[40] Bendix, *Max Weber,* p. 79.

[41] *Ibid,* p. 79. See also Weber, *The Protestant Ethic,* pp. 45, 97-98, 183; and Max Weber, "Anticritical Last Word on *The Spirit of Capitalism*" (trans. with an introduction by Wallace M. Davis), *American Journal of Sociology,* Vol. 83, 1978, pp. 1105-1131 (first published in German in 1910). Weber's profound interest in theological formulations stands in sharp contrast to Durkheim's lack of concern with the specific content of religious doctrines. See chapter four and Parsons, *Structure of Social Action,* p. 437.

[42] Max Weber, "Kritische Bemerkungen zu den vorstehenden 'Kritischen Beiträgen'," *Archiv für Sozialwissenschaft,* Vol. 25, 1907, p. 248. This article is quoted in Bendix, *Max Weber,* p. 79.

[43] *Ibid,* p. 79.
[44] Weber, *The Protestant Ethic,* p. 45.
[45] Bendix, *Max Weber,* p. 80.
[46] Weber, *The Protestant Ethic,* p. 79.
[47] *Ibid,* p. 79.
[48] *Ibid,* p. 80.
[49] *Ibid,* p. 80.
[50] *Ibid,* p. 80.
[51] *Ibid,* p. 81.
[52] *Ibid,* p. 81.
[53] *Ibid,* p. 83.
[54] *Ibid,* p. 87. On the importance of the sect in the generation of the "Spirit of Capitalism," see Bendix, *op. cit.,* pp. 87-89; Weber, "The Protestant Sects and the Spirit of Capitalism," in Gerth and Mills, *op. cit.,* pp. 302-322; and Stephen D. Berger, "The Sects and the Breakthrough into the Modern World: On the Centrality of the Sects in Weber's Protestant Ethic Thesis," *The Sociological Quarterly,* Vol. 12, 1971, pp. 486-499. Weber notes that in the sixteenth and seventeenth centuries "and in general even today" predestination was considered Calvinism's "most characteristic dogma." (*The Protestant Ethic,* p. 98.)
[55] Quoted in Weber, *The Protestant Ethic,* pp. 99-100.
[56] Parsons, *Structure of Social Action,* p. 522.
[57] See Weber, *The Protestant Ethic,* pp. 102-103. Weber observes that the "interest of it is solely in God, not in man; God does not exist for men, but men for the sake of God." This, of course, is the theological perspective Feuerbach overturned. (See Chapter Three.)
[58] Weber, *The Protestant Ethic,* p. 103.
[59] *Ibid,* pp. 103-104.
[60] *Ibid,* pp. 113-114.
[61] Parsons, *Structure of Social Action,* p. 524.
[62] Weber, *The Protestant Ethic,* p. 121.
[63] *Ibid,* p. 121.
[64] *Ibid,* pp. 121-122.
[65] See Bendix, *Max Weber,* pp. 276-282. Weber infers a psychological state from an analysis of doctrines and institutions and then uses this inference to link the theological doctrines of ascetic Protestantism with the spirit of capitalistic enterprise. This solution to the paradox of the affinity between Protestantism and capitalism rests, therefore, in the view of some critics, on an unwarranted psychological reconstruction that utilizes an appropriately forged intervening variable to make an otherwise implausible connection.
[66] Weber, *The Protestant Ethic,* pp. 117-118.
[67] *Ibid,* p. 117.
[68] *Ibid,* p. 118.
[69] Bendix, *Max Weber,* p. 81.
[70] Parsons, *Structure of Social Action,* p. 524.
[71] Bendix, *Max Weber,* p. 81.
[72] Weber, *The Protestant Ethic,* pp. 109-110.
[73] Parsons, *Structure of Social Action,* p. 524.
[74] Weber, *The Protestant Ethic,* p. 110.
[75] *Ibid,* p. 110.
[76] Parsons, *Structure of Social Action,* p. 525.
[77] Weber, *The Protestant Ethic,* pp. 111-112.
[78] *Ibid,* pp. 114-115.
[79] *Ibid,* p. 115.
[80] *Ibid,* p. 104.
[81] *Ibid,* pp. 105-106.

[82] *Ibid*, pp. 105-106 and p. 112.

[83] Parsons, *Structure of Social Action*, p. 526.

[84] Weber, *The Protestant Ethic*, pp. 115 and 117.

[85] Parsons, *Structure of Social Action*, p. 526.

[86] *Ibid*, p. 526.

[87] *Ibid*, pp. 526-527; and Weber, *The Protestant Ethic*, pp. 117-122, 171-172.

[88] Weber, *The Protestant Ethic*, pp. 121-125 and p. 172; Parsons, *Structure of Social Action*, p. 527; and Bendix, *Max Weber*, pp. 72-73.

[89] Weber, *The Protestant Ethic*, p. 180.

[90] *Ibid*, p. 181. For English-speaking readers the "iron cage" has become one of Weber's best known metaphors. See, for example, Arthur Mitzman, *The Iron Cage: An Historical Interpretation of Max Weber*, New York: Knopf, 1969. The metaphor appears to owe more to Talcott Parsons, who translated *The Protestant Ethic*, than to Weber, however, and "iron shell" or "iron casing" would seem to be more literal renderings. On this issue, see Edward A. Tiryakian, "The Sociological Import of a Metaphor: Tracking the Source of Max Weber's 'Iron Cage'," *Sociological Inquiry*, Vol. 51, 1981, pp. 27-33; Stephen P. Turner, "Bunyan's Cage and Weber's 'Casing'," *Sociological Inquiry*, Vol. 52, 1982, pp. 84-87; and Stephen A. Kent, "Weber, Goethe, and the Nietzschean Allusion: Capturing the Source of the 'Iron Cage' Metaphor," *Sociological Analysis* (forthcoming, 1983).

[91] Weber, *The Protestant Ethic*, p. 182.

[92] See Parsons, *Structure of Social Action*, p. 529; and Bendix, *Max Weber*, pp. 84-85. Parsons does not use the term "elective affinity" in his translation of *The Protestant Ethic*, preferring the less colourful terms "correlation" or "relationship." (Compare his translation of the passage on pp. 91-92 with the translation offered by Bendix in his biography of Weber, pp. 84-85). Yet the notion of "elective affinity," which is borrowed from Goethe, is used frequently by Weber, as Bendix notes, and is now inextricably associated with his work, expressing, as it does, "the dual aspect of ideas, ie. that they were created or chosen by one individual ('elective') and that they fit in with his material interests ('affinity')." See Bendix, *Max Weber*, p. 85n. See also Johann Wolfgang Von Goethe, *Elective Affinities: A Novel*, New York: Frederick Ungar Publishing Co., 1962 (first published in German in 1807.) Interestingly, the English translation of Durkheim's *Elementary Forms* (cited above) uses the term "elective affinities" in the context of primitive classification (p. 174).

[93] Bendix, *Max Weber*, p. 84.

[94] Weber, *The Protestant Ethic*, pp. 91-92.

[95] *Ibid*, p. 97.

[96] Parsons, *Structure of Social Action*, p. 528.

[97] On Weber's view of causal adequacy and adequacy at the level of meaning, see Bendix, *Max Weber*, p. 85; Parsons, *Structure of Social Action*, pp. 532-533 and pp. 624-636; Weber, *The Theory of Social and Economic Organization* (cited above), pp. 89-100; and Weber, *The Methodology of the Social Sciences* (cited above), pp. 67-72. The nature of *The Protestant Ethic* as an element in a vast, ambitious enterprise of comparative sociology is manifest in the author's introduction included in the English translation (pp. 13-31). Benjamin Nelson argues that this essay "is perhaps the strongest general statement Weber offers us of his mature awareness that the realization of his master purposes as a sociologist was not possible without a definite commitment to a perspective he himself called 'universal historical' and which I prefer to describe as 'differential historical sociological' and, indeed, 'comparative civilizational'." (Nelson, "Max Weber's 'Author's Introduction'," p. 271.) Weber is thus prepared to risk "falling under the anathema: 'dilettantes compare'" (see letter to Von Below quoted in G. Roth, Introduction to *Economy and Society*, cited above, p. lvii.) Weber might well have echoed Müller's aphorism that "he who knows one knows none." See Chapter Three; see also Eric J. Sharpe, *Comparative Religion: A History*, London: Duckworth, 1975.

[98] Weber, *The Protestant Ethic*, p. 35.

[99] *Ibid,* pp. 37-40.

[100] *Ibid,* p. 27.

[101] Parsons, *Structure of Social Action,* pp. 532-533.

[102] *Ibid,* p. 533; and Weber, *The Protestant Ethic,* p. 27.

[103] Weber, *The Protestant Ethic,* p. 27; and Parsons, *Structure of Social Action,* p. 533.

[104] Weber, *The Protestant Ethic,* pp. 25-26; and Bendix, *Max Weber,* p. 90, pp. 103-104.

[105] Parsons, *Structure of Social Action,* p. 533.

[106] Weber, *The Protestant Ethic,* pp. 26-27.

[107] *Ibid,* p. 27; and Parsons, *Structure of Social Action,* p. 557. The series of studies called the "Economic Ethics of the World Religions," which was to include volumes on Medieval Catholicism, Islam and Early Christianity as well as Hinduism, Confucianism, Buddhism, and Ancient Judaism, remained incomplete at the time of Weber's death. However, some idea of its scope may be gained from investigation of Weber's works on *The Religion of China, The Religion of India,* and *Ancient Judaism* (cited above). See also Bendix, *Max Weber,* pp. 117-264; Nelson, "Review Article" (cited above), pp. 598-599; Parsons, *Structure of Social Action,* pp. 539-563; Bryan S. Turner, *Weber On Islam,* London: Routledge and Kegan Paul, 1976; and S.N. Eisenstadt, "The Implications of Weber's Sociology of Religion . . ." in Glock and Hammond, *op. cit.,* pp. 131-180.

[108] Weber, *The Protestant Ethic,* p. 27.

[109] Parsons, *Structure of Social Action,* p. 540.

[110] *Ibid,* p. 540.

[111] *Ibid,* p. 540.

[112] *Ibid,* pp. 541-542.

[113] Weber, *The Protestant Ethic,* p. 13. See the discussion of the meaning of this phrase in Nelson, "Weber's 'Author's Introduction' . . . ."

[114] See Parsons, Introduction to Weber, *Sociology of Religion,* pp. xix-xx and p. 1x. Claiming that "the most central focus of Weber's thought lay in the field of religion," Parsons sees his analysis of religion as the "strategically central part of a generally evolutionary view of the development of human society." Luckmann, *op. cit.,* notes the centrality of Weber's studies of religion and Nelson likewise accords them a crucial place in Weber's comparative "sociology of the social and cultural depths" ("Review Article," pp. 595-599). In this regard, see much of the work discussed in Seyfarth, *op. cit.,* and Kalberg, *op. cit.*

[115] See Roland Robertson, *The Sociological Interpretation of Religion,* New York: Schocken Books, 1970, p. 3.

[116] Parsons, Introduction to Weber, *The Sociology of Religion,* p. 11.

[117] *Ibid,* p. xx.

[118] Luckmann, *op. cit.,* p. 11.

[119] See discussion in later notes and consult Weber, *The Sociology of Religion,* p. 1.

[120] In this context see Weber, "The Social Psychology of the World Religions," in Gerth and Mills, *op. cit.,* pp. 267-301; Parsons, Introduction to Weber, *The Sociology of Religion,* p. xxiii; Weber, *The Methodology of the Social Sciences;* Bendix, *Max Weber,* pp. 276-282; Outhwaite, *op. cit.;* and Martin E. Spencer, "The Social Psychology of Max Weber," *Sociological Analysis,* Vol. 40, 1979, pp. 240-253.

[121] Parsons, Introduction to Weber, *The Sociology of Religion,* p. xxx.

[122] See the discussion of Durkheim's emphasis on social stability and integration in chapter four.

[123] Luckmann, *op. cit.,* pp. 11-12.

[124] *Ibid,* p. 11.

[125] Weber, *The Protestant Ethic,* p. 183.

[126] *Ibid,* p. 183.

[127] *Ibid,* p. 183. For a similar attack on one-sided interpretations of culture see Weber, *Methodology of the Social Sciences,* pp. 67-71.

[128] These are all themes that are taken up in Weber, *Sociology of Religion.* See also the discussion in subsequent notes.

[129] Ephraim Fischoff, translator's preface to *Ibid,* p. xiii. See also Parsons, introduction to the same work, pp. lxi-lxii; Parsons, *Structure of Social Action,* pp. 500-502; Nelson, "Weber's Protestant Ethic . . ."; and Nelson, "Weber's 'Author's Introduction' . . . ."

[130] Parsons, Introduction to Weber, *Sociology of Religion,* p. lx.

[131] Parsons, *Structure of Social Action,* p. 500.

[132] *Ibid,* p. 500.

[133] *Ibid,* pp. 500-501; and see chapter four.

[134] *Ibid,* p. 501.

[135] Parsons, Introduction to Weber, *Sociology of Religion,* p. lx.

[136] *Ibid,* p. lx.

[137] *Ibid,* p. lx.

[138] MacRae, *op. cit.,* pp. 80-81.

[139] Luckmann, *op. cit.,* p. 12.

[140] See Weber, *Sociology of Religion,* pp. 3-5. Weber's discussion in this section is entirely in line with the Tylorian or "neo-Tylorian" substantivism discussed in chapters two and three. See Melford E. Spiro, "Religion: Problems of Definition and Explanation," in Michael Banton (ed.), *Anthropological Approaches to the Study of Religion,* London: Tavistock Publications, 1966; Robin Horton, "A Definition of Religion and its Uses," *Journal of the Royal Anthropological Institute,* Vol. 90, 1960, pp. 201-226; Jack Goody, "Religion and Ritual: the Definitional Problem," *British Journal of Sociology,* Vol. 12, 1961, pp. 142-164; and Robin Horton, "Neo-Tylorianism: Sound Sense or Sinister Prejudice?" in *Man: The Journal of the Royal Anthropological Institute,* New Series, Vol. 3, 1968, pp. 625-634.

[141] Weber, *Sociology of Religion,* p. 4. See also Durkheim's discussion of totemism in *Elementary Forms,* and the discussion in chapter four.

[142] Weber, *Sociology of Religion,* p. 5. This definition bears an uncanny resemblance to those of modern neo-Tylorians such as Horton and Goody.

[143] Theodore M. Steeman, "Max Weber's Sociology of Religion," *Sociological Analysis,* Vol. 25, 1964, p. 56.

[144] *Ibid,* p. 56.

[145] *Ibid,* p. 56. On Weber's notion of ideal and material interests, see Parsons, *Structure of Social Action,* pp. 520-521; Parsons, Introduction to Weber, *Sociology of Religion,* p. lx; Bendix, *Max Weber,* pp. 84-85; Weber, *The Protestant Ethic,* pp. 91-92; and Werner Stark, "Max Weber's Sociology of Religious Belief," *Sociological Analysis,* Vol. 25, 1964, pp. 41-46.

[146] Steeman, *op. cit.,* pp. 56-57. See Parsons' discussions of the problem of meaning in Introduction to Weber, *The Sociology of Religion,* pp. xlv-xlviii; and also Luckmann, *op. cit.,* pp. 12-13 for similar views.

[147] Steeman, *op. cit.,* p. 57. See Weber, *The Protestant Ethic,* pp. 91-92, p. 183; and Weber, *The Methodology of the Social Sciences,* pp. 67-71.

[148] Parsons, Introduction to Weber, *The Sociology of Religion,* p. xlvii.

[149] Steeman, *op. cit.,* p. 57.

[150] It has been noted that Durkheim's concern with the functions of religion in general results in a lack of interest in the details of specific religions. As Bendix notes: "Durkheim devotes much attention to problems of definition, to the supposed origins of religious phenomena, and correspondingly little or no attention to religious functionaries or theological doctrines. With Weber it is the other way around." (Bendix in Bendix and Roth, *op. cit.,* p. 292.) Yet Weber's "omnivorous appetite for detail and for piling up masses of fact" only serves to emphasize his interest in religion in general "as a determinant of action in the very heart of a culture . . . as a fundamental fact of human existence, as the central feature of a culture, and

as the prime moving force in social evolution." (Parsons, *Structure of Social Action*, pp. 500-501; and Steeman, *op. cit.*, p. 57.)

[151] See the discussion of broad, inclusive functional definitions of religion in chapter two. Weber is clearly aware of the inevitability of naming as "religious" those phenomena that, in common usage, are perceived as non-religious or even anti-religious, if an inclusive functional view is adopted. See his wry joke about atheistic religion in his reference to the "religion (or perhaps better, irreligion)" of Confucianism cited in Runciman, *op. cit.*, p. 165n.

[152] See chapter two. Luckmann has gained fame (or notoriety) by taking Weber's analysis to its logical conclusion in what some critics regard as a *reductio ad absurdum*. See Thomas Luckmann, *The Invisible Religion: The Problem of Religion in Modern Society*, New York: Macmillan Co., 1967. For examples of functionalism that occasionally strays back into "ordinary-usage" substantivism, see Talcott Parsons, "Religion in a Modern Pluralistic Society," *Review of Religious Research*, Vol. 7, 1966, pp. 125-146; Elizabeth K. Nottingham, *Religion and Society*, New York: Random House, 1962; Thomas F. O'Dea, *The Sociology of Religion*, Englewood Cliffs, N.J.: Prentice-Hall, Inc., 1966; and J. Milton Yinger, *Religion, Society and the Individual*, New York: Macmillan Co., 1957.

[153] Luckmann, "Theories of Religion and Social Change" (cited above), p. 12.

[154] *Ibid*, p. 12. On the process of rationalization, see also discussions in Steeman, *op. cit.*; Seyfarth, *op. cit.*; Kalberg, *op. cit.*; Nelson, "Max Weber's 'Author's Introduction'", and Parsons, Introduction to Weber, *Sociology of Religion*. Recent important works in this regard are Wolfgang Schluchter, *The Rise of Western Rationalism: Max Weber's Developmental History* (trans. G. Roth), Berkeley: University of California Press, 1981; and Guenther Roth and Wolfgang Schluchter, *Max Weber's Vision of History: Ethics and Methods*, Berkeley: University of California Press, 1979.

[155] Luckmann, "Theories of Religion and Social Change," pp. 13-14.

[156] *Ibid*, p. 14.

[157] *Ibid*, p. 14.

[158] *Ibid*, p. 14.

[159] *Ibid*, p. 12. Weber adopts the phrase *Entzauberung der Welt*, used by the German poet and playwright Schiller, and sees the "disenchantment of the world" as the distinguishing feature of Western culture. On the broad process of rationalization see Weber, *The Protestant Ethic*, pp. 13-26, pp. 76-78 and pp. 182-183.

[160] Parsons, Introduction to *The Sociology of Religion*, p. xxxii.

[161] *Ibid*, p. xxxii.

[162] *Ibid*, pp. xxxii-xxxiii.

[163] *Ibid*, p. xxxiii.

[164] See Friedrich H. Tenbruck, "The Problem of Thematic Unity in the Works of Max Weber," *British Journal of Sociology*, Vol. 31, 1980, pp. 316-351; and Stephen Kalberg, "The Search for Thematic Orientations in a Fragmented Oeuvre . . .", pp. 127-133 (cited in footnote 19 of this chapter). See also sources cited in footnote 154 of this chapter.

[165] Steeman, "Max Weber's Sociology of Religion," p. 57.

[166] *Ibid*, p. 57.

[167] *Ibid*, p. 53.

[168] *Ibid*, p. 53.

[169] See Constans Seyfarth, "The West German Discussion of Max Weber's Sociology of Religion," cited in footnote 20 of this chapter, pp. 12-20.

[170] Steeman, "Max Weber's Sociology of Religion," p. 54.

[171] *Ibid*, p. 53.

[172] MacRae, *Weber*, p. 81.

[173] *Ibid*, p. 81.

[174] Especially "traditional" orders. See Parsons' comment on the "sanctification" of traditional rule in his *Structure of Social Action*, pp. 659-600. See also Weber, *Theory of Social and Economic Organization*, pp. 324-392, cited in footnote 9 of this chapter.

[175] Weber's terminology is adopted as appropriate here. See Weber, *The Protestant Ethic*, p. 27.

[176] Weber, *Sociology of Religion*, p. 44. It is interesting to compare Weber's distinction between religion and magic with the distinctions made by Frazer and Durkheim. See chapters three and four. The religion-magic dichotomy is still an issue for social-scientific debate. See, for example, Mischa Titiev, "A Fresh Approach to the Problem of Magic and Religion," *Southwestern Journal of Anthropology*, Vol. 16, 1960, pp. 292-298.

[177] *Ibid*, p. 1. Weber is quoting Deuteronomy 4:40.

[178] Weber, *Sociology of Religion*, p. 27.

[179] *Ibid*, p. 27.

[180] Parsons, Introduction to Weber's *Sociology of Religion*, p. xxviii.

[181] *Ibid*, p. xxviii.

[182] Weber, *Sociology of Religion*, p. 30.

[183] *Ibid*, p. 28.

[184] *Ibid*, p. 28.

[185] See his *Religion of China* and *Religion of India*, cited in footnote 13.

[186] Bendix, *Max Weber*, p. 152.

[187] Weber, *Religion of China*, p. 227.

[188] *Ibid*, p. 228.

[189] Bendix, *Max Weber*, pp. 152-153.

[190] Weber, *Religion of China*, p. 227.

[191] *Ibid*, p. 240.

[192] Weber, *The Religion of India*, p. 336.

[193] *Ibid*, p. 118.

[194] *Ibid*, p. 119.

[195] *Ibid*, p. 119.

[196] *Ibid*, p. 119.

[197] *Ibid*, p. 121.

[198] *Ibid*, pp. 121-122.

[199] *Ibid*, p. 131.

[200] *Ibid*, p. 131.

[201] *Ibid*, p. 132.

[202] *Ibid*, p. 122.

[203] *Ibid*, p. 123.

[204] *Ibid*, p. 123.

[205] *Ibid*, p. 122.

[206] Parsons, Introduction to Weber's *Sociology of Religion*, p. xxx.

[207] See Weber, *The Protestant Ethic*, p. 27, and Parsons, *Structure of Social Action*, p. 539.

[208] Parsons, Introduction to Weber's *Sociology of Religion*, p. xxxi.

[209] *Ibid*, p. xxxii.

[210] Steeman, "Max Weber's Sociology of Religion," p. 54.

[211] *Ibid*, p. 54.

[212] Parsons, Introduction to Weber's *Sociology of Religion*, p. xlvi.

[213] *Ibid*, p. xlvii.

[214] *Ibid*, p. xlvii.

[215] An indication that this is of contemporary concern is the best-selling status of Harold Kushner's book, *When Bad Things Happen to Good People*, New York: Avon Books, 1983 (first published 1981). See also Parsons, Introduction to Weber's *Sociology of Religion*, p. xlvii.

[216] Weber, *Sociology of Religion*, p. 117.

[217] Parsons, Introduction to Weber's *Sociology of Religion*, p. xlvii.

[218] *Ibid*, p. xxxii.

[219] *Ibid*, p. xlviii.

[220] Weber, *Sociology of Religion*, p. 205.

[221] Parsons, Introduction to Weber's *Sociology of Religion*, p. xlix.

[222] MacRae, *Weber*, p. 82.

[223] Parsons, Introduction to Weber's *Sociology of Religion*, p. xlix. See also p. l.

[224] *Ibid*, p. l.

[225] Weber, *Sociology of Religion*, p. 149.

[226] *Ibid*, p. 149.

[227] *Ibid*, p. 149.

[228] *Ibid*, p. 150.

[229] *Ibid*, p. 149.

[230] *Ibid*, p. 149.

[231] *Ibid*, p. 149.

[232] Parsons, Introduction to Weber's *Sociology of Religion*, p. li.

[233] Weber, *Sociology of Religion*, p. 103. See also Parsons' Introduction to this work, pp. lii-liii.

[234] Weber, *Sociology of Religion*, p. 204.

[235] *Ibid*, p. 204.

[236] *Ibid*, pp. 205-206.

[237] *Ibid*, p. 220.

[238] *Ibid*, p. 205.

[239] *Ibid*, p. 205.

[240] Parsons, Introduction to Weber's Sociology of Religion, p. lii.

[241] See Weber, "The Protestant Sects and the Spirit of Capitalism" in Gerth and Mills (eds.), *From Max Weber*, pp. 302-322, (cited in footnote 13 of this chapter); Weber, *Theory of Social and Economic Organization*, pp. 152 and 157; Bendix, *Max Weber*, pp. 87-89; and Stephen Berger, "The Sects and the Breakthrough into the Modern World," cited in footnote 54 of this chapter. Weber contrasts the voluntary nature of the sect with the compulsory nature of the church, to which one is affiliated by birth. His distinction is taken up and developed in the classic work of his colleague, Troeltsch. See Ernst Troeltsch, *The Social Teaching of the Christian Churches* (trans. Olive Wyon), London: George Allen and Unwin, 1931 (two volumes; first published in German in 1911).

[242] Parsons, Introduction to Weber's *Sociology of Religion*, p. xxxviii. Actually, Weber uses this metaphor himself. See, for example, his *Sociology of Religion*, p. 100.

[243] Parsons, Introduction to Weber's *Sociology of Religion*, p. xxxviii.

[244] Weber, *Sociology of Religion*, pp. 80-91. For a highly critical view of Weber's attempt to link religion with classes, castes and estates see Werner Stark, "Max Weber's Sociology of Religious Belief," especially p. 46.

[245] Weber, *Sociology of Religion*, p. 106.

[246] *Ibid*, p. 107.

[247] *Ibid*, p. 106. In this context see Karl Mannheim, *Ideology and Utopia* (trans. L. Wirth and E. Shils), London: Routledge and Kegan Paul, 1936.

[248] Weber, *Sociology of Religion*, p. 106.

[249] *Ibid*, p. 107.

[250] *Ibid*, p. 108.

[251] *Ibid*, p. 109.

[252] *Ibid*, p. 109.

[253] *Ibid*, p. 107.

[254] *Ibid*, p. 96.

[255] *Ibid*, p. 96.

[256] *Ibid*, pp. 83-84.

[257] *Ibid*, p. 97.

[258] *Ibid*, p. 97.
[259] *Ibid*, p. 97.
[260] *Ibid*, p. 97. Consideration of the idea of "compensation" leads Weber to examine the relevance of "resentment" (*ressentiment*) as formulated by Nietzsche. See Weber, *Sociology of Religion*, pp. 115-116; and Max Scheler, *Ressentiment* (ed. Lewis A. Coser and trans. William W. Holdheim), New York: The Free Press, 1961.
[261] Weber, *Sociology of Religion*, p. 98.
[262] *Ibid*, p. 98.
[263] *Ibid*, p. 100.
[264] *Ibid*, p. 100.
[265] *Ibid*, p. 100.
[266] *Ibid*, p. 101.
[267] *Ibid*, p. 101.
[268] *Ibid*, p. 99.
[269] *Ibid*, p. 100.
[270] *Ibid*, pp. 116-117. Weber devotes special attention to the role of women in religious movements. See his *Sociology of Religion*, pp. 104-106.
[271] Parsons, Introduction to Weber's *Sociology of Religion*, p. xlii.
[272] *Ibid*, pp. xlii-xliii.
[273] Weber, *Sociology of Religion*, p. 117.
[274] *Ibid*, pp. 124-125.
[275] *Ibid*, p. 125.
[276] *Ibid*, p. 125.
[277] *Ibid*, p. 125.
[278] *Ibid*, p. 125.
[279] *Ibid*, pp. 125-126.
[280] Parsons, Introduction to Weber's *Sociology of Religion*, pp. xliii-xliv.
[281] Weber, *Sociology of Religion*, p. 126.
[282] Parsons, Introduction to *Weber's Sociology of Religion*, p. xlv.
[283] Weber, *Sociology of Religion*, p. 101.
[284] *Ibid*, p. 126.
[285] *Ibid*, p. 126.
[286] *Ibid*, p. 136.
[287] *Ibid*, pp. 136-137.
[288] *Ibid*, p. 137.
[289] *Ibid*, p. 137.
[290] *Ibid*, p. 137.
[291] *Ibid*, p. 137.
[292] See Albert Salamon, "Max Weber's Political Ideas," *Social Research*, Vol. 2, 1935, pp. 368-370; and sources cited in footnote 27. In the present context, Weber is specifically concerned with refuting the views of Kautsky. See Karl Kautsky, *The Foundations of Christianity* (trans. Henry F. Mins), New York: S.A. Russell, 1953 (first published in English in 1925); and Parsons, Introduction to Weber's *Sociology of Religion*, p. xli. Weber decisively rejects Kautsky's contention that early Christianity was essentially a movement of proletarian economic protest and that Jesus was the leader of a proletarian liberation movement. For a recent discussion of Weber's work on stratification, see Jack M. Barbalet, "Principles of Stratification in Max Weber: An Interpretation and Critique," *British Journal of Sociology*, Vol. 31, 1980, pp. 401-417.
[293] Parsons, Introduction to Weber's *Sociology of Religion*, p. xxxviii. See also p. xxii; and Parsons, *Structure of Social Action*, p. 533. If Weber is not an idealistic 'emanationist," neither is he, however, merely an epigone of Marx in his treatment of religion and social stratification. See Nelson, "Max Weber's 'Author's Introduction' . . .", p. 275.

[294] Weber, *The Protestant Ethic*, p. 183.

[295] *Ibid*, p. 27.

[296] *Ibid*, pp. 26-27.

[297] *Ibid*, p. 26.

[298] *Ibid*, p. 27.

[299] See footnote 92. See also Richard Herbert Howe, "Max Weber's Elective Affinities: Sociology Within the Bounds of Pure Reason," *American Journal of Sociology*, Vol. 84, 1978, pp. 336-385; and the rather idealistic interpretation in Stark, "Max Weber's Sociology of Religious Belief," p. 45.

[300] Steeman, "Max Weber's Sociology of Religion," pp. 56-57.

[301] Bendix, *Max Weber*, p. 270.

[302] Parsons, Introduction to Weber's *Sociology of Religion*, p. lx.

[303] *Ibid*, p. xli.

[304] *Ibid*, p. xli.

[305] *Ibid*, p. xxxiii.

[306] *Ibid*, p. xxix.

[307] Weber, *Sociology of Religion*, p. 46.

[308] Parsons, Introduction to Weber's *Sociology of Religion*, p. xxxiii. See also Weber, *Theory of Social and Economic Organization*, pp. 358-386; Weber, *Sociology of Religion*, pp. 2 and 46; and Parsons, *Structure of Social Action*, pp. 564-567, 658-672. Other relevant material includes Peter L. Berger, "Charisma and Religious Innovation: the Social Location of Israelite Prophecy," *American Sociological Review*, Vol. 28, 1963, pp. 940-950; and Wolfgang Lipp, "Charisma-Deviation, Leadership and Cultural Change," *Annual Review of the Social Sciences of Religion*, Vol. 1, 1977, pp. 59-77.

[309] Parsons, *Structure of Social Action*, p. 662.

[310] Weber, *Sociology of Religion*, p. 2.

[311] Parsons, *Structure of Social Action*, p. 663. See also p. 564.

[312] *Ibid*, p. 663. See also Bendix and Roth, *Scholarship and Partisanship*, p. 297.

[313] Steeman, "Max Weber's Sociology of Religion," p. 53.

[314] *Ibid*, p. 53.

[315] Parsons, *Structure of Social Action*, p. 663.

[316] *Ibid*, p. 567.

[317] *Ibid*, p. 567.

[318] Weber, *Theory of Social and Economic Organization*, p. 358-359.

[319] *Ibid*, p. 360.

[320] *Ibid*, p. 361.

[321] *Ibid*, pp. 362-363.

[322] *Ibid*, p. 363.

[323] Parsons, Introduction to Weber's *Sociology of Religion*, pp. xxxiii-xxxiv.

[324] *Ibid*, p. xxxv.

[325] Weber, *Sociology of Religion*, p. 49.

[326] *Ibid*, p. 46.

[327] *Ibid*, pp. 46-47.

[328] *Ibid*, p. 47.

[329] *Ibid*, pp. 49-50.

[330] *Ibid*, p. 52.

[331] *Ibid*, p. 52.

[332] *Ibid*, p. 53.

[333] *Ibid*, p. 55.

[334] Parsons, Introduction to Weber's *Sociology of Religion*, p. xxxv.

[335] Weber, *Sociology of Religion*, p. 55.

[336] *Ibid*, p. 55.

[337] *Ibid,* p. 55.

[338] *Ibid,* pp. 55-58.

[339] *Ibid,* pp. 58-59.

[340] *Ibid,* p. 59.

[341] *Ibid,* p. 59.

[342] *Ibid,* p. 59.

[343] *Ibid,* p. 51.

[344] Weber, *Theory of Social and Economic Organization,* p. 363.

[345] *Ibid,* p. 364.

[346] *Ibid,* p. 364. See also Parsons, *Structure of Social Action,* p. 663.

[347] Weber, *Theory of Social and Economic Organization,* p. 364.

[348] *Ibid,* p. 361.

[349] On charisma and the sacred, see Weber, *Theory of Social and Economic Organization,* p. 361n; Parsons, Introduction to Weber's *Sociology of Religion,* p. xxxiv; Parsons, *Structure of Social Action,* pp. 564-567, 662-663; and Edward A. Tiryakian, "Durkheim's 'Elementary Forms' as 'Revelation'" in Buford Rhea, *The Future of the Sociological Classics,* London: George Allen and Unwin, 1981, p. 135.

[350] Weber, *The Protestant Ethic,* p. 175.

[351] *Ibid,* p. 175.

[352] In the political sphere the notion of "permanent revolution" is most associated with the name of Leon Trotsky. See Isaac Deutscher (ed.), *The Age of Permanent Revolution: A Trotsky Anthology,* New York: Dell Publishing Co., 1964. In its original conception, "revolution" assumed a cyclical process of history.

[353] Steeman, "Max Weber's *Sociology of Religion,*" p. 53.

[354] *Ibid,* p. 53.

[355] *Ibid,* p. 54.

[356] Henri Desroche has noted in a different context that "musicologists are not necessarily musicians. And conversely." It might perhaps be said that Weber was a musicologist rather than a musician in the sphere of religion. See Henri Desroche, *Jacob and the Angel: An Essay in Sociologies of Religion* (trans. John K. Savacool), Amherst: University of Massachusetts Press, 1973, p. 105.

[357] It is significant that both social action and religion are defined by Weber in terms of meaning.

[358] See footnote 159. Compare also Weber's treatment of the "disenchantment" carried through by Puritanism, and the preservation of the "magic garden" by Taoism and Confucianism. See Weber, *Religion of China,* pp. 226-227.

[359] For recent considerations of rationalization, individualism and freedom, see Stephen Kalberg, "Max Weber's Types of Rationality: Cornerstones for the Analysis of Rationalization Processes in History," *American Journal of Sociology,* Vol. 85, 1980, pp. 1145-1179; Steven Seidman and Michael Gruber, "Capitalism and Individualism in the Sociology of Max Weber," *British Journal of Sociology,* Vol. 28, 1977, pp. 498-508; and Donald N. Levine, "Rationality and Freedom; Weber and Beyond," *Sociological Inquiry,* Vol. 51, 1981, pp. 5-26.

[360] Weber, *The Protestant Ethic,* p. 182.

[361] See chapters three and four.

[362] See, for example, MacRae, *Max Weber,* p. 81; and Stark, "Max Weber's Sociology of Religious Belief," pp. 46-49.

[363] Parsons, Introduction to Weber's *Sociology of Religion,* p. lxvii.

[364] Benjamin Nelson, review of Weber's *Sociology of Religion,* p. 598, cited in footnote 19. The fact that Weber's work in the sociology of religion is still capable of inspiring scholars is exemplified by a number of recent articles. See François Houtart, "Weberian Theory and the Ideological Function of Religion," *Social Compass,* Vol. 23, 1976, pp. 345-354; Jere Cohen, "Rational Capitalism in Renaissance Italy," *American Journal of Sociology,* Vol. 85, 1980, pp.

1340-1355; Stephen Molloy, "Max Weber and the Religion of China: Any Way Out of the Maze?" *British Journal of Sociology,* Vol. 31, 1980, pp. 378-399; Tony Fahey, "Max Weber's *Ancient Judaism,*" *American Journal of Sociology,* Vol. 88, 1982, pp. 62-87; David L. Petersen, "Max Weber and the Sociological Study of Ancient Israel" in Harry M. Johnson (ed.), *Religious Change and Continuity,* San Francisco: Jossey-Bass, 1979, pp. 117-149; David Gellner, "Max Weber, Capitalism and the Religion of India," *Sociology,* Vol. 16, 1982, pp. 526-543; and Gordon Marshall, "The Dark Side of the Weber Thesis: the Case of Scotland," *British Journal of Sociology,* Vol. 31, 1980, pp. 419-440. For many contemporary sociologists of religion the title of an important article by Edward Tiryakian expresses their assessment of the utility of the classic tradition. See Edward A. Tiryakian, "Neither Marx Nor Durkheim . . . Perhaps Weber?" in *American Journal of Sociology,* Vol. 81, 1975, pp. 1-33.

CHAPTER SIX

THE SOCIOLOGY OF RELIGION: A BRIEF GUIDE TO SOME PROBLEMS AND LITERATURE

Such unity and consensus as existed in the discipline of sociology during the two decades following World War Two largely disappeared in the theoretical and methodological strife of the late nineteen-sixties and early nineteen-seventies. It is not one world in sociology anymore, as Howard S. Becker rightly comments,[1] and any serious appraisal of a particular sociological sub-division must acknowledge this fact as the *sine qua non* of informed investigation.

Due perhaps to the marginality and relatively lowly academic status of their sub-disciplinary enterprise,[2] sociologists of religion appear to have remained relatively sheltered from the most vigorous scholarly exchanges and animosities of the discipline at large. Moreover, by contrast with their colleagues in other sub-disciplines, they seem to have been rather slow and reluctant to embrace novel perspectives or revolutionary scientific "paradigms."[3] Thus, with the major exception of its somewhat circumspect incorporation of Marxian ideas, and the minor exception of its rather reserved reception of phenomenological insights, the sociology of religion exhibits a remarkable continuity of concern.[4] If its unbroken links with its long-acknowledged founding fathers are combined with its belated recognition of the contribution of Karl Marx, the sociology of religion appears essentially rooted in what C. Wright Mills called the "classic tradition" of sociology.[5]

Alfred North Whitehead's observation that "a science which hesitates to forget its founders is lost" is frequently cited within the social sciences as a rallying cry against scholasticism and intellectual inertia.[6] Doubtless the sociology of religion has witnessed its share of scholarly traditionalism and timidity and, in this regard, its failure to transcend the perspectives of its founding fathers may be a cause for concern. Yet if, following Alvin Gouldner's advice, we recall that it is not possible to forget something until it is really known in the first place, the seeming stagnation or stolidity of this sub-discipline takes on a remarkably different aspect.[7] Thus, it may be suggested that the persisting preoccupation of sociologists of religion with the ideas of the classic thinkers is a simple function of the very richness of these ideas. Mills notes of the classic thinkers that, in general, "our immediate generation of social scientists is still living off their work."[8] This is a true *a fortiori* of contemporary sociologists of religion, for whom the writings of Durkheim and Weber in particular "have been a point of orientation" of direct relevance to current work.[9] This is by no means to imply that all sociologists of religion work consciously and consistently in the classic tradition, modelling their projects on those of the giants of sociology. Such is, of course, far from being the case.[10] The sub-discipline of the sociology of religion undoubtedly exhibits more than its share of intellectual parochialism, theoretical indifference, scholarly shallowness, academic mediocrity and abstracted empiricism.[11] Nonetheless, if, at its worst, this sub-discipline's pronounced link with the past is explainable in terms of caution, conservatism and lack of creativity; at its best, it reflects a sustained concern with some of the most central and fundamental questions of sociological theory. Whatever the reason for its commitment to the classics, however, it may be suggested that the sociology of religion is intellectually the richer for it. We may understand why this must inevitably be the case by a brief consideration of the characteristics of the classic tradition in sociology.

Of this intellectual heritage, C. Wright Mills has written:

> The classic tradition . . . may not be defined by any one specified method, certainly not by the acceptance of any one theory of society, history or human nature . . . . [It] is most readily defined by the character of the questions that have guided and do now guide those who are part of it. These questions are generally of wide scope: they concern total societies, their transformations, and the varieties of individual men and women that inhabit them. The answers given by classic sociologists provide conceptions about society, about history and about biography, and in their work these three are usually linked closely together. The structure of society and the mechanics of history are seen within this perspective, and within this perspective changes in human nature are also defined.[12]

In Mills's view, the work of the classic thinkers "represents the best that has been done by later nineteenth and earlier twentieth century sociologists, and remains directly relevant to the best work that is being done today."[13] This is so because it is "not of the sort that can readily be shaped for precise testing."[14] The fruits of the classic tradition are "interpretive ideas orienting us to various ways of looking at social realities:"

> They are attempts to state the general historical trend, the main drift of modern society . . . the "state and fate" of societies. . . . They are attempts to make sense of what is happening in the world and to gauge what may be going to happen in the near future.[15]

If much in the sociology of religion is, like sociology in general, characterized by "plain and fancy retreats from the tasks which classic sociologists confronted so boldly,"[16] yet in its basic hesitation to forget its founders, this sub-discipline has avoided total immersion in smaller problems as part of a "tacit conspiracy of the mediocre."[17] By continuing their enterprise within the frameworks established by their founding fathers, sociologists of religion have, at least, retained the opportunity of pondering those grand and profound questions that Mills so insightfully and accurately identifies. In the discussion that follows, brief treatment of the main contemporary themes in the sociology of religion is integrated with a sketch of the legacy of the classic tradition in an effort to indicate how far the scholarly sub-disciplinary conversation of the present is still dominated by the voices of the past.

The Definitional Problem

In Chapter Two of this book, a short account of classic and contemporary sociological attempts at defining religion was presented. Even a cursory review of this definitional literature reveals the extent to which current debates are conducted according to rules laid down in the formative years of sociology. Hence, though the impatience and frustration engendered by the lack of terminological consensus periodically find expression in attempts to "set matters straight" either through persuasion or legislation, such proposals go largely unheeded.[18] This is because, by and large, such definitional proposals tend to be variations on familiar themes that, as such, are unlikely to woo the devotees of no less familiar and equally popular intellectual harmonies. Intrepid explorers of the definitional labyrinth appear doomed inevitably to retrace the steps of one or other of their forebears, and to emerge with similar insights at the ends of their journeys. For this reason, the most radical promulgations of recent years have also been the most steeped in social-scientific tradition. Thus, the resurgence of "substantivist" definitions naturally involved the resurrection of Tylor's minimal definition of religion and a revival of interest in nineteenth-century British anthropological evolutionism.[19] By the same token, Luckmann's controversially inclusive definition is rooted in a functional fundamentalism that, by its author's own admission, is inspired by the implicit definitional strategy of Max Weber in particular.[20]

It requires no extraordinary insight to discern the influence of a Durkheimian inclusivist functionalism in many sociological definitions in currency at the present time. Nor does it take a highly tuned ear to detect echoes of Durkheim and Weber in contemporary debates regarding implicit and explicit definitional stances and deductive and inductive definitional strategies. Through the babel of definitional debate and dispute, the voices of the past still ring loudly and clearly as they intermittently rise above the almost continuous expression of profound disagreement.[21]

Before turning from purely definitional matters it is worth noting that, where they are regarded as worthwhile undertakings, contemporary efforts to distinguish magic from religion are heavily indebted to the analytical distinctions proposed by classic thinkers. In particular, the dichotomies of Durkheim and Weber, and the tripartite scheme suggested by Frazer, frequently find their way into the background of more recent blueprints no matter how critically they may be appraised.[22]

Marxism: An Ambiguous Legacy

A distinguishing mark of a "classic" intellectual proposition or perspective is, according to Mills, its susceptibility to "a variety of interpretations."[23] Certainly no perspective on human society has been subject to such a range of interpretations as Marxism, and within the confines of the sociology of religion its legacy is a decidedly ambiguous one.[24]

In chapter three Marx's view of religion is briefly examined in terms of its origin in the critique of Ludwig Feuerbach and the German "Young Hegelians." Given its intellectual lineage, it is not surprising that the work of Marx, particularly his early writing, has come to hold a considerable fascination for many modern theologians. In one sense at least, Marxism may be perceived as originating in a theological as much as a political or economic context.[25] If theologians have, understandably, been slow to appreciate Marx's relevance to their enterprise, this is no less true of sociologists of religion, especially in a North American context. Thus, a general neglect of Marxism in American and Canadian sociology was only remedied after the collapse of the structural-functionalist intellectual hegemony in the nineteen-sixties.[26] This state of affairs was accurately reflected in the intellectual temper of the sociology of religion, within whose confines Marx was more likely to be appreciated as the founder of a new world religion rather than as a pioneer contributor to the sub-discipline. From this perspective, any sociological relevance of Marxism for the understanding of religion appeared to be restricted to the observation that religion is "the opium of the people." In short, Marxism was dismissed, and to a considerable extent justifiably, as an unduly deterministic, dogmatic and arid perspective with little or nothing to add to a field dominated by the powerful presence of Emile Durkheim.[27]

In the last two decades, however, the role of Marxism within sociology, particularly on this continent, has undergone a transformation. Thus, changes within the discipline of sociology and within Marxism itself have resulted in Marxian insights playing a more significant though by no means central part in the deliberations of sociologists of religion.[28] In this way, the sub-discipline, or at least a segment of it, has belatedly accorded scholarly recognition to one of its pioneers.

Closer sociological scrutiny of the Marxist conception of religion reveals a far more circumspect, multi-faceted and sophisticated viewpoint than would be stereotypically suggested. Thus, while Marx is undoubtedly interested in the ideological functions of religion in preserving the status quo and maintaining the domination of a ruling class, his analysis is by no means confined to this area of inquiry. The fact that religion is far from being in all cases a drug administered by oppressors for the purpose of inducing resignation and inaction among the oppressed has long been clear to Marxists as well as to others. The existence of "another side" to religion was evidently recognized by Marx himself, and the work of his close collaborator, Friedrich Engels, and his immediate heirs makes no sense unless this alternative aspect of religion is acknowledged to be part of a Marxist framework.[29] Thus, repetition of a crude opium-of-the-people thesis has no scholarly justification, least of all if presented as *the* Marxist view of religion.[30] Beginning with the work of Engels, Marxists have undoubtedly recognized the active rôle that may be played by religion in effecting revolutionary social change. Though more recent work is better known, the research of Eduard Bernstein on the communistic sects of the English civil-war period, and Karl Kautsky's investigation of early Christianity, provide almost classic statements of religion's revolutionary rôle.[31] Indeed, among Marxists in the early years of the century, so taken for granted was this aspect of religion that the ancestry of modern socialism and communism was unashamedly traced to the revolutionary religious movements of classical, medieval and pre-industrial times.[32] Regarded, therefore, as expressing, in religious language, the yearnings and aspirations of the oppressed, these frequently violent and millennial protest movements were perceived as the liberation movements of their time; the creations of the economically and politically disprivileged and disinherited.[33] Engels notes, for example:

> One good thing, however, Ernest Renan has said: "When you want to get a distinct idea of what the first Christian communities were, do not compare them to the parish congregation of our day; they were rather like local sections of the International Working Man's Association." And this is correct. Christianity got hold of the masses, exactly as modern socialism does, under the shape of a variety of sects. . . .[34]

Incidentally, as this quotation suggests, Marxism may be credited with developing its own tradition of analysis of sectarianism, although most sociologists have remained understandably unaware of its existence.[35]

Although there is thus a venerable Marxist tradition in which the "other side" of religion is investigated, it must be said that, from the standpoint both of modern sociology in general and contemporary Marxist scholarship in particular, the major foundations of this tradition are somewhat shaky. Rooted in a narrow view of historical materialism that interprets religion as ultimately a mere epiphenomenal reflection of economic infra-structure, many of the works in this genre appear partial and incomplete by the standards of modern commentary. It may be sugested, therefore, that a major intellectual "loosening-up" of Marxism was a necessary pre-condition for a state of affairs in which non-Marxist sociologists of religion began to take Marxian ideas seriously. Moreover, it may also be asserted that such scholarly revisionism was an absolute prerequisite of a genuine and fruitful Marxist theory of religion.

It is now possible to detect, within the sociology of religion, a growing tolerance for and interest in a Marxist interpretation of religion. Indeed, though it has clearly taken root more readily in Europe than in North America, it is possible to speak of the existence of a "Marxist sociology of religion," at least in embryonic form.[36] This enterprise is characterized by a theoretical and methodological openness and diversity, and appears to reject, or at least circumscribe, Engels' blunt assertion of the ultimate determination of religion by the relations of production.[37] Taking their lead from earlier work, Marxist sociologists of religion adopt a broad view of the social rôle of religion and a "dialectical conception of culture," arguing that while both are implicit in Marxism they have hitherto been inadequately maintained and developed.[38] Thus, a leading spokesman for this viewpoint, Otto Maduro, observes:

> . . . the struggle of the oppressed to free themselves also takes place on the level of culture and cultural apparatus (school, church, et cetera). The ideas of the dominant, even at apparently, the most stable level of consolidating their power within a social formation, are never the only existing ones. Nor do these ideas exist without conflicting with the ideas that express (whether in the form of muteness, glossolalia or hysterical cries) the protest of the oppressed.[39]

Viewing Engels' formula of ultimate determination as merely underlining "*one* of the aspects of the relationship between class structure and religious structures," Maduro comments:

> He left in the dark the aspect of the variable relative autonomy of the religious field and its particular (also variable) effectiveness within the social structure and class struggles pertaining to it.[40]

So broadly, indeed, is a Marxist theory of religion interpreted by some writers, and so decisively is any form of economic determinism rejected, that a hybrid viewpoint labelled "Marxist-Weberian" has emerged.[41] Some critics have, however, suggested that such a formulation does a double disservice, by depriving Marxism of its distinctiveness and by relegating Weber to the status of an epigone of Marx.[42].

It may be regarded as significant that the most comprehensive bibliography of "Marxist analysis and sociology of religions" is preceded by the following quotation from Mao Tse-tung:

> We need books, but we must rid ourselves of the worship we accord them in defiance of reality. If we put all our trust in books, it's better not to have them at all.[43]

While doubtless intended as a caveat for present and future practitioners of a Marxist sociology of religion, it also appears to endorse the manner in which recent Marxist scholarship has attempted to eschew dogmatism and embrace reality in recent decades. A Marxist theory of religion is now at least able to appreciate and analyze such phenomena as the religious character of Polish trade-unionism, the Islamic fundamentalism of Iranian revolutionaries and the religious inspiration of Latin-American liberation movements.[44] An earlier brand of Marxism would undoubtedly have dismissed or defined away comparable phenomena that seemed to contradict the one-dimensional analogy of religion as an opiate, or that suggested "the relative autonomy of the religious field" as a respectable hypothesis:

> . . . it must be noted that up until the sixties practically all the Marxist works on religion came under the influence of this triple unilateral tendency which only sees the types of conditioning that the social structure exerts on the content of various religions, the conservative functions of religions and the "inevitability" that religions will disappear. This is an evolutionist-teleological-scientistic vision, the most representative sample of which can be found in much of the Marxist research done on religion in the socialist countries of Eastern Europe.[45]

The concern, and indeed preoccupation, of contemporary Marxists and neo-Marxists with problems of superstructure and culture has profoundly encouraged the forging of a Marxist sociology of religion.[46] A short sketch clearly cannot do justice to the richness and variety of recent and current work in this area, but it may, perhaps, outline the main contours of theory and research that is beginning to accumulate. The merits of this new approach compared to its predecessor may perhaps be most concisely summed up in an appraisal of a recent Marxist analysis of the religion of East African herdsmen.[47] This study appears to exhibit in microcosm the most positive characteristics of a Marxist scholarship with a human face:

> Pierre Bonte in his study of the Masai gives us a valuable critique of the ravages done by dogmatism and ethnocentrism, notably in the "reflection" theory so often linked with the Marxist Theory of Religion. Emphasizing the necessity of situating the study of religious phenomena inside the societies where they are observable, Bonte shies away from a certain type of Marxism which would know in advance the functions of a religion in any society. Bonte points out how religion can even be a

"dominant instance" in a society like that of the Masai so much so that "certain original transformations, particularly the genesis of class relationships, can only be explained by this dominance."[48]

Under the intellectual umbrella of this new Marxism, therefore, scholars have abandoned a traditional reductionism that conceives of religion as "a totally dependent variable, externally and mechanically determined by the economic system of each society" while, at the same time, they attempt to preserve "all of the Marxian contributions to the sociology of religions."[49] Thus, an attempt is made to overcome reductionism, while at the same time retaining a Marxist standpoint. This is accomplished primarily through the affirmation of the "relative autonomy of religion," a strategy involving:

> . . . an approach in which religious systems have to be studied in themselves and to be situated within a specific macro-social context in a historical perspective, thus trying to establish the complex mutual influences between social structure and religious systems.[50]

The ways in which the assumptions of this approach part company with those of the classic Marxist perspective on religion have been usefully summarized as follows:

1. Religion is not a mere passive effect of the social relations of production; it is an active element of social dynamics, both conditioning and conditioned by social processes.
2. Religion is not always a subordinate element within social processes; it may often play an important part in the birth and consolidation of a particular social structure.
3. Religion is not necessarily a functional, reproductive or conservative factor in society; it often is one of the main (and sometimes the only) available channel to bring about a social revolution.
4. The scientific study of religion is not an easy task; it requires a many-sided empirical approach whose results cannot be either substituted or anticipated by theoretical constructs.[51]

Critics of this approach might, of course, argue that its proponents aspire to have their cake and eat it by explicitly retaining a Marxist identity previously associated with economic reductionism, whilst implicitly espousing what is essentially a Weberian point of view. Responses to this accusation, however, are generally couched in terms of an essential continuity rather than conflict between the views of Marx and Weber.[52]

The boundaries of the Marxist sociology of religion are indistinct so that this enterprise shades off naturally into the domains of anthropology, sociology of culture, sociology of knowledge and general sociological theory. Within its vague confines may be encountered a wide range of concerns, from broad theoretical speculations regarding the nature of religion and ideology in industrial-capitalist society to minute empirical analyses of religious practices in primitive tribal settings.[53] The interests of Marxist sociologists of religion thus include many diverse topics, such as the potential religious contribution to the political mobilization of the proletariat, the significance of religious conceptions in the struggles of contemporary peasantry in the Third World, and the links between heresy, prophecy and the changing class-structure of pre-industrial Europe.[54] Overlapping with Weberian scholarship, and even on occasion straying into alien Durkheimian territory,[55] the new Marxist sociology of religion draws heavily on the insights of the Frankfurt school of "critical theory," whose leading spokesmen are Adorno, Horkheimer and Habermas.[56] Another important element in the formation of the intellectual outlook of a Marxian sociology of religion, however, has been the so-called "Christian-Marxist Dialogue," which began in earnest approximately two decades ago.[57] Although commitment to this venture appears to have waned and even evaporated in recent years, at least at a formal level, the legacy of an earlier enthusiastic interchange is evident both in the serious and sympathetic reception currently accorded Marxist ideas in Christian theological circles, and in the theological literacy and sensitivity increasingly exhibited by Marxist studies of religion.[58] This dialogue contributed to the removal of a "theoretical block" so that:

> . . . sociologists of religion were able to rid themselves of the prejudices of evolutionist scientism or have access to Marxist theory and put it to work in their research without being frightened by the dogmatic atheism so easily associated with it.[59]

The fruit of this detente, or the synthesis of this dialectic, are well illustrated by the work of Henri Desroche and Otto Maduro, among others.[60]

A decade ago, Norman Birnbaum depicted the Christian-Marxist dialogue as "a movement of thought and action so contemporary that it may be described as a mood or temper."[61] Such a description now seems decidedly appropriate to the emergence of a Marxist sociology of religion in North America. The unprecedented inroads made by Marxist ideas in recent years have had an important impact upon American and Canadian sociology in general and on a number of sub-disciplines in particular.[62] Within the sub-discipline of the sociology of religion, however, Marxian thought has been slow to take root, although eminent and influential scholars have undoubtedly been influenced by the new wave of Marxist philosophical and social-scientific inquiry.[63] Though there is certainly evidence of a growing interest in their novel approaches to the study of religion, it remains unclear to what extent the work of European Marxian sociologists will fundamentally or permanently affect North American scholarship.

So far, it may be suggested that Marxist sociology of religion has made three broad contributions that might be pondered within the sub-discipline in North America. It has emphasized that Marxism is a more ambiguous legacy than hitherto generally supposed, and that a Marxian framework need not involve a rigid reductionist determinism in the analysis of religious phenomena. Moreover, in abandoning a narrow functionalist perspective that was preoccupied with the conservative, adaptive or compensatory aspects of religion, it has strongly underlined the importance of religion in major social conflict and revolutionary social change. Like its rejection of a one-sided materialism, this strategy has inevitably brought it closer to a Weberian perspective.[64] Finally, it has suggested the ability of Marxism to generate new interpretations, to provoke new insights and to inspire new lines of inquiry.

Within the sociology of religion, therefore, a minority challenges the majority to take Marx more seriously. In so doing, it affirms his importance in the classic tradition of sociology, promotes his claim to recognition as a founder of the sub-discipline and asserts the relevance of his ideas for current research. Whether or not Marx achieves wider recognition within the sub-displine, it is clear that his ideas already possess the power to stimulate scholarship within its ranks. Thus, among some sociologists of religion at least, his work is perceived as a pioneering contribution to the scientific study of religion; a rich intellectual capital to be drawn upon by scholars now and in the future.[65]

Durkheim and Beyond

Though the proposition is sometimes questioned, it is generally considered that the work of Durkheim has had a more profound effect on the sociology of religion than that of any other thinker.[66] As a founding father of the school of structural-functionalism, Durkheim has exerted an influence on North American sociology that has been ubiquitous, deep and lasting. His impact on the sociology of religion, moreover, has been, if anything, even more pronounced, as any casual survey of textbooks published since World War Two will confirm.[67]

It should be evident from earlier chapters of this book that, whereas the chief interest of Marx and Weber lay in social change and conflict, Durkheim's prime concern was with the process of social integration. Thus, it is primarily, though by no means exclusively, through the concepts of integration, stability, consensus and continuity that contemporary Durkheimianism makes its contribution to the sociological study of religion.[68]

Though they have been subject to the attacks of generations of social-scientific critics, Durkheim's major insights into religion and society continue to hold an attraction for certain scholars, despite or perhaps because of their ambiguous, elusive and elliptical character. Thus, while Durkheim's functional definition of religion is reviled by its detractors as overly-inclusive, vague and ultimately circular, it is defended by many of its admirers for these self-same reasons.[69] By the same token, Durkheim's theory of religion and social integration is assailed by its critics as an unwarranted generalization on the basis of the single case of a simple society, while to its defenders it represents a brilliantly insightful extrapolation of universal social validity.[70] If, therefore, as Phillip Hammond has noted, the "richness of his offering has always been mixed with a serving of confusion,"[71] it seems possible that Durkheim's persisting importance may derive, at least in part, from this element of confusion. Thus, if as Mills suggests, a "distinguishing mark of the classic is that it is subject to a variety of interpretations," Durkheim's sociology of religion must be considered a classic perspective *par excellence.*[72] Like Marx, Durkheim has bequeathed an ambiguous legacy, and generated very different forms of social inquiry.

Durkheim's influence on structural-functional sociology and social anthropology is well-known, as is his rôle as a progenitor of various forms of French structuralism.[73] In the present context, however, it seems appropriate to draw attention to contemporary "materialist" and "idealist" interpretations of Durkheim's theory of religion in order to indicate the fundamentally different ways in which his identification of God with society is understood.[74]

Durkheim holds that the "chief aim of religious symbolism is to reproduce society." It is hardly surprising, therefore, that at times he appears to assert "a straightforward representational or objective theory of religious symbols" in which "religious symbols stand for society and particular symbols stand for particular groups."[75] In contemporary sociology, the best example of an "objective representational" interpretation of Durkheim's view of religion is provided by the work of Guy E. Swanson.[76] Building upon a reading of Durkheim that is arguably reductionist in emphasis, Swanson is concerned not with the general functions of religion, but with the "identification of the 'true' (societal) referents of one class of religious statements . . . those about a god or gods."[77] In pondering the question of the referent of religious symbols, Swanson provides an answer that underscores an implicit convergence between Durkheim's sociologism and Marx's historical materialism:[78]

> Swanson accepts Durkheim's basic tenet that theistic assertions are metaphorical representations or symbols of social facts, and advances the Durkheimian formulations by describing the specific components of society which he holds to be the referents of theistic beliefs.[79]

Thus, Swanson asserts that the "true referents of theistic discourse are specific components of society rather than society as a whole."[80] Where Marx would see the economic component as crucial, however, Swanson believes that the true referent of the gods is to be found in the political realm. Claiming that, to the extent that it possesses sovereignty, a group may furnish the model for conceptions of a god, he argues that gods are modelled on the "social arrangements which constitute sovereignty."[81] These arrangements, which Swanson terms "constitutional structures" are, in his opinion, "what men often conceptualize as personified and supernatural beings:"[82]

> Thus, "god," in Swanson's view, is a metaphoric representation or symbol which parallels not the total society, as Durkheim argues, but the "structures by which goals are chosen, and rewards and responsibilities allocated," the structures by which decisions are made in the areas of legitimate concern to the society's sovereign groups. That is, "god" is a metaphorical representation of the structure of the political regime. The properties attributed to the gods have their parallels in the structures of the regime.[83]

Swanson's variation on a Durkheimian theme has been taken up by other scholars, notably by Winter, who prefers to regard this approach as metaphoric parallelism rather than as symbolic reductionism.[84] Though open to strong criticism on both theoretical and empirical grounds, it may be expected that this insightful line of neo-Durkheimian inquiry will provoke further research and heated discussion in the coming years.[85]

A very different interpretation of Durkheim's theory of religion results in a perspective termed "symbolic realism" and associated primarily with the name of Robert Bellah.[86] Dissatisfied with a reductionist view that portrays Durkheim's theory as a version of a simplistic form of historical materialism, Bellah refuses to regard religious symbols as merely reflections of underlying social-structural realities. Drawing special inspirations from his essay on "Value Judgements and Judgements of Reality,"[87] he discerns in Durkheim's later writings "a more active, forming, imaginative role for religious symbolism than Durkheim's amoral epistemology admits."[88] Durkheim's suggestion that ideals of value do not merely "express the reality to which they adhere" but, on the contrary, "transfigure the realities to which they relate," seems to Bellah to presage the position of symbolic realism:[89]

> This position openly asserts the autonomous creative function of religious symbolism operating in a different way from the cognitive symbolism of science.[90]

Because they seek to explain religion by presupposing a set of principles more universal and objective than those of religion itself, most scientific studies of religion are reductionist, in Bellah's view. This situation is not to Bellah's liking, given that "religious symbolization and religious experience are inherent in human existence."[91] Thus, he asserts that social scientists must abandon "their assumption that they speak from a higher level of truth" than the religions they investigate; and that, therefore, "all reductionism must be eliminated."[92] Acknowledging that Durkheim perceived society as the reality behind religious symbolism, Bellah also stresses the fact that he "came to see that society itself is a symbolic reality."[93] Coupling Durkheim with Freud in the camp of symbolic reductionism, Bellah conceives that:

. . . the theories of the classical symbolic reductionists manifest a fundamental destructive contradiction; they purport to "explain" religious symbols and derive them from more authentic realities, yet their theories actually point to the irreducible *reality* of spiritual symbols.[94]

Thus, Bellah contends that "implicit in the work of the great symbolic reductionists was another possible position with entirely different implications," a position he terms "symbolic realism."[95] In a passage that is evocative of Durkheim's essay, "Value Judgements and Judgements of Reality,"[96] he affirms:

The canons of empirical science apply primarily to symbols that attempt to express the nature of objects, but there are nonobjective symbols that express the feelings, values, and hopes of subjects, or that organize and regulate the flow of interaction between subjects and objects, or that attempt to sum up the whole subject-object complex or even point to the context or ground of that whole. The symbols, too, express reality and are not reducible to empirical propositions. This is the position of symbolic realism.[97]

If religion is defined as "that symbol system that serves to evoke . . . the totality that includes subject and object and provides the context in which life and action finally have meaning," then, proclaims Bellah:

I am prepared to claim that as Durkheim said of society, religion is a reality *sui generis*. To put it bluntly, religion is true.[98]

This is, by no means, to maintain that "every religious symbol is equally valid any more than every scientific theory is equally valid," but it is to insist that symbolic realism is "the only adequate basis for the scientific study of religion."[99] In Bellah's view, the truth-claims of science and religion are not in conflict because they involve different kinds of truth. Science is unable to falsify religion, just as it is incapable of undermining religious truths by revealing their social and historical origins:

Perhaps the first fruit of symbolic realism, of taking seriously noncognitive symbols and the realms of experience they express, is to introduce a note of skepticism about all talk of reality. . . . We must develop multiple schemes of interpretation with respect not only to others but ourselves. We must realize with Alfred Schutz that there are multiple realities and that human growth requires the ability to move easily between them and will be blocked by setting up one as a despot to tyrannize over the others.[100]

Any one medium or symbol, observes Bellah, has "many meanings and many contexts of interpretation."[101]

In positing a universal need for non-objective symbol systems, Bellah suggests an underlying unity of religion:

I believe that those of us who study religion must have a kind of double vision; at the same time as we study religious systems as objects we need also to apprehend them as ourselves religious subjects. Neither evolutionist nor historical relativist nor theological triumphalist positions should allow us to deny that religion is one. I don't mean to say that all religions are saying the same thing in doctrinal or ethical terms; obviously they are not. But religion is one for the same reason that science is one — though in different ways — because man is one.[102]

While it echoes Durkheim's view of the universality of religion and his conviction that religion cannot be rooted in an error and a lie,[103] Bellah's promulgation of the doctrine of symbolic realism involves a complete rejection of the positivist subjection of religion to science. Denying that science can truly explain religion, it raises fundamental issues regarding social science and religion in its blunt affirmation of religious truth.

Questioning the belief that the truth-claims of religion are unverifiable, and therefore irrelevant to the sociologist, Bellah's perspective has challenged one of the most cherished assumptions of "value-free" social science, thus provoking a vigorous controversy.[104] Rooted in a Durkheimian insight, symbolic realism comprises an idealist interpretation of religion which, in the new agenda it sketches for sociological and theological interchange, would doubtless intrigue its progenitor. In this form at least, contemporary Durkheimianism can hardly be identified with a simple strategy of agnostic symbolic reduction. Bellah's proposal continues to generate heated discussion among sociologists of religion.[105] It thereby underscores the persisting significance of Durkheim's thought within the subdiscipline.

Another variation on the Durkheimian theme is contained in Bellah's stimulating and contentious "civil-religion" thesis. Although the notion originates with Rousseau,[106] Bellah's utilization of the concept of civil religion is decidedly and undeniably Durkheimian in inspiration.[107] Obviously impressed with Durkheim's insight that society is a religious phenomenon as much as religion is a social phenomenon,[108] Bellah is in clear agreement with "his insistence on the essential, 'sacred' elements in all social relationships."[109] This insistence has, as Hammond notes, "helped alert sociology to the binding potential in all social institutions," as well as emphasizing that the very existence of society *ipso facto* implies religion.[110] Like Durkheim, Bellah sees in religion the expression of an integrated society. Appreciating that those "who feel themselves united, partially by bonds of blood, but still more by a community of interest and tradition, assemble and become conscious of their moral unity,"[111] he recognizes that the phenomenon of social cohesion has a religious quality. Such a viewpoint, naturally, goes beyond the common interpretation of Durkheim's thesis, in which a society is thought to be integrated to the extent that it exhibits a common religion.

Focussing his attention on American society, Bellah attempts, in an essay that has now become a classic in its own right, "both to classify and redefine a perspective, emerging out of the 1950s, that viewed Americanism as increasingly the real or operative faith of the American people."[112]

While some have argued that Christianity is the national faith, and others that church and synagogue celebrate only the generalized religion of "the American Way of Life," few have realized that there actually exists alongside of and rather clearly differentiated from the churches an elaborate and well-institutionalized civil religion in America.[113]

Arguing not only that a civil religion exists in the United States, but that it possesses a "seriousness and integrity," Bellah maintains:

. . . the separation of church and state has not denied the political realm a religious dimension. Although matters of personal religious belief, worship, and association are considered to be strictly private affairs, there are, at the same time, certain common elements of religious orientation, that the great majority of Americans share.[114]

These common elements have played, according to Bellah, a "crucial rôle in the development of American institutions," and supply "a religious dimension for the whole fabric of American life, including the political sphere."[115] The "public religious dimension," as Bellah calls it, comprises the "American Civil Religion."[116] It is expressed in a set of beliefs, symbols and rituals, and the presidential inauguration represents its most central ceremonial act of religious legitimation in the political sphere. In an especially Durkheimian passage, Bellah observes:

What we have, then, from the earliest years of the republic is a collection of beliefs, symbols and rituals with respect to sacred things and institutionalized in a collectivity. This religion — there seems no other word for it — while not antithetical to, and indeed sharing much in common with, Christianity, was neither sectarian nor in any specific sense Christian.[117]

Viewing the civil religion as a "genuine vehicle of national religious self-understanding,"[118] he maintains that:

(1) it is hardly surprising that a society should sacralize its dominant values (and the events, personages, and artifacts representative of these values) and (2) merely to attack this civil faith as vulgar nationalism is to overlook its profound and indispensable contribution to maintaining a cohesive and viable national society.[119]

Taking the argument further, however, Bellah proclaims:

. . . the civil religion at its best is a genuine apprehension of universal and transcendent religious reality as seen in or, one could almost say, as revealed through the experience of the American people.[120]

If, as Bellah suggests, Durkheim may be considered "a theologian of the French civil religion,"[121] the honour of being the leading contemporary theologian of the American civil religion must undoubtedly go to Bellah himself. Inspired by a Durkheimian concern with the socially integrative, cohesive and reproductive functions of religion, the civil-religion thesis represents a special variant of a neo-Durkheimian approach that postulates the existence of a wide range of secular, political and nationalistic ideologies serving as "functional equivalents" of religion in their respective societies.[122] Thus, although Bellah is preoccupied with the analysis of American society, he emphasizes the wider utility of the civil-religion concept when he notes:

> It would seem that the problem of civil religion is quite general in modern societies and that the way it is solved or not solved will have repercussions in many spheres.[123]

Summing up the particular character of the American civil religion, Bellah states:

> Behind the civil religion at every point lie Biblical archetypes: Exodus, Chosen People, Promised Land, New Jerusalem, Sacrificial Death and Rebirth. But it is also genuinely American and genuinely new. It has its own prophets and its own martyrs, its own sacred events and sacred places, its own solemn rituals and symbols. It is concerned that America be a society as perfectly in accord with the will of god as men can make it, and a light to all the nations.[124]

More generally, however, Bellah's thesis is completely in accord with the view expressed in the classic structural-functional treatment of American society:

> Every functioning society has, to an important degree, a common religion. The possession of a common set of ideas, (ideals), rituals and symbols can supply an overarching sense of unity even in a society otherwise riddled with conflict.[125]

Over the last decade and a half, Bellah has refined and reformulated his thesis in the light of political events that threatened to shatter the fabric of the American nation. Meanwhile, other scholars have followed Bellah's lead, appropriating the civil-religion concept, applying it to settings other than the United States, and thereby reaffirming an essentially Durkheimian view of religion and society.[126] Applied in the contexts of Northern Ireland, Italy, Mexico, Canada and other nations,[127] the concept of civil religion has even been introduced into discussions of the phenomenon of the "New Religious Movements."[128] Though regarded by some critics as an unoriginal and unfruitful concept characterized by vagueness, circularity and a singular lack of insight into the real nature of modern societies, Bellah's civil-religion thesis is arguably a seminal work, "one of the most prodigious ideas to come from the social sciences in many years."[129] It has begotten a significant literature and given rise to one of the most important contemporary debates in the sociology of religion. The civil-religion thesis may indeed be old Durkheimian wine in a new bottle, but it is clear that its potency for scholars within the sub-discipline is undiminished.

Although Durkheim's legacy may be discerned most readily in those perspectives just sketched, the influence of Durkheim on the sociology of religion is certainly not confined to them. Students of both secularization and the "new religious movements," for example, have clearly been affected by Durkheim's monumental struggle to comprehend and control the forces that bind or rend apart modern societies.[130] Both note his interest in the achievement of national solidarity through a secular political or civil religion transmitted through a system of compulsory public education. On the other hand, both ponder the hint of religious rebirth that is explicit in his attempt to envision the future by rising above the moral coldness and mediocrity of his own age.[131]

Durkheim's influence on individual leading scholars of our own day is also profound. Thus, for example, within the sociology of religion, Durkheim's influence may undoubtedly be detected in the work of Peter Berger and Thomas Luckmann, whose separate and joint ventures have themselves achieved classic status in the field.[132] Finally, though its importance should not be exaggerated, there appears to be a new interest in Durkheim among Marxist scholars.[133] To what degree Durkheimians and Marxists may find common ground within the sociology of religion remains at present, however, a matter for speculation.

One Marxist commentator has observed that, for Durkheim, religious symbolism "transforms human dependence upon society into a different set of meanings":[134]

> The sociology of religion is, in effect, a venture in interpretation employing symbolic rationality to establish the underlying rationality of social control. Marx proposed that religion be transcended as part of a process of transcending a given and oppressive state of society. Durkheim proposed that religion be understood so that the true source of morality (and personal integration) could be known.[135]

This appraisal naturally stresses Durkheim's conservatism and indicates its inextricability from his theory of religion. It thus provokes a final brief consideration of issues of consensus, conflict and change in his sociology of religion. Although a concern with change is not entirely absent from Durkheim's analysis of religion, there is no doubt that his primary interest involves social stability and integration rather than change and conflict. In this, of course, he differs fundamentally from Marx and Weber. In a contemporary sociological climate, obsessed with issues of change and conflict, Durkheim's perspective now possesses a somewhat deviant character. Yet this by no means implies its irrelevance. As Bellah rightly observes:

> Each great thinker has his own angle of vision and his own blind spots. It is fashionable to read Durkheim to discover the ways he is not Marx or not Weber.

From such a reading there will be very little instruction. In Durkheim there is to be found a moral vision, a return to the depths of social existence, which is in some ways more radical than that of either of his rivals.[136]

Thus, while the study of social change and conflict is undisputably a worthy cause, this does not mean that the study of social stability has no justification or merit. The undeniable fact that some societies do not change, or change little relative to others, is surely of concern to the sociologist. Integration, persistence and continuity are no less inherently worthy of analysis and investigation than disintegration, conflict and change. In the sociology of religion, as in the field of sociology as a whole, it appears intellectually myopic to study social dynamics to the utter neglect of social statics.[137] The richness of Durkheim's analysis of religion illustrates the truth of this statement eloquently and decisively. Moreover, the degree to which Durkheim's ideas continue to influence the thinking of sociologists of religion demonstrates clearly that, whatever their limitations, their considerable merits do not go unappreciated among members of this sub-discipline. This state of affairs, at least, seems unlikely to change in the forseeable future.

Beyond Weber

Though Parsons' assessment that Weber's writings have been the greatest single influence on the sociology of religion seems of doubtful validity, there can be no doubt that their impact has been both widespread and profound.[138] In the long run, moreover, it seems extremely likely that Weber's work will, indeed, comprise the major source of inspiration for scholars in the sub-discipline. Thus, though it is false as a statement about the past, Parsons' declaration is probably true if converted into a prediction about the future. A sketch of Weber's legacy involves a virtual inventory of areas of research within the sociology of religion; a situation that is not surprising if the vast, encyclopaedic range of Weber's investigations is contemplated. Weber's impact upon North American sociology of religion may be viewed as a two-stage process. The first stage, occurring from the 1930s to the 1950s, primarily involved a quarter-century of assimilation of the arguments propounded in the celebrated work *The Protestant Ethic and the Spirit of Capitalism,* a process by no means completed.[139] The second stage may roughly be said to have begun with the first publication in English of the section of Weber's *Wirtschaft und Gesellschaft* devoted to the sociology of religion.[140]

It is sometimes lamented that, due to linguistic insularity, Weber is still known to many English-speaking scholars primarily as the advocate of the controversial "Protestant Ethic" thesis. It is arguable, however, that posterity has not been wrong in perceiving this provocative, scholarly *tour de force* as centrally important in Weber's enterprise.[141] To underscore this point, it may be noted that Weber's analysis of Protestantism and capitalism has also been the overwhelming concern of Weberian scholarship in his own country.[142] The scholarly dissection of Weber's Protestant Ethic argument is almost a sociological sub-discipline in its own right. Though clearly highly relevant to it, it is understandably by no means confined to the sociology of religion. Nonetheless, sociologists of religion retain a special interest in new research on this topic and make a significant contribution to the continuing and apparently interminable debate.[143] While it has naturally provoked research by sociologists of religion into Puritanism, capitalism, marginality and the links among them, *The Protestant Ethic and the Spirit of Capitalism* has also generated interest in much broader concerns, contributing to the most fundamental assumptions of those within the sub-discipline.[144] However interpreted, it is clear that Weber's thesis asserts the vital importance of religion in human society and the necessity of analyzing it sociologically. This view is essentially the first article of the creed of a sociologist of religion. Furthermore, Weber's stress on the rôle of religion as an independent variable in social change has led sociologists of religion to a more general appreciation of the importance of ideas, values and culture in social order and social change. This fact is illustrated nowhere better than in some of the studies of modernization that have been undertaken in recent years.[145] As a corollary of this observation, it may be observed that the profound influence of Weber's Protestant Ethic thesis has been responsible, at least in part, for the rather cool reception afforded Marxist ideas by sociologists of religion. It seems worthy of note that in the growing convergence between Marxian and Weberian ideas within the sub-discipline, it is Marxism that seems to be undergoing the greater transformation.[146]

A brief review of the other ways in which Weber's influence is felt by contemporary sociologists of religion should undoubtedly begin with a consideration of his still widely imitated definitional stance. Continuing to exert a broad appeal despite the periodic assaults of substantivist critics,[147] Weber's implicit functional identification of religion with the provision of meaning is so inclusive that it co-exists and converges with a Durkheimian perspective in many contemporary formulations.[148] Its breadth and inclusivity have encouraged research into civil, political and secular religion at the same time as they have generated such a radical formulation as Luckmann's "invisible religion," the most inclusive of all sociological definitions of religion.[149] It is hard to decide whether the current definitional situation in the sub-discipline owes more to Durkheim or Weber. Certainly, in the occasional attempt to distinguish magic from religion, the dichotomies of both classic thinkers are equally discernible in the background.[150]

As the founding father of "church-sect theory," Weber's influence is considerable. A veritable sub-disciplinary cottage industry, the analysis of the main types of religious organization, especially sectarianism, has been rivalled over the years only by research into the Protestant Ethic thesis.[151] By providing the original tense conceptual distinction between church and sect, Weber may rightly be regarded as having inspired a venerable tradition of theory and research that remains of central significance within the sub-discipline.[152] While at its worst this enterprise has seemed obsessed with sterile typologizing for its own sake, at its best it has generated insights that have utility far beyond the boundaries of the sociology of religion.[153] Within the tradition of church-sect studies, it should be stressed, Weber is no remote ancestor or patron saint. Ever more elaborate formulations often seem to wend their way back inexorably toward reconsideration of his original, simple dichotomy.[154] Likewise, in a tradition that has been frequently preoccupied with the effect of the inclusive society upon the exclusive sect, the rediscovery of Weber's concern with the impact of the sect on the wider society has been of some significance.[155] Those working within the church-sect tradition appear to be primarily engaged both in the dissection of the classic writings of Troeltsch, Niebuhr and Wach, and in the investigation of the classificatory schemes of such contemporary scholars as Yinger, Wilson, Johnson and Swatos.[156] They nonetheless remain acutely aware of the origins of their enterprise in the tensions and complexities of Weberian analysis.

Clearly overlapping the study of sectarianism, research into religious movements of revolutionary or evolutionary social change is also heavily indebted to Weber, particularly to his discussions of salvation, prophecy and charisma.[157] Although this field is strongly contested by Marxism,[158] the investigation of millenarian, messianic, nativistic and revitalizing movements in contemporary and historical settings owes much to Weber's pioneering researches.[159] Indeed, the best recent work on religious movements in underdeveloped and primitive social contexts explicitly affirms its Weberian inspiration.[160] Meanwhile, students of the so-called "New Religious Movements" that have arisen in the very different conditions of modernized, industrialized, and otherwise secularized societies have also incurred debts to Weber.[161] It is worth remarking, moreover, that a number of scholars have recently exhibited a serious interest in Weber's analysis of mysticism, a topic for so long overshadowed by scholarly pre-occupation with the nature of ascetism.[162] In investigating the social and economic roots of radical religious movements, contemporary research invokes either Marx or Weber, and possibly both. Weber's explorations of the rôle of class and status in the genesis of salvation-religion remains, for many scholars, an indispensable mine of evidence and insight with far more than an antiquarian interest.[163] The brilliance, delicacy and sophistication of Weber's comparative and historical treatment of the relative significance of ideal and material interests in the connections between specific segments of society and particular forms of religiosity still provides a unique model for students approaching this thorny topic undogmatically.[164]

Whether or not Weber is perceived as an advocate of the view that religious decline is an inevitable and irreversible feature of modern society, it is clear that his conception of rationalization is relevant to contemporary work on the process of secularization.[165] Inasmuch as rationalization is increasingly perceived as the unifying theme of Weber's view of society and history, the interest of sociologists of religion in his account of the "disenchantment" or de-mystification of the world appears likely to continue unabated.[166] In particular, his portrait of an intellectualized, systematized, specialized and utilitarian world, whose processes "simply 'are' and 'happen' but no longer signify anything," still provides an incomparable starting-point for any discussion of the nature of a secular society.[167]

Finally, though Weber is clearly alert to the importance of religion in the maintenance of social order, his primary interest is in the rôle of religion in social conflict and social change.[168] Given the prevailing bias of contemporary sociology towards social dynamics as opposed to social statics, Weber's stock seems likely to continue to rise among sociologists of religion for this reason if for no other. But, of course, members of the sub-discipline have more than enough reasons to view Weber's study of religion with profound admiration and gratitude. Amenable, in its scholarly richness, to a variety of scholarly interpretations and reinterpretations, Weber's classic framework for the sociology of religion is characterized by what Parsons terms an "enduring greatness."[169] If its main weakness is that its "application to concrete problems requires such flexibility and such a fund of knowledge as Weber possessed,"[170] Weber's work in this area must nonetheless be mastered by anyone seeking to understand the fate of man in the twentieth century and the rôle of religion in determining that fate. For the sociologist of religion, "a very thorough coming to terms with the nature and implications of Weber's work"[171] is an absolute scholarly essential. In this regard, Parsons' assessment of two decades ago is still as profoundly valid as when it was written:

> Weber's scheme, in the sociology of religion and generally, constituted a great advance in its time, has provided a foundation for further progress in sociology, and remains relevant at its broadest morphological levels. Though Weber's conceptual scheme is certainly far from complete or definitive, it seems unlikely that the broadest outline of the evolutionary pattern of the development of religious orientations . . . will be radically invalidated.[172]

In short, it is true that sociologists of religion are still living off Weber's ideas, and it is right that they should do so.

Classic Themes and Contemporary Issues

It was noted at the beginning of this chapter that the "classic tradition" in sociology is characterized by the character of the questions that have guided those who are part of it. These questions are "generally of wide scope: they concern total societies, their transformations, and the varieties of individual men and women which inhabit them."[173] According to Mills, the answers given by classic sociologists "provide conceptions about society, about history and about biography," and in their work these three are usually linked closely together.[174] Though contemporary sociologists of religion have recently begun to move in a number of very different theoretical directions,[175] it is arguable that the main concerns of students in the sub-discipline are still inspired by the classic tradition. Moreover, at its best, scholarly discussion of the main contemporary themes of the sociology of religion itself exhibits the characteristics of classic sociology.

The theme of "secularization," as the process by which "religious thinking, practice and institutions lose social significance,"[176] is, of course, a venerable one. Just as the process has long been perceived by the man in the street, it has long concerned sociologists of religion and theologians. It is, of course, a major theme in the work of Marx, and equally so in the perspectives of Durkheim and Weber. Yet, if secularization is obvious to the common man, and the "decline of religion" is, with some reservations, an accepted insight of classic sociology, the "secularization thesis" is by no means endorsed universally within the sociology of religion.[177] Though the details of this frequently subtle debate cannot be reviewed in this brief comment, it may be remarked that sociologists of religion are engaged in an extremely important theoretical exchange concerning the nature of what many commentators perceive to be a fundamental and characteristic process of large-scale modern societies.[178] Furthermore, in engaging in such discussion, scholars are led unavoidably to ask the most basic questions about the nature of religion and the character of human society itself. By considering to what extent religion is a societal necessity and whether a purely secular society is possible, sociologists of religion inevitably raise issues that are of central theoretical importance not merely for their sub-discipline but for the sociological enterprise as a whole.[179]

The theme of "civil religion," inspired by Durkheim and infused into the discourse of the sub-discipline by Robert Bellah, has also provoked intense thought about fundamental sociological issues.[180] Like the debate over the "secularization thesis," the arguments about civil religion tackle the most rudimentary questions about the way in which modern societies cohere and persist. Thus, if proponents of the secularization thesis refuse to accord those "values, norms, conventions and orientations to the world laid deep in the socialization process"[181] a religious character in the functionalist manner, opponents of the civil-religion hypothesis are no less reluctant to do so. The argument about civil religion thus reveals fundamental disagreement about the ways in which modern societies work. It is, therefore, of great significance, not just for the sociology of religion but for general sociological theory.[182]

If the study of the "New Religious Movements" that have emerged in recent years is occasionally tainted with an interpretive abstracted empiricism and voyeurism, this enterprise also raises questions of the most profound sort both for sociologists of religion and sociological theorists.[183] Drawing on the insights of Durkheim and Weber and writing an entirely new chapter in "church-sect" study, this recently blossoming field has undoubtedly revitalized the sub-discipline in terms of both research and theory.[184] The range of theoretical opinion on these non-traditional and frequently exotic social movements is immense, and impossible to catalogue here.[185] It must be emphasized, however, that many of these serious sociological attempts to understand the origins, appeals and impact of such organizations raise the most general questions about the modern industrialized societies in which they have emerged. Thus, in its most theoretically sophisticated form, the study of new religious movements may indeed offer a perspective for understanding society as a whole,[186] whether in terms of its integration, disintegration or transformation.[187] It may also offer insight into the crucial problem of individual identity in large-scale, complex societies, a classic sociological issue *par excellence.*[188] Thus, whether they are regarded as the vanguard of a new "Great Awakening" that will shake the foundations of contemporary social order, or perceived merely as a "highly privatized preference that reduces religion to the significance of pushpin, poetry or popcorns,"[189] the new religious movements have undoubtedly provoked some hard theoretical thinking among sociologists of religion. Moreover, the results of this intellectual activity are of relevance to students of collective behaviour, social movements and general sociological theory as well as to sociologists of religion.

Thomas Luckmann's "invisible religion" thesis has generated a heated controversy by offering a radical reformulation of the problem of religion in modern society.[190] Explicitly drawing on the classic views of Durkheim and Weber, Luckmann puts forward an all-inclusive "anthropological" definition of religion in order to rescue sociologists of religion from the clutches of institutionalized churches, sects and denominations.[191] Luckmann's effort to expunge parochialism from the sub-discipline has possibly led him to theoretical excess, and has certainly led him to energetic intellectual confrontation.[192] Nonetheless, his thesis and the discussion it has provoked have made the sociology of religion the locus of a theoretical debate that is of central concern to all sociologists. Observing significantly that the "relevance of sociology for contemporary man derives primarily from its search for an understanding of the fate of the person in the structure of modern society,"[193] Luckmann suggests that the "sociologist today need look no further than the 'classical' traditions of his own discipline to find illumination in this search."[194] Perceiving a convergence in the thinking of Durkheim and Weber, Luckmann attempts to use their insights to solve "the problem of personal existence in society" and to analyze the "changing social . . . basis of religion in modern society."[195] Thus, where Durkheim and Weber "sought the key to an understanding of the social location of the individual in the study of religion," he also perceives the problem of individual existence in society in "religious" terms.[196] Essentially identifying religion with "culture,"[197] Luckmann posits the "emergence of a new social form of religion which . . . is determined by a radical transformation in the relation of the individual to the social order."[198] In so doing, he provides a brilliant theoretical essay on the nature of modern industrial society and its overarching symbolic sacred cosmos. Though they have received a severe reception from some critics, his views on the relation of religion to individual autonomy, individualism, privatization, socialization and dehumanization deserve a hearing far beyond the confines of the sociology of religion.[199] It is to be hoped that the controversy that still surrounds the "invisible religion" thesis within this sub-discipline will attract greater attention from general sociological theorists than has so far been accorded it. Luckmann's work is thus an explicit attempt to give general theoretical sociological significance to the sociology of religion by utilizing the classic tradition. Specifically, it involves a reaffirmation of "Weber's and Durkheim's view of religion as the key to the understanding of society."[200]

Conclusion

At its best, the sociology of religion is a scholarly enterprise that seeks answers to the most fundamental questions regarding "total societies, their transformations and the varieties of men and women that inhabit them."[201] Sharing the view of the founding fathers that religion is a "central issue" for sociology,[202] its practitioners attempt the exercise of a sociological imagination that will enable them to "grasp history and biography and the relations between the two within society."[203] If, therefore, the sociology of religion is theoretically central to the pursuit of sociology as a whole, it may be expected to remain so to the degree that it preserves and extends the classic tradition.

Footnotes to Chapter Six

[1] Howard S. Becker, "What's Happening to Sociology?" *Society,* Vol. 16, No. 5, 1979, p. 24.

[2] See David Martin, "The Sociology of Religion: A Case of Status Deprivation," *British Journal of Sociology,* Vol. 17, 1966, pp. 353-359.

[3] The term "paradigm," frequently misused, gained currency with the publication of Thomas S. Kuhn's *The Nature of Scientific Revolutions,* Chicago: University of Chicago Press, 1962. See also Robert Friedrichs, *The Sociology of Sociology,* New York: The Free Press, 1970.

[4] On the reception of Marxist ideas, see the section on Marxism in this chapter. For recent examples of the phenomenological genre, see Anthony J. Blasi, "Definition of Religion and Phenomenological Approach Toward a Problematic," *Cahiers du CRSR,* Vol. 3, 1980, pp. 55-70; and A.J. Blasi and A.J. Weigert, "Toward a Sociology of Religion: An Interpretive Sociology Approach," *Sociological Analysis,* Vol. 37, 1976, pp. 189-204.

[5] See C. Wright Mills (ed.), *Images of Man,* New York: George Braziller, Inc., 1960, pp. 1-17. In somewhat similar vein, see Robert A. Nisbet, *The Sociological Tradition,* New York: Basic Books, Inc., 1966.

[6] A typical example is Lawrence W. Sherman, "Uses of the Masters," *The American Sociologist,* Vol. 9, 1974, pp. 176-181.

[7] See Alvin W. Gouldner, "Introduction," in Emile Durkheim, *Socialism and Saint-Simon,* (trans. C. Sattler), Yellow Springs, Ohio: The Antioch Press, 1958 (first published in French in 1928). Gouldner observes: "A Science *ignorant* of its founders does not know how far it has travelled nor in what direction; it, too, is lost" (p. vi).

[8] Mills, *Images of Man,* p. 4.

[9] *Ibid,* p. 4.

[10] See Mills, *Images of Man,* pp. 5-7; and Thomas Luckmann, *The Invisible Religion: The Transformation of Symbols in Industrial Society,* New York: The Macmillan Company, 1967, pp. 17-18.

[11] The term "abstracted empiricism" was coined by Mills. See C. Wright Mills, *The Sociological Imagination,* New York: Oxford University Press, 1959, pp. 50-75. For overviews of the field, consult J. Milton Yinger, "The Present Status of the Sociology of Religion," in Richard D. Knudten (ed.), *The Sociology of Religion: An Anthology,* New York: Appleton-Century-Crofts, 1967; David O. Moberg, "Some Trends in the Sociology of Religion in the U.S.A.," *Social Compass,* Vol. 13, 1966, pp. 237-243; D.O. Moberg, "The Sociology of Religion in Western Europe and America," *Social Compass,* Vol. 13, 1966, pp. 193-204; K. Dobbelaere, "Trend Report of the State of The Sociology of Religion: 1965-1966," *Social Compass,* Vol. 15, 1968, pp. 329-365; J.K. Hadden and E.F. Heenan, "Empirical Studies in the Sociology of Religion: An Assessment of the Past Ten Years," *Sociological Analysis,* Vol. 31, 1970, pp. 153-171; Thomas F. O'Dea, "The Sociology of Religion Reconsidered," *Sociological Analysis,* Vol. 31, 1970, pp. 145-151; and Louis Schneider, "The Sociology of Religion: Some Areas of Theoretical Potential," *Sociological Analysis,* Vol. 31, 1970, pp. 131-143. For an overview of Canadian material, see the postscript to this book.

[12] Mills, *Images of Man,* p. 4.

[13] *Ibid,* p. 2.

[14] *Ibid,* p. 2.

[15] *Ibid,* pp. 2-2.

[16] *Ibid,* p. 5.

[17] *Ibid,* p. 5.

[18] See, for example, comment by James Dagenais, "The Scientific Study of Myth and Ritual: A Lost Cause," *The Human Context,* Vol. 6, 1974, p. 617, and James Beckford in a review of an essay in B.R. Wilson (ed.), *The Social Impact of New Religious Movements,* in *Sociology,* Vol. 16, 1982, p. 321.

[19] See the discussion in chapter two of this book.

[20] See Luckmann, *The Invisible Religion*, pp. 18 and 49. The influence of Durkheim is also clear.

[21] This should be clear from chapter two of this book. In particular, the frequent reappearance of the definitional strategies of Tylor, Durkheim and Weber may be noted.

[22] For more recent discussions of magic and religion see Mischa Titiev, "A Fresh Approach to the problem of Magic and Religion," *Southwestern Journal of Anthropology*, Vol. 15, 1960, pp. 292-298; Louis Schneider, "The Scope of 'The Religious Factor' and the Sociology of Religion: Notes on Definition, Idolatry and Magic," *Social Research*, Vol. 41, 1974, pp. 340-361; and Eli Sagan, "Religion and Magic: A Developmental View," in Harry M. Johnson (ed.), *Religious Change and Continuity*, San Francisco: Jossey-Bass, 1979, pp. 87-116.

[23] Mills, *Images of Man*, p. 2.

[24] See Sidney Hook (ed.), *Marx and the Marxists: The Ambiguous Legacy*, New York: Van Nostrand, 1955.

[25] See the discussion of Marx in chapter three of this book, noting especially his connection with Feuerbach and the "Young Hegelians."

[26] See Friedrichs, *The Sociology of Sociology*; and Elizabeth and Tom Burns (eds.), *Sociology of Literature and Drama*, Harmondsworth: Penguin Books, 1973, p. 10.

[27] This situation was completely in line with the general sociological judgement expressed by Talcott Parsons. See Talcott Parsons, *The Structure of Social Action*, Glencoe: The Free Press, 1949 (first published in 1937), pp. 488-495. In his 1968 introduction to the paperback edition of this work, Parsons reiterated his view that the contributions of Marx "belong properly on the wings rather than at the core" of sociological theory (p. xiv).

[28] On the general impact of Marxism, see Tom Bottomore, *Marxist Sociology*, London: Macmillan, 1975; and Peter Worsley, *Marx and Marxism*, London: Tavistock Publications, 1982. Canadian introductory sociology textbooks have notably incorporated Marxist ideas and perspectives. See, for example, Robert Hagedorn (ed.), *Sociology*, Toronto: Holt, Rinehart and Winston, 1980.

[29] The notion of "another side" of the causal chain is, of course, appropriated from Max Weber, *The Protestant Ethic and the Spirit of Capitalism*, London: George Allen and Unwin, 1930, p. 27. A less "deterministic" view of Marxism is characteristic of contemporary Marxian scholarship as a whole. See, for example, Irving M. Zeitlin, "Karl Marx: Aspects of His Social Thought and their Contemporary Relevance" in Buford Rhea (ed.) , *The Future of the Sociological Classics*, London: George Allen and Unwin, 1981, pp. 1-15; George Lichtheim, *Marxism: An Historical and Critical Study* (second edition), New York: Praeger Publishers, 1965; E.J. Hobsbawm, "Introduction" to E.J. Hobsbawm (ed.), *Karl Marx: Precapitalist Economic Formations* (trans. J. Cohen), New York: International Publishers, 1965; and Randall Collins, "Reassessments of Sociological History: The Empirical Validity of the Conflict Tradition," *Theory and Society*, Vol. 1, 1974, pp. 147-178.

[30] Typical of such repetition is Archibald Robertson, *Socialism and Religion: An Essay*, London: Lawrence and Wishart, 1960. The classic polemical source is V.I. Lenin, *Lenin On Religion*, Moscow: Foreign Languages Publishing House (many editions).

[31] See Eduard Bernstein, *Cromwell and Communism* (trans. M.J. Stenning), New York: Schocken Books, 1963 (first published in German in 1895); Karl Kautsky, *Foundations of Christianity* (trans. H.F. Mims), New York: Russell and Russell, 1953; and Delos B. McKown, *The Classical Marxist Critiques of Religion: Marx, Engels, Lenin, Kautsky*, The Hague: Martinus Nijhoff, 1975. For recent Marxist work in this area see, for example, E.J. Hobsbawm, *Primitive Rebels*, New York: Norton Library, 1965; Peter Worsley, *The Trumpet Shall Sound* (second edition), New York: Schocken Books, 1968; and later citations in this chapter.

[32] See, for example, Karl Kautsky, *Communism in Central Europe at the Time of The Reformation* (trans. J.L. and E.G. Mulliken), London: T. Fisher Unwin, 1897; Max Beer, *Social*

Struggles and Socialist Forerunners (trans. H.J. Stenning), New York: International Publishers, 1929; and E. Belfort Bax, *The Social Side of The Reformation in Germany* (3 vols), London: Swan Sonnenschein and Co., 1894-1903. For further discussion of this topic, see Roger O'Toole, *The Precipitous Path,* Toronto: PMA Associates, 1977, especially chapter one.

[33] In chapter five of this book, it was noted that Weber was opposed to this neat characterization, particularly as expressed in the work of Kautsky.

[34] Karl Marx and Frederick Engels, *Selected Works,* Moscow: Foreign Languages Publishing House, 1958, Vol. 2, pp. 205-206.

[35] See Roger O'Toole, "'Underground' Traditions in the Study of Sectarianism: Non-Religious Uses of the Concept 'Sect'," *Journal for the Scientific Study of Religion,* Vol. 15, 1976, pp. 145-156.

[36] See, for example, the discussion in Norman Birnbaum, "Beyond Marx in the Sociology of Religion?" in Charles Glock and Phillip Hammond (eds.), *Beyond the Classics: Essays in the Scientific Study of Religion,* New York: Harper and Row, 1973, pp. 3-70; and the special issue of the journal *Social Compass,* Vol. 22, Nos. 3-4, 1975, devoted to "Marxism and the Sociology of Religion." This publication contains a large bibliography compiled by Otto Maduro.

[37] For insight into Engels' view of religion, see especially his *The Peasant War in Germany,* Moscow: Foreign Languages Publishing House, 1958; and selections in Karl Marx and Frederick Engels, *On Religion,* Moscow: Foreign Languages Publishing House, 1958. The openness of the new approach is characterized in Otto Maduro, "Marxist Analysis and the Sociology of Religion: An Introduction," *Social Compass,* Vol. 22, 1975, pp. 305-322.

[38] Otto Maduro, "Marxist Analysis and the Sociology of Religion," p. 314.

[39] *Ibid,* p. 313.

[40] *Ibid,* p. 312.

[41] See, for example, Jean-Guy Vaillancourt, *Papal Power: A Study of Vatican Control Over Lay Catholic Elites,* Berkeley: University of California Press, 1980; François Houtart and Geneviève Lemercinier, "Weberian Theory and the Ideological Function of Religion," *Social Compass,* Vol. 23, 1976, pp. 345-354; François Houtart, *Religion and Ideology in Sri Lanka,* Maryknoll, New York: Orbis Books, 1980.

[42] This is not to suggest, however, that there are no convergences between the two thinkers or that interchange between Marxists and Weberians is undesirable, but certainly Weber would find "Marxist-Weberianism" a strange combination. On the notion of Weber as an epigone of Marx, see George Lichtheim, *Marxism,* p. 385n; and Benjamin Nelson, "Max Weber's 'Author's Introduction': A Master Clue to His Main Aims," *Sociological Inquiry,* Vol. 44, 1974, p. 275. See also Collins, "Reassessments of Sociological History."

[43] See Otto Maduro, "Marxist Analysis and Sociology of Religions: An Outline of International Bibliography up to 1975," *Social Compass,* Vol. 22, 1975, p. 401.

[44] See, for example, Otto Maduro, *Religion and Social Conflicts,* Maryknoll, New York: Orbis Books, 1982; and Oleg Mandić, "A Marxist Perspective on Contemporary Religious Revivals," *Social Research,* Vol. 37, 1970, pp. 237-258.

[45] Maduro, "Marxist Analysis and the Sociology of Religion," p. 315.

[46] At least in Western Marxism, attention in recent years has shifted away from a concern with economic infra-structure toward such topics as art, literature, ideology and cultural production. It is sometimes commented that some discussions are neo-Hegelian more than neo-Marxist. Within such analysis, the notion of culture as a simple reflection of economic or social structure is heavily criticized, as for example in the works of Lukacs, Goldmann, Gramsci and Korsch. In a different vein, the works of Althusser are also relevant to this theme. See Perry Anderson, *Western Marxism,* London: New Left Books, 1976.

[47] Pierre Bonte, "Cattle for God: An Attempt at a Marxist Analysis of East African Herdsmen," *Social Compass,* Vol. 22, 1975, pp. 381-396.

[48] Maduro, "Marxist Analysis and the Sociology of Religion," pp. 320-321.

[49] Otto Maduro, "New Marxist Approaches to the Relative Autonomy of Religion," *Sociological Analysis,* Vol. 38, 1977, p. 359.

[50] *Ibid,* p. 359.

[51] *Ibid,* p. 366.

[52] See footnote 41 of this chapter. On the relationship between Marx and Weber, see for example, Karl Löwith, *Max Weber and Karl Marx* (ed. Tom Bottomore and William Outhwaite; trans. Hans Fantel), London: George Allen and Unwin, 1982 (first published in German in 1960), especially pp. 102-107; Lucien Goldmann, *The Hidden God* (trans. Philip Thody), London: Routledge and Kegan Paul, 1964 (first published in French in 1955); Terry Lovell, "Weber, Goldmann and the Sociology of Beliefs," *European Journal of Sociology,* Vol. 14, 1973, pp. 304-323; Jean Seguy, "The Marxist Classics and Ascetism," *Annual Review of the Social Sciences of Religion,* Vol. 1, 1977, pp. 79-101; Norman Birnbaum, "Conflicting Interpretations of the Rise of Capitalism: Marx and Weber," *British Journal of Sociology,* Vol. 4, 1953, pp. 289-310; and Bryan S. Turner, "Class Solidarity and System Integration," *Sociological Analysis,* Vol. 38, 1977, pp. 345-358.

[53] See for example, Marko Kersevan, "Religion and the Marxist Concept of Social Formation," *Social Compass,* Vol. 22, 1975, pp. 323-342; Daniel Vidal, "Pour une lecture marxiste du prophétisme: champ autre et champ outre," *Social Compass,* Vol. 22, 1975, pp. 355-380; Arnaldo Nesti, "Gramsci et la religion populaire," *Social Compass,* Vol. 22, 1975, pp. 343-354; Pierre Bonte, "Cattle for God"; and Maurice Godelier, *Perspectives in Marxist Anthropology,* Cambridge: Cambridge University Press, 1979. See also Maduro, "New Marxist Approaches" for discussion of the works of Maurice Godelier, Hughes Portelli and Pierre Bourdieu.

[54] See the articles by Nesti and Vidal cited in footnote 53; and works by Houtart and Lemercinier cited in footnote 41. See also Trevor Ling, *Karl Marx and Religion in Europe and India,* New York: Barnes and Noble, 1980.

[55] See, for example, Sheelagh Strawbridge, "Althusser's Theory of Ideology and Durkheim's Account of Religion: An Examination of Some Striking Parallels," *The Sociological Review,* Vol. 30, 1982, pp. 125-140. More generally, see Tom Bottomore, "A Marxist Consideration of Durkheim," *Social Forces,* Vol. 59, 1981, pp. 902-917.

[56] On the Frankfurt School see Martin Jay, *The Dialectical Imagination,* London: Heinemann, 1973; Trent Schroyer, *The Critique of Domination,* New York: George Braziller, 1973; Raymond Geuss, *The Idea of a Critical Theory,* Cambridge: Cambridge University Press, 1981; Philip Slater, *Origins and Significance of the Frankfurt School,* London: Routledge and Kegan Paul, 1977; and John O'Neill (ed.), *On Critical Theory,* New York: Seabury Press, 1976. A useful collection of writings is Andrew Arato and Eike Gebhart (eds.), *The Essential Frankfurt School Reader,* Oxford: Basil Blackwell, 1978. Representative works of the Frankfurt School are: Jürgen Habermas, *Knowledge and Human Interests,* Boston: Beacon Press, 1971; J. Habermas, *Toward a Rational Society,* Boston: Beacon Press, 1970; J. Habermas, *Theory and Practice,* Boston: Beacon Press, 1973; J. Habermas, *Legitimation Crisis,* Boston: Beacon Press, 1975; Max Horkheimer, *Critical Theory,* New York: Herder and Herder, 1972; Max Horkheimer and Theodor Adorno, *Dialectic of Enlightenment,* New York: Herder and Herder, 1972; and T.W. Adorno, "Theses Upon Art and Religion Today," *Kenyon Review,* Vol. 7, 1945, pp. 677-681. See also Ingo Morth, "La Sociologie de la religion comme Théorie Critique," *Social Compass,* Vol. 27, 1980, pp. 27-50; Rudolf J. Siebert, *Horkheimer's Critical Sociology of Religion,* Washington, D.C.: University Press of America, 1979; and Cary J. Nederman and James Wray Goulding, "Popular Occultism and Critical Social Theory: Exploring some Themes in Adorno's Critique of Astrology and the Occult," *Sociological Analysis,* Vol. 42, 1982, pp. 325-332.

[57] On this topic, see Birnbaum, "Beyond Marx in the Sociology of Religion?" pp. 60-62; A. Van Der Bent, *The Christian-Marxist Dialogue,* Geneva: World Council of Churches, 1969; Peter Hebblethwaite, *The Christian-Marxist Dialogue,* New York: Paulist Press, 1977; Roger

Garaudy, *The Alternative Future: A Vision of Christian Marxism* (trans. Leonard Mayhew), New York: Simon and Schuster, Inc., 1974; Dale Vree, *On Synthesizing Marxism and Christianity*, New York: John Wiley and Sons, 1976; Roger Garaudy, *From Anathema to Dialogue*, New York: Vintage Books, 1968; and William W. Mayrl, "The Christian-Marxist Encounter: From Dialogue to Detente," *Sociological Analysis*, Vol. 39, 1978, pp. 84-89. The work of Ernst Bloch has been important in this context. See for example, Ernst Bloch, *A Philosophy of the Future* (trans. John Cumming), New York: Herder and Herder, 1970.

[58] See, for example, Gregory Baum, *Religion and Alienation: A Theological Reading of Sociology*, New York: Paulist Press, 1975; Jürgen Moltmann, *Theology of Hope*, New York: Harper and Row, 1967; and J. Moltmann, *Religion, Revolution and the Future*, New York: Scribner's, 1969.

[59] Maduro, "Marxist Analysis and the Sociology of Religion," p. 315.

[60] See Maduro, *Religion and Social Conflicts*; Maduro, "Catholic Church, State Power and Popular Movements," paper presented to the 1982 Meeting of the Society for the Scientific Study of Religion; and Henri Desroche, *Jacob and the Angel: An Essay in Sociologies of Religion* (trans. J.K. Savacool), Amherst: University of Massachusetts Press, 1973.

[61] Birnbaum, "Beyond Marx in the Sociology of Religion?" p. 61.

[62] The sub-disciplines of political sociology and the sociology of deviance have been notably affected.

[63] For example, Peter L. Berger, *The Sacred Canopy*, Garden City, N.Y.: Doubleday and Company, 1967.

[64] See footnotes 41 and 52. Contemporary Marxist sociologists of religion refuse to see their standpoint as summarized in the phrase "religion is the opium of the people." In this context, see Gary Marx, "Religion: Opiate or Inspiration of Civil Rights Militancy Among Negroes?" in *American Sociological Review*, Vol. 32, 1967, pp. 64-72; and H. Wesley Perkins, "Organized Religion as Opiate or Prophetic Stimulant: A Study of American and English Assessments of Social Justice in Two Settings," *Review of Religious Research*, Vol. 24, 1983, pp. 206-224.

[65] This is so whether or not Marx's ideas are perceived as belonging to the core of sociological theory.

[66] Parsons questions this view, perceiving Durkheim as having been too far ahead of his time to be sufficiently acclaimed. See Talcott Parsons, "Durkheim on Religion Revisited: Another Look at the Elementary Forms of the Religious Life" in Glock and Hammond, *Beyond the Classics?* p. 174.

[67] See, for example, Kingsley Davis, *Human Society*, New York: Macmillan and Company, 1949, pp. 509-548; Elizabeth Nottingham, *Religion and Society*, New York: Random House, Inc., 1962; Thomas F. O'Dea, *The Sociology of Religion*, Englewood Cliffs, N.J.: Prentice-Hall, Inc., 1966; and J. Milton Yinger, *Religion, Society and the Individual*, New York: The Macmillan Co., 1957. See also R. Dale Givens, "The Treatment of Religion in Introductory Sociology Texts," *Journal for the Scientific Study of Religion*, Vol. 5, 1965, pp. 59-63; Joseph B. Tamney, "Textbooks in the Sociology of Religion: A Review Article," *Sociological Analysis*, Vol. 27, 1966, pp. 106-112; and Richard L. Means, "Textbooks in the Sociology of Religion: A Review Article," *Sociological Analysis*, Vol. 27, 1966, pp. 101-105.

[68] As noted in chapter four of this book, a concern with social change is not entirely absent from Durkheim's perspective but it is undoubtedly overshadowed.

[69] See, for example, the discussion of functionalist definitions in chapter two of this book.

[70] Critics have taken particular exception to Durkheim's "leap" from a primitive to a modern context and his assumption that religion functions identically in both cases. This view, incidentally, seems to contradict the view of "mechanical" and "organic" solidarity expressed in his *Division of Labour*. See Emile Durkheim, *The Elementary Forms of The Religious Life* (trans. J.W. Swain), New York: Collier Books, 1961; and Emile Durkheim, *The Division of*

Labour in Society (trans. George Simpson), New York: The Free Press, 1933. See also Phillip E. Hammond, "Religious Pluralism and Durkheim's Integration Thesis," in Allan W. Eister (ed.), *Changing Perspectives in the Scientific Study of Religion,* New York: John Wiley and Sons, 1974, pp. 115-142.

[71] Hammond, "Religious Pluralism and Durkheim's Integration Thesis," p. 113.

[72] Mills, *Images of Man,* p. 2. For a recent re-interpretation of this classic, see Edward A. Tiryakian, "Durkheim's 'Elementary Forms' as 'Revelation'," in Buford Rhea, *The Future of the Sociological Classics,* pp. 114-135.

[73] See, for example, the remarks in Parsons, "Durkheim on Religion Revisited," p. 175. Parsons traces Durkheim's influence on both Lévi-Strauss and Piaget. Durkheim's influence on structural-functionalism is mediated by A.R. Radcliffe-Brown and to the greatest extent by Parsons himself.

[74] This loose designation of two main lines of interpretation of Durkheim was utilized in Chapter Four of this book. See also Dean R. Gerstein, "Reading Durkheim," *Sociological Inquiry,* Vol. 51, 1981, p. 69.

[75] See Robert N. Bellah (ed.), *Emile Durkheim: On Morality and Society,* Chicago: University of Chicago Press, 1973, p. l.

[76] See mainly Guy E. Swanson, *The Birth of the Gods,* Ann Arbor: University of Michigan Press, 1964; G.E. Swanson, *Religion and Regime,* Ann Arbor: University of Michigan Press, 1967; and G.E. Swanson, "Interpreting the Reformation," *Journal of Interdisciplinary History,* Vol. 1, 1971, pp. 419-446.

[77] See J. Alan Winter, "The Metaphoric Parallelist Approach to the Sociology of Theistic Belief: Theme, Variations and Implications," *Sociological Analysis,* Vol. 34, 1973, p. 213.

[78] Durkheim was, of course, aware that it was possible to read such a convergence into his work. See Durkheim, *Elementary Forms,* p. 471. On parallels and convergence between Marx and Durkheim see Winter, "The Metaphoric Parallelist Approach," pp. 218-219; Tom Bottomore, "A Marxist Consideration of Durkheim;" and Sheelagh Strawbridge, "Althusser's Theory of Ideology and Durkheim's Account of Religion."

[79] Winter, "The Metaphoric Parallelist Approach," p. 215.

[80] *Ibid,* pp. 218.

[81] *Ibid,* pp. 216.

[82] Swanson, *Birth of the Gods,* p. 27.

[83] Winter, "The Metaphoric Parallelist Approach," p. 216.

[84] *Ibid,* p. 213, note 3. Winter denies that this approach is necessarily reductionist.

[85] See, for example, J. Alan Winter, "Immanence and Regime in the Kingdom of Judah: A Cross-Disciplinary Study of a Swansonian Hypothesis," *Sociological Analysis,* Vol. 44, 1983 (forthcoming); Ralph Underhill, "Economic and Political Antecedents of Monotheism: A Cross-Cultural Study," *American Journal of Sociology,* Vol. 80, 1975, pp. 841-861; G.E. Swanson, "Monotheism, Materialism, and Collective Purpose: An Analysis of Underhill's Correlations," *American Journal of Sociology,* Vol. 80, 1975, pp. 862-869; R. Underhill, "Economy, Polity, and Monotheism: Reply to Swanson," *American Journal of Sociology,* Vol. 82, 1976, pp. 418-421; G.E. Swanson, "Comment on Underhill's Reply," *American Journal of Sociology,* Vol. 82, 1976, pp. 421-423; John H. Simpson, "Sovereign Groups, Subsistence Activities, and the Presence of a High God in Primitive Societies," in Robert Wuthnow (ed.), *The Religious Dimension: New Directions in Quantitative Research,* New York: Academic Press, Inc., 1979, pp. 299-310; and Randall Collins, "The Sociology of God," in R. Collins, *Sociological Insight: An Introduction to Non-Obvious Sociology,* New York: Oxford University Press, 1982.

[86] See Robert N. Bellah, "Between Religion and Social Science," in R.N. Bellah, *Beyond Belief: Essays on Religion in a Post-Traditional World,* New York: Harper and Row, 1970, pp. 237-259; and R.N. Bellah, "Comment on 'The Limits of Symbolic Realism,'" *Journal for the Scientific Study of Religion,* Vol. 13, 1974, pp. 487-489.

[87] R.N. Bellah, introduction to R.N. Bellah (ed.), *Emile Durkheim: On Morality and Society,* pp.li-liii. For Durkheim's essay, see Emile Durkheim, *Sociology and Philosophy* (trans. D.F. Pocock), London: Cohen and West Ltd., 1953, pp. 80-97 (essay first published in French in 1911).

[88] Bellah, introduction to *Emile Durkheim: On Morality and Society,* p. 1ii.

[89] *Ibid,* p. 1ii.

[90] *Ibid,* p. lii.

[91] Bellah, *Beyond Belief,* p. 253.

[92] *Ibid,* p. 253.

[93] *Ibid,* p. 251.

[94] Dick Anthony and Thomas Robbins, "From Symbolic Realism to Structuralism," *Journal for the Scientific Study of Religion,* Vol. 14, 1975, p. 403.

[95] Bellah, *Beyond Belief,* pp. 250-251.

[96] See footnote 87.

[97] Bellah, *Beyond Belief,* p. 252.

[98] *Ibid,* pp. 252-253. See also Durkheim, *Elementary Forms,* pp. 28-29.

[99] *Ibid,* p. 253.

[100] *Ibid,* p. 254.

[101] *Ibid,* p. 254.

[102] *Ibid,* p. 256.

[103] Durkheim, *Elementary Forms,* p. 14.

[104] In particular, the idea that Bellah attempts to use social science to vindicate religion has infuriated some scholars. Others have perceived Bellah as carrying the detente between sociology and theology too far into the sphere of theology. See, for example, Anthony and Robbins, "From Symbolic Realism to Structuralism;" Thomas Robbins, Dick Anthony and Thomas Curtis, "The Limits of Symbolic Realism: Problems of Empathic Field Observation in a Sectarian Context," *Journal for the Scientific Study of Religion,* Vol. 12, 1973, pp. 259-271; Dick Anthony, Thomas Robbins and Thomas Curtis, "Reply to Bellah," *Journal for the Scientific Study of Religion,* Vol. 13, 1974, pp. 491-495; and Benton Johnson, "Sociological Theory and Religious Truth," *Sociological Analysis,* Vol. 38, 1977, pp. 368-388.

[105] See Robert N. Bellah, "Christianity and Symbolic Realism," *Journal for the Scientific Study of Religion,* Vol. 9, 1970, pp. 89-96 (reprinted as part two of the essay "Between Religion and Social Science" and published in Bellah, *Beyond Belief*); Samuel Z. Klausner, "Scientific and Humanistic Study of Religion: A Comment on 'Christianity and Symbolic Realism,'" *Journal for the Scientific Study of Religion,* Vol. 9, 1970, pp. 100-106; Benjamin Nelson, "Is the Sociology of Religion Possible? A Reply to Robert Bellah," *Journal for the Scientific Study of Religion,* Vol. 9, 1970, pp. 107-111; Robert N. Bellah, "Response to Comments on 'Christianity and Symbolic Realism,'" *Journal for the Scientific Study of Religion,* Vol. 9, 1970, pp. 112-115; Daniel L. Hodges, "Breaking a Scientific Taboo: Putting Assumptions About the Supernatural Into Scientific Theories of Religion," *Journal for the Scientific Study of Religion,* Vol. 13, 1974, pp. 393-408; William C. Shepherd, "Religion and the Social Sciences: Conflict or Reconciliation?" *Journal for the Scientific Study of Religion,* Vol. 11, 1972, pp. 230-239; William C. Shepherd, "Robert Bellah's Sociology of Religion: The Theoretical Elements," *Journal for the Scientific Study of Religion,* Vol. 14, 1975, pp. 395-402; Ralph Burhoe, "The Phenomenon of Religion Seen Scientifically," in Allan W. Eister (ed.), *Changing Perspectives in the Scientific Study of Religion,* pp. 15-40; and, most recently, Michael A. Cavanaugh, "Pagan and Christian: Sociological Euhemerism Versus American Sociology," *Sociological Analysis,* Vol. 43, 1982, pp. 109-130. On the relations between sociology and theology, see Robert W. Friedrichs, "Social Research and Theology: End of the Detente?" *Review of Religious Research,* Vol. 15, 1974, pp. 113-127; and David Martin, John O. Mills and W.S.F. Pickering, *Sociology and Theology: Alliance and Conflict,* New York: St. Martins

Press, 1980. Roland Robertson has coined the term "sociotheologian." See R. Robertson, "Sociologists and Secularization," *Sociology,* Vol. 5, 1971, p. 309.

[106] See Jean-Jacques Rousseau, *The Social Contract,* any edition, Chapter 8, Book 4.

[107] See the comments in Parsons, "Durkheim on Religion Revisited," pp. 175-176; and Robert E. Stauffer, "Bellah's Civil Religion," *Journal for the Scientific Study of Religion,* Vol. 14, 1975, p. 390.

[108] See Parsons, *Structure of Social Action,* p. 427.

[109] See Hammond, "Religious Pluralism and Durkheim's Integration Thesis," p. 115.

[110] *Ibid,* pp. 115 and 117.

[111] Durkheim, *Elementary Forms,* p. 432.

[112] Stauffer, "Bellah's Civil Religion," p. 390. Most notable among Bellah's predecessors in this regard is Will Herberg, *Protestant-Catholic-Jew,* Garden City, New York: Doubleday and Co., 1959 (revised edition). Perceiving the "American Way of Life" as the "common religion" and "operative faith" of the American people (p. 75), Herberg adds that this "'common faith' of American society is not merely a civic religion to celebrate the values and convictions of the American people as a corporate entity" (p. 89). See also W. Lloyd Warner, *The Living and the Dead: A Study in the Symbolic Life of Americans,* New Haven, Connecticut: Yale University Press, 1959. For parallel British discussions of the 1950s see Edward Shils and Michael Young, "The Meaning of the Coronation," *Sociological Review,* Vol. 1, 1953, pp. 63-81; and Norman Birnbaum, "Monarchs and Sociologists: A Reply to Professor Shils and Mr. Young," *Sociological Review,* Vol. 3, 1955, pp. 5-23. Bellah's essay created a stir on its appearance in 1967. See Robert N. Bellah, "Civil Religion in America," *Daedalus,* Vol. 96, 1967, pp. 1-21. (Page references below are to its reprinting in Bellah, *Beyond Belief.*)

[113] Bellah, *Beyond Belief,* p. 168.

[114] *Ibid,* p. 171.

[115] *Ibid,* p. 171.

[116] *Ibid,* p. 171.

[117] *Ibid,* p. 175.

[118] *Ibid,* p. 176.

[119] Stauffer, "Bellah's Civil Religion," p. 390.

[120] Bellah, *Beyond Belief,* p. 179.

[121] Bellah, introduction to *Emile Durkheim: On Morality and Society,* p. xvii.

[122] Bellah notes his indebtedness to the "Durkheimian notion that every group has a religious dimension" in the first footnote to his essay. See *Beyond Belief,* p. 187. See, for example, J. Milton Yinger, *Religion, Society and the Individual,* pp. 117-124; Sally F. Moore and Barbara G. Meyerhoff (eds.), *Secular Ritual,* Assen/Amsterdam: Van Gorcum, 1977; Donald MacRae, "The Bolshevik Ideology" in D.G. MacRae, *Ideology and Society,* London: Heinemann, 1961, pp. 181-197; George Urban (ed.), *The Miracles of Chairman Mao: A Compendium of Devotional Literature, 1966-1970,* London: Tom Stacy Ltd., 1971; Albert James Bergeson, "A Durkheimian Theory of 'Witch Hunts' with the Chinese Cultural Revolution of 1966-1969 as an Example," *Journal for the Scientific Study of Religion,* Vol. 17, 1978, pp. 19-29; Nina Tumarkin, *Lenin Lives! The Lenin Cult in Soviet Russia,* Cambridge: Harvard University Press, 1983; Lewis Lipsitz, "If, as Verba says, the State functions as a religion, what are we to do to save our souls?" *American Political Science Review,* Vol. 62, 1968, pp. 527-535; Morris R. Cohen, "Baseball as a National Religion" in M.R. Cohen, *The Faith of a Liberal,* New York: Henry Holt, 1946, pp. 334-336; and Tom Sinclair-Faulkner, "Hockey in Canada: A Puckish Reflection on Religion in Canada," in Peter Slater (ed.), *Religion and Culture in Canada,* Waterloo, Ontario: Wilfrid Laurier University Press, 1977, pp. 383-405.

[123] Bellah, *Beyond Belief,* p. 181.

[124] *Ibid,* p. 186.

[125] Robin M. Williams, *American Society: A Sociological Interpretation,* New York: Alfred A. Knopf, 1952, p. 312.

[126] Bellah's other writings on this topic include "Response to Commentaries on 'Civil Religion in America,'" in Donald R. Cutler (ed.), *The Religious Situation: 1968,* Boston; Beacon Press, 1968, pp. 388-393; "American Civil Religion in the 1970s," in Russell E. Richey and Donald G. Jones (eds.), *American Civil Religion,* New York: Harper and Row, 1974, pp. 255-272; and *The Broken Covenant: American Civil Religion in Time of Trial,* New York: Seabury Press, 1975; "Religion and Legitimation in the American Republic" in Thomas Robbins and Dick Anthony (eds.), *In Gods We Trust: New Patterns of Religious Pluralism in America,* New Brunswick, N.J.: Transaction Books, 1981; and R.N. Bellah and Phillip E. Hammond, *Varieties of Civil Religion,* New York: Harper and Row, 1980. The most useful collection of papers on the topic is Richey and Jones (eds.), *American Civil Religion.* A recent monograph is Gail Gehrig, *American Civil Religion: An Assessment,* Storrs, Connecticut: Society for the Scientific Study of Religion, 1979. See also John A. Coleman, "Civil Religion," *Sociological Analysis,* Vol. 31, 1970, pp. 67-77; William A. Cole and Phillip E. Hammond, "Religious Pluralism, Legal Development, and Societal Complexity: Rudimentary Forms of Civil Religion," *Journal for the Scientific Study of Religion,* Vol. 13, 1974, pp. 177-189; and Ellis M. West, "A Proposed Neutral Definition of Civil Religion," *Journal of Church and State,* Vol. 22, 1980, pp. 23-40. Extensive bibliography is to be found in Boardman Kathan and Nancy Fuchs-Kreimer, "Civil Religion in America," *Religious Education,* Vol. 70, 1975, pp. 451-550; and Phillip E. Hammond, "The Sociology of American Civil Religion: A Bibliographic Essay," *Sociological Analysis,* Vol. 37, 1976, pp. 169-182.

[127] See, for example, Bellah and Hammond, *Varieties of Civil Religion,* Part 2, "Civil Religion in Comparative Perspective," pp. 27-118; Meredith B. McGuire, *Religion: The Social Context,* Belmont, California: Wadsworth Publishing Co., 1981, pp. 149-179; Jennifer McDowell, "Soviet Civil Ceremonies," *Journal for the Scientific Study of Religion,* Vol. 13, 1974, pp. 265-279, 1974; and Pamela M. Jolicoeur and Louis K. Knowles, "Fraternal Associations and Civil Religion: Scottish Rite Freemasonry," *Review of Religious Research,* Vol. 20, 1978, pp. 3-22. The most recent articles in the comparative genre are: John Markoff and Daniel Regan, "The Rise and Fall of Civil Religion: Comparative Perspectives," *Sociological Analysis,* Vol. 42, 1982, pp. 333-352; Lilly Weissbrod, "Religion as National Identity in a Secular Society," *Review of Religious Research,* Vol. 24, 1983, pp. 188-205; and Michael C. Kearl and Anoel Rinaldi, "The Political Uses of the Dead as Symbols in Contemporary Civil Religions," *Social Forces,* Vol. 61, 1983, pp. 693-708. On civil religion in Canada, see William A. Stahl, "Civil Religion and Canadian Confederation," unpublished doctoral dissertation, Graduate Theological Union, Berkeley, California, 1981; Robert Blumstock, "Civil Uncivility: Non-Civil Religion in Canada," paper presented to the Annual Meeting of the Society for the Scientific Study of Religion, 1977; Peter Slater, "On the Apparent Absence of Civil Religion in Canada" (mimeographed); John H. Simpson, "Ethnic Groups and Church Attendance in the United States and Canada" in Andrew M. Greeley and Gregory Baum (eds.), *Ethnicity,* New York: Seabury Press, 1977, pp. 16-22; Hans Mol, *Faith and Fragility,* Chapter 16, "National Identity," Waterloo, Ontario: Wilfrid Laurier University Press (forthcoming); and Roger O'Toole, "Some Good Purpose: Notes on Religion and Political Culture in Canada," *Annual Review of the Social Sciences of Religion,* Vol. 6, 1982 (forthcoming).

[128] See, for example, Bellah and Hammond, *Varieties of Civil Religion,* Part 4, "Civil Religion and New Religious Movements," pp. 167-205; and the discussion of "new civil-religious sects" in Robbins and Anthony (eds.), *In Gods We Trust,* pp. 17-24, 161-243.

[129] Jeffrey Hadden, introduction to Review Symposium, "The Sociology of Religion of Robert Bellah," *Journal for the Scientific Study of Religion,* Vol. 14, 1975, p. 386. For a dissenting view on the utility of the civil-religion concept in advanced societies, see Richard K. Fenn, "Toward a New Sociology of Religion," *Journal for the Scientific Study of Religion,* Vol. 11, 1972, pp. 16-32. Fenn argues cogently that rather than eliminating religion from society, secularization fosters a kind of religion "which has no major function for the *entire* society" (p. 31). He thus questions the assumption that "religion or its functional alternatives inevitably

provides the basis for the cultural integration of all societies" (p. 16). See also R.K. Fenn, "The Process of Secularization: A Post-Parsonian View," *Journal for the Scientific Study of Religion,* Vol. 9, 1970, pp. 117-136.

[130] See, for example, Hammond, "Religious Pluralism and Durkheim's Integration Thesis"; David E. Greenwald, "Durkheim on Society, Thought and Ritual," *Sociological Analysis,* Vol. 34, 1973, pp. 157-158; Ruth A. Wallace, "The Secular Ethic and the Spirit of Patriotism," *Sociological Analysis,* Vol. 34, 1973, pp. 3-11; Frances Westley, " 'The Cult of Man': Durkheim's Predictions and New Religious Movements," *Sociological Analysis,* Vol. 39, 1978, pp. 135-145; and Thomas Robbins and Dick Anthony, "New Religious Movements and the Social System: Integration, Disintegration and Transformation," *Annual Review of the Social Sciences of Religion,* Vol. 2, 1978, pp. 1-28.

[131] See Durkheim, *Elementary Forms,* p. 475; and Bellah, introduction to *Emile Durkheim: On Morality and Society,* p. xlvii.

[132] See, for example, Peter L. Berger, *The Sacred Canopy;* Thomas Luckmann, *The Invisible Religion;* and Peter L. Berger and Thomas Luckmann, *The Social Construction of Reality,* Garden City, New York: Doubleday and Co., 1966. See also Durkheim's influence on the anthropologist Clifford Geertz in C. Geertz, *The Interpretation of Cultures,* New York: Basic Books, 1973.

[133] See, for example, Bottomore, "A Marxist Consideration of Durkheim"; and Strawbridge, "Althusser's Theory of Ideology and Durkheim's Account of Religion."

[134] Birnbaum, "Beyond Marx in the Sociology of Religion?" p. 35.

[135] *Ibid,* p. 35.

[136] Bellah, introduction to *Emile Durkheim: On Morality and Society,* p. liv.

[137] The terms "social dynamics" and "social statics" were utilized by both Comte and Spencer in their early programmes of sociology.

[138] See Parsons, "Durkheim on Religion Revisited," p. 174.

[139] *Ibid,* p. 174. See Max Weber, *The Protestant Ethic.*

[140] See Max Weber, *The Sociology of Religion* (trans. E. Fischoff), Boston: Beacon Press, 1963 (first published in German in 1922). See also the review of this translation by Benjamin Nelson in *American Sociological Review,* Vol. 30, 1965, pp. 595-599.

[141] See the comment by Donald MacRae in D.G. MacRae, *Weber,* London: Fontana Books, 1974, p. 78.

[142] See Constans Seyfarth, "The West German Discussion of Max Weber's Sociology of Religion Since the 1960s," *Social Compass,* Vol. 27, 1980, pp. 5-8.

[143] For brief reviews of the topic, incorporating extensive bibliography, see Benjamin Nelson, "Weber's Protestant Ethic: Its Origins, Wanderings and Forseeable Futures," in Glock and Hammond (eds.), *Beyond the Classics?* pp. 71-130; and S.N. Eisenstadt, "The Implications of Weber's Sociology of Religion for Understanding Processes of Change in Contemporary Non-European Societies and Civilizations," in Glock and Hammond, *Beyond the Classics?* pp. 131-155.

[144] Karl H. Hertz, "Max Weber and American Puritanism," *Journal for the Scientific Study of Religion,* Vol. 1, 1961-62, pp. 189-197; Benton Johnson, "Max Weber and American Protestantism," *Sociological Quarterly,* Vol. 12, 1971, pp. 473-485; Paul Gustafson, "Exegesis on the Gospel According to St. Max," *Sociological Analysis,* Vol. 34, 1973, pp. 12-25; Richard L. Means, "American Protestantism and Max Weber's Protestant Ethic," *Religious Education,* Vol. 60, 1965, pp. 90-98; Dennis P. Forcese, "Calvinism, Capitalism and Confusion: the Weberian Thesis Revisited," *Sociological Analysis,* Vol. 29, 1968, pp. 193-201; and David Little, "Max Weber and the Comparative Study of Religious Ethics," *Journal of Religious Ethics,* Vol. 2, 1974, pp. 5-40. See chapter five of this book for further bibliography.

[145] See, for example, S.N. Eisenstadt (ed.), *The Protestant Ethic and Modernization,* New York: Basic Books, 1968; and Bellah, *Beyond Belief,* Part Two, pp. 151-167.

[146] Weberianism has certainly made no concession comparable to the abandonment of economic determinism.

[147] For criticisms of Weber see Peter L. Berger, *The Sacred Canopy,* Appendix I, pp. 175-177; and Peter L. Berger, "Some Second Thoughts on Substantive Versus Functional Definitions of Religion," *Journal for the Scientific Study of Religion,* Vol. 13, 1974, pp. 125-133. See also Andrew J. Weigert, "Functional, Substantive, or Political? A Comment on Berger's 'Second Thoughts on Defining Religion,'" *Journal for the Scientific Study of Religion,* Vol. 13, 1974, pp. 483-486. See also the discussion of functional and substantive definitions in chapter two of this text.

[148] The convergence of Weber and Durkheim in this respect has been a crucial foundation of Parsonian structural-functionalism as well as of the "invisible-religion" thesis of Thomas Luckmann. See Luckmann, *The Invisible Religion,* p. 19 and see the discussion of this theme later in this chapter.

[149] See footnote 192 of this chapter and Luckmann, *The Invisible Religion,* p. 69.

[150] See footnote 22 of this chapter.

[151] See Max Weber, "The Protestant Sects and the Spirit of Capitalism," in H.H. Gerth and C.W. Mills (trans. and ed.), *From Max Weber: Essays in Sociology,* London: Routledge and Kegan Paul, 1948, pp. 305-306; and Max Weber, *The Theory of Social and Economic Organization* (trans. A.M. Henderson and T. Parsons), New York: The Free Press, 1947, p. 157. Weber contrasts the "obligatory" nature of the church with the "voluntary" nature of the sect. Membership in the church he sees as proving nothing; membership in the sect denotes religious and moral qualification.

[152] Some of the major works in this tradition are: Ernst Troeltsch, *The Social Teaching of the Christian Churches* (trans. Olive Wyon), London: Allen and Unwin, 1931; H. Richard Niebuhr, *The Social Sources of Denominationalism,* Cleveland: World Publishing Company, 1957 (first published in 1929); J. Milton Yinger, *Religion in the Struggle for Power,* Durham, North Carolina: Duke University Press, 1946; and Bryan R. Wilson, *Sects and Society,* London: Heinemann, 1961. As noted, the literature on sectarianism is immense, but the following may give something of its flavour. See B.R. Wilson, *Religious Sects,* New York: McGraw Hill, 1970; B.R. Wilson (ed.), *Patterns of Sectarianism,* London: Heinemann, 1967; Roy Wallis (ed.), *Sectarianism: Analyses of Religious and Non-Religious Sects,* London: Peter Owen Ltd., 1975; James A. Beckford, *Religious Organization,* The Hague: Mouton and Co., 1975; H.R. Niebuhr, "Sects" in *Encyclopaedia of the Social Sciences,* Vol. 13, New York: Macmillan, 1937, pp. 624-631; Thomas F. O'Dea, "Sects and Cults," *Encyclopaedia of the Social Sciences,* Vol. 14, New York: Macmillan, 1968, pp. 130-136; Wellman J. Warner, "Sect" in Julius Gould and William L. Kolb (eds.), *A Dictionary of the Social Sciences,* New York: The Free Press, 1964, pp. 624-625; and Peter L. Berger, "The Sociological Study of Sectarianism," *Social Research,* Vol. 21, 1954, pp. 467-485.

[153] See, for example, J.A. Beckford, *Religious Organization,* p. 97; Roland Robertson, *The Sociological Interpretation of Religion,* New York: Schocken Books, 1971, p. 120; Roland Robertson, "Religious Movements and Modern Societies: Toward a Progressive Problemshift," *Sociological Analysis,* Vol. 40, 1979, pp. 297-314; William H. Swatos, "Weber or Troeltsch? Methodology, Syndrome and the Development of Church-Sect Theory," *Journal for the Scientific Study of Religion,* Vol. 15, 1976, pp. 129-144; Roland Robertson, "Church-Sect and Rationality: Reply to Swatos," *Journal for the Scientific Study of Religion,* Vol. 16, 1977, pp. 197-200; W.H. Swatos, "Quo Vadis: Reply to Robertson," *Journal for the Scientific Study of Religion,* Vol. 16, 1977, pp. 201-204. See also Wallis (ed.), *Sectarianism;* Roger O'Toole, "'Underground' Traditions in the Study of Sectarianism"; and Roger O'Toole, *The Precipitous Path: Studies in Political Sects,* Toronto: PMA Associates, 1977.

[154] See, for example, Robertson, "Religious Movements and Modern Societies," p. 298.

[155] See Stephen Berger, "The Sects and the Breakthrough into the Modern World: On the Centrality of Sects in Weber's Protestant Ethic Thesis," *Sociological Quarterly*, Vol. 12, 1971, pp. 486-499. See also Benton Johnson, "Church and Sect Revisited," *Journal for the Scientific Study of Religion*, Vol. 10, 1971, pp. 124-137.

[156] See Troeltsch, *Social Teaching of the Christian Churches;* Niebuhr, *Social Sources of Denominationalism;* Yinger, *Religion in the Struggle for Power;* Joachim Wach, *The Sociology of Religion*, Chicago: University of Chicago Press, 1944, pp. 196-205; Bryan R. Wilson, "An Analysis of Sect Development," *American Sociological Review*, Vol. 24, 1959, pp. 3-15; Allan W. Eister, "H. Richard Niebuhr and the Paradox of Religious Organization: A Radical Critique," in Glock and Hammond (eds.), *Beyond the Classics?* pp. 355-408; Allan W. Eister, "Toward a Radical Critique of Church-Sect Typologizing," *Journal for the Scientific Study of Religion*, Vol. 6, 1967, pp. 85-90; Benton Johnson, "A Critical Appraisal of The Church-Sect Typology," *American Sociological Review*, Vol. 22, 1957, pp. 88-92; Benton Johnson, "On Church and Sect," *American Sociological Review*, Vol. 28, 1963, pp. 539-549; and William H. Swatos, "Monopolism, Pluralism, Acceptance, and Rejection: An Integrated Model for Church-Sect Theory," *Review of Religious Research*, Vol. 16, 1975, pp. 174-183. See also, as examples of the genre: Rodney Stark and William S. Bainbridge, "Of Churches, Sects, and Cults: Preliminary Concepts for a Theory of Religious Movements," *Journal for the Scientific Study of Religion*, Vol. 18, 1979, pp. 117-133; Calvin Redekop, "A New Look at Sect Development," *Journal for the Scientific Study of Religion*, Vol. 13, 1974, pp. 345-352; John B. Snook, "An Alternative to Church-Sect," *Journal for the Scientific Study of Religion*, Vol. 13, 1974, pp. 191-204; and John A. Coleman, "Church-Sect Typology and Organizational Precariousness," *Sociological Analysis*, Vol. 29, 1968, pp. 55-66.

[157] See, for example, Guenther Roth, "Religion and Revolutionary Beliefs: Sociological and Historical Dimensions in Max Weber's Work," *Social Forces*, Vol. 55, 1976, pp. 257-272; Wolfgang Lipp, "Charisma-Social Deviation, Leadership and Cultural Change," *Annual Review of the Social Sciences of Religion*, Vol. 1, 1977, pp. 59-77; William H. Swatos, "The Disenchantment of Charisma: A Weberian Assessment of Revolution in a Rationalized World," *Sociological Analysis*, Vol. 42, 1981, pp. 119-136; Martin E. Spencer, "What is Charisma?" *British Journal of Sociology*, Vol. 24, 1973, pp. 341-354; W.G. Runciman, "Charismatic Legitimacy and One-Party Rule in Ghana," *European Journal of Sociology*, Vol. 4, 1963, pp. 148-165; Thomas E. Dow, "The Role of Charisma in Modern African Development," *Social Forces*, Vol. 46, 1968, pp. 328-338; William H. Friedland, "For a Sociological Concept of Charisma," *Social Forces*, Vol. 43, 1964, pp. 18-36; Barry Schwartz, "George Washington and the Whig Conception of Heroic Leadership," *American Sociological Review*, Vol. 48, 1983, pp. 18-33; Roy Wallis, "The Social Construction of Charisma," *Social Compass*, Vol. 29, 1982, pp. 25-39; Roy Wallis (ed.), *Millennialism and Charisma*, Belfast: The Queen's University, 1982; and Roy Wallis, *Salvation and Protest: Studies of Social and Religious Movements*, New York: St. Martin's Press, 1979.

[158] See, for example, Peter Worsley, *The Trumpet Shall Sound;* and E.J. Hobsbawm, *Primitive Rebels*.

[159] See, for example, Yonina Talmon, "Millenarian Movements," *Archives Européennes de Sociologie*, Vol. 7, 1966, pp. 159-200; Roy Wallis, introduction to *Millennialism and Charisma;* Yonina Talmon, "Pursuit of the Millennium: the Relation Between Religious and Social Change," *Archives Européennes de Sociologie*, Vol. 3, 1962, pp. 125-148; Anthony F.C. Wallace, "Revitalization Movements," *American Anthropologist*, Vol. 58, 1956, pp. 264-281; Norman Cohn, *The Pursuit of the Millennium* (revised and expanded edition), New York: Oxford University Press, 1970 (first published in 1957), p. 51; and Guenter Lewy, *Religion and Revolution*, New York: Oxford University Press, 1974, pp. 57-274.

[160] See Bryan R. Wilson, *Magic and the Millennium*, London: Heinemann, 1973; and Bryan R. Wilson, *The Noble Savages: The Primitive Origins of Charisma and its Contemporary Survival*, Berkeley: University of California Press, 1975.

[161] See, for example, Roy Wallis, "Charisma, Commitment and Control in a New Religious Movement," in Wallis (ed.), *Millennialism and Charisma*, pp. 73-141; Doyle Paul Johnson, "Dilemmas of Charismatic Leadership: the Case of the People's Temple," *Sociological Analysis*, Vol. 40, 1979, pp. 315-323; Donald Stone, "The Charismatic Authority of Werner Erhard," in Wallis (ed.), *Millennialism and Charisma*, pp. 141-175; Robert S. Ellwood, "Emergent Religion in America: An Historical Perspective," in Jacob Needleman and George Baker (eds.), *Understanding the New Religions*, New York: Seabury Press, 1978, pp. 267-284; and Randall H. Alfred, "The Church of Satan," in Charles Y. Glock and Robert N. Bellah (eds.), *The New Religious Consciousness*, Berkeley: University of California Press, 1976, pp. 191 and 197. For similar work in a more "traditional" sectarian setting, see Robin Theobald, "The Role of Charisma in the Development of Social Movements: Ellen White and the Emergence of Seventh Day Adventism," *Archives de Sciences Sociales des Religions*, Vol. 49, 1980, pp. 83-100.

[162] See Roland Robertson, "On the Analysis of Mysticism: Pre-Weberian, Weberian and Post-Weberian Types," *Sociological Analysis*, Vol. 36, 1975, pp. 241-266; Allan W. Eister, "Comment on 'Max Weber on Church, Sect, and Mysticism,'" *Sociological Analysis*, Vol. 36, 1975, pp. 227-228; William R. Garrett, "Maligned Mysticism: The Maledicted Career of Troeltsch's Third Type," *Sociological Analysis*, Vol. 36, 1975, pp. 205-223; Paul M. Gustafson, "The Missing Member of Troeltsch's Trinity: Thoughts Generated by Weber's Comments," *Sociological Analysis*, Vol. 36, 1975, pp. 224-226; and Theodore M. Steeman, "Church, Sect, Mysticism, Denomination: Periodological Aspects of Troeltsch's Types," *Sociological Analysis*, Vol. 36, 1975, pp. 181-204. See also Max Weber, "On Church, Sect and Mysticism" (trans. J. Gittleman), *Sociological Analysis*, Vol. 34, 1973, pp. 140-149; and William H. Swatos, "Church-Sect and Cult: Bringing Mysticism Back In," *Sociological Analysis*, Vol. 42, 1981, pp. 17-26.

[163] This analysis converges with Marxist concerns, though Weber refuses to see religious ideas as simple reflections of class or status position.

[164] This includes many "neo-Marxist" sociologists of religion.

[165] See, for example, Seyfarth, "The West German Discussion of Max Weber's Sociology of Religion," pp. 12-20.

[166] The term "de-magification" is also sometimes used despite its inelegance. On Weber's continued relevance to the sociology of secularization, see Thomas Luckmann, "Theories of Religion and Social Change," *Annual Review of the Social Sciences of Religion*, Vol. 1, 1977, pp. 15-21.

[167] Weber, *Sociology of Religion*, p. 125.

[168] See Luckmann, "Theories of Religion and Social Change," pp. 11-12; and Parsons, Introduction to Weber, *Sociology of Religion*, p. xxx.

[169] Parsons, Introduction to Weber, *Sociology of Religion*, p. lxi.

[170] *Ibid*, p. lxi.

[171] *Ibid*, p. lxi.

[172] *Ibid*, p. lxv. In his review of Weber's *Sociology of Religion*, Benjamin Nelson estimated that "another fifty years may be required to say we have fully assimilated Weber's work according to his lights" (p. 596). See also Roland Robertson, "Weber, Religion and Modern Sociology," in R. Robertson, *Meaning and Change*, New York: New York University Press, 1978, pp. 50-102.

[173] Mills, *Images of Man*, p. 4.

[174] *Ibid*, p. 4.

[175] See, for example, R.K. Fenn, "A New Sociology of Religion"; Charles C. Lemert, "Social Structure and the Absent Centre: An Alternative to New Sociologies of Religion," *Sociological Analysis*, Vol. 36, 1975, pp. 95-107; John A. Saliba, "The New Ethnography and the Study of Religions," *Journal for the Scientific Study of Religion*, Vol. 13, 1974, pp.

145-159; and Joseph Michael Ryan, "Ethnoscience and Problems of Method in the Social Scientific Study of Religion," *Sociological Analysis,* Vol. 39, 1978, pp. 241-249.

[176] Bryan R. Wilson, *Religion in Secular Society: A Comment,* Harmondsworth: Penguin Books, 1969, p. 14.

[177] For opposition to the notion of secularization, see, for example, Andrew M. Greeley, *Unsecular Man: the Persistence of Religion,* New York: Dell Publishing Co., 1972; Andrew M. Greeley and Gregory Baum (eds.), *The Persistence of Religion,* New York: Herder and Herder, 1973; and David Martin, "Towards Eliminating The Concept of Secularization," in Julius Gould (ed.), *Penguin Survey of the Social Sciences,* Harmondsworth: Penguin Books, 1965, pp. 169-182. Some definitions of religion, of course, entail the possibility of the existence of a completely secular society.

[178] The literature on secularization is vast, but see: Bryan R. Wilson, *Religion in Secular Society;* B.R. Wilson, "The Debate Over 'Secularization,'" *Encounter,* Vol. 45, October 1975, pp. 77-83; B.R. Wilson, "The Return of the Sacred," *Journal for the Scientific Study of Religion,* Vol. 18, 1979, pp. 268-280; Daniel Bell, "The Return of the Sacred? The Argument on the Future of Religion," *British Journal of Sociology,* Vol. 28, 1977, pp. 419-449; Daniel Bell, "Religion in the Sixties," *Social Research,* Vol. 38, 1971, pp. 447-497; Talcott Parsons, "Religion in Postindustrial America: The Problem of Secularization," *Social Research,* Vol. 41, 1974, pp. 193-225; Horace M. Kallen, "Secularism as the Common Religion of a Free Society," *Journal for the Scientific Study of Religion,* Vol. 4, 1965, pp. 145-151; Victor M. Lidz, "Secularization, Ethical Life, and Religion in Modern Societies," in H.M. Johnson (ed.), *Religious Change and Continuity,* pp. 191-217; Peter E. Glasner, *The Sociology of Secularization: A Critique of a Concept,* London: Routledge and Kegan Paul, 1977; Richard K. Fenn, *Toward a Theory of Secularization,* Storrs, Connecticut: Society for the Scientific Study of Religion, 1978; David Martin, *A General Theory of Secularization,* Oxford: Basil Blackwell, 1978; and Benton Johnson, "A Fresh Look at Theories of Secularization," in Hubert M. Blalock (ed.), *Sociological Theory and Research: A Critical Approach,* New York: The Free Press, 1980, pp. 314-331.

[179] See, for example, Bryan R. Wilson, *Contemporary Transformations of Religion,* Oxford: Oxford University Press, 1976; B.R. Wilson, *Religion in Sociological Perspective,* Oxford: Oxford University Press, 1982; R.K. Fenn, "The Process of Secularization"; and Roland Robertson, "Secularization and the Sociologists." Wilson observes that it "may well be that an integrated culture is now a thing of the past in the West" (*Contemporary Transformations of Religion,* p. 115), and that the "process of societalization, which I believe brings secularization and demoralization, may threaten the continuity of those basic dispositions on which human society of any sort depends." (*Religion in Sociological Perspective,* p. 178).

[180] The civil-religion thesis assumes that religion provides the basis for the cultural integration of society. This view is seriously questioned by many scholars. See, for example, R.K. Fenn, "A New Sociology of Religion."

[181] Wilson, *Religion in Secular Society,* pp. 256-257.

[182] Through the notion of civil religion, the general utility of Durkheimian and functional perspectives may be assessed.

[183] See Roland Robertson, "Religious Movements and Modern Societies"; Roy Wallis, "The Rebirth of the Gods? Reflections on the New Religions in the West," Inaugural Lecture published by The Queen's University of Belfast, 1978; Thomas Robbins and Dick Anthony, "New Religious Movements and the Social System"; Dick Anthony and Thomas Robbins, "Culture Crisis and Contemporary Religion" in Robbins and Anthony (eds.), *In Gods We Trust,* pp. 9-31; Benton Johnson, "A Sociological Perspective on the New Religions" in Robbins and Anthony (eds.), *In Gods We Trust,* pp. 51-66; James Davison Hunter, "The New Religions: Demodernization and the Protest Against Modernity" in Bryan Wilson (ed.), *The Social Impact of New Religious Movements,* New York: Rose of Sharon Press, 1981, pp. 1-19; and Eileen Barker, "New Religious Movements: A Perspective for Understanding Society," in

Eileen Barker (ed.), *New Religious Movements: A Perspective for Understanding Society,* New York and Toronto: The Edwin Mellen Press, 1982, pp. ix-xxv; and Bryan Wilson, "The New Religions: Some Preliminary Considerations," in E. Barker (ed.), *New Religious Movements,* pp. 16-31.

[184] See Thomas Robbins, Dick Anthony and James Richardson, "Theory and Research on Today's 'New Religions,'" *Sociological Analysis,* Vol. 39, 1978, pp. 95-122; and Dick Anthony, Thomas Robbins and Paul Schwartz, "Contemporary Religious Movements and the Secularization Premise," *Concilium: International Review of Theology,* Vol. 161, 1983, pp. 1-8.

[185] Useful collections of materials are contained in Bryan Wilson (ed.), *The Social Impact of New Religious Movements;* Eileen Barker (ed.), *New Religious Movements;* Jacob Needleman and George Baker (eds.), *Understanding the New Religions;* Charles Y. Glock and Robert N. Bellah (eds.), *The New Religious Consciousness;* and Thomas Robbins and Dick Anthony (eds.), *In Gods We Trust.* See also David G. Bromley and Anson D. Shupe, *Strange Gods: The Great American Cult Scare,* Boston: Beacon Press, 1981; David G. Bromley and Anson D. Shupe, *"Moonies" in America: Cult, Church and Crusade,* Beverley Hills, California: Sage Publications, 1970; Anson D. Shupe and David G. Bromley, *The New Vigilantes: Deprogrammers, Anticultists and the New Religions,* Beverley Hills, California: Sage Publications, 1980; David G. Bromley and James T. Richardson, *The Brainwashing/Deprogramming Controversy,* New York and Toronto: Edwin Mellen Press, 1983 (forthcoming); Robert Wuthnow, *The Consciousness Reformation,* Berkeley: University of California Press, 1976; and Robert Wuthnow, *Experimentation in American Religion,* Berkeley: University of California Press, 1978. There are many case-studies: see, for example, John Lofland, *Doomsday Cult* (revised edition), New York: Irvington Publishers, 1978; Roy Wallis, *The Road to Total Freedom: A Sociological Analysis of Scientology,* New York: Colombia University Press, 1977; and James T. Richardson, M. Stewart and R.B. Simmonds, *Organized Miracles: A Sociological Study of a Jesus Movement Organization,* New Brunswick, New Jersey: Transaction Books, 1978. For a Canadian example see Frederick Bird, "Comparative Analysis of The Rituals Used by Some Contemporary 'New' Religions and Para-Religious Movements" in Peter Slater (ed.), *Religion and Culture in Canada,* pp. 447-469; and Frederick Bird and William Reimer, "New Religious and Para-Religious Movements in Montreal" in Stewart Crysdale and Les Wheatcroft (eds.), *Religion in Canadian Society,* Toronto: Macmillan of Canada, 1976, pp. 307-320.

[186] See Barker, *New Religious Movements: A Perspective for Understanding Society.*

[187] See Thomas Robbins and Dick Anthony, "New Religious Movements and the Social System: Integration, Disintegration and Transformation."

[188] See Ralph C. Beals, "Religion and Identity," *International Yearbook for The Sociology of Knowledge and Religion,* Vol. 11, 1978, pp. 147-161; Roland Robertson and Burkart Holzner (eds.), *Identity and Authority: Explorations in the Theory of Society,* New York: St. Martin's Press, 1979; Hans Mol, *Identity and the Sacred,* Oxford: Basil Blackwell, 1976; and Hans Mol (ed.), *Identity and Religion: International, Cross-Cultural Approaches,* Beverley Hills, California: Sage Publishers, 1978.

[189] B.R. Wilson, *Contemporary Transformations of Religion,* p. 96. For another view of the significance of the "New Religions," see Andrew M. Greeley, "Implications for the Sociology of Religion of Occult Behaviour in the Youth Culture" in Edward A. Tiryakian (ed.), *On the Margin of the Visible,* New York: John Wiley and Sons, 1973, pp. 295-302; and J. Milton Yinger, "Countercultures and Social Change," *American Sociological Review,* Vol. 42, 1977, pp. 833-853; and Daniel Bell, "The Return of the Sacred?" For other general assessments of the "New Religious Movements" see Steven M. Tipton, "New Religious Movements and the Problem of a Modern Ethic" in H.M. Johnson (ed.), *Religious Change and Continuity,* pp. 286-339; Steven M. Tipton, *Getting Saved from the Sixties,* Berkeley: University of California Press, 1982; Colin Campbell, "The Secret Religion of the Educated Classes," *Sociological*

Analysis, Vol. 39, 1978, pp. 146-156; Donald Stone, "New Religious Consciousness and Personal Religious Experience," *Sociological Analysis,* Vol. 39, 1978, pp. 123-134; and Anthony, Robbins and Schwartz, "Contemporary Religious Movements and the Secularization Premise."

[190] See Thomas Luckmann, *The Invisible Religion.* See also T. Luckmann, "On Religion in Modern Society: Individual Consciousness, World View, Institution," *Journal for the Scientific Study of Religion,* Vol. 2, 1963, pp. 147-162; and T. Luckmann, "Belief, Unbelief and Religion," in Rocco Caporale and Antonio Grumelli (eds.), *The Culture of Unbelief,* Berkeley: University of California Press, 1971, pp. 21-37.

[191] Luckmann, *The Invisible Religion,* pp. 17-27, 41-49.

[192] Many sociologists have felt, of course, that Luckmann's conception of religion is so broad as to be useless. Luckmann, however, anticipates this criticism, reaffirming his view of religion as an "all-encompassing phenomenon." See Luckmann, *The Invisible Religion,* p. 49. In this context see Bryan R. Wilson, *Contemporary Transformation of Religion,* p. 4; Andrew J. Weigert, "Whose Invisible Religion? Luckmann Revisited," *Sociological Analysis,* Vol. 35, 1974, pp. 181-188; C. Buehler, G. Hesser and A.J. Weigert, "A Study of Articles on Religion in Major Sociology Journals: Some Preliminary Findings," *Journal for the Scientific Study of Religion,* Vol. 11, 1972, pp. 165-170; and Charles C. Lemert, "Defining Non-Church Religion," *Review of Religious Research,* Vol. 16, 1975, pp. 186-197.

[193] Luckmann, *The Invisible Religion,* p. 12.

[194] *Ibid,* p. 12.

[195] *Ibid,* p. 18.

[196] *Ibid,* p. 12.

[197] In an anthropological sense. Luckmann notes: "It is in keeping with an elementary sense of the concept of religion to call the transcendence of biological nature by the human organism a religious phenomenon" (*The Invisible Religion,* p. 49).

[198] Luckmann, *The Invisible Religion,* p. 114.

[199] *The Invisible Religion* may thus be read as an important work of social theory. See especially pp. 107-117.

[200] Luckmann, *The Invisible Religion,* p. 18.

[201] Mills, *Images of Man,* p. 4.

[202] Michael Hill, *A Sociology of Religion,* London: Heinemann, 1973, p. 1.

[203] Mills, *The Sociological Imagination,* p. 6. For recent work that links the sociology of religion with broader themes in sociological theory see R.K. Fenn, "A New Sociology of Religion"; Roland Robertson, *Meaning and Change;* Charles C. Lemert, "Social Structure and the Absent Centre; An Alternative to New Sociologies of Religion"; Mary Douglas, "The Effects of Modernization on Religious Change," *Daedalus,* Vol. 111, 1982, pp. 1-19; Roland Robertson, "Individualism, Societalism, Worldliness, Universalism: Thematizing Theoretical Sociology of Religion," *Sociological Analysis,* Vol. 38, 1977, pp. 281-308; and Bryan S. Turner, *Religion and Social Theory,* London: Heinemann, 1983 (forthcoming). See also Phillip E. Hammond, "The Gap Between Theory and Research in the Sociology of Religion," in H.M. Blalock, *Sociological Theory and Research,* pp. 332-338. Robertson notes that "there has been in recent years a revival of interest in religion among sociologists dealing with 'mainstream' questions of sociological theory" (Robertson, "Individualism, Societalism, Worldliness, Universalism," p. 281). He notes especially the work of Bell, Collins, Gouldner, Habermas, Luhman and Touraine. Robertson's article illustrates the vitality of the classics in contemporary sociology of religion. Lewis Coser notes that, for some time to come, "recourse to the classics will continue to be necessary," while Talcott Parsons observes "without an intellectually rich tradition to revisit, I do not think that disciplines like our own, with all their difficulties and complexities could continue to advance." See Lewis A. Coser, "The Uses of Classical Sociological Theory" in Buford Rhea (ed.), *The Future of the Sociological Classics,* p. 182; and

Talcott Parsons, "Revisiting the Classics Throughout a Long Career," *in Buford Rhea (ed.), The Future of the Sociological Classics,* p. 193. These comments are of special relevance for the sociology of religion.

POSTSCRIPT

REFLECTIONS ON THE SOCIOLOGY OF RELIGION IN CANADA

During recent decades, sociologists have sought after many strange gods.[1] Crazes and cults have come and gone as theoretical and methodological prophets have scrambled for hegemony.[2] Meanwhile, the fortunes of particular sub-disciplines have waxed and waned in response to the magnetic power of funds.

Amidst the uproar, at least one sociological sub-discipline has remained relatively undisturbed. The sociology of religion has, at least in Canada, remained unembarassed by riches: whether in the shape of numerous zealous recruits, in the guise of inflammatory intellectual blueprints or in the more prosaically tangible form of coin of the realm. This has proven a mixed blessing. On the one hand, practitioners within the discipline have perhaps been spared the unreadable plethora of trivia that appears to be a frequent consequence of current practices in large-scale research support; and have likewise been denied the dubious benefits of the dogmatic tracts of academic faddists and transients. On the other hand, their position on the academic sidelines of sociology has placed them in danger of intoxication from the stale air of the cloister.

Like their counterparts in other lands, Canadian sociologists of religion repress the doubts and complexes accompanying their status deprivation[3] by repetition of the first article of their creed, which affirms that the scientific study of religion is an enterprise that is not merely intrinsically interesting, but central to the discipline of sociology as a whole. The comments below renew this Act of Faith, and do so by noting the degree to which Canadian society affords a particularly hospitable environment for analysis of the socio-cultural importance of the phenomenon of religion. In this regard, the discussion that follows also contains the ingredients of an Act of Hope.

The Scope of the Sociology of Religion in Canada

In this brief review, it is impossible to provide full characterization, let alone critical synthesis, of all the diverse strands of research and teaching that might appropriately be labelled "Canadian Sociology of Religion."[4] Scrutiny of a mass of publications and conference proceedings, together with relevant bibliographical sources, reveals, however, that the work of Canadian scholars is a fairly typical product of the sub-discipline considered as an international enterprise. With few exceptions, Canadian sociologists of religion are indistinguishable from their American, British, French and German colleagues with respect to their perceptions of key concepts, "classic" literature and theoretical issues; as well as in the context of their past and present empirical concerns and the methods by which these are exploited.

Thus, Canadian sociologists of religion build upon foundations laid primarily by Weber and Durkheim (and to a lesser extent by Marx).[5] They exhibit a methodological bias toward quantitative-survey research, while providing occasional and useful exceptions to this rule in the form of qualitative "participant-observation" studies.[6] Focussing primarily upon "institutional" forms of religion,[7] they explore the links between formal religious affiliation and the social, economic and cultural attributes of individuals and groups.[8] Having scrutinized religious *virtuosi* or "professionals,"[9] and traced the fortunes of sundry churches, denominations and sects, they now exhibit fascination with the "new religious consciousness" manifested in various, largely imported, sects and cults of recent vintage.[10] More rarely, they take the broader view, ruminating theoretically upon general social or social-psychological aspects of religion,[11] and posing again the question that is the alpha and omega of the sub-discipline: what is religion?[12]

Despite the breadth and variety of such Canadian work in recent decades, an explicit or implicit common underlying theme may be discerned. Predictably, it is the same theme that dominates analysis of religion in the rest of the Western world: secularization, the process whereby, in Bryan Wilson's succinct definition, "religious thinking, practice and institutions lose social significance."[13]

That Canadian sociologists have been drawn to the concept of secularization, despite its eloquent critics, should surprise no one.[14] The delayed decline of organized religion in this country has been characterized by a bewildering swiftness and intensity that has tempted more than one observer to discern "the end of a religion."[15] Indeed, so taken for granted is the tightening grip of secularization, even (and perhaps especially) in the formerly "priest-ridden" province of Quebec, that dissenters to this novel orthodoxy snatch at straws in their haste to proclaim "the return of the sacred,"[16] hanging their weighty thesis upon the extremely fragile peg of "the new religious consciousness."[17]

The bemusement with which sociologists have apprehended this northern twilight of the gods underscores a fundamental point that is in danger of neglect. In their anxiety to understand a world in which documentation and analysis of traditional religious organizations appears akin to recording the qualities of exotic endangered species, observers of the Canadian religious scene may be inclined to forget to what extent in the very recent past such phenomena appeared as natural and perhaps necessary elements of Canadian life.

Notwithstanding this danger, the rapid "disenchantment" of Canadian society has contributed to the demystification of many students of religion.[18] By causing them to pause and take their theoretical bearings by renewed intellectual meditation on the nature of religion, it has engendered a serious receptivity to perspectives that require painful re-thinking, and demand arduous re-exploration of the definitional labyrinth. For example, the response to Professor Luckmann's provocative "invisible-religion" thesis may, whatever the merits of its attendant debate, be understood and appreciated in this light.[19]

This informed and wary openness to theoretical innovation fused with a sophisticated sensitivity to the impact of secularization is the prime requisite of the Canadian sociologist of religion in the closing decades of the present century. But, as previously observed, awareness of actual and potential changes in traditional religion, alertness to the possibility of novel species of religiosity, or even the capacity to visualize the nature of a society without religion are not, of themselves, sufficient. These undoubted qualities require, as their foundation, thorough appreciation of the vital rôle played by institutional forms of religion in the creation and development of this society.[20] The nurturing of such appreciation appears, moreover, to be of more than academic importance: an undertaking relevant to all citizens of a fragile federation[21] perched precariously on the brink of political, regional, social and economic fragmentation.

Footnotes

[1] Professor C.B. Macpherson has used this phrase of political scientists. See C.B. Macpherson, "After Strange Gods: Canadian Political Science 1973" in T.N. Guinsburg and G.L. Reuber (eds.), *Perspectives on the Social Sciences in Canada,* Toronto: University of Toronto Press, 1974, pp. 52-76.

[2] For overviews, see for example, Scott G. McNall (ed.), *Theoretical Perspectives in Sociology*, New York: St. Martin's Press, 1979; John Rex (ed.), *Approaches to Sociology*, London: Routledge and Kegan Paul, 1974; and Edmund Ions, *Against Behaviouralism*, Oxford: Basil Blackwell, 1977.

[3] This is David Martin's phrase. See David Martin, "The Sociology of Religion: A Case of Status Deprivation?" *British Journal of Sociology*, Vol. 17, 1966, pp. 353-359.

[4] Useful bibliographical sources and overviews include Stewart Crysdale and Jean-Paul Montminy, *La Religion au Canada/Religion in Canada: Annotated Inventory of Scientific Studies of Religion (1945-1972)*, Downsview, Ontario: York University and Québec: Les Presses de l'Université Laval, 1974; Stewart Crysdale, "Historical Change and Conflict Perspectives in the Sociology of Religion in English-Speaking Canada," paper presented at the annual meeting of the Society for the Scientific Study of Religion, Chicago, 1977; Harry Hiller, "The Sociology of Religion in Canadian Context" in G.N. Ramu and S.D. Johnson (eds.), *Introduction to Canadian Society: Sociological Analysis*, Toronto: Macmillan of Canada, 1976, pp. 349-400; Paul Stryckman, "Theory and Research in Quebec: Qualitative Appraisal and Perspectives," paper presented at the annual meeting of the Society for the Scientific Study of Religion, Chicago, 1977; Jean-Charles Falardeau, "Les recherches de sociologie religieuse au Canada" in *Lumen Vitae*, Vol. 6, Nos. 1-2, 1950-51, pp. 127-142; J-C. Falardeau, "Les recherches religieuses au Canada Français" in *Recherches Sociographiques*, Vol. 3, Nos. 1-2, 1962, pp. 209-228; Fernand Dumont, "La Sociologie religieuse au Canada Français" in *Sociologie religieuse, Sciences Sociales, Actes de IVe Congrès International*, Paris: Editions Economie et Humanisme, 1955, pp. 150-152; F. Dumont, *La Situation presente de la Théorie dans la sociologie des religions*, Ottawa, Editions du Musée de l'Homme, 1958; Harold Fallding, "Canada" in Hans Mol (ed.), *Western Religion: A Country by Country Sociological Inquiry*, The Hague: Mouton, 1972, pp. 101-115; Reginald W. Bibby, "Numbers and Northeners: Survey Research in the Sociology of Religion in Canada," paper presented at the annual meeting of the Society for the Scientific Study of Religion, Chicago, 1977; and Harry Hiller, "The Sociology of Religion in Western Canada: An Assessment," paper presented at the annual meeting of the Canadian Sociology and Anthropology Association, Quebec City, 1976; and Paul Stryckman, "Reflexions et Perspectives sur le Sociologie de la Religion au Québec," *Les Cahiers du CRSR*, Québec: Centre de Recherches en Sociologie Religieuse, Université Laval, Vol. 1, 1977, pp. 145-183 (this article contains a useful bibliography.) A useful enterprise involving inventory of the teaching of courses with religious subject-matter in Canadian universities was unfortunately discontinued. See C.P. Anderson and T.A. Nosanchuck, *The 1967 Guide to Religious Studies in Canada*, Canadian Society for the Study of Religion, 1967; and C.P. Anderson, *The 1969 Guide to Religious Studies in Canada*, Canadian Society for the Study of Religion, 1969. Useful historical sources are N.K. Clifford, "Religion and the Development of Canadian Society: An Historiographical Analysis," *Church History*, Vol. 38, 1969, pp. 506-523; and N.K. Clifford, "History of Religion in Canada," *The Ecumenist*, Vol. 18, No. 5, 1980, pp. 65-69.

[5] On Weber, see primarily Max Weber, *The Sociology of Religion* (trans. E. Fischoff), Boston: Beacon Press, 1963 (first published in German in 1922); Max Weber, *The Protestant Ethic and the Spirit of Capitalism* (trans. T. Parsons), London: George Allen and Unwin, 1930 (first published 1904-5). See also Weber's studies of the religions of China, India and ancient Judaism. On Durkheim, see Emile Durkheim, *The Elementary Forms of the Religious Life* (trans. J.W. Swain), London: George Allen and Unwin, 1915 (first published in French in 1912); and W.S.F. Pickering (ed.), *Durkheim on Religion*, London: Routledge and Kegan Paul, 1975.

On Marx, see Karl Marx and Frederick Engels, *On Religion*, Moscow: Foreign Languages Publishing House, 1958; and D.B. McKown, *The Classical Marxist Critiques of Religion: Marx, Engels, Lenin, Kautsky*, The Hague: Martinus Nijhoff, 1975.

[6] A useful indication of the main biases of the sociology of religion in Canada may be found in Stewart Crysdale and Les Wheatcroft (eds.), *Religion in Canadian Society*, Toronto: Macmillan of Canada, 1976; ten of the selections in this volume utilize sample surveys while three utilize the method of participant-observation. See pp. 40-41 and *passim*. For a useful bibliography of survey research on religion in Canada see Bibby, *op. cit.*

[7] In the sense that Luckmann attacks as a "church-oriented" conception of religion. See Thomas Luckmann, *The Invisible Religion: The Transformation of Symbols in Industrial Society*, New York: The Macmillan Company 1967 (first published in German in 1963).

[8] See, for example, the useful summary by Hans Mol, "Major Correlates of Churchgoing in Canada" in Crysdale and Wheatcroft, *op. cit.*, pp. 241-254.

[9] See, for example, Paul Stryckman, *Les Prêtres du Québec d'aujourd'hui*, Québec: Université Laval, Centre de Recherches en Sociologie Religieuse, 1970; Paul Stryckman and Robert Gaudet, "Priests Under Stress" in Crysdale and Wheatcroft, *op. cit.*, pp. 336-345; and P. Stryckman and R. Gaudet, *Priests in Canada, 1971: A Report on English-Speaking Clergy*, Québec: Centre de Recherches en Sociologie Religieuse, Université Laval, 1971.

[10] The Crysdale and Wheatcroft collection and the Crysdale and Montminy bibliography provide evidence of the range of studies on various churches, denominations and sects. On the "new religious consciousness," see Charles Y. Glock and Robert N. Bellah (eds.), *The New Religious Consciousness*, Berkeley and Los Angeles: University of California Press, 1976; Robert Wuthnow, *The Consciousness Reformation*, Berkeley and Los Angeles: University of California Press, 1976. For Canadian material, see John Whitworth and Martin Shiels, "From Across the Black Water: Two Imported Varieties of Hinduism" in Eileen Barker (ed.), *New Religious Movements*, New York and Toronto: Edwin Mellen Press, 1982, pp. 155-172; Fred Bird, "A Comparative Analysis of the Rituals Used by Some Contemporary 'New' Religious and Para-Religious Movements" in Peter Slater (ed.), *Religion and Culture in Canada/Religion et Culture au Canada*, Canadian Corporation for Studies in Religion, 1977, pp. 447-469; Jordan Paper, "A Shaman in Contemporary Toronto" in Slater, *op. cit.*, pp. 471-489; Fred Bird and William Reimer, "New Religious and Para-Religious Movements in Montreal" in Crysdale and Wheatcroft, *op. cit.*, pp. 307-320.

[11] See, for example, Hans Mol, "The Origin and Function of Religion," *Journal for the Scientific Study of Religion*, Vol. 18, No. 4, 1979, pp. 379-389; Hans Mol, *Identity and the Sacred: A Sketch for a New Social Scientific Theory of Religion*, Agincourt, Ontario: The Book Society of Canada, 1976; Harold Fallding, *The Sociology of Religion*, Toronto: McGraw-Hill Ryerson, 1974; and Harry Hiller, "The New Theology and the Sociology of Religion," *Canadian Review of Sociology and Anthropology*, Vol. 6, No. 3, 1969, pp. 179-187; T. Rennie Warburton, "Critical Theory and the Sociology of Religion," paper presented at the annual meeting of the Society for the Scientific Study of Religion, Milwaukee, 1975; T.R. Warburton, "A Dialectical Theory of Religion" (mimeographed); and Ralph C. Beals, "Religion and Identity," *International Yearbook for the Sociology of Knowledge and Religion*, Vol. 11, 1978, pp. 147-162. Of course, differences between Canada's "two sociologies" (French and English), as Hubert Guindon has termed them, must not be overlooked. Crysdale and Wheatcroft, *op. cit.*, pp. 42-44, offer some useful comments on this matter, but see also the Crysdale and Montminy bibliography, cited above.

[12] Of the many discussions of the definitional dilemma, see Melford W. Spiro, "Religion: Problems of Definition and Explanation" in Michael Banton (ed.), *Anthropological Approaches to the Study of Religion*, London: Tavistock Publications, 1966, pp. 85-126; Robin Horton, "A Definition of Religion and its Uses," *Journal of the Royal Anthropological Institute*, Vol. 90, 1960, pp. 201-226; Jack Goody, "Religion and Ritual: The Definitional Problem," *British Journal of Sociology*, Vol. 12, 1961, pp. 142-146; Peter Berger, *The Sacred Canopy*, New York: Doubleday Anchor Books, 1969, pp. 175-177; Peter Berger, "Some Second Thoughts on Substantive versus Functional Definitions of Religion," *Journal for the Scientific Study of Religion*, Vol. 13, 1974, pp. 125-133; F.J. Streng, "Studying Religion:

Possibilities and Limitations of Different Definitions," *Journal of the American Academy of Religion,* Vol. 40, No. 2, 1972, pp. 217-237. The classic problem of definition is posed by Weber in *The Sociology of Religion* (see p. 1), and the most controversial recent re-definition of the concept is in Luckmann, *op. cit.* For recent Canadian excursions into this labyrinth, see Reginald Richard, "Le Concept de Religion: Specificité ou Homologie," in *Les Cahiers du CRSR,* Québec: Centre de Recherches en Sociologie Religieuse, Université Laval, Vol. 2, 1978, pp. 3-17; Anthony J. Blasi, "Definition of Religion and Phenomenological Approach Towards a Problematic" in *Les Cahiers du CRSR,* Vol. 3, 1980, pp. 55-70, and chapter two of the present work.

[13] See Bryan R. Wilson, *Religion in Secular Society: A Sociological Comment,* Harmondsworth: Penguin Books, 1969, p. 14. See also his *Contemporary Transformations of Religion,* Oxford: Oxford University Press, 1976. The literature on secularization is vast but the following are useful sources: Alasdair Macintyre, *Secularization and Moral Change,* Oxford: Oxford University Press, 1967; David Martin, *A General Theory of Secularization,* New York: Harper and Row, 1978; Richard K. Fenn, *Toward a Theory of Secularization,* Society for the Scientific Study of Religion Monographs, No. 1, 1978; and Peter E. Glasner, *The Sociology of Secularization: A Critique of a Concept,* London: Routledge and Kegan Paul, 1977.

[14] For such criticism, see David Martin, "Towards Eliminating the Concept of Secularization," in Julius Gould (ed.), *Penguin Survey of the Social Sciences,* Harmondsworth: Penguin Books, 1965, pp. 169-182; Andrew Greeley and Gregory Baum (eds.), *The Persistence of Religion,* New York: Herder and Herder, 1973; and Andrew Greeley, *Unsecular Man: The Persistence of Religion,* New York: Schocken Books, 1972.

[15] See Colette Moreux, *Fin d'une religion?,* Montreal: Les Presses de l'Université de Montréal, 1969. For discussion of the decline of traditional religion in Canada, see Crysdale and Wheatcroft, *op. cit.,* pp. 3-14; S. Crysdale, "Some Problematic Aspects of Religion in Canada," *Sociological Focus,* Vol. 9, 1976, pp. 137-148; Henry MacLeod, "The Religious Situation in Canadian Society," paper presented to the annual meeting of the Canadian Sociology and Anthropology Association, Saskatoon, 1979; Reginald W. Bibby, "Religion and Modernity: The Canadian Case," *Journal for the Scientific Study of Religion,* Vol. 18, No. 1, 1979, pp. 1-17; R.W. Bibby, "The State of Collective Religiosity in Canada," *Canadian Review of Sociology and Anthropology,* Vol. 16, 1979, pp. 105-116; R.W. Bibby, "Religion" in Robert Hagedorn (ed.), *Sociology,* Toronto: Holt, Rinehart and Winston, 1980, pp. 422-425; R.W. Bibby, "The Nature of Religiosity in Canada" in Stewart Crysdale and Christopher Beattie (eds.), *Sociology Canada: Readings* (second edition), Toronto: Butterworth, 1977; and S. Crysdale, "Religion and Secularization" in S. Crysdale and C. Beattie, *Sociology Canada: An Introductory Text,* Toronto: Butterworth, 1973, pp. 267-290.

[16] The phrase is Daniel Bell's. See his "The Return of the Sacred?" in *British Journal of Sociology,* Vol. 28, No. 4, 1977, pp. 419-449.

[17] See Glock and Bellah, *The New Religious Consciousness,* cited above.

[18] "Disenchantment" and "demystification" are both used to refer to the process of emancipation from magic that "Weber regarded as the distinguishing peculiarity of Western culture." See Reinhard Bendix, *Max Weber: An Intellectual Portrait,* London: Heinemann, 1960, p. 90.

[19] See Luckmann, *op. cit.*

[20] It is necessary to consider, for example, whether there is any Canadian historical parallel to de Tocqueville's view of American religion as an "institution which powerfully contributes to the maintenance of a democratic republic." See Alexis de Tocqueville, *Democracy in America,* New York: Alfred Knopf, 1948, Vol. 1, p. 300. (See also Vol. 1, pp. 300-314, Vol. 2, pp. 20-28.) In pursuing such a strategy they might be regarded as behaving in a "characteristically" Canadian manner, for if any one thing might be thought to distinguish Canadian from United States sociology it would be the former's historical bias. In a famous phrase,

Bishop Strachan declared "It is not what we are, but what we may become." See J.L.H. Henderson, *John Strachan 1778-1867,* Toronto: University of Toronto Press, 1969, p. 47. The importance of understanding what we were as a basis for sociological investigation has been stressed by S.D. Clark: "The sociologist in whatever he may attempt to do in the study of the Canadian community must place himself under a heavy obligation to the historian" in "Introduction," *The Developing Canadian Community,* Toronto: University of Toronto Press, revised edition, 1968, p. xiv. Elsewhere he observes: "It is hard to believe that the sociologist who has turned to history will remain for long so little curious about the facts of history that he will be content to leave to others the task of historical research. The sociologist who uses history is bound in the end to find himself doing history" in "History and the Sociological Method" in *The Developing Canadian Community,* p. 294. For further discussion of sociology and history, see Seymour Martin Lipset and Richard Hofstadter (eds.), *Sociology and History: Methods,* New York: Basic Books, 1968; Werner Jacob Cahnman and Alvin Boskoff (eds.), *Sociology and History: Theory and Research,* New York: The Free Press, 1964; Peter Burke, *Sociology and History,* London: Allen and Unwin, 1980; and Charles Tilly, *As Sociology Meets History,* New York: Academic Press, Inc., 1981.

[21] See Lorna R. Marsden and Edward B. Harvey, *Fragile Federation: Social Change in Canada,* Toronto: McGraw-Hill Ryerson, 1979. The authors have adopted Mordecai Richler's description of Canada as "a fragile, loosely knit confederation."

BIBLIOGRAPHY

This bibliography comprises mainly works referred to in the text, though a few useful and related titles have also been included.

Abel, Theodore. "The Operation Called *Verstehen.*" *American Journal of Sociology* 54: 212-218, 1948.

Abercrombie, Nicholas, Stephen Hill and Bryan S. Turner. *The Dominant Ideology Thesis.* London: Allen and Unwin, 1980.

Abrahamson, Mark. *Functionalism.* Englewood Cliffs, N.J.: Prentice-Hall, Inc., 1978.

Abramowski, Günter. "Meaningful Life in a Disenchanted World." *Journal of Religious Ethics* 10: 121-134, 1982.

Absalom, Francis. "The Historical Development of the Study of the Sociology of Religion." *The Expository Times* 82(4): 105-109, 1971.

Acquaviva, S.S. *The Decline of the Sacred in Industrial Society.* Translated by P. Lipscomb. Oxford: Basil Blackwell, 1979 (first published in Italian in 1966).

Adorno, Theodor W. "Theses Upon Art and Religion Today." *Kenyon Review* 7: 677-681, 1945.

Alatas, Syed Hussein. "Problems of Defining Religion." *International Social Science Journal* 29: 213-234, 1977.

Alfred, Randall H. "The Church of Satan," in C.Y. Glock and R.N. Bellah (eds.), *The New Religious Consciousness,* pp. 180-202. Berkeley: University of California Press, 1976.

Alpert, Harry. *Emile Durkheim and His Sociology.* New York: Columbia University Press, 1961 (first published in 1939).

Anderson, C.P. *The 1969 Guide to Religious Studies in Canada.* Waterloo: Canadian Society for the Study of Religion, 1969.

______ and Nosanchuk, T.A. (eds.). *The 1967 Guide to Religious Studies in Canada.* Waterloo: Canadian Society for the Study of Religion, 1967.

Anderson, Perry. *Western Marxism.* London: New Left Books, 1976.

Andreski, Stanislav (ed.). *Herbert Spencer: Structure, Function and Evolution.* London: Nelson, 1971.

Anthony, Dick; Robbins, Thomas; and Curtis, Thomas. "Reply to Bellah." *Journal for the Scientific Study of Religion* 13: 491-495, 1974.

______ and Robbins, Thomas. "From Symbolic Realism to Structuralism." *Journal for the Scientific Study of Religion* 14: 403-414, 1975.

______ Robbins, Thomas; and Schwartz, Paul. "Contemporary Religious Movements and the Secularization Premise." *Concilium: International Review of Theology* 161: 1-8, 1983.

______ and Robbins, Thomas. "Culture Crisis and Contemporary Religion," in T. Robbins and D. Anthony (eds.), *In Gods We Trust: New Patterns of Religious Pluralism in America,* pp. 9-31. New Brunswick, N.J.: Transaction Books, 1981.

Arato, Andrew and Gebhardt, Eike (eds.). *The Essential Frankfurt School Reader.* Oxford: Basil Blackwell, 1978.

Argyle, Michael and Beit-Hallahmi, Benjamin. *The Social-Psychology of Religion.* London: Routledge and Kegan Paul, 1975.

Aron, Raymond. *German Sociology.* Translated by T. Bottomore. Glencoe: The Free Press, 1957.

______ *Main Currents in Sociological Thought* (two volumes). Translated by R. Howard and H. Weaver. New York: Basic Books, 1967.

Baird, Robert D. (ed.). *Methodological Issues in Religious Studies.* Chico: New Horizons Press, 1975.

Banton, Michael (ed.). *Anthropological Approaches to the Study of Religion.* London: Tavistock Publications, 1966.

Barbalet, Jack M. "Principles of Stratification in Max Weber: An Interpretation and Critique." *British Journal of Sociology* 31: 401-417, 1980.

Barbour, Ian G. *Issues in Science and Religion.* New York: Harper & Row, 1966.

______ *Myths, Models and Paradigms: A Comparative Study in Science and Religion.* New York: Harper and Row, 1974.

Barker, Eileen (ed.). *New Religious Movements: A Perspective for Understanding Society.* New York and Toronto: The Edwin Mellen Press, 1982.

Barnhart, Joseph E. "Is One's Definition of 'Religion' Always Circular?" *International Yearbook for the Sociology of Knowledge and Religion* 9: 122-135, 1975.

______ *The Study of Religion and its Meaning.* The Hague: Mouton, 1977.

Baum, Gregory. *Religion and Alienation: A Theological Reading of Sociology.* New York: The Paulist Press, 1975.

______ (ed.). *Sociology and Human Destiny.* New York: The Seabury Press, 1980.

______ "Definitions of Religion in Sociology," in Mircea Eliade and David Tracy (eds.), *What is Religion? An Inquiry for Christian Theology* (*Concilium* No. 136): 25-32. New York: The Seabury Press, 1980.

______ "Liberation Theology and the 'Supernatural'." *The Ecumenist* 19: 81-87, 1981.

Beals, Ralph C. "Religion and Identity." *International Yearbook for the Sociology of Knowledge and Religion* 11: 147-161, 1978.

Becker, Howard S. "What's Happening to Sociology?" *Society* 16(5): 19-24, 1979.

Beckford, James A. *Religious Organization.* The Hague: Mouton and Co., 1975.

Beer, Max. *Social Struggles and Socialist Forerunners.* Translated by H.J. Stenning. New York: International Publishers, 1929.

Beidelman, T.O. *W. Robertson Smith and the Sociological Study of Religion.* Chicago: University of Chicago Press, 1974.

Belfort Bax, E. *The Social Side of the Reformation in Germany* (3 volumes). London: Swan Sonnenschein and Co., 1894-1903.

Bell, Daniel. "Religion in the Sixties." *Social Research* 38: 447-497, 1971.

______ "The Return of the Sacred? The Argument on the Future of Religion." *British Journal of Sociology* 28: 419-449, 1977.

Bellah, Robert N. *Tokugawa Religion.* Glencoe: The Free Press, 1957.

______ "Religious Evolution." *American Sociological Review* 29: 358-374, 1964.

______ (ed.). *Religion and Progress in Modern Asia.* New York: The Free Press, 1965.

______ "Civil Religion in America." *Daedalus* 96: 1-21, 1967.

______ "Response to Commentaries on 'Civil Religion in America'," in D.R. Cutler

(ed.), *The Religious Situation: 1968,* pp. 388-393. Boston: Beacon Press, 1968.
______ "Civil Religion in America," in R.N. Bellah, *Beyond Belief: Essays on Religion in a Post-Traditional World,* pp. 168-189. New York: Harper and Row, 1970 (essay first published in 1967).
______ *Beyond Belief: Essays on Religion in a Post-Traditional World.* New York: Harper and Row, 1970.
______ "Christianity and Symbolic Realism." *Journal for the Scientific Study of Religion* 9: 89-96, 1970.
______ "Response to Comments on 'Christianity and Symbolic Realism'." *Journal for the Scientific Study of Religion* 9: 112-115, 1970.
______ (ed.). *Emile Durkheim: On Morality and Society.* Chicago: University of Chicago Press, 1973.
______ "Comment on 'The Limits of Symbolic Realism'." *Journal for the Scientific Study of Religion* 13: 487-489, 1974.
______ "American Civil Religion in the 1970's," in R.E. Richey and D.G. Jones (eds.), *American Civil Religion,* pp. 255-272. New York: Harper and Row, 1974.
______ *The Broken Covenant: American Civil Religion in Time of Trial.* New York: The Seabury Press, 1975.
______ and Hammond, Phillip E. *Varieties of Civil Religion.* San Francisco: Harper and Row, 1980.
______ "Religion and Legitimation in the American Republic," in T. Robbins and D. Anthony (eds.), *In Gods We Trust: New Patterns of Religious Pluralism in America,* pp. 35-49. New Brunswick, N.J.: Transaction Books, 1981.
Bendix, Reinhard. *Max Weber: An Intellectual Portrait.* London: Heinemann, 1960.
______ and Roth, Guenther. *Scholarship and Partisanship: Essays on Max Weber.* Berkeley: University of California Press, 1971.
______ "Two Sociological Traditions," in R. Bendix and G. Roth, *Scholarship and Partisanship,* pp. 291-298. Berkeley: University of California Press, 1971.
Berger, Peter L. "The Sociological Study of Sectarianism." *Social Research* 21: 467-485, 1954.
______ "Charisma and Religious Innovation: The Social Location of Israelite Prophecy." *American Sociological Review* 28: 940-950, 1963.
______ *The Sacred Canopy: Elements of a Sociological Theory of Religion.* Garden City, N.Y.: Doubleday and Co., 1967.
______ "Religious Institutions," in N.J. Smelser (ed.), *Sociology: An Introduction,* pp. 329-379. New York: John Wiley and Sons, 1967.
______ "A Sociological View of The Secularization of Theology." *Journal for the Scientific Study of Religion* 6: 3-16, 1967.
______ *A Rumour of Angels: Modern Society and the Rediscovery of the Supernatural.* Garden City, N.Y.: Doubleday and Co., 1970.
______ "Some Second Thoughts on Substantive Versus Functional Definitions of Religion." *Journal for the Scientific Study of Religion* 13: 125-133, 1974.
______ "Religion and the American Future," in S.M. Lipset (ed.), *The Third Century,* pp. 65-77. Chicago: University of Chicago Press, 1979.
______ *The Heretical Imperative: Contemporary Possibilities of Religious Affirmation.* Garden City, N.Y.: Doubleday and Co., 1979.
______ (ed.). *The Other Side of God: A Polarity in World Religions.* Garden City,

N.Y.: Doubleday and Co., 1981.

______ and Luckmann, Thomas. *The Social Construction of Reality*. Garden City, N.Y.: Doubleday and Co., 1966.

Berger, Stephen D. "The Sects and the Breakthrough into the Modern World: On the Centrality of the Sects in Weber's Protestant Ethic Thesis." *The Sociological Quarterly* 12: 486-499, 1971.

Bergeson, Albert James. "A Durkheimian Theory of 'Witch Hunts' with the Chinese Cultural Revolution of 1966-1969 as an Example." *Journal for the Scientific Study of Religion* 17: 19-29, 1978.

Bernard, L.L. "The Sociological Interpretation of Religion." *The Journal of Religion* 18: 1-18, 1938.

______ "The Definition of Definition." *Social Forces* 19: 500-510, 1941.

Bernstein, Eduard. *Cromwell and Communism*. Translated by M.J. Stenning. New York: Schocken Books, 1963 (first published in 1895).

Bettis, Joseph Dabney (ed.). *Phenomenology of Religion*. New York: Harper and Row, 1969.

Bibby, Reginald W. "The Nature of Religiosity in Canada," in S. Crysdale and C. Beattie (eds.), *Sociology Canada: Readings* (second edition). Toronto: Butterworths, 1977.

______ "Numbers and Northerners: Survey Research in the Sociology of Religion in Canada." Paper presented at the Annual Meeting of the Society for the Scientific Study of Religion, 1977.

______ "Religion and Modernity: The Canadian Case." *Journal for the Scientific Study of Religion* 18: 1-17, 1979.

______ "The State of Collective Religiosity in Canada." *Canadian Review of Sociology and Anthropology* 16: 105-116, 1979.

______ "Religion," in R. Hagedorn (ed.), *Sociology*, pp. 422-425. Toronto: Holt, Rinehart and Winston, 1980.

Bird, Frederick. "Comparative Analysis of the Rituals Used by Some Contemporary 'New' Religious and Para-Religious Movements," in P. Slater (ed.), *Religion and Culture in Canada*, pp. 447-469. Waterloo: Canadian Corporation for Studies in Religion, 1977.

______ and Reimer, William. "New Religious and Para-Religious Movements in Montreal," in S. Crysdale and L. Wheatcroft (eds.), *Religion in Canadian Society*, pp. 307-320. Toronto: Macmillan of Canada, 1976.

Birnbaum, Norman. "Conflicting Interpretations of the Rise of Capitalism: Marx and Weber." *British Journal of Sociology* 4: 125-141, 1953.

______ "Monarchs and Sociologists: A Reply to Professor Shils and Mr. Young." *Sociological Review* 3: 5-23, 1955.

______ "Beyond Marx in the Sociology of Religion?", in C.Y. Glock and P.E. Hammond (eds.), *Beyond the Classics? Essays in the Scientific Study of Religion*, pp. 3-70. New York: Harper and Row, 1973.

______ and Lenzer, Gertrud (eds.). *Sociology and Religion*. Englewood Cliffs, N.J.: Prentice-Hall Inc., 1969.

Blalock, Hubert M. (ed.). *Sociological Theory and Research: A Critical Approach*. New York: The Free Press, 1980.

Blasi, Anthony J. "Definition of Religion and Phenomenological Approach Toward a Problematic." *Cahiers du CRSR* 3: 55-70, 1980.

_____ and Weigert, Andrew J. "Toward a Sociology of Religion: An Interpretive Sociology Approach." *Sociological Analysis* 37: 189-204, 1976.

Bloch, Ernst. *A Philosophy of the Future*. Translated by J. Cumming. New York: Herder and Herder, 1970.

Blumstock, Robert. "Civil Uncivility: Non-Civil Religion in Canada." Paper presented to the Annual Meeting of the Society for the Scientific Study of Religion, 1977.

Bonte, Pierre. "Cattle for God: An Attempt at a Marxist Analysis of East African Herdsmen." *Social Compass* 22: 381-396, 1975.

Bosk, Charles L. "The Routinization of Charisma: The Case of the Zaddik," in H.M. Johnson (ed.), *Religious Change and Continuity*, pp. 150-167. San Francisco: Jossey-Bass, 1979.

Bottomore, Tom. *Marxist Sociology*. London: Macmillan, 1975.

_____ "A Marxist Consideration of Durkheim." *Social Forces* 59: 902-917, 1981.

Boulard, F. *An Introduction to Religious Sociology: Pioneer Work in France*. Translated by M.J. Jackson. London: Darton, Longman and Todd, 1960.

Bowker, John. *Problems of Suffering in Religions of the World*. Cambridge: Cambridge University Press, 1970.

Bramson, Leon. *The Political Context of Sociology*. Princeton, N.J.: Princeton University Press, 1961.

Bromley, David G., and Shupe, Anson D. *"Moonies" in America: Cult, Church and Crusade*. Beverley Hills, California: Sage Publications, 1970.

_____ and Shupe, Anson D. *Strange Gods: The Great American Cult Scare*. Boston: Beacon Press, 1981.

_____ and Richardson, James T. *The Brainwashing/Deprogramming Controversy*. New York and Toronto: The Edwin Mellen Press, 1983 (forthcoming).

Brothers, Joan (ed.). *Readings in the Sociology of Religion*. Oxford: Pergamon Press, 1967.

Brown, L.B. (ed.). *Psychology and Religion*. Harmondsworth: Penguin Books, 1973.

Buber, Martin. *I and Thou*. Translated by W. Kaufman. New York: Charles Scribner's Sons, 1970.

Buehler, C.; Hesser, G.; and Weigert, A.J. "A Study of Articles on Religion in Major Sociology Journals: Some Preliminary Findings." *Journal for the Scientific Study of Religion* 11: 165-170, 1972.

Burhoe, Ralph. "The Phenomenon of Religion Seen Scientifically," in A.W. Eister (ed.), *Changing Perspectives in the Scientific Study of Religion*, pp. 15-40. New York: John Wiley and Sons, 1974.

Burke, Peter. *Sociology and History*. London: Allen and Unwin, 1980.

Burns, Elizabeth and Tom Burns (eds.). *Sociology of Literature and Drama*. Harmondsworth: Penguin Books, 1973.

Cahnman, Werner Jacob and Boskoff, Alvin (eds.). *Sociology and History: Theory and Research*. New York: The Free Press, 1964.

Campbell, Colin. "The Secret Religion of the Educated Classes." *Sociological Analysis* 39: 146-156, 1978.

_____ "Romanticism and the Consumer Ethic: Intimations of a Weber-Style Thesis." *Sociological Analysis* 44, 1983 (forthcoming).

Caporale, Rocco and Grumelli, Antonio (eds.). *The Culture of Unbelief*. Berkeley: University of California Press, 1971.

Cavanaugh, Michael. "Pagan and Christian: Sociological Euhemerism Versus American Sociology." *Sociological Analysis* 43: 109-130, 1982.

Chadwick, Owen. *The Secularization of the European Mind in the Nineteenth Century*. Cambridge: Cambridge University Press, 1975.

Chalfant, H. Paul; Beckley, Robert E.; and Palmer, C. Eddie. *Religion in Contemporary Society*. Sherman Oaks, California: Alfred Publishing Co. Inc., 1981.

Clark, S.D. *Church and Sect in Canada*. Toronto: University of Toronto Press, 1948.

______ *The Developing Canadian Community* (revised and expanded edition). Toronto: University of Toronto Press, 1968.

Clark, W.H. "How Do Social Scientists Define Religion?" *Journal of Social Psychology* 47: 143-147, 1958.

Clifford, N. Keith. "Religion and the Development of Canadian Society: An Historiographical Analysis." *Church History* 38: 506-523, 1969.

______ "History of Religion in Canada." *The Ecumenist* 18(5): 65-69, 1980.

Cogley, John. *Religion in a Secular Age: The Search for Final Meaning*. London: Pall Mall Press, 1968.

Cohen, Jere. "Rational Capitalism in Renaissance Italy." *American Journal of Sociology* 85: 1340-1355, 1980.

Cohen, Morris R. "Baseball as a National Religion," in M.R. Cohen, *The Faith of a Liberal*, pp. 334-336 (essay first published 1919). New York: Henry Holt, 1946.

Cohn, Norman. *The Pursuit of The Millennium* (revised and expanded edition). New York: Oxford University Press, 1970.

Cohn, Werner. "Is Religion Universal? Problems of Definition." *Journal for the Scientific Study of Religion* 2: 25-33, 1962.

Cole, William A. and Hammond, Phillip E. "Religious Pluralism, Legal Development, and Societal Complexity: Rudimentary Forms of Civil Religion." *Journal for the Scientific Study of Religion* 13: 177-189, 1974.

Coleman, John A. "Church-Sect Typology and Organizational Precariousness." *Sociological Analysis* 29: 55-66, 1968.

______ "Civil Religion." *Sociological Analysis* 31: 67-77, 1970.

Collins, Randall. "Reassessments of Sociological History: The Empirical Validity of the Conflict Tradition." *Theory and Society* 1: 147-178, 1974.

______ *Sociological Insight: An Introduction to Non-Obvious Sociology*. New York: Oxford University Press, 1982.

Comte, Auguste. *A General View of Positivism*. New York: Robert Speller and Sons, 1957.

Coser, Lewis A. "Durkheim's Conservatism and its Implications for His Sociological Theory," in K.H. Wolff (ed.), *Emile Durkheim: Essays on Sociology and Philosophy*, pp. 211-232. New York: Harper and Row, 1964.

______ "The Uses of Classical Sociological Theory," in B. Rhea (ed.), *The Future of the Sociological Classics*, pp. 170-182. London: George Allen and Unwin, 1981.

Crysdale, Stewart. "Religion and Secularization," in S. Crysdale and C. Beattie, *Sociology Canada: An Introductory Text*, pp. 267-290. Toronto: Butterworths, 1973.

______ "Some Problematic Aspects of Religion in Canada." *Sociological Focus* 9: 137-148, 1976.

______ "Historical Change and Conflict Perspectives in the Sociology of Religion in English-Speaking Canada." Paper presented at the Annual Meeting of the Society for the Scientific Study of Religion, 1977.

______ and Montminy, Jean-Paul. *La Religion au Canada/Religion in Canada: Annotated Inventory of Scientific Studies of Religion (1945-1972).* Downsview: York University and Québec: Les Presses de l'Université Laval, 1974.

______ and Wheatcroft, Les (eds.). *Religion in Canadian Society.* Toronto: Macmillan of Canada, 1976.

Cutler, Donald R. (ed.). *The Religious Situation: 1968.* Boston: Beacon Press, 1968.

Dagenais, James G. "The Scientific Study of Myth and Ritual: A Lost Cause." *The Human Context* 6: 586-620, 1974.

Dahrendorf, Ralf. "Out of Utopia: Toward a Reorientation of Sociological Analysis." *American Journal of Sociology* 64: 115-127, 1958.

Daiber, Karl-Fritz. "Introduction." *Social Compass* (Issue on "La religion dans les grands courants de la sociologie allemande") 27: 5-8, 1980-81.

Davies, J.G. *Christians. Politics and Violent Revolution.* London: SCM Press, 1976.

Davis, Kingsley. *Human Society.* New York: The Macmillan Co., 1948.

DeKadt, Emmanuel. *Catholic Radicals in Brazil.* London: Oxford University Press, 1970.

Demerath, N.J. and Peterson, Richard A. (eds.). *System, Change and Conflict.* New York: The Free Press, 1967.

Desroche, Henri. *Jacob and the Angel: An Essay in Sociologies of Religion.* Translated by J.K. Savacool. Amherst: University of Massachusetts Press, 1973 (first published in French 1968).

Deutscher, Isaac (ed.). *The Age of Permanent Revolution: A Trotsky Anthology.* New York: Dell Publishing Co., 1964.

Dimock, H.S. "Trends in the Redefinition of Religion." *Journal of Religion* 8: 434-452, 1928.

Dobbelaere, Karel. "Trend Report of The State of the Sociology of Religion: 1965-1966." *Social Compass* 15: 329-365, 1968.

______ and Lauwers, Jan. "Definition of Religion: A Sociological Critique." *Social Compass* 20: 535-551, 1973-74.

Dorson, Richard M. *The British Folklorists: A History.* Chicago: University of Chicago Press, 1968.

Douglas, Mary. *Purity and Danger.* Harmondsworth: Penguin Books, 1966.

______ "The Effects of Modernization on Religious Change." *Daedalus* 111: 1-19, 1982.

Dow, Thomas E. "The Role of Charisma in Modern African Development." *Social Forces* 46: 328-338, 1968.

Dumont, Fernand. "La sociologie religieuse au Canada Français," in *Sociologie Religieuse, Sciences Sociales, Actes de IVe Congrès International,* pp. 150-152. Paris: Editions Economie et Humanisme, 1955.

______ *La Situation présente de la Théorie dans la sociologie des religions.* Ottawa: Editions du Musée de l'Homme, 1958.

Durkheim, Emile. *The Division of Labour in Society.* Translated by G. Simpson. Glencoe: The Free Press, 1933 (first published in 1893).

______ *The Rules of Sociological Method.* Translated by S.A. Solovay and J.H.

Mueller. Glencoe: The Free Press, 1950 (first published in 1895).

______ *Suicide: A Study in Sociology.* Translated by J.A. Spaulding and G. Simpson. Glencoe: The Free Press, 1951 (first published in 1897).

______ *Sociology and Philosophy.* Translated by D.F. Pocock. Glencoe: The Free Press, 1953 (first published in 1911).

______ *Socialism and Saint-Simon.* Translated by C. Sattler. Yellow Springs, Ohio: The Antioch Press, 1958 (first published in French in 1928).

______ *The Elementary Forms of the Religious Life.* Translated by J.W. Swain. New York: Collier Books, 1961 (first published in 1912).

Eisenstadt, S.N. (ed.). *The Protestant Ethic and Modernization: A Comparative View.* New York: Basic Books, 1968.

______ "The Implications of Weber's Sociology of Religion for Understanding Processes of Change in Contemporary Non-European Societies and Civilizations," in C.Y. Glock and P.E. Hammond (eds.), *Beyond the Classics? Essays in the Scientific Study of Religion,* pp. 131-155. New York: Harper and Row, 1973.

Eister, Allan W. "Values, Sociology and the Sociologists." *Sociological Analysis* 25: 108-112, 1964.

______ "Toward a Radical Critique of Church-Sect Typologizing." *Journal for the Scientific Study of Religion* 6: 85-90, 1967.

______ "H. Richard Niebuhr and the Paradox of Religious Organization: A Radical Critique," in C.Y. Glock and P.E. Hammond (eds.), *Beyond the Classics? Essays in the Scientific Study of Religion,* pp. 355-408. New York: Harper and Row, 1973.

______ "Comment on 'Max Weber on Church, Sect and Mysticism'." *Sociological Analysis* 36: 227-228, 1975.

______ (ed.). *Changing Perspectives in the Scientific Study of Religion.* New York: John Wiley and Sons, 1974.

Ellwood, Robert S. "Emergent Religion in America: An Historical Perspective," in J. Needleman and G. Baker (eds.), *Understanding the New Religions,* pp. 267-284. New York: The Seabury Press, 1978.

Engels, Frederick. *The Peasant War in Germany.* Moscow: Foreign Language Publishing House, 1958.

Evans-Pritchard, E.E. *The Institutions of Primitive Society.* Oxford: Basil Blackwell, 1954.

______ *Nuer Religion.* Oxford: Oxford University Press, 1956.

______ *Theories of Primitive Religion.* Oxford: The Clarendon Press, 1965.

Fahey, Tony. "Max Weber's *Ancient Judaism.*" *American Journal of Sociology* 88: 62-87, 1982.

Falardeau, Jean-Charles. "Les recherches de sociologie religieuse au Canada." *Lumen Vitae* 6(1-2): 127-142, 1950-51.

______ "Les recherches religieuses au Canada Français." *Recherches Sociographiques* 3(1-2): 209-228, 1962.

Fallding, Harold. "Canada," in H. Mol (ed.), *Western Religion,* pp. 101-115. The Hague: Mouton, 1972.

______ *The Sociology of Religion.* Toronto: McGraw-Hill Ryerson, 1974.

Fenn, Richard K. "The Death of God: An Analysis of Ideology Crisis." *Review of Religious Research* 9: 171-181, 1968.

_____ "Max Weber on the Secular: A Typology." *Review of Religious Research* 10: 159-169, 1969.
_____ "The Process of Secularization: A Post-Parsonian View." *Journal for the Scientific Study of Religion* 9: 117-136, 1970.
_____ "Toward a New Sociology of Religion." *Journal for the Scientific Study of Religion* 11: 16-32, 1972.
_____ *Toward a Theory of Secularization.* Storrs, Connecticut: Society for the Scientific Study of Religion, 1978.
Ferrarotti, Franco. *Max Weber and the Destiny of Reason.* Translated by J. Fraser. Armonk, N.Y.: M.E. Sharpe Inc., 1982 (first published in Italian in 1965).
Ferré, Frederick. "The Definition of Religion." *Journal of the American Academy of Religion* 38: 3-16, 1970.
Feuerbach, Ludwig. *The Essence of Christianity.* Translated by G. Eliot. New York: Harper and Row, 1957 (first published in 1841).
Firth, Raymond. "Problem and Assumption in an Anthropological Study of Religion." *Journal of the Royal Anthropological Institute* 89: 130-148, 1959.
Forcese, Dennis P. "Calvinism, Capitalism and Confusion: The Weberian Thesis Revisited." *Sociological Analysis* 29: 193-201, 1968.
Frazer, James George. *The Golden Bough* (twelve volumes). London: The Macmillan Press, 1980.
_____ *The New Golden Bough.* Edited by T.H. Gaster. Garden City, N.Y.: Doubleday and Co., 1961.
_____ *The Illustrated Golden Bough.* Edited by S. MacCormack. London: Macmillan, 1978.
Freedman, Maurice (ed.). *Social Organization: Essays Presented to Raymond Firth.* London: Cass, 1967.
Freud, Sigmund. *The Future of an Illusion.* London: Hogarth Press, 1934.
_____ *Civilization and its Discontents.* London: Hogarth Press, 1939.
_____ *Moses and Monotheism.* Translated by K. Jones. New York: Vintage Books, 1967 (first published in English in 1939).
_____ *Totem and Taboo.* Translated by J. Strachey. London: Routledge and Kegan Paul, 1950 (first published in English in 1919).
Freund, Julien. *The Sociology of Max Weber.* Translated by M. Ilford. New York: Vintage Books, 1969.
Friedland, William H. "For a Sociological Concept of Charisma." *Social Forces* 43: 18-36, 1964.
Friedrichs, Robert W. *The Sociology of Sociology.* New York: The Free Press, 1970.
_____ "Social Research and Theology: End of the Detente?" *Review of Religious Research* 15: 113-127, 1974.
Friess, Horace L. "Comment on J. Paul Williams' 'The Nature of Religion'." *Journal for the Scientific Study of Religion* 1: 15-17, 1962.
Garaudy, Roger. *From Anathema to Dialogue.* New York: Vintage Books, 1968.
_____ *The Alternative Future: A Vision of Christian Marxism.* Translated by L. Mayhew. New York: Simon and Schuster Inc., 1974.
Garrett, William R. "Maligned Mysticism: The Maledicted Career of Troeltsch's Third Type." *Sociological Analysis* 36: 205-223, 1975.
Geertz, Clifford. *The Interpretation of Cultures.* New York: Basic Books, 1973.

Gehrig, Gail. *American Civil Religion: An Assessment*. Storrs, Connecticut: Society for the Scientific Study of Religion, 1979.

Gellner, David. "Max Weber, Capitalism and the Religion of India." *Sociology* 16: 526-543, 1982.

Gellner, Ernest. *Words and Things*. Harmondsworth: Penguin Books, 1968.

Gerstein, Dean R. "Reading Durkheim." *Sociological Inquiry* 51: 69, 1981.

Geuss, Raymond. *The Idea of a Critical Theory*. Cambridge: Cambridge University Press, 1981.

Giddens, Anthony. "Marx, Weber and the Development of Capitalism." *Sociology* 4: 289-310, 1970.

Gillispie, C.C. *Genesis and Geology: The Impact of Scientific Discoveries Upon Religious Beliefs in the Decades Before Darwin*. New York: Harper and Row, 1959.

Gittus, Elizabeth (ed.). *Key Variables in Social Research, Vol. 1: Religion, Housing, Locality*. London: Heinemann, 1972.

Givens, R. Dale. "The Treatment of Religion in Introductory Sociology Texts." *Journal for the Scientific Study of Religion* 5: 59-63, 1965.

Glasner, Peter E. *The Sociology of Secularization: A Critique of a Concept*. London: Routledge and Kegan Paul, 1977.

Glock, Charles Y. (ed.). *Religion in Sociological Perspective: Essays in the Empirical Study of Religion*. Belmont, California: Wadsworth Publishing Co., 1973.

______ and Stark, Rodney. *Religion and Society in Tension*. Chicago: Rand McNally and Co., 1965.

______ and Bellah, Robert N. (eds.). *The New Religious Consciousness*. Berkeley: University of California Press, 1976.

______ and Hammond, Phillip E. (eds.). *Beyond the Classics: Essays in the Scientific Study of Religion*. New York: Harper and Row, 1973.

Godelier, Maurice. *Perspectives in Marxist Anthropology*. Cambridge: Cambridge University Press, 1979.

Goethe, Johann Wolfgang Von. *Elective Affinities: A Novel*. New York: Frederick Ungar Publishing Co., 1962 (first published in German in 1807).

Goldenweiser, A.A. "Review of Emile Durkheim's *Elementary Forms*." *American Anthropologist* 17: 719-735, 1915.

______ "Religion and Society: A Critique of Durkheim's Theory of the Origin and Nature of Religion." *Journal of Philosophy, Psychology and Scientific Methods* 12, 1917.

Goldmann, Lucien. *The Hidden God*. Translated by P. Thody. London: Routledge and Kegan Paul, 1964 (first published in French in 1955).

Goode, William J. *Religion Among the Primitives*. New York: The Free Press, 1951.

Goodenough, Ward H. "Toward an Anthropologically Useful Definition of Religion," in A.W. Eister (ed.), *Changing Perspectives in the Scientific Study of Religion*, pp. 165-184. New York: John Wiley and Sons, 1974.

Goody, Jack. "Religion and Ritual: The Definitional Problem." *British Journal of Sociology* 12: 142-164, 1961.

Grafton, Thomas H. "Religious Origins and Sociological Theory." *American Sociological Review* 10: 726-739, 1945.

Greeley, Andrew M. *Unsecular Man: The Persistence of Religion*. New York: Dell Publishing Co., 1972.

______ "Implication for the Sociology of Religion of Occult Behaviour," in E.A. Tiryakian (ed.), *On the Margin of the Visible.* New York: John Wiley and Sons, 1973.

______ and Baum, Gregory (eds.). *The Persistence of Religion.* New York: Herder and Herder, 1973.

Green, Robert W. (ed.). *Protestantism and Capitalism: The Weber Thesis and its Critics.* Boston: D.C. Heath and Co., 1959.

Greenwald, David E. "Durkheim on Society, Thought and Ritual." *Sociological Analysis* 34: 157-168, 1973.

Grossman, Nathan. "Comment: On Peter Berger's Definition of Religion." *Journal for the Scientific Study of Religion* 14: 289-292, 1975.

Guindi, Fadwa El. *Religion in Culture.* Dubuque, Iowa: William C. Brown Company, 1977.

Gustafson, Paul M. "Exegesis on the Gospel According to St. Max." *Sociological Analysis* 34: 12-25, 1973.

Habermas, Jürgen. *Toward a Rational Society.* Boston: Beacon Press, 1970.

______ *Knowledge and Human Interests.* Boston: Beacon Press, 1971.

______ *Theory and Practice.* Boston: Beacon Press, 1973.

______ *Legitimation Crisis.* Boston: Beacon Press, 1975.

Hadden, Jeffrey. "Introduction" to Symposium on "The Sociology of Religion of Robert Bellah." *Journal for the Scientific Study of Religion* 14: 385-390, 1975.

______ and Heenan, E.F. "Empirical Studies in the Sociology of Religion: An Assessment of the Past Ten Years." *Sociological Analysis* 31: 153-171, 1970.

Hagedorn, Robert (ed.). *Sociology.* Toronto: Holt, Rinehart and Winston, 1980.

Halle, Louis J. "Marx's Religious Drama." *Encounter* 25(4): 29-37, 1965.

Hammond, Phillip E. "Religious Pluralism and Durkheim's Integration Thesis," in A.W. Eister (ed.), *Changing Perspectives in the Scientific Study of Religion,* pp. 115-142. New York: John Wiley and Sons, 1974.

______ "The Sociology of American Civil Religion: A Bibliographic Essay." *Sociological Analysis* 37: 169-182, 1976.

______ "The Gap Between Theory and Research in the Sociology of Religion," in H.M. Blalock (ed.), *Sociological Theory and Research,* pp. 332-338. New York: The Free Press, 1980.

Hargrove, Barbara. *The Sociology of Religion: Classical and Contemporary Approaches.* Arlington Heights, Illinois: AHM Publishing Corporation, 1979.

Harrison, Jane E. *Themis: A Study of the Social Origins of Greek Religion.* Cambridge: Cambridge University Press, 1912.

Hasler, A.B. *How the Pope Became Infallible: Pius IX and the Politics of Persuasion.* Translated by P. Heinegg. Garden City, N.Y.: Doubleday and Co., 1981 (first published in German in 1979).

Hebblethwaite, Brian. *Evil, Suffering and Religion.* New York: Hawthorn Books, Inc., 1976.

Hebblethwaite, Peter. *The Runaway Church: Post-Conciliar Growth or Decline.* New York: The Seabury Press, 1975.

______ *The Christian-Marxist Dialogue.* New York: Paulist Press, 1977.

Hegel, Georg W.F. *On Art, Religion, Philosophy.* Edited by J.G. Gray. New York: Harper and Row, 1970.

Hempel, Carl G. *Fundamentals of Concept Formation in Empirical Science.*

Chicago: University of Chicago Press, 1952.

Henderson, J.L.H. *John Strachan 1778-1867*. Toronto: University of Toronto Press, 1969.

Herberg, Will. *Protestant-Catholic-Jew: An Essay in American Religious Sociology* (revised edition). Garden City, N.Y.: Doubleday and Co., 1960.

______ "America's Civil Religion: What it is and Whence it Comes," in R.E. Richey and D.G. Jones (eds.), *American Civil Religion*, pp. 76-88. New York: Harper and Row, 1974.

Hertz, Karl H. "Max Weber and American Puritanism." *Journal for the Scientific Study of Religion* 1: 189-197, 1961-62.

Hill, Michael. *A Sociology of Religion*. London: Heinemann Books, 1973.

Hiller, Harry. "The New Theology and the Sociology of Religion." *Canadian Review of Sociology and Anthropology* 6: 179-187, 1969.

______ "The Sociology of Religion in Canadian Context," in G.N. Ramu and S.D. Johnson (eds.), *Introduction to Canadian Society: Sociological Analysis*. Toronto: Macmillan of Canada, 1976.

______ "The Sociology of Religion in Western Canada: An Assessment." Paper presented at the Annual Meeting of the Canadian Sociology and Anthropology Association, 1976.

Hobsbawm, Eric J. *Primitive Rebels*. New York: The Norton Library, 1965.

______ (ed.). *Karl Marx: Precapitalist Economic Formations*. Translated by J. Cohen. New York: International Publishers, 1965.

Hodges, Daniel L. "Breaking a Scientific Taboo: Putting Assumptions about the Supernatural into Scientific Theories of Religion." *Journal for the Scientific Study of Religion* 13: 393-408, 1974.

Holmes, J. Derek. *The Triumph of the Holy See*. London: Burns and Oates, 1978.

Homans, George C. "Anxiety and Ritual: The Theories of Malinowski and Radcliffe-Brown." *American Anthropologist* 43: 164-172, 1941.

Hook, Sidney (ed.). *Marx and the Marxists: The Ambiguous Legacy*. New York: Van Nostrand, 1955.

______ *From Hegel to Marx*. Ann Arbor: University of Michigan Press, 1962.

Horkheimer, Max. *Critical Theory*. New York: Herder and Herder, 1972.

______ and Adorno, Theodor. *Dialectic of Enlightenment*. New York: Herder and Herder, 1972.

Horowitz, Irving Louis. "Consensus, Conflict and Co-operation: A Sociological Inventory." *Social Forces* 41: 177-188, 1962.

Horton, Robin. "A Definition of Religion and its Uses." *Journal of the Royal Anthropological Institute* 90: 201-226, 1960.

______ "Neo-Tylorianism: Sound Sense or Sinister Prejudice?" *Man: The Journal of the Royal Anthropological Institute* (new series) 3: 625-634, 1968.

Houtart, François. *Religion and Ideology in Sri Lanka*. Maryknoll, N.Y.: Orbis Books, 1980.

______ and Lemercinier, Geneviève. "Weberian Theory and the Ideological Function of Religion." *Social Compass* 23: 345-354, 1976.

Howe, Richard Herbert. "Max Weber's Elective Affinities: Sociology Within The Bounds of Pure Reason." *American Journal of Sociology* 84: 336-385, 1978.

Hughes, Everett Cherrington. "The Early and the Contemporary Study of Religion." *American Journal of Sociology* 60: (supplement) i-iv, 1955.

Hume, David. *Dialogues Concerning Natural Religion.* Indianapolis and New York: The Bobbs-Merrill Co. Inc., 1974 (first published in 1779).

Hunter, James Davison. "The New Religions: Demodernization and the Protest Against Modernity," in B.R. Wilson (ed.), *The Social Impact of New Religious Movements,* pp. 1-19. New York: Rose of Sharon Press, 1981.

Iggers, Georg G. (trans. and ed.). *The Doctrine of Saint-Simon: An Exposition.* New York: Schocken Books, 1972.

Inglis, K.S. *Churches and the Working Classes in Victorian England.* London: Routledge and Kegan Paul, 1963.

Ions, Edmund. *Against Behaviouralism.* Oxford: Basil Blackwell, 1977.

James, William. *The Varieties of Religious Experience.* London: Collins, 1960 (first published in 1902).

Jarvie, Ian C. *The Revolution in Anthropology.* London: Routledge and Kegan Paul, 1964.

Jay, Martin. *The Dialectical Imagination.* London: Heinemann, 1973.

Johnson, Benton. "A Critical Appraisal of the Church-Sect Typology." *American Sociological Review* 22: 88-92, 1957.

______ "On Church and Sect." *American Sociological Review* 28: 539-549, 1963.

______ "Church and Sect Revisited." *Journal for the Scientific Study of Religion* 10: 124-137, 1971.

______ "Max Weber and American Protestantism." *Sociological Quarterly* 12: 473-485, 1971.

______ "Sociological Theory and Religious Truth." *Sociological Analysis* 38: 368-388, 1977.

______ "A Fresh Look at Theories of Secularization," in H.M. Blalock (ed.), *Sociological Theory and Research: A Critical Approach,* pp. 314-331. New York: The Free Press, 1980.

______ "A Sociological Perspective on the New Religions," in T. Robbins and D. Anthony (eds.), *In Gods We Trust,* pp. 51-66. New Brunswick, N.J.: Transaction Books, 1981.

Johnson, Doyle Paul. "Dilemmas of Charismatic Leadership: the Case of the People's Temple." *Sociological Analysis* 40: 315-323, 1979.

Johnson, Harry M. *Sociology: An Introduction.* New York: Harcourt, Brace and World, 1960.

______ (ed.). *Religious Change and Continuity.* San Francisco: Jossey-Bass, 1979.

Johnstone, Ronald L. *Religion and Society in Interaction.* Englewood Cliffs, N.J.: Prentice-Hall, Inc., 1975.

Jolicoeur, Pamela M., and Knowles, Louis K. "Fraternal Associations and Civil Religion: Scottish Rite Freemasonry." *Review of Religious Research* 20: 3-22, 1978.

Jung, Carl G. *Psychology and Religion: West and East.* Translated by R.F.C. Hull. London: Routledge and Kegan Paul, 1958.

Kalberg, Stephen. "The Search for Thematic Orientations in a Fragmented Oeuvre: The Discussion of Max Weber in Recent German Sociological Literature." *Sociology* 13: 127-139, 1979.

______ "Max Weber's Types of Rationality: Cornerstones for the Analysis of Rationalization Processes in History." *American Journal of Sociology* 85: 1145-1179, 1980.

Kallen, Horace M. "Secularism as the Common Religion of a Free Society." *Journal for the Scientific Study of Religion* 4: 145-151, 1965.

Kaplan, Abraham. *The Conduct of Inquiry*. San Francisco: Chandler Publishing Co., 1964.

Kathan, Boardman and Fuchs-Kreimer, Nancy. "Civil Religion in America." *Religious Education* 70: 451-550, 1975.

Kautsky, Karl. *Communism in Central Europe at the Time of the Reformation*. Translated by J.L. and E.G. Mulliken. London: T. Fisher Unwin, 1897.

______ *Foundations of Christianity*. Translated by M.F. Mims. New York: Russell and Russell, 1953 (first published in English in 1925).

Kearl, Michael C. and Rinaldi, Anoel. "The Political Uses of the Dead as Symbols in Contemporary Civil Religions." *Social Forces* 61: 643-708, 1983.

Kee, Alistair (ed.). *A Reader in Political Theology*. London: SCM Press, 1974.

Kent, Stephen A. "Weber, Goethe, and the Nietzschean Allusion: Capturing the Source of the 'Iron Cage' Metaphor." *Sociological Analysis* 44, 1983 (forthcoming).

Kersevan, Marko. "Religion and the Marxist Concept of Social Formation." *Social Compass* 22: 323-342, 1975.

Klausner, Samuel Z. "Scientific and Humanistic Study of Religion: A Comment on 'Christianity and Symbolic Realism'." *Journal for the Scientific Study of Religion* 9: 100-106, 1970.

Kneale, W.C. *Probability and Induction*. Oxford: Oxford University Press, 1952.

Knudten, Richard D. (ed.). *The Sociology of Religion: An Anthology*. New York: Appleton-Century-Crofts, 1967.

Kuhn, Thomas S. *The Nature of Scientific Revolutions*. Chicago: University of Chicago Press, 1962.

Kushner, Harold. *When Bad Things Happen to Good People*. New York: Avon Books, 1983.

Leach, Edmund R. "Golden Bough or Gilded Twig?" *Daedalus* 90: 371-387, 1961.

______ "Frazer and Malinowski." *Encounter* 25(5): 24-36, 1965.

______ (ed.). *The Structural Study of Myth and Totemism*. London: Tavistock Publications, 1967.

Le Bon, Gustave. *The Crowd: A Study of the Popular Mind*. New York: Viking Press, 1960 (first published in 1895).

Lemert, Charles C. "Social Structure and the Absent Centre: An Alternative to New Sociologies of Religion." *Sociological Analysis* 36: 95-107, 1975.

______ "Defining Non-Church Religion." *Review of Religious Research* 16: 186-197, 1975.

Lenin, Vladimir Ilych. *Lenin on Religion*. London: Martin Lawrence, undated.

Lenzer, Gertrud (ed.). *Auguste Comte and Positivism*. New York: Harper and Row, 1975.

Lessa, William A., and Vogt, Evon Z. (eds.). *Reader in Comparative Religion*. Evanston, Illinois: Row, Peterson and Co., 1958.

______ *Reader in Comparative Religion* (fourth edition). New York: Harper and Row, 1979.

Levine, David H. *Religion and Politics in Latin America: The Catholic Church in Venezuela and Colombia*. Princeton, N.J.: Princeton University Press, 1981.

Levine, Donald N. "Rationality and Freedom: Weber and Beyond." *Sociological Inquiry* 51: 5-26, 1981.

Lévi-Strauss, Claude. *Totemism.* London: Merlin Press, 1964.

______ *The Savage Mind.* London: Weidenfeld and Nicolson, 1966.

Lévy-Bruhl, Lucien. *Primitive Mentality.* Translated by L.A. Clare. London: Allen and Unwin, 1923.

______ *How Natives Think.* Translated by L.A. Clare. New York: Washington Square Press, 1966.

Lewy, Guenter. *Religion and Revolution.* New York: Oxford University Press, 1974.

Lichtheim, George. *Marxism: An Historical and Critical Study* (second edition). New York: Praeger Publishers, 1965.

Lidz, Victor M. "Secularization, Ethical Life, and Religion in Modern Societies," in H.M. Johnson (ed.), *Religious Change and Continuity,* pp. 191-217. San Francisco: Jossey-Bass, 1979.

Ling, Trevor. *Karl Marx and Religion in Europe and India.* New York: Barnes and Noble, 1980.

Lipp, Wolfgang. "Charisma-Deviation, Leadership and Cultural Change." *Annual Review of the Social Sciences of Religion* 1: 59-77, 1977.

Lipset, Seymour Martin (ed.). *The Third Century: America as a Post-Industrial Society.* Chicago: University of Chicago Press, 1979.

______ and Hofstadter, Richard (eds.). *Sociology and History: Methods.* New York: Basic Books, 1968.

Lipsitz, Lewis, "If, as Verba says, the State functions as a religion, what are we to do to save our souls?" *American Political Science Review* 62: 527-535, 1968.

Little, David. "Max Weber and the Comparative Study of Religious Ethics." *Journal of Religious Ethics* 2: 5-40, 1974.

Lofland, John. *Doomsday Cult* (revised edition). New York: Irvington Publishers, 1978.

Lonergan, Bernard J.F. *Insight: A Study of Human Understanding.* New York: Harper and Row, 1978 (first published in 1958).

Lovell, Terry. "Weber, Goldmann and the Sociology of Beliefs." *European Journal of Sociology* 14: 304-323, 1973.

Lowie, Robert H. *Primitive Religion* (revised edition). New York: Liveright Publishing Co., 1948 (first published in 1924).

Löwith, Karl. *Max Weber and Karl Marx.* Edited by T. Bottomore and W. Outhwaite. Translated by H. Fantel. London: George Allen and Unwin, 1982 (first published in German in 1960).

Luckmann, Thomas. "On Religion in Modern Society: Individual Consciousness, World View, Institution." *Journal for the Scientific Study of Religion* 2: 147-162, 1963.

______ *The Invisible Religion: The Problem of Religion in Modern Society.* New York: The Macmillan Co., 1967 (first published in German in 1963).

______ "Belief, Unbelief and Religion," in R. Caporale and A. Grumelli (eds.), *The Culture of Unbelief,* pp. 21-37. Berkeley: University of California Press, 1971.

______ "Theories of Religion and Social Change." *Annual Review of the Social Sciences of Religion* 1: 1-28, 1977.

Luethy, Herbert. "Once Again: Calvinism and Capitalism." *Encounter* 22(1): 26-38, 1964.

______ "Max Weber - Luethy's Reply." *Encounter* 24(1): 92-94, 1965.

Lukes, Steven. *Emile Durkheim: His Life and Work.* Harmondsworth: Penguin Books, 1975.

McCaffery, Peter G. "A Sociological Analysis of the Concerns of Pressure Groups in the Roman Catholic Church in the Netherlands and in England," in *The Contemporary Metamorphosis of Religion?* (Acts of the 12th International Conference on the Sociology of Religion), pp. 239-255. Lille, France: C.I.S.R. Secretariat, 1973.

McDonald, Lynn. *The Sociology of Law and Order.* Toronto: Methuen, 1979.

McDowell, Jennifer. "Soviet Civil Ceremonies." *Journal for the Scientific Study of Religion* 13: 265-279, 1974.

McGuire, Meredith B. *Religion: The Social Context.* Belmont, California: Wadsworth Publishing Co., 1981.

Machalek, Richard. "Definitional Strategies in the Study of Religion." *Journal for the Scientific Study of Religion* 16: 395-401, 1977.

Macintyre, Alasdair. "Weber At His Weakest." *Encounter* 25(5): 85-87, 1965.

______ *Secularization and Moral Change.* Oxford: Oxford University Press, 1967.

McKown, Delos B. *The Classical Marxist Critique of Religion: Marx, Engels, Lenin, Kautsky.* The Hague: Martinus Nijhoff, 1975.

MacLeod, Henry. "The Religious Situation in Canadian Society." Paper presented to the Annual Meeting of the Canadian Sociology and Anthropology Association, 1979.

McLeod, Hugh. *Religion and the People of Western Europe, 1789-1970.* Oxford: Oxford University Press, 1981.

McLoughlin, William G., and Bellah, Robert N. (eds.). *Religion in America.* Boston: Beacon Press, 1968.

McNall, Scott G. (ed.). *Theoretical Perspectives in Sociology.* New York: St. Martin's Press, 1979.

Macpherson, C.B. "After Strange Gods: Canadian Political Science 1973," in T.N. Guinsberg and G.L. Reuber (eds.), *Perspectives on the Social Sciences in Canada,* pp. 52-76. Toronto: University of Toronto Press, 1974.

MacRae, Donald G. *Ideology and Society: Papers in Sociology and Politics.* London: Heinemann, 1961.

______ *Weber.* London: Collins, 1974.

McSweeney, Bill. *Roman Catholicism: The Search for Relevance.* Oxford: Basil Blackwell, 1980.

Maddock, Kenneth. *The Australian Aborigines: A Portrait of their Society.* Harmondsworth: Penguin Books, 1972.

Maduro, Otto. "Marxist Analysis and the Sociology of Religion: An Introduction." *Social Compass* 22: 305-322, 1975.

______ "Marxist Analysis and Sociology of Religions: An Outline of International Bibliography up to 1975." *Social Compass* 22: 401-482, 1975.

______ "New Marxist Approaches to the Relative Autonomy of Religion." *Sociological Analysis* 38: 359-367, 1977.

______ *Religion and Social Conflicts.* Maryknoll, N.Y.: Orbis Books, 1982.

______ "Catholic Church, State Power and Popular Movements." Paper presented to the 1982 Meeting of the Society for the Scientific Study of Religion.

Malefijt, Annemarie De Waal. *Religion and Culture: An Introduction to Anthropology of Religion*. New York: The Macmillan Co., 1968.

Malinowski, Bronislaw. "Review of Durkheim's *Elementary Forms*." *Folklore* 24: 525-553, 1913.

______ "Sir James George Frazer: A Biographical Appreciation," in B. Malinowski (ed.), *A Scientific Theory of Culture*, pp. 177-221. Chapel Hill: University of North Carolina Press, 1944.

______ *A Scientific Theory of Culture*. Chapel Hill: University of North Carolina Press, 1944.

______ *Magic, Science and Religion and Other Essays*. Glencoe: The Free Press, 1948.

Mandic, Oleg. "A Marxist Perspective on Contemporary Religious Revivals." *Social Research* 37: 237-258, 1970.

Mannheim, Karl. *Ideology and Utopia*. Translated by L. Wirth and E. Shils. London: Routledge and Kegan Paul, 1936.

Manuel, Frank. *The Prophets of Paris: Turgot, Condorcet, Saint-Simon and Comte*. New York: Harper and Row, 1965.

______ *The Eighteenth Century Confronts the Gods*. New York: Atheneum, 1967 (first published in 1959).

Markoff, John and Daniel Regan. "The Rise and Fall of Civil Religion: Comparative Perspectives." *Sociological Analysis* 42: 333-352, 1982.

Marsden, Lorna R., and Harvey, Edward B. *Fragile Federation: Social Change in Canada*. Toronto: McGraw-Hill Ryerson, 1979.

Marshall, Gordon. "The Dark Side of the Weber Thesis: The Case of Scotland." *British Journal of Sociology* 31: 419-440, 1980.

______ *In Search of the Spirit of Capitalism: An Essay on Max Weber's Protestant Ethic Thesis*. New York: Columbia University Press, 1982.

Martin, David. "Towards Eliminating the Concept of Secularization," in J. Gould (ed.), *Penguin Survey of the Social Sciences*, pp. 169-182. Harmondsworth: Penguin Books, 1965.

______ "The Sociology of Religion: A Case of Status Deprivation." *British Journal of Sociology* 17: 353-359, 1966.

______ *The Religious and the Secular: Studies in Secularization*. London: Routledge and Kegan Paul, 1969.

______ *A General Theory of Secularization*. Oxford: Basil Blackwell, 1978.

______ John Orme Mills and W.S.F. Pickering (eds.). *Sociology and Theology: Alliance and Conflict*. New York: St. Martin's Press, 1980.

Martindale, Don. *The Nature and Types of Sociological Theory*. London: Routledge and Kegan Paul, 1960.

Marx, Gary. "Religion: Opiate or Inspiration of Civil Rights Militancy Among Negroes." *American Sociological Review* 32: 64-72, 1967.

Marx, Karl. *Karl Marx: Early Writings*. Translated and edited by T.B. Bottomore. New York: McGraw-Hill, 1964.

______ and Engels, Frederick. *Selected Works* (two volumes). Moscow: Foreign Languages Publishing House, 1948.

______ and Engels, Frederick. *Selected Correspondence.* Moscow: Foreign Languages Publishing House, 1956.

______ and Engels, Frederick. *On Religion.* Moscow: Foreign Languages Publishing House, 1958.

______ and Engels, Frederick. *The German Ideology.* London: Lawrence and Wishart, 1965.

Mayo, H.B. "Marxism and Religion." *The Hibbert Journal* 51: 226-233, 1953.

Mayrl, William W. "The Christian-Marxist Encounter: From Dialogue to Detente." *Sociological Analysis* 39: 84-89, 1978.

Means, Richard L. "American Protestantism and Max Weber's Protestant Ethic." *Religious Education* 60: 90-98, 1965.

______ "Textbooks in the Sociology of Religion: A Review Article." *Sociological Analysis* 27: 101-105, 1966.

Merton, Robert K. *Social Theory and Social Structure* (revised edition). Glencoe: The Free Press, 1957.

______ *Science, Technology and Society in Seventeenth-Century England.* New York: Harper and Row, 1970 (first published in 1938).

Mills, C. Wright. *The Sociological Imagination.* New York: Oxford University Press, 1959.

______ (ed.). *Images of Man.* New York: George Braziller, 1960.

Mitzman, Arthur. *The Iron Cage: An Historical Interpretation of Max Weber.* New York: Alfred Knopf, 1969.

Moberg, David O. "The Sociology of Religion in Western Europe and America." *Social Compass* 13: 193-204, 1966.

______ "Some Trends in the Sociology of Religion in the U.S.A." *Social Compass* 13: 237-243, 1966.

Mol, Hans (ed.). *Western Religion: A Country by Country Sociological Enquiry.* The Hague: Mouton, 1972.

______ "Marginality and Commitment as Hidden Variables in the Jellinek/Weber/Merton Theses on the Calvinist Ethic." *Current Sociology* 22: 279-297, 1974.

______ "Major Correlates of Churchgoing in Canada," in S. Crysdale and L. Wheatcroft (eds.), *Religion in Canadian Society,* pp. 241-254. Toronto: Macmillan of Canada, 1976.

______ *Identity and the Sacred: A Sketch for a New Social-Scientific Theory of Religion.* Agincourt: The Book Society, 1976.

______ "The Origin and Function of Religion: A Critique of, and Alternative to, Durkheim's Interpretation of the Religion of the Australian Aborigines." *Journal for the Scientific Study of Religion* 18: 379-389, 1979.

______ *The Firm and the Formless: Religion and Identity in Aboriginal Australia.* Waterloo: Wilfrid Laurier University Press, 1982.

______ *Faith and Fragility.* Waterloo: Wilfrid Laurier University Press (forthcoming).

______ (ed.). *Identity and Religion: International, Cross-Cultural Approaches.* Beverley Hills, California: Sage Publishers, 1978.

Molloy, Stephen. "Max Weber and the Religions of China: Any Way Out of the Maze?" *British Journal of Sociology* 31: 378-399, 1980.

Moltmann, Jürgen. *Theology of Hope.* New York: Harper and Row, 1967.

______ *Religion, Revolution and the Future.* New York: Charles Scribner's Sons, 1969.

Moore, Sally F., and Myerhoff, Barbara G. (eds.). *Secular Religion.* Assen/Amsterdam: Van Gorcum, 1977.

Moreux, Collette. *Fin d'une Religion?* Montréal: Les Presses de l'Université de Montréal, 1969.

Morth, Ingo. "La Sociologie de la religion comme Théorie Critique." *Social Compass* 27: 27-50, 1980.

Mueller, Gert H. "Asceticism and Mysticism." *International Yearbook for the Sociology of Religion* 8: 68-132, 1973.

______ "The Notion of Rationality in the Work of Max Weber." *Archives Européennes de Sociologie* 20: 149-171, 1979.

Müller, F. Max. *Lectures on the Science of Language* (first series). London: Longmans, Green and Co., 1866.

______ *Lectures on the Science of Language* (second series). London: Longmans, Green and Co., 1868.

______ *The Life and Letters of the Right Honourable Friedrich Max Müller: Edited by his Wife* (two volumes). Longmans, Green and Co., 1902.

______ *The Six Systems of Indian Philosophy.* London: Longmans, Green and Co., 1919.

______ (ed.). *The Sacred Books of the East: Volume 32, The Vedic Hymns.* Translated by F.M. Müller. Oxford: The Clarendon Press, 1891.

Mullins, Nicholas C. *Theory and Theory Groups in Contemporary American Sociology.* New York: Harper and Row, 1973.

Nadel, S.F. *Nupe Religion.* London: Routledge and Kegan Paul, 1954.

Nederman, Gary J., and Goulding, James Wray. "Popular Occultism and Critical Social Theory: Exploring Some Themes in Adorno's Critique of Astrology and the Occult." *Sociological Analysis* 42: 325-332, 1982.

Needleman, Jacob and George Baker (eds.). *Understanding the New Religions.* New York: The Seabury Press, 1978.

Nelson, Benjamin. "In Defence of Max Weber." *Encounter* 23(2): 94-95, 1964.

______ "Review Article on Weber's *Sociology of Religion.*" *American Sociological Review* 30: 595-599, 1965.

______ "Is the Sociology of Religion Possible? A Reply to Robert Bellah." *Journal for the Scientific Study of Religion* 9: 107-111, 1970.

______ "Weber's Protestant Ethic: Its Origins, Wanderings, and Forseeable Futures," in C.Y. Glock and P.E. Hammond (eds.), *Beyond the Classics? Essays in the Scientific Study of Religion,* pp. 71-130. New York: Harper and Row, 1973.

______ "Max Weber's 'Author's Introduction' (1920): A Master Clue to his Main Aims." *Sociological Inquiry* 44: 269-278, 1974.

______ "On Orient and Occident in Max Weber." *Social Research* 43: 114-129, 1976.

Nesti, Arnaldo. "Gramsci et la religion populaire." *Social Compass* 22: 343-354, 1975.

Newman, William M. (ed.). *The Social Meanings of Religion: An Integrated Anthology.* Chicago: Rand McNally, 1974.

Niebuhr, H. Richard. *The Social Sources of Denominationalism.* Cleveland: World Publishing Co., 1957 (first published in 1929).

______ "Sects." *Encyclopaedia of the Social Sciences* 13: 624-631, New York: Macmillan, 1937.

Nisbet, Robert A. "Conservatism and Sociology." *American Journal of Sociology* 58: 167-175, 1952.

______ (ed.). *Emile Durkheim*. Englewood Cliffs, N.J.: Prentice-Hall Inc., 1965.

______ *The Sociological Tradition*. New York: Basic Books Inc., 1966.

______ *The Sociology of Emile Durkheim*. New York: Oxford University Press, 1974.

Norbeck, Edward. *Religion in Primitive Society*. New York: Harper and Row, 1961.

______ *Religion in Human Life: Anthropological Views*. New York: Holt, Rinehart and Winston, 1974.

Nottingham, Elizabeth. *Religion and Society*. New York: Random House, 1954.

O'Dea, Thomas F. *The Sociology of Religion*. Englewood Cliffs, N.J.: Prentice-Hall, Inc., 1966.

______ "Sects and Cults." *Encyclopaedia of the Social Sciences* 14: 130-136, New York: Macmillan, 1968.

______ "The Sociology of Religion Reconsidered." *Sociological Analysis* 31: 145-151, 1970.

______ and O'Dea, Janet K. (eds.). *Readings on the Sociology of Religion*. Englewood Cliffs, N.J.: Prentice-Hall, Inc., 1973.

Oliver, Ivan. "The Limits of the Sociology of Religion: A Critique of the Durkheimian Approach." *British Journal of Sociology* 27: 461-473, 1976.

O'Neill, John (ed.). *On Critical Theory*. New York: The Seabury Press, 1976.

O'Toole, Roger. " 'Underground' Traditions in the Study of Sectarianism: Non-Religious Uses of the Concept 'Sect'." *Journal for the Scientific Study of Religion* 15: 145-156, 1976.

______ *The Precipitous Path: Studies in Political Sects*. Toronto: P.M.A. Associates, 1977.

______ "Some Good Purpose: Notes on Religion and Culture in Canada." *Annual Review of the Social Sciences of Religion* 6: 1982 (forthcoming).

Otto, Rudolf. *The Idea of the Holy: An Inquiry into the Non-Rational Factor in the Idea of the Divine and its Relation to the Rational*. Translated by J.W. Harvey. London: Humphrey Milford and Oxford University Press, 1926 (first published in German in 1917).

Outhwaite, William. *Understanding Social Life: The Method Called Verstehen*. London: George Allen and Unwin, 1975.

Paine, Thomas. *The Age of Reason*. New York: The Liberal Arts Press, 1957 (first published in 1794).

Paper, Jordan. "A Shaman in Contemporary Toronto," in P. Slater (ed.), *Religion and Culture in Canada*, pp. 471-489. Waterloo: Canadian Corporation for Studies in Religion, 1977.

Park, Robert E. *On Social Control and Collective Behaviour*. Edited by R.H. Turner. Chicago: University of Chicago Press, 1967.

______ and Burgess, Ernest W. *Introduction to the Science of Sociology*. Chicago: University of Chicago Press, 1924.

Parkin, Frank. *Max Weber*. London: Tavistock Publications, 1982.

Parsons, Talcott. "The Theoretical Development of the Sociology of Religion: A

Chapter in the History of Modern Social Science." *Journal of the History of Ideas* 5: 176-190, 1944.

______ *The Social System*. Glencoe: The Free Press, 1951.

______ *The Structure of Social Action*. Glencoe: The Free Press, 1949 (first published in 1937).

______ *Structure and Process in Modern Societies*. Glencoe: The Free Press, 1960.

______ et al. (eds.). *Theories of Society* (two volumes). Glencoe: The Free Press, 1961.

______ "Introduction" to Max Weber, *The Sociology of Religion*. Translated by E. Fischoff. Boston: Beacon Press, 1963.

______ "Evolutionary Universals in Society." *American Sociological Review* 29: 339-357, 1964.

______ "Durkheim's Contribution to the Theory of Integration of Social Systems," in K.H. Wolff (ed.), *Emile Durkheim: Essays on Sociology and Philosophy*, pp. 118-153. New York: Harper and Row, 1964.

______ "Religion in a Modern Pluralistic Society." *Review of Religious Research* 7: 125-146, 1966.

______ "Christianity and Modern Industrial Society," in E.A. Tiryakian (ed.), *Sociological Theory, Values and Sociocultural Change*, pp. 33-70. New York: Harper and Row, 1967.

______ "Durkheim on Religion Revisited: Another Look at the Elementary Forms of the Religious Life," in C.Y. Glock and P.E. Hammond (eds.), *Beyond the Classics: Essays in the Scientific Study of Religion*, pp. 156-180. New York: Harper and Row, 1973.

______ "Religion in Postindustrial America: The Problem of Secularization." *Social Research* 41: 193-225, 1974.

______ "Revisiting the Classics Throughout a Long Career," in B. Rhea (ed.), *The Future of the Sociological Classics*, pp. 183-194. London: George Allen and Unwin, 1981.

Peel, J.D.Y. *Herbert Spencer: The Evolution of a Sociologist*. London: Heinemann, 1971.

Penner, Hans H. "The Problem of Semantics in the Study of Religion," in R.D. Baird (ed.), *Methodological Issues in Religious Studies*. Chico: New Horizons Press, 1975.

______ "Lost Causes: A Reply to James Dagenais." *The Human Context* 7: 136-141, 1975.

______ and Yonan, Edward A. "Is a Science of Religion Possible?" *The Journal of Religion* 52: 107-133, 1972.

Pepper, George. "Religion and Evolution." *Sociological Analysis* 31: 78-91, 1970.

Perkins, H. Wesley. "Organized Religion as Opiate or Prophetic Stimulant: A Study of American and English Assessments of Social Justice in Two Settings." *Review of Religious Research* 24: 206-224, 1983.

Petersen, David L. "Max Weber and the Sociological Study of Ancient Israel," in H.M. Johnson (ed.), *Religious Change and Continuity*, pp. 117-149. San Francisco: Jossey-Bass, 1979.

Pickering, W.S.F. (ed.). *Durkheim on Religion*. London: Routledge and Kegan Paul, 1975.

Pope, Whitney; Cohen, Jere; and Hazelrigg, Lawrence E. "On the Divergence of Weber and Durkheim." *American Sociological Review* 40: 417-427, 1975.

Prades, Jose A. "Sur le concept de religion." *Studies in Religion/Sciences Religieuses* 3: 47-62, 1973.

Pruyser, Paul. *A Dynamic Psychology of Religion*. New York: Harper and Row, 1968.

Radin, Paul. *Primitive Religion: Its Nature and Origin*. New York: Dover Publications, 1957 (first published in 1937).

Raison, Timothy (ed.). *The Founding Fathers of Social Science*. Harmondsworth: Penguin Books, 1969.

Reardon, B.M.G. *Religious Thought in the Nineteenth Century*. Cambridge: Cambridge University Press, 1966.

Redekop, Calvin. "A New Look at Sect Development." *Journal for the Scientific Study of Religion* 13: 345-352, 1974.

Rex, John A. *Key Problems of Sociological Theory*. London: Routledge and Kegan Paul, 1961.

______ (ed.). *Approaches to Sociology*. London: Routledge and Kegan Paul, 1974.

Rhea, Buford (ed.). *The Future of the Sociological Classics*. London: George Allen and Unwin, 1981.

Richard, Reginald. "Le concept de religion: specificité ou homologie." *Cahiers du CRSR* 2: 3-17, 1978.

Richardson, James T.; Stewart, M.; and Simmonds, R.B. *Organized Miracles: A Sociological Study of a Jesus Movement Organization*. New Brunswick, N.J.: Transaction Books, 1978.

Richey, Russell E., and Jones, Donald E. (eds.). *American Civil Religion*. New York: Harper and Row, 1974.

Robbins, Thomas; Anthony, Dick; and Curtis, Thomas. "The Limits of Symbolic Realism: Problems of Empathic Field Observation in a Sectarian Context." *Journal for the Scientific Study of Religion* 12: 259-271, 1973.

______ and Anthony, Dick. "New Religious Movements and the Social System: Integration, Disintegration and Transformation." *Annual Review of the Social Sciences of Religion* 2: 1-28, 1978.

______ Anthony, Dick; and Richardson, James. "Theory and Research on Today's 'New Religions'." *Sociological Analysis* 39: 95-122, 1978.

______ and Anthony, Dick. (eds.). *In Gods We Trust: New Patterns of Religious Pluralism in America*. New Brunswick, N.J.: Transaction Books, 1981.

Robertson, Archibald. *Socialism and Religion: An Essay*. London: Lawrence and Wishart, 1960.

Robertson, Roland. *The Sociological Interpretation of Religion*. New York: Schocken Books, 1970.

______ "Basic Problems of Definition," in K. Thompson and J. Tunstall (eds.), *Sociological Perspectives*, pp. 365-378. Harmondsworth: Penguin Books, 1971.

______ "Sociologists and Secularization." *Sociology* 5: 297-312, 1971.

______ "Religious and Sociological Factors in the Analysis of Secularization," in A.W. Eister (ed.), *Changing Perspectives in the Scientific Study of Religion*, pp. 41-60. New York: John Wiley and Sons, 1974.

______ "On the Analysis of Mysticism: Pre-Weberian, Weberian and Post-Weberian Types." *Sociological Analysis* 36: 241-266, 1975.

______ "Individualism, Societalism, Worldliness, Universalism: Thematizing Theoretical Sociology of Religion." *Sociological Analysis* 38: 281-308, 1977.

______ "Church-Sect and Rationality: Reply to Swatos." *Journal for the Scientific Study of Religion* 16: 197-200, 1977.

______ "Weber, Religion and Modern Sociology," in R. Robertson, *Meaning and Change*, pp. 50-102. New York: New York University Press, 1978.

______ *Meaning and Change*. New York: New York University Press, 1978.

______ "Religious Movements and Modern Societies: Toward a Progressive Problemshift." *Sociological Analysis* 40: 297-314, 1979.

______ (ed.). *Sociology of Religion: Selected Readings*. Harmondsworth: Penguin Books, 1969.

______ and Holzner, Burkhart (eds.). *Identity and Authority: Explorations in the Theory of Society*. New York: St. Martin's Press, 1979.

Robinson, John A.T. *Honest to God*. London: SCM Press, 1963.

Roth, Guenther. "Religion and Revolutionary Beliefs: Sociological and Historical Dimensions in Max Weber's Work." *Social Forces* 55: 257-272, 1976.

______ and Schluchter, Wolfgang. *Max Weber's Vision of History: Ethics and Methods*. Berkeley: University of California Press, 1979.

Royle, Edward (ed.). *The Infidel Tradition: From Paine to Bradlaugh*. Toronto: Macmillan of Canada and Maclean Hunter Press, 1976.

Rumney, Jay. *Herbert Spencer's Sociology*. New York: Atherton Press, 1966 (first published in 1937).

Runciman, W.G. "Charismatic Legitimacy and One-Party Rule in Ghana." *European Journal of Sociology* 4: 148-165, 1963.

______ "The Sociological Explanation of 'Religious' Beliefs." *Archives Européennes de Sociologie* 10: 149-191, 1969.

______ *A Critique of Max Weber's Philosophy of Social Science*. Cambridge: Cambridge University Press, 1972.

______ (ed.). *Weber: Selections in Translation*. Translated by E. Matthews. Cambridge: Cambridge University Press, 1978.

Ryan, Joseph Michael. "Ethnoscience and Problems of Method in the Social Scientific Study of Religion." *Sociological Analysis* 39: 241-249, 1978.

Sagan, Eli. "Religion and Magic: A Developmental View," in H.M. Johnson (ed.), *Religious Change and Continuity*, pp. 87-116. San Francisco: Jossey-Bass, 1979.

Saint-Simon, Henri de. *Social Organization, the Science of Man and Other Writings*. Translated and edited by F. Markham. New York: Harper and Row, 1964.

Salamon, Albert. "Max Weber's Political Ideas." *Social Research* 2: 368-370, 1935.

Saliba, John A. "The New Ethnography and the Study of Religions." *Journal for the Scientific Study of Religion* 13: 145-159, 1974.

Sapir, Edward. *Culture, Language and Personality: Selected Essays*. Berkeley: University of California Press, 1964.

Scharf, Betty R. *The Sociological Study of Religion*. London: Hutchinson, 1970.

Scheler, Max. *Ressentiment*. Edited by L.A. Coser and translated by W.W. Holdheim. New York: The Free Press, 1961.

Schluchter, Wolfgang. *The Rise of Western Rationalism: Max Weber's Developmental History*. Translated by G. Roth. Berkeley: University of California Press, 1981.

Schneider, Louis. "The Sociology of Religion: Some Areas of Theoretical Potential." *Sociological Analysis* 31: 131-143, 1970.

______ (ed.). *Religion, Culture and Society: A Reader in the Sociology of Religion.* New York: John Wiley and Sons, 1964.

______ *Sociological Approach to Religion.* New York: John Wiley and Sons, 1970.

______ "The Scope of 'The Religious Factor' and the Sociology of Religion: Notes on Definition, Idolatry and Magic." *Social Research* 41: 340-361, 1974.

Schroyer, Trent. *The Critique of Domination.* New York: George Braziller, 1973.

Schwartz, Barry. "George Washington and the Whig Conception of Heroic Leadership." *American Sociological Review* 48: 18-33, 1983.

Seguy, Jean. "The Marxist Classics and Asceticism." *Annual Review of the Social Sciences of Religion* 1: 79-101, 1977.

Seidman, Steven. "Modernity, Meaning and Cultural Pessimism in Max Weber." *Sociological Analysis* 44: 1983 (forthcoming).

______ and Gruber, Michael. "Capitalism and Individualism in the Sociology of Max Weber." *British Journal of Sociology* 28: 498-508, 1977.

Seyfarth, Constans. "The West German Discussion of Max Weber's Sociology of Religion Since the 1960's." *Social Compass* 27: 9-25, 1980-81.

Sharpe, Eric J. "Some Problems of Method in the Study of Religion." *Religion* 1: 1-14, 1971.

______ *Comparative Religion: A History.* London: Duckworth, 1975.

Shepherd, William C. "Religion and the Social Sciences: Conflict or Reconciliation?" *Journal for the Scientific Study of Religion* 11: 230-239, 1972.

______ "Robert Bellah's Sociology of Religion: The Theoretical Elements." *Journal for the Scientific Study of Religion* 14: 395-402, 1975.

Sherman, Lawrence W. "Uses of the Masters." *The American Sociologist* 9: 176-181, 1974.

Shils, Edward and Michael Young. "The Meaning of the Coronation." *Sociological Review* 1: 63-81, 1953.

Shupe, Anson D., and Bromley, David G. *The New Vigilantes: Deprogrammers, Anticultists and the New Religions.* Beverley Hills, California: Sage Publications, 1980.

Siebert, Rudolf J. *Horkheimer's Critical Sociology of Religion.* Washington, D.C.: University Press of America, 1979.

Sighele, Scipio. *Psychologie des Sectes.* Paris: Giard et Brière, 1898.

Simmel, Georg. "A Contribution to the Sociology of Religion." Translated by W.W. Elwang. *American Journal of Sociology* 10: 359-376, 1905; and reprinted in 60: (Supplement) 1-18, 1955.

______ *Sociology of Religion.* Translated by C. Rosenthal. New York: The Philosophical Library, 1959 (first published in 1905).

Simpson, George. *Auguste Comte: Sire of Sociology.* New York: Thomas Y. Crowell Company, 1969.

Simpson, John H. "Ethnic Groups and Church Attendance in the United States and Canada," in A.M. Greeley and G. Baum (eds.), *Ethnicity,* pp. 16-22. New York: The Seabury Press, 1977.

______ "Sovereign Groups, Subsistence Activities, and the Presence of a High God in Primitive Societies," in R. Wuthnow (ed.), *The Religious Dimension,* pp. 299-310. New York: Academic Press Inc., 1979.

______ "Is There a Moral Majority?" Paper presented at the Annual Meeting of the Society for the Scientific Study of Religion. Baltimore, 1981.

______ "Some Observations on the Current Vitality of Conservative Religion." Paper presented at the Annual Meeting of the American Association for the Advancement of Science. Toronto, 1981.

Sinclair-Faulkner, Tom. "A Puckish Reflection on Religion in Canada," in P. Slater (ed.), *Religion and Culture in Canada,* pp. 407-420. Waterloo: Canadian Corporation for Studies in Religion, 1977.

Sissons, Peter L. "The Sociological Definition of Religion." *The Expository Times* 82(5): 132-137, 1971.

Slater, Peter (ed.). *Religion and Culture in Canada/Religion et Culture au Canada.* Waterloo: Canadian Corporation for Studies in Religion, 1977.

______ "On the Apparent Absence of Civil Religion in Canada." (mimeographed).

Slater, Philip. *Origins and Significance of the Frankfurt School.* London: Routledge and Kegan Paul, 1977.

Smith, J.Z. "When the Bough Breaks." *History of Religions* 12: 342-371, 1973.

Smith, W. Robertson. *Lectures on the Religion of the Semites.* New York: Schocken Books, 1972 (first published in 1889).

Snook, John B. "An Alternative to Church-Sect." *Journal for the Scientific Study of Religion* 13: 191-204, 1974.

Sorokin, Pitirim A. *Fads and Foibles in Modern Sociology.* Chicago: Henry Regnery Co., 1956.

Spencer, Herbert. *The Principles of Sociology* (two volumes) (third edition). New York: D. Appleton and Co., 1892.

______ *The Study of Sociology.* Ann Arbor: University of Michigan Press, 1961 (first published in 1873).

Spencer, Martin E. "What is Charisma?" *British Journal of Sociology* 24: 341-354, 1973.

______ "The Social Psychology of Max Weber." *Sociological Analysis* 40: 240-253, 1979.

Spinks, G. Stephens. *Psychology and Religion: An Introduction to Contemporary Views.* London: Methuen and Co., 1963.

Spiro, Melford E. "Religion: Problems of Definition and Explanation," in M. Banton (ed.), *Anthropological Approaches to the Study of Religion,* pp. 85-126. London: Tavistock Publications, 1966.

Stackhouse, Reginald. "Darwin and a Century of Conflict," in R.D. Knudten (ed.), *The Sociology of Religion: An Anthology,* pp. 430-435. New York: Appleton-Century-Crofts, 1967.

Stahl, William A. "Civil Religion and Canadian Confederation." Unpublished doctoral dissertation. Graduate Theological Union, Berkeley, California, 1981.

Stanner, W.E.H. "Reflections on Durkheim and Aboriginal Religion," in Maurice Freedman (ed.), *Social Organization: Essays Presented to Raymond Firth,* pp. 217-240. London: Cass, 1967.

Stark, Rodney and William S. Bainbridge. "Of Churches, Sects and Cults: Preliminary Concepts for a Theory of Religious Movements." *Journal for the Scientific Study of Religion* 18: 117-133, 1979.

Stark, Werner. "Max Weber's Sociology of Religious Belief." *Sociological Analysis* 25: 41-46, 1964.

——— *The Sociology of Religion: A Study of Christendom* (five volumes). London: Routledge and Kegan Paul, 1966-72.

Stauffer, Robert E. "Bellah's Civil Religion." *Journal for the Scientific Study of Religion* 14: 390-394, 1975.

Steeman, Theodore M. "Max Weber's Sociology of Religion." *Sociological Analysis* 25: 50-58, 1964.

——— "Church, Sect, Mysticism, Denomination: Periodological Aspects of Troeltsch's Types." *Sociological Analysis* 36: 181-204, 1975.

Stone, Donald. "New Religious Consciousness and Personal Religious Experience." *Sociological Analysis* 39: 123-134, 1978.

——— "The Charismatic Authority of Werner Erhard," in R. Wallis (ed.), *Millennialism and Charisma*, pp. 141-175. Belfast: The Queen's University, 1982.

Strawbridge, Sheelagh. "Althusser's Theory of Ideology and Durkheim's Account of Religion: An Examination of Some Striking Parallels." *The Sociological Review* 30: 125-140, 1982.

Streng, F.J. "Studying Religion: Possibilities and Limitations of Different Definitions." *Journal of the American Academy of Religion* 40: 219-237, 1972.

Stryckman, Paul. *Les prêtres du Québec d'aujourd'hui.* Québec: Université Laval, Centre de Recherches en Sociologie Religieuse, 1970.

——— "Réflexions et perspectives sur la sociologies de la religion au Québec." *Les Cahiers du CRSR* 1: 145-183, 1977.

——— "Theory and Research in Quebec: Qualitative Appraisal and Perspectives." Paper presented at the Annual Meeting of the Society for the Scientific Study of Religion, 1977.

——— and Gaudet, Robert. *Priests in Canada, 1971: A Report On English-Speaking Clergy*. Québec: Université Laval, Centre de Recherches en Sociologie Religieuse, 1971.

——— and Gaudet, Robert. "Priests Under Stress," in S. Crysdale and L. Wheatcroft (eds.), *Religion in Canadian Society*, pp. 336-345. Toronto: Macmillan of Canada, 1976.

Swanson, Guy E. *The Birth of the Gods.* Ann Arbor: University of Michigan Press, 1960.

——— *Religion and Regime.* Ann Arbor: University of Michigan Press, 1967.

——— "Interpreting the Reformation." *Journal of Interdisciplinary History* 1: 419-446, 1971.

——— "Monotheism, Materialism, and Collective Purpose: An Analysis of Underhill's Correlations." *American Journal of Sociology* 80: 862-869, 1975.

——— "Comment on Underhill's Reply." *American Journal of Sociology* 82: 421-423, 1976.

Swatos, William H. "Monopolism, Pluralism, Acceptance, and Rejection: An Integrated Model for Church-Sect Theory." *Review of Religious Research* 16: 174-183, 1975.

——— "Weber or Troeltsch? Methodology, Syndrome and the Development of Church-Sect Theory." *Journal for the Scientific Study of Religion* 15: 129-144, 1976.

——— "Quo Vadis: Reply to Robertson." *Journal for the Scientific Study of Religion* 16: 201-204, 1977.

______ "Church-Sect and Cult: Bringing Mysticism Back In." *Sociological Analysis* 42: 17-26, 1981.

______ "The Disenchantment of Charisma: A Weberian Assessment of Revolution in a Rationalized World." *Sociological Analysis* 42: 119-136, 1981.

______ "Enchantment and Disenchantment in Modernity: the Significance of 'Religion' as a Sociological Category." *Sociological Analysis* 44: 1983 (forthcoming).

Talmon, Yonina. "Pursuit of the Millennium: The Relation Between Religious and Social Change." *Archives Européennes de Sociologie* 3: 125-148, 1962.

______ "Millennarian Movements." *Archives Européennes de Sociologie* 7: 159-200, 1966.

Tamney, Joseph B. "Textbooks in the Sociology of Religion: A Review Article." *Sociological Analysis* 27: 106-112, 1966.

Tenbruck, Friedrich H. "The Problem of Thematic Unity in the Works of Max Weber." *British Journal of Sociology* 31: 316-351, 1980.

Theobald, Robin. "The Role of Charisma in the Development of Social Movements: Ellen White and the Emergence of Seventh Day Adventism." *Archives de Sciences Sociales de Religions* 49: 83-100, 1980.

Thompson, Kenneth. *Emile Durkheim.* London: Tavistock Publications, 1982.

______ and Tunstall, Jeremy (eds.). *Sociological Perspectives.* Harmondsworth: Penguin Books, 1971.

Thorman, Donald J. "The Sociological Concept of Religion." *American Catholic Sociological Review* 12: 148-153, 1951.

Thouless, Robert H. *An Introduction to the Psychology of Religion.* Cambridge: Cambridge University Press, 1961 (first published in 1923).

Tillich, Paul. *The Protestant Era.* Chicago: University of Chicago Press, 1948.

______ *Biblical Religion and the Search for Ultimate Reality.* Chicago: University of Chicago Press, 1955.

______ *The Courage To Be.* New Haven: Yale University Press, 1959.

Tilly, Charles. *As Sociology Meets History.* New York: Academic Press, Inc., 1981.

Tipton, Steven M. "New Religious Movements and the Problem of a Modern Ethic," in H.M. Johnson (ed.), *Religious Change and Continuity,* pp. 286-339. San Francisco: Jossey-Bass, 1979.

______ *Getting Saved from the Sixties.* Berkeley: University of California Press, 1982.

Tiryakian, Edward A. *Sociologism and Existentialism.* Englewood Cliffs, N.J.: Prentice-Hall Inc., 1962.

______ "Neither Marx Nor Durkheim . . . Perhaps Weber?" *American Journal of Sociology* 81: 1-33, 1975.

______ "The Sociological Import of a Metaphor: Tracking the Source of Max Weber's 'Iron Cage'." *Sociological Inquiry* 51: 27-33, 1981.

______ "Durkheim's 'Elementary Forms' as 'Revelation'," in B. Rhea (ed.), *The Future of the Sociological Classics,* pp. 114-135. London: George Allen and Unwin, 1981.

______ (ed.). *Sociological Theory, Values and Sociocultural Change.* New York: Harper and Row, 1967 (first published in 1963).

______ (ed.). *On the Margin of the Visible.* New York: John Wiley and Sons, 1973.

Titiev, Mischa. "A Fresh Approach to the Problem of Magic and Religion." *Southwestern Journal of Anthropology* 16: 292-298, 1960.

Tocqueville, Alexis de. *Democracy in America* (two volumes). New York: Alfred Knopf, 1948.

Towler, Robert. *Homo Religiosus*. New York: St. Martin's Press, 1974.

Tremmel, William Calloley. *Religion: What Is It?* New York: Holt, Rinehart and Winston, 1976.

Trevor-Roper, Hugh R. *Historical Essays*. London: Macmillan, 1967.

______ *Religion, The Reformation and Social Change* (second edition). London: Macmillan, 1972.

Troeltsch, Ernst. *The Social Teaching of the Christian Churches* (two volumes). Translated by O. Wyon. London: George Allen and Unwin, 1931 (first published in German in 1911).

Tucker, Robert C. *Philosophy and Myth in Karl Marx*. Cambridge: Cambridge University Press, 1961.

Tumarkin, Nina. *Lenin Lives! The Lenin Cult in Soviet Russia*. Cambridge: Harvard University Press, 1983.

Turner, Bryan S. *Weber and Islam*. London: Routledge and Kegan Paul, 1974.

______ "Class Solidarity and System Integration." *Sociological Analysis* 38: 345-358, 1977.

______ *Religion and Social Theory*. London: Heinemann, 1983 (forthcoming).

Turner, Stephen P. "Bunyan's Cage and Weber's 'Casing'." *Sociological Inquiry* 52: 84-87, 1982.

Tylor, Edward. *Primitive Culture* (2 volumes). London: John Murray, 1871.

Udehn, Lars. "The Conflict Between Methodology and Rationalization in the Work of Max Weber." *Acta Sociologica* 24: 131-147, 1981.

Underhill, Ralph. "Economic and Political Antecedents of Monotheism: A Cross-Cultural Study." *American Journal of Sociology* 80: 841-861, 1975.

______ "Economy, Polity and Monotheism: Reply to Swanson." *American Journal of Sociology* 82: 418-421, 1976.

Urban, George. *The Miracles of Chairman Mao: A Compendium of Devotional Literature, 1966-1970*. London: Tom Stacy Ltd., 1971.

Vaillancourt, Jean-Guy. *Papal Power: A Study of Vatican Control Over Lay Catholic Elites*. Berkeley: University of California Press, 1980.

Van der Bent, A. *The Christian Marxist Dialogue*. Geneva: World Council of Churches, 1969.

Vernon, Glenn M. *Sociology of Religion*. New York: McGraw-Hill Book Co., 1962.

Vidal, Daniel. "Pour une lecture marxiste du prophétisme: champ autre et champ outre." *Social Compass* 22: 355-380, 1975.

Vree, Dale. *On Synthesizing Marxism and Christianity*. New York: John Wiley and Sons, 1976.

Wach, Joachim. *The Sociology of Religion*. Chicago: University of Chicago Press, 1944.

______ *Types of Religious Experience: Christian and Non-Christian*. Chicago: University of Chicago Press, 1951.

Waismann, Friedrich. "How I See Philosophy," in A.J. Ayer (ed.), *Logical Positivism*, pp. 345-380. New York: The Free Press, 1959.

Wallace, Anthony F.C. "Revitalization Movements." *American Anthropologist* 58: 264-281, 1956.

______ *Religion: An Anthropological View*. New York: Random House, 1966.

Wallace, Ruth A. "The Secular Ethic and the Spirit of Patriotism." *Sociological Analysis* 34: 3-11, 1973.

Wallis, Roy. *The Road to Total Freedom: A Sociological Analysis of Scientology*. New York: Columbia University Press, 1977.

______ "The Rebirth of the Gods? Reflections on the New Religions in the West." Inaugural Lecture, The Queen's University of Belfast (New Lecture Series No. 108), 1978.

______ *Salvation and Protest: Studies of Social and Religious Movements*. New York: St. Martin's Press, 1979.

______ "Charisma, Commitment and Control in a New Religious Movement," in R. Wallis (ed.), *Millennialism and Charisma*, pp. 73-141. Belfast: The Queen's University, 1982.

______ "The Social Construction of Charisma." *Social Compass* 29: 25-39, 1982.

______ (ed.). *Sectarianism: Analyses of Religious and Non-Religious Sects*. London: Peter Owen Ltd., 1975.

______ (ed.), *Millennialism and Charisma*. Belfast: The Queen's University, 1982.

Wallis, W.D. "Durkheim's View of Religion." *Journal of Religious Psychology* 7: 252-267, 1914.

Wallwork, Ernest. *Durkheim: Morality and Milieu*. Cambridge: Harvard University Press, 1972.

Warburton, T. Rennie. "Critical Theory and the Sociology of Religion." Paper presented at the Annual Meeting of the Society for the Scientific Study of Religion, 1975.

______ "A Dialectical Theory of Religion." Paper presented at the Annual Meeting of the American Association for the Advancement of Science, 1981.

Warner, Wellman J. "Sect," in J. Gould and W.L. Kolb (eds.), *A Dictionary of the Social Sciences*, pp. 624-625. New York: The Free Press, 1964.

Warner, W. Lloyd. *The Living and the Dead: A Study in the Symbolic Life of Americans*. New Haven, Connecticut: Yale University Press, 1959.

Weber, Max. *The Protestant Ethic and the Spirit of Capitalism*. Translated by T. Parsons. London: George Allen and Unwin, 1930 (first published in German in 1904-05).

______ *The Theory of Social and Economic Organization*. Translated by A.M. Henderson and T. Parsons. Glencoe: The Free Press, 1947.

______ *From Max Weber: Essays in Sociology*. Translated and edited by H.H. Gerth and C.W. Mills. London: Routledge and Kegan Paul, 1948.

______ *The Methodology of the Social Sciences*. Translated by E.A. Shils and H.A. Finch. Glencoe: The Free Press, 1949 (essays first published in German in 1903-1917).

______ *The Religion of China: Confucianism and Taoism*. Translated by H.M. Gerth. Glencoe: The Free Press, 1951.

______ *The Religion of India: The Sociology of Hinduism and Buddhism*. Translated and edited by H.H. Gerth and D. Martindale. New York: The Free Press, 1952.

——— *The Sociology of Religion*. Translated by E. Fischoff. Boston: Beacon Press, 1963 (first published in German in 1922).

——— *Economy and Society: An Outline of Interpretive Sociology* (3 volumes). Edited by G. Roth and C. Wittich. New York: The Bedminster Press, 1968.

——— "On Church, Sect and Mysticism." Translated by J. Gittleman and introduced by B. Nelson. *Sociological Analysis* 34: 140-149, 1973.

——— "Anticritical Last Word on *The Spirit of Capitalism*." Translated and with an introduction by W.M. Davis. *American Journal of Sociology* 83: 1105-1131, 1978 (first published in German in 1910).

Weigert, Andrew J. "Functional, Substantive or Political? A Comment on Berger's 'Second Thoughts on Defining Religion'." *Journal for the Scientific Study of Religion* 13: 483-486, 1974.

——— "Whose Invisible Religion? Luckmann Revisited." *Sociological Analysis* 35: 181-188, 1974.

Weisinger, Herbert. "The Branch That Grew Full Straight." *Daedalus* 90: 388-399, 1961.

Weissbrod, Lilly. "Religion as National Identity in a Secular Society." *Review of Religious Research* 24: 188-205, 1983.

Wells, A.R. "Is Supernatural Belief Essential in a Definition of Religion?" *Journal of Philosophy* 18: 269-275, 1921.

West, Ellis M. "A Proposed Neutral Definition of Civil Religion." *Journal of Church and State* 22: 23-40, 1980.

Westley, Frances. " 'The Cult of Man': Durkheim's Predictions and New Religious Movements." *Sociological Analysis* 39: 135-145, 1978.

White, A.D. *A History of the Warfare of Science with Theology in Christendom* (2 volumes). New York: Dover Publications, 1960 (first published in 1896).

Whitworth, John and Martin Shiels. "From Across the Black Water: Two Imported Varieties of Hinduism," in E. Barker (ed.), *New Religious Movements*, pp. 155-172. New York and Toronto: The Edwin Mellen Press, 1982.

Williams, J. Paul. "The Nature of Religion." *Journal for the Scientific Study of Religion* 1: 3-14, 1962.

Williams, Robin M. *American Society: A Sociological Interpretation*. New York: Alfred A. Knopf, 1952.

Wilson, Bryan R. "An Analysis of Sect Development." *American Sociological Review* 24: 3-15, 1959.

——— *Sects and Society*. London: Heinemann, 1961.

——— (ed.). *Patterns of Sectarianism*. London: Heinemann, 1967.

——— *Religion in Secular Society: A Sociological Comment*. Harmondsworth: Penguin Books, 1969.

——— *Religious Sects*. New York: McGraw-Hill, 1970.

——— *Magic and the Millennium*. London: Heinemann, 1973.

——— *The Noble Savages: The Primitive Origins of Charisma and its Contemporary Survival*. Berkeley: University of California Press, 1975.

——— "The Debate Over 'Secularization'." *Encounter* 45(10): 77-83, 1975.

——— *Contemporary Transformations of Religion*. London: Oxford University Press, 1976.

——— "The Return of the Sacred." *Journal for the Scientific Study of Religion* 18: 268-280, 1979.

______ (ed.). *The Social Impact of New Religious Movements.* New York: Rose of Sharon Press, 1981.

______ "The New Religions: Some Preliminary Considerations," in E. Barker (ed.), *New Religious Movements,* pp. 16-31. New York and Toronto: The Edwin Mellen Press, 1982.

______ *Religion in Sociological Perspective.* Oxford: Oxford University Press, 1982.

Wilson, John. *Religion.* London: Heinemann, 1972.

Wiltshire, David. *The Social and Political Thought of Herbert Spencer.* Oxford: Oxford University Press, 1978.

Winter, J. Alan. "The Metaphoric Parallelist Approach to the Sociology of Theistic Beliefs: Theme Variations and Implications." *Sociological Analysis* 34: 212-229, 1973.

______ *Continuities in the Sociology of Religion: Creed, Congregation and Community.* New York: Harper and Row, 1977.

______ "Immanence and Regime in the Kingdom of Judah: A Cross-Disciplinary Study of a Swansonian Hypothesis." *Sociological Analysis* 44: 1983 (forthcoming).

Wolff, Kurt H. (ed.). *Emile Durkheim: Essays on Sociology and Philosophy.* New York: Harper and Row, 1964.

Worsley, Peter. *The Trumpet Shall Sound* (second edition). New York: Schocken Books, 1968.

Wrong, Dennis H. (ed.). *Max Weber.* Englewood Cliffs, N.J.: Prentice-Hall Inc., 1970.

Wuthnow, Robert. *The Consciousness Reformation.* Berkeley: University of California Press, 1976.

______ *Experimentation in American Religion: The New Mysticisms and Their Implications for the Churches.* Berkeley: University of California Press, 1978.

______ (ed.). *The Religious Dimension: New Directions in Quantitative Research.* New York: Academic Press Inc., 1979.

Yinger, J. Milton. *Religion in the Struggle for Power.* Durham, N.C.: Duke University Press, 1946.

______ *Religion, Society and the Individual.* New York: The Macmillan Co., 1957.

______ *Sociology Looks at Religion.* New York: The Macmillan Co., 1961.

______ "The Present Status of the Sociology of Religion," in R.D. Knudten (ed.), *The Sociology of Religion: An Anthology,* pp. 26-38. New York: Appleton-Century-Crofts, 1967.

______ *The Scientific Study of Religion.* New York: Macmillan Publishing Co., 1970.

______ "Countercultures and Social Change." *American Sociological Review* 42: 833-853, 1977.

Zaretsky, Irving I., and Leone, Mark P. (eds.). *Religious Movements in Contemporary America.* Princeton, N.J.: Princeton University Press, 1974.

Zeitlin, Irving M. "Karl Marx: Aspects of His Social Thought and their Contemporary Relevance," in B. Rhea (ed.), *The Future of the Sociological Classics,* pp. 1-15. London: George Allen and Unwin, 1981.

INDEX

Acknowledgements

Page 15: Quote from *Nupe Religion* by S.F. Nadel reprinted by permission of Routledge & Kegan Paul Ltd. Pages 16, 32, 33, 34: Quotes from "A Definition of Religion and Its Uses" by Robin Horton in *Journal of the Royal Anthropological Institute,* Vol. 90, 1960, pp. 201, 211. Reprinted by permission of the Royal Anthropological Institute of Great Britain and Ireland. Page 16: Excerpt from THE SACRED CANOPY by Peter L. Berger. Copyright © 1967 by Peter L. Berger. Reprinted by permission of Doubleday & Company Ltd. Reprinted by permission of Faber and Faber Ltd. from THE SOCIAL REALITY OF RELIGION by Peter L. Berger. Page 21: Quote from Thomas F. O'Dea, THE SOCIOLOGY OF RELIGION, © 1966, p. 6. Reprinted by permission of Prentice-Hall, Inc., Englewood Cliffs, New Jersey. Page 23: Quote from *Religion, Society and the Individual:* Reprinted with permission of Macmillan Publishing Company, from RELIGION, SOCIETY AND THE INDIVIDUAL by J. Milton Yinger. Copyright © 1957 by Macmillan Publishing Company. Quote from *The Invisible Religion: The Problem of Religion in Modern Society,* 1967, by Thomas Luckmann. Reprinted by permission. Pages 29, 42: Quotes from *The Varieties of Religious Experience* by William James. Reprinted by permission of the publisher, Fount Paperbacks, London. Pages 35, 36: Quotes from "Religion: Problems of Definition and Explanation" in Michael Banton (ed.), *Anthropological Approaches to the Study of Religion.* Reproduced by permission of the publishers, Tavistock Publications Ltd. Page 37: Quote from "Theories of Religion and Social Change" reprinted by permission of the author. Pages 38, 40: Quotes by Peter L. Berger reprinted by permission of the Society for the Scientific Study of Religion, Inc. Pages 55, 57: Quotes from *Theories of Primitive Religion* by E.E. Evans-Pritchard, © Oxford University Press. Reprinted by permission of Oxford University Press. Pages 59, 60, 61: Quotes from *The New Golden Bough* by Sir James George Fraser (T.H. Gaster, ed.) reprinted by permission of University Books Inc. Pages 63, 64, 65: Quotes from *The Essence of Christianity* by Ludwig Feuerbach, translated by George Eliot reprinted by permission of Routledge & Kegan Paul, Limited. Page 66: Quote from *Karl Marx: Early Writings,* T.B. Bottomore, ed. Reprinted by permission of McGraw-Hill Book Company. Pages 66, 67: Quotes reprinted from *The German Ideology* (1965) by Karl Marx. Reprinted by permission of Lawrence & Wishart Ltd. Pages 66, 67: Quotes reprinted from *On Religion* (1958) by Karl Marx and Friedrich Engels. Reprinted by permission of Lawrence & Wishart Ltd. Pages 77-88, 98, 99: Quotes from Emile Durkheim. Reprinted with permission of Macmillan Publishing Company from *The Elementary Forms of the Religious Life* by Emile Durkheim. New York: The Free Press, 1963. Reprinted with permission of George Allen & Unwin (Publishers) Ltd. Page 89: Quote from *Comparative Religion: A History* by Eric J. Sharpe reprinted by permission of the publisher, Gerald Duckworth & Co. Ltd. Page 91: Quote from *Sociology and Philosophy:* Reprinted with permission of Macmillan Publishing Company from *Sociology and Philosophy* by Emile Durkheim. New York: The Free Press, 1953. Reprinted with permission of Routledge & Kegan Paul. Quote from Tom Bottomore: Reprinted from *Social Forces,* Vol. 59:4 (June 1981). "A Marxist Consideration of Durkheim"